In selecting *To End a War* as one
of the Year, *The New Yo.*

"Diplomacy is the grungiest job. . . . But it must be satisfying because this en-thralling book is also a heartfelt call to America to use its power when soci-eties break down and to become a steady global force resisting human rights abuses everywhere. It is filled with anecdotes and sharp pictures of the wily Balkan leaders Holbrooke had to deal with, as well as with shrewd and seldom flattering analyses of the personalities and motivations of timid American and NATO military commanders. . . . His re-creation of battles over principle and tactics with Western generals and State Department and White House officials are dramatic, and his description of a rudderless administration during the early days of his efforts is astonishingly candid, and convincing. His combat-iveness may offend the pinstripe set, but it is wonderfully refreshing on the page. It is a very rare book on diplomacy that makes you feel you were in the midst of it, and excited to be there."   —*The New York Times Book Review*

More praise for *To End a War*

"One of the most important and readable diplomatic memoirs of recent times. . . . His account should restore some respect to the much maligned art of diplomacy."   —*The Washington Post*

"A compelling account of a life-and-death negotiation—the personal dynam-ics, the theatrical gestures, the unexpected snags, the leaks. . . . A classic exercise in lockup, great-power diplomacy. *To End a War* is a riveting book."
                                                                                —*Time*

"Engaging, witty, and dramatic. . . . Holbrooke paints a picture of an adminis-tration so inattentive and rudderless that it was often unclear what policy, if any, it had adopted."   —*The New York Times Book Review*

"Holbrooke is brilliant, forceful, determined, focused. . . . In his intuitive feel for the realities of power diplomacy and his strategic vision, he is the heir to Henry Kissinger in American diplomacy."   —*New York Post*

"Of all the many excellent books that have been written on Bosnia, *To End a War* may turn out to be the most important. Holbrooke has written a superb

book, one that is clear and honest. Bosnia needed a Holbrooke; perhaps more importantly, so did Washington, if it was to redeem its besmirched honor."
—MICHAEL ELLIOTT, *Newsweek*

"Easily the best book of recent years on how to carry off a diplomatic negotiation. . . . We can only hope that the White House, Congress and the public are listening, and that generations of Americans will read Holbrooke's book."
—*The Philadelphia Inquirer*

"A first-rate piece of diplomatic history. . . . Holbrooke portrays the inner circle of the Clinton administration at work . . . and makes as powerful a case for the use of tactical force as is ever likely to appear in print."
—*The New York Times*

"A natural writer, Holbrooke uses poetic license to dramatize events into an absorbing read. We have him bluffing, shouting at, or cursing Balkan politicians, negotiating deals of great consequence on the fly, stitching things together as he goes along."
—*The Boston Globe*

"A roller-coaster ride, from the driver's seat. . . . The going is rambunctious and fascinating."
—*Foreign Affairs*

"A bravura performance, fascinating, informative and powerfully argued."
—*The New Republic*

"Peppered with amusing anecdotes and shrewd insights. . . . Richard Holbrooke is the Quentin Tarantino of diplomacy."
—*The Economist*

"*To End a War* should be read by anyone who still believes that the relationship between the United States military and its political overseers is healthy."
—THOMAS E. RICKS, *The Washington Monthly*

"The first detailed insider account of foreign policy battles in the Clinton presidency. An unsettling, prophetic book."
—JIM HOAGLAND, *The Washington Post*

"Riveting and forthright. . . . Holbrooke's memoir is both highly literate and informed, as well as notably readable. It is steeped in the tradition of diplomatic memoirs by eminent diplomat/authors such as Henry Kissinger and Harold Nicolson."
—*Kirkus Reviews* (starred)

"Holbrooke on Bosnia is legendary." —*The Christian Science Monitor*

"One of the most important memoirs written about a post–cold war crisis. . . . Historians, diplomats and foreign policy experts will surely read *To End a War* in an attempt to understand the intricacies of how American actions were decisive in bringing an end to the worst tragedy to occur on European soil since World War II. Holbrooke gives riveting accounts of the meetings between members of the Principal's Committee who, with President Clinton, made life-and-death decisions over NATO bombing and the timing of peace negotiations. The author also takes the reader on a tour de force of intense negotiations between the infamous figures who share responsibility for the demise of the Balkans. Like other memoirs written about historic negotiations, *To End a War* will take on greater importance as leaders try to 'learn from history.' *To End a War* is a vital starting point to understanding the success and failures of building peace." —*The Georgetown Public Policy Review*

"Absorbing. . . . What mattered [to Holbrooke] was the exercise of American leadership in setting the post–cold war global pace, in keeping the peace in Europe, and in strengthening a Western alliance badly strained by what was otherwise regarded as a second-tier regional problem. . . . Holbrooke has been hailed for prodigies of imperial shrewdness, manipulation, and overall orchestration. Yet his willingness to second-guess some of his own tactics along the way adds to the credibility of his account."
—STEPHEN S. ROSENFELD, *World Policy Journal*

"The Dayton Agreement provided much-needed relief from the horrible war that preceded it, and it is largely to the credit of Richard Holbrooke that there is any agreement at all. He has now given us, in *To End a War,* his memoir of this crucially important negotiation, the crowning achievement (so far) of an impressive diplomatic career. The book makes compelling reading."
—PAUL WOLFOWITZ, *The National Interest*

"*To End a War* is a good book, well written and very readable. . . . It is invaluable to have such a substantial contribution to the public record, written by a principal player so soon after the event."
—PAULINE NEVILLE-JONES, *Prospect*

"*To End a War* goes a long way toward revealing a much more human and thoughtful figure behind the brash, pushy image. Though Holbrooke was presented in the media as a sort of diplomatic Lone Ranger, one of the constant themes of this book is the teamwork on which he always depended. The point is made in a dramatic and tragic way in his opening chapter, in which he describes how three of his closest colleagues lost their lives when their armored vehicle rolled off a mountain track on the outskirts of Sarajevo. . . . This is one of several genuinely moving moments in *To End a War*."

—NOEL MALCOLM, *Los Angeles Times Book Review*

"A graphic and insightful account of one of the most difficult problems the United States has faced since the end of World War II."

—WARREN CHRISTOPHER

"This brilliant and remarkable book is both an absorbing firsthand narrative of the Balkan conflict and an invaluable contribution to the history of our time. This is more than a book about Bosnia. There will be more Bosnias in our future, and *To End a War* offers basic guidance about the uses of American power in a dangerous world."

—ARTHUR SCHLESINGER, JR.

"What Richard Holbrooke has given us in this impressive diplomatic memoir is a vivid and well-written account of the heroic efforts put forth by the author himself and the small team he headed to spare the troubled Balkan region further bloodshed and horror, and to bring the endangered peoples of Bosnia hope, security, and normalcy of life."

—GEORGE F. KENNAN

"Whether one agrees with him or not on Bosnia, Richard Holbrooke's book is must reading."

—HENRY KISSINGER

ALSO BY RICHARD HOLBROOKE

Counsel to the President
(with Clark Clifford)

TO END
A WAR

RICHARD HOLBROOKE

TO END A WAR

THE MODERN LIBRARY

NEW YORK

Originally published in hardcover by Random House, Inc., in 1998.

Grateful acknowledgment is made to the following for permission
to reprint previously published material:

Éditions Bernard Grasset: Excerpt from *Le Lys et la Cendre* by
Bernard-Henri Lévy (Paris: Éditions Bernard Grasset, 1996). Reprinted
by permission of Éditions Bernard Grasset.

Harcourt Brace & Company and Faber and Faber Limited: Excerpt from
"The Hollow Men" from *Collected Poems 1909–1962* by T. S. Eliot.
Copyright © 1936 by T. S. Eliot. Copyright © 1964, 1963 by T. S. Eliot.
Rights outside of the United States are controlled by Faber and Faber Limited.
Reprinted by permission of Harcourt Brace & Company and Faber
and Faber Limited.

Random House, Inc.: Fifty-one lines from "New Year's Day" by W. H. Auden.
Copyright © 1941, 1969 by W. H. Auden. Four lines from "Danse Macabre"
by W. H. Auden. Copyright © 1940, 1968 by W. H. Auden. Both poems are
published in *Collected Poems* (New York: Random House, Inc., 1945).
Reprinted by permission of Random House, Inc.

Photo of Joseph Kruzel (p. vii): Scott Davis/U.S. Army Visual
Information Center

Library of Congress Cataloging-in-Publication Data
Holbrooke, Richard C.
To end a war /
Richard Holbrooke.
p.   cm.
Originally published: New York : Random House, ©1998.
Includes bibliographical references and index.
ISBN 0-375-75360-5
1. Holbrooke, Richard C.   2. Yugoslav War, 1991–1995—Diplomatic history.
3. Yugoslav War, 1991–1995—Peace.   4. Yugoslav War, 1991–1995—Bosnia
and Hercegovina.   5. Yugoslav War, 1991–1995—Personal narratives,
American. 6. Bosnia and Hercegovina—History—1992–   I. Title.
DR1313.7.D58H65   1999
949.703—dc21   98-55520

Modern Library website address: www.modernlibrary.com
Printed in the United States of America
68975

This book is dedicated to three cherished colleagues
who did not reach Dayton.

Robert C. Frasure

Joseph Kruzel

S. Nelson Drew

No words men write can stop the war
Or measure up to the relief
Of its immeasurable grief. . . .
May an Accord be reached, and may
This aide-mémoire on what they say,
Be the dispatch that I intend;
Although addressed to a Whitehall,
Be under Flying Seal to all
Who wish to read it anywhere,
And, if they open it, En Clair.

—W. H. AUDEN, *New Year Letter*

Contents

BOOK III: DAYTON

BOOK IV: IMPLEMENTATION

List of Maps

Note to the Reader

BETWEEN 1991 AND 1995, CLOSE TO three hundred thousand people were killed in the former Yugoslavia. The international response to this catastrophe was at best uncertain and at worst appalling. While both the United States and the European Union initially viewed the Balkan wars as a European problem, the Europeans chose not to take a strong stand, restricting themselves to dispatching U.N. "peacekeepers" to a country where there was no peace to keep, and withholding from them the means and the authority to stop the fighting. Finally, in late 1995, in the face of growing atrocities and new Bosnian Serb threats, the United States decided to launch a last, all-out negotiating effort. This is the story of how, belatedly and reluctantly, the United States came to intervene and how that intervention brought the war in Bosnia to an end.

In the last two years, many people have asked me what the negotiations were really like. This cannot be answered with a dry account of positions taken and agreements reached. The fourteen weeks that form the core of this story were filled with conflict, confusion, and tragedy before their ultimate success. The negotiations were simultaneously cerebral and physical, abstract and personal, something like a combination of chess and mountain climbing. This was not a theoretical game between nation-states, but a dangerous and unpredictable process.

This account of the Bosnia negotiations is written from the perspective of the negotiating team, but to broaden it I have interviewed many of my former colleagues and associates, as well as other experts on the region, who offered their own recollections of important events. Physical descriptions, anecdotes, and the personal background of participants are integral to the story; in diplomacy, as in architecture, details matter. Many events happened far from the negotiating team, in Washington, in the Balkans, in the United Nations, and in the major European capitals. I have included most of them, but, by necessity,

they are discussed in less detail. Of special importance were the parallel negotiations with Moscow, conducted primarily by Secretary of Defense
William Perry and Deputy Secretary of State Strobe Talbott, which resulted in
the unprecedented deployment of Russian troops to Bosnia under American
command as part of a NATO-led peacekeeping force.

Government service is always a collective effort; we were only part of a
much larger team headed by President Clinton, Vice President Gore, and Secretary of State Warren Christopher, without whose support we would have
failed. A list of acknowledgments can be found at the end of this book, but it
is not long enough to credit everyone who made the shuttle and Dayton possible. The opinions and views expressed in this book are nonetheless solely
those of the author and do not necessarily represent the official views of the
Department of State or the United States Government.

Today, public service has lost much of the aura that it had when John F.
Kennedy asked us what we could do for our country. To hear that phrase before it became a cliché was electrifying and led many in my generation to
enter public service. For me it was the Foreign Service, which I joined right
after graduating from college. Less than a year later I found myself in Saigon.
It seems like yesterday, but this was almost thirty-six years ago. I do not wish
to suggest that in some distant "golden age" all was altruism and that today
idealism is dead. Such easy myths may satisfy, but they are not true; every era
has both heroes and scandals. But in an age when the media pays more attention to personalities than to issues, Americans may conclude that public service is either just another job, or a game played for personal advancement.

The public sector contains countless men and women who, whether liberal
or conservative, still believe in hard work, high ethical standards, and patriotism. This book is dedicated to three of them. As this story demonstrates,
public service can make a difference. If this book helps inspire a few young
Americans to enter the government or other forms of public service, it will
have achieved one of its goals.

My own government experiences over the last thirty-five years have led me to
conclude that most accounts of major historical events, including memoirs, do
not convey how the process felt at the time to those participating in it. This de-
rives, in part, from the historian's need to compress immensely complicated
and often contradictory events into a coherent narrative whose outcome the
reader (unlike the participants at the time) already knows. Other, more subtle
factors are also at work: the natural tendency of memoirists to present themselves in a favorable light; a faulty memory or incomplete knowledge; and the
distorting effect of perfect hindsight. A memoir sits at the dangerous intersec-

tion of policy, ambition, and history, where it is tempting to focus on instances of good judgment, and to blur or forget times when one made a mistake.

Hindsight tends to give historical narrative a sense of inevitability. But there was nothing predetermined about the outcome of the Bosnia negotiations. In August 1995, when they began, it was almost universally believed that they would fail, as all previous efforts had. And we knew that if we failed, the war would continue.

RICHARD HOLBROOKE
New York
April 1998

Prologue

But often, in the world's most crowded streets,
But often, in the din of strife,
There rises an unspeakable desire
After the knowledge of our buried life;
A thirst to spend our fire and restless force
In tracking out our true, original course;
A longing to inquire
Into the mystery of this heart which beats
So wild, so deep in us—to know
Whence our lives come and where they go.

—MATTHEW ARNOLD, *The Buried Life*

THE FIRST TIME I SAW SARAJEVO, I placed my feet for a moment in the cement footprints pressed into the sidewalk on the spot where Gavrilo Princip
stood when he fired the bullets that killed Archduke Franz Ferdinand. This
was in the summer of 1960. I was hitchhiking across southeastern Europe with
a friend, and I was nineteen years old. Suddenly, a guide appeared and offered
to translate the words engraved in Serbian on the wall above the footprints.
"Here, on June 28, 1914," read the plaque (or so I remember it), "Gavrilo Princip struck the first blow for Serbian liberty."

I can still recall my astonishment. "Serbian liberty?" What was this all
about? Every college student knew Princip's act had started Europe's slide
into two world wars and contributed to the rise of both communism and fascism. How could anyone hail it as heroic? And "Serbia" no longer existed as
an independent country; it was part of communist Yugoslavia, teeming, or so
it seemed to a nineteen-year-old in Eastern Europe for the first time, with
grim-faced soldiers and policemen. I never forgot that first brush with extreme nationalism, and it came back to me vividly when Yugoslavia fell
apart.

By the time I saw Sarajevo again, in 1992, thirty-two years had passed.
Bosnia had become the worst killing ground in Europe since World War II,
and a new phrase had entered the English language: "ethnic cleansing."

With Bosnia on the brink of collapse, I visited the region twice on fact-finding missions for the International Rescue Committee. On the second trip I finally returned to Sarajevo, traveling illegally across Serb lines in a Danish armored personnel carrier. The city, no longer a beautiful and cosmopolitan combination of Muslim, Catholic, and Eastern Orthodox cultures, had turned into a desperate hellhole, under heavy mortar, artillery, and sniper attacks. Children gathered twigs for firewood, and people piled shattered buses into makeshift barriers as protection against the constant sniper threat.

When I reached the war-torn city, I ran into John Burns, the great war correspondent of *The New York Times,* and asked if he could take me to Princip's footprints in the pavement. Impossible, he said with a laugh: they had been destroyed by the Bosnian Muslims. But the spirit behind their inscription had been revived—murderously so.*

---

* According to Rebecca West in *Black Lamb and Grey Falcon,* the inscription, engraved on "a very modest black tablet," actually read, "Here, in this historical place, Gavrilo Princip was the initiator of liberty, on the day of St. Vitus, the 28th of June, 1914." In *The Unknown War,* Winston Churchill referred to this inscription as "a monument erected by his fellow countrymen [which] records his infamy and their own." West, pro-Serb throughout her famous book, objected to Churchill's characterization, and described the words on the plaque as "remarkable in their restraint . . . [and] justified by their literal truth."

TO END
A WAR

CHAPTER 1

The Most Dangerous
Road in Europe

(August 15–21, 1995)

> For all of us there is a twilight zone between history and memory;
> between the past as a generalized record which is open to relatively
> dispassionate inspection and the past as a remembered part of, or
> background to, one's own life.
>
> —ERIC HOBSBAWM, *The Age of Empire: 1875–1914*

THE MOUNT IGMAN ROUTE TO SARAJEVO was often described as the most
dangerous road in Europe. Parts of the road, a narrow, winding red-dirt track
originally used only by farmers and shepherds, were controlled by Serb machine gunners, who regularly shot at U.N. vehicles trying to reach the Bosnian
capital. The roadbed itself had little foundation and no reinforcement along its
sides, and in several of its narrower sections it was difficult for two cars to
pass each other. The wreckage of vehicles that had slid off the road or been hit
by Serb gunners littered the steep slopes and ravines. In the summer of 1995,
however, with the airport closed by Serb artillery, the two-hour drive over
Mount Igman was the only way to reach Sarajevo without going through
Bosnian Serb lines.

The chief European negotiator, Carl Bildt of Sweden, had been shot at
crossing Serb territory only weeks earlier. He urged us not to use the Igman
road. But without visiting Bosnia's beleaguered capital we could not carry out
our mission. On August 15, we made our first attempt, taking a United Nations helicopter from the Croatian coastal town of Split to a landing zone high
on Mount Igman, after which we would drive in armored vehicles to Sarajevo.
Our helicopter was unable to find a break in the heavy clouds over the landing
site. After circling for several unpleasant hours, we returned, frustrated and
tired, to Split.

Hearing that we could not reach Sarajevo, Bosnian Foreign Minister
Muhamed Sacirbey, accompanied by the senior American diplomat in

Bosnia, John Menzies, drove over Mount Igman to meet us at the Split airport. Known to most Americans via television as the eloquent face of his embattled new nation, Sacirbey was perhaps proudest of the fact that he had been a first-string defensive back at Tulane University. He was tough, strong, and fit. Still, the long and bumpy road trip had tired him, and he was as exhausted as we were. To avoid being overheard, we squeezed into the cabin of our small Air Force jet as it sat on the tarmac, and briefed him on our plans. I stressed that while our mission had the full backing of President Clinton, and represented a last, best hope for peace in the Balkans, there was no guarantee of its success. Our discussion finished as darkness fell over the Balkans, and we flew on to Zagreb, the capital of Croatia, to meet Croatian President Franjo Tudjman. After a day in Zagreb, we arrived in Belgrade on August 17 to meet the key actor in this stage of the drama, President Slobodan Milosevic of Serbia.

Although I knew the other major leaders in the region, this would be my first meeting with the man who, in our view, bore the heaviest responsibility for the war. I approached the meeting with great uncertainty and was guided by my deputy, Robert Frasure, who had spent many hours negotiating with Milosevic earlier that spring.

Frasure's main bargaining chip with Milosevic had been the economic sanctions that the United Nations had imposed in 1992 against the "Federal Republic of Yugoslavia," the name by which Serbia and Montenegro called themselves even though the four other republics of the original Yugoslavia—Slovenia, Croatia, Macedonia, and Bosnia-Herzegovina—had declared themselves independent nations. The sanctions had seriously damaged Serbia's economy, and Milosevic wanted them ended. But for more than sixteen months he had refused to offer anything concrete in return for our suspending or lifting them.

Our first meeting with Milosevic, on August 17, lasted almost six hours. He was smart, evasive, and tricky. Warren Zimmermann, our last Ambassador to Yugoslavia, would later write: "Milosevic makes a stunning first impression on those who do not have the information to refute his often erroneous assertions. Many is the U.S. senator or congressman who has reeled out of his office exclaiming, 'Why, he's not nearly as bad as I expected!' "[1] His English was excellent, and he was playing word games devoid of substance—focusing on inconsequential changes in draft documents over which he and Frasure had been arguing since the beginning of the year. His goal remained to get the sanctions lifted at no cost.

Our most important point concerned whom we would negotiate with. The United States, we said, would never again deal directly with the Bosnian Serbs who rained artillery and racist rhetoric down upon the Muslims and the Croats from their mountain capital of Pale. "You must speak for Pale," I said. "We won't deal with them ever again."*

Frasure thought the meeting had gone well, but it left me dissatisfied. I decided to see Milosevic again the next morning to let him know that we would not continue the cat-and-mouse game he had played with previous negotiators. To emphasize this, it was necessary to change the ground rules a bit. Our entire team of six people had attended the first meeting, but Milosevic had had only two people with him—his new Foreign Minister, Milan Milutinovic, and his chief of staff, Goran Milinovic. Nine people were simply too many to establish the sort of direct relationship necessary for a frank dialogue.

Early on the morning of August 18, before our second meeting with Milosevic, I met with Frasure and Rudy Perina, the senior American diplomat in Belgrade,† in the garden of the ambassadorial residence. As we walked between the imposing old stone house and the tennis court, under magnificent chestnut trees and presumably out of the range of prying microphones, I said that I planned to throw a controlled fit to make clear to Milosevic that what he was doing was unacceptable. Because of this plan, I added, the next meeting needed to be smaller.

Apologizing to Rudy, I asked him to drop out of the meeting. Returning to the house, I asked the other two members of our team—Joseph Kruzel, the Senior Deputy Assistant Secretary of Defense; and Lieutenant General Wesley Clark, the Chief of Plans for the Joint Chiefs of Staff—to drop out as well. I would take only Frasure and Nelson Drew, an Air Force colonel who, as the National Security Council staff member on our team, represented the White House. Frasure concurred with this suggestion.

Nothing generates more heat in the government than the question of who is chosen to participate in important meetings. My request ran against a diplomatic custom I greatly respected—that the senior resident American diplomatic representative should attend every official meeting with a head of government. But although unhappy, all three men agreed without objection. It could have been a difficult moment; I was deeply gratified by this early sign of our cohesiveness as a team.

---

* Many earlier negotiating efforts of both the United States and the Europeans, including an American probe as late as January 1995, had dealt with the Bosnian Serbs as a separate entity.

† Our diplomatic presence in Belgrade was unique in the world: it was a fully functioning diplomatic mission, yet it was accredited to no one. Neither the United States nor the European Union recognized the claim of Serbia and Montenegro that they still constituted the "Federal Republic of Yugoslavia." However, because of the value of continuing contacts with the Serbians, we maintained an Embassy in Belgrade even though we did not recognize the country it was in.

.   .   .

Less than an hour later Frasure, Drew, and I were seated in a high-ceilinged meeting room in the Presidential Palace—one of Tito's old offices—in Belgrade. It was a room we would come to know well in the next seven months. Like other such meeting rooms in communist and former communist countries from Beijing to Bratislava, the room tried to make up for its lack of charm by a drab giganticism. The three of us sat on a long sofa. Milosevic took an armchair a few feet from where I sat at the end of the sofa. Foreign Minister Milutinovic chose another soft chair facing us directly, and Goran Milinovic, always the loyal staff officer, sat at the edge of the group, taking notes.

As we talked, I thought of the difficulties and dangers we would face each time we tried to reach Sarajevo. It was annoying that we had to depend on U.N. helicopters, the uncertain weather—and that awful road.

"It is disgraceful," I said, "that President Clinton's peace mission has to travel to Sarajevo by such a slow and dangerous route. In order to negotiate we must be able to move rapidly between here and Sarajevo. We have already been in the area for almost a week and we haven't been able to get there. It is ridiculous. You claim to want peace. I ask you now to arrange for us to fly to Sarajevo or to guarantee that we can use a safer land route without any interference from the Bosnian Serbs."

Milosevic stared at us for a moment with a penetrating gaze, as if no one had ever made this request before. Then he replied, "You're right. I'll try." He spoke sharply in Serbian to Goran, who almost ran out of the room. Milosevic said, "I'm sending a message to General Mladic. Let's see what he can do."

Bob, Nelson, and I watched with fascination, looking for clues as to how the enigmatic relationship between Milosevic and Mladic worked. This was the first time we had evidence of what was to become a recurring pattern during the diplomatic shuttle: direct communication between Milosevic and Ratko Mladic, the commander of the Bosnian Serb forces, who had recently been indicted by the International War Crimes Tribunal for direct or indirect responsibility for the murder of thousands of Bosnian Muslims and Croats.

Less than twenty minutes later, Goran returned and handed a piece of paper to Milosevic. "Mladic says the airport is too dangerous," Milosevic said. "He cannot guarantee that you would not be shot down by Muslim or Croat soldiers." This was an absurd statement: everyone knew, I said heatedly, that the only danger to people at the Sarajevo airport was from the Serb gunners ringing the hills around it. But Milosevic was not finished. "Mladic says you can fly to Kiseljak and go in by road from there. You will be completely safe."

I knew that road. Its flat terrain and paved surface made it a much easier drive than the route over Mount Igman. But the road ran through Bosnian Serb territory—"Indian country," as Bob Frasure called it. I had traveled down it as a private citizen almost three years earlier, on December 31, 1992, huddled in the forward seat of a Danish armored personnel carrier, trying to appear inconspicuous under a U.N. helmet and a heavy blue flak jacket. We had been stopped a half-dozen times by heavily armed Serbs who poked machine guns around the inside of the APC while checking our ID cards (to make things worse, mine was a crude forgery). Less than two weeks later, the Serbs had killed a Bosnian Deputy Prime Minister during a search of a French APC not far from where we'd been.

"We can only consider using that road," I said, "if you give us your personal guarantee that we will not be stopped by the Bosnian Serbs."

"I can't give you that guarantee," Milosevic said, "but I'll ask Mladic for one—"

"That's out of the question, Mr. President. We can't possibly accept guarantees from Mladic, only from you."

Sitting next to me on the long couch, Bob Frasure leaned over and whispered, "We have no choice except Igman."

That night we flew to Split. Four days earlier, we had stayed in the lovely old Kastile Hotel, directly on the water, where we had dared Joe Kruzel and Wes Clark to dive in from their third-story windows. The two men had leaped into the water, proud of their courage. But the Kastile was forty minutes away from the airport, too far for our exhausted team, and we opted for a dreary hotel near the airport with chalk-white walls and blue lights.

On the short bus trip from our plane to the hotel, Kruzel and Frasure hung on the hand straps and improvised a reggae lyric in anticipation of the trip we were going to make the next day; its refrain was something about "Goin' up Mount Igman, mon, tryin' to make da peace, mon." It wasn't much to listen to, they cheerfully admitted, as they danced in the bus to their own song. We ate dinner in the bleak hotel dining room, almost alone and unnoticed. I sat with Frasure, Kruzel, and Clark; my executive assistant, Rosemarie Pauli, sat at the next table with Nelson Drew.

We talked at length about a mutual friend, Frank Wisner, who had recently become Ambassador to India. When it came to personnel in the State Department, Frank was always the first person I consulted. When I became Assistant Secretary of State for European and Canadian Affairs in the summer of 1994, he recommended Bob Frasure for the deputy's job. Frasure had worked for him in the Bureau of African Affairs ten years earlier. After one meeting with Bob, then finishing a tour as America's first Ambassador to Estonia, I offered him the job and asked him to reorganize the European Bureau's Central European division so as to reflect the new emphasis we wished to place on that region.*

Frasure, fifty-three years old, was a craggy, cynical professional diplomat who loved his work, while grumbling continually about it. He walked—almost shuffled—with a slight stoop, as if about to fall over, but he had enormous energy, great patience, and a strategic sense unusual in career Foreign Service officers. His cables were widely read in the Department of State not just for their content but for their wit and descriptive powers. His reports of negotiating with Milosevic over lengthy dinners of lamb and plum brandy were classics for both their conciseness and their humor—two qualities not much in evidence in most State Department telegrams.

Bob's greatest joy was to retreat to his farm in the Shenandoah and, with his wife, Katharina, and his two daughters, Sarah and Virginia, paint his barn. At the end of 1994, with the situation in Bosnia continuing to deteriorate, Secretary Christopher—who greatly admired Frasure's cool detachment, fierce loyalty, and patriotism—suggested we add to his portfolio the job of chief Bosnia negotiator. Although Bob had earlier said he did not want direct responsibility for Bosnia, he accepted this enormous additional burden without complaint. But by the summer of 1995, he was visibly worn out by the constant and frustrating travel to the Balkans, and we had agreed that after this trip he would remain at home to backstop our efforts. Frasure wondered constantly if, in its post-Vietnam, post-Somalia mood, our nation would have the nerve and strength to stand up to what he called the "junkyard dogs and skunks of the Balkans." He believed in the need to use airpower, but doubted that the United States had the political will to do so.

Joe Kruzel was shorter and stockier than Frasure. At fifty, his sharp mind combined in equal measure theoretical and practical ability. He often wore his eyeglasses on the lower part of his nose and peered over them, in a manner that emphasized his academic background. He was equally proud of his undergraduate days at the United States Air Force Academy and his Ph.D. from Harvard. Kruzel had a certain playfulness into which he could switch effortlessly from his somber, serious demeanor. After our dinner in Split, Joe volunteered to rewrite our presentation for the Bosnians. Reading his memo the next morning, I saw he had slipped in a one-liner, perhaps to see if we were paying attention: "We will need a mini–Marshall Plan (you know Minnie Marshall, George's sister)."

* We abolished the outdated Office of Eastern European Affairs on our first day in office in September 1994, and created in its place three new offices that reflected the post–Cold War realities of Europe. One combined the Nordic countries and the three newly independent Baltic states. We also banished the phrase "Eastern Europe" from our official vocabulary, replacing it with the historically and geographically more accurate "Central Europe." Unfortunately, most people, including the media, still use the outmoded phrase.

As we talked, General Wesley Clark joined us. He was in a complicated position on our team. A West Pointer, a Rhodes scholar from Arkansas, and a Vietnam veteran, he had been one of the fastest rising officers in the United States Army—the youngest brigadier general at the time he got his first star. He had a personal relationship, although not close, with another Rhodes scholar from Arkansas who was now our Commander in Chief. With three stars, Clark was at the crossroads of his career; this assignment would lead him either to a fourth star—every general officer's dream—or to retirement. Assignment to a diplomatic negotiating team offered some exciting possibilities, but it could be hazardous duty for a military officer, since it might put him into career-endangering conflicts with more senior officers. Clark's boyish demeanor and charm masked, but only slightly, his extraordinary intensity. No one worked longer hours or pushed himself harder than Wes Clark. Great things were expected of him—and he expected them of himself.

Of the people at the hotel that evening, the one I knew least was Samuel Nelson Drew, a forty-seven-year-old Air Force colonel who had recently joined the National Security Council staff. In civilian clothes he seemed less like a military officer than an academic. (He had a doctorate from the University of Virginia.) A devoted family man with a strong Christian faith, he had worked for almost four years at NATO headquarters, where, among other responsibilities, he had headed a special crisis task force on Yugoslavia.

In our first meeting with Milosevic, Nelson hung back, saying almost nothing. But near the end of dinner, Milosevic began to pay close attention to him. Sensing that he could become a vital part of our team, I took him aside that night, and urged him to speak up more. As we prepared for the next day's trip, he seemed subdued, and spent part of the evening writing a long letter to his wife.

On Saturday, August 19, we ate breakfast early and returned to the French air base. The French helicopter had room for only six passengers, but we were seven, counting Rosemarie Pauli and General Clark's executive assistant, Lieutenant Colonel Dan Gerstein. So Rosemarie, who had visited Sarajevo on two earlier trips with me, offered her seat to Gerstein.

The helicopter ride was relatively uneventful, although swooping between hills and looking for breaks in the clouds can never be entirely routine. Nelson Drew, seeing the savage land for the first time, stared silently out the small window. After about ninety minutes, we landed in a soccer field at Veliko Polje, near the Mount Igman pass. Our greeting party was headed by Lieutenant Colonel Randy Banky, the senior American military liaison officer with the U.N. forces in Sarajevo. Two vehicles waited for us on the soccer field—a large, heavy French armored personnel carrier, painted U.N. white, and a U.S. Army Humvee.

General Clark talked to Colonel Banky for a moment. Then he turned to me and yelled over the roar of the helicopter, "Have you ever been in one of our new Humvees? You ought to see how much better it is than the jeeps you were used to in Vietnam."

The French armored personnel carrier, or APC, would take the rest of the party to Sarajevo. As we walked to the APC, I asked Kruzel what the attitude of the Pentagon would be if the United States sent troops to Bosnia as part of a peace settlement. "They wouldn't like it," he said in his half-sardonic, half-joking style, "because it would disrupt their training schedule."

Another American introduced himself at the doors of the APC: Pete Hargreaves, a security officer in the American Embassy in Sarajevo. The doors on the back of the massive vehicle swung open and everyone took seats on the side benches, Bob Frasure at the front left, the others facing each other, Gerstein and Hargreaves in the seats nearest the back doors. "Think hard about how we handle the meeting with Izetbegovic," I said to Bob Frasure. He gave an ironic laugh and, as I turned back toward the Humvee, the doors of the APC slammed shut.

Clark sat to my right in the backseat of the Humvee. Colonel Banky and the driver, an American sergeant, took the two seats in front. The vehicle was heavily armored and the windows, which could be opened, were almost two inches thick. Nonetheless, Clark insisted that we buckle our seat belts and put on flak jackets and helmets. In the August heat, our colleagues in the APC did not take these precautions.

For almost an hour we traveled toward Sarajevo through seemingly peaceful woods, although the road was bumpy and in poor condition. The French military, in whose sector Sarajevo and Mount Igman fell, had recently begun upgrading the road and patrolling it with tanks, part of the new and powerful Rapid Reaction Force (RRF) established by French President Jacques Chirac to show the Serbs that France intended to pursue a more aggressive policy.

The road emerged from the woods and reached a steep incline above the Sarajevo valley, where, hugging the mountain wall, it suddenly narrowed. On our left was a nearly vertical wall, to our right a sharp drop-off. We were approaching the most dangerous part of the road, where we would be directly exposed to Serb machine gunners. But in these well-armored cars we felt safe. It was about 9:30 in the morning.

The Humvee rounded a corner. On the left, a French convoy going the other way had pulled over against the inside wall to let us pass on the outside. As we approached the last French tank, we saw a soldier yelling and gesturing, but we couldn't hear what he was saying through the thick windows. Our driver got out of the car, looking puzzled. "I don't understand this guy," he said. "He's speaking French." I jumped out of the Humvee to help, but I couldn't quite grasp what the French soldier was saying, something about a vehicle behind us going over the edge of the road. I thought that I had misunderstood him. Behind us was—nothing. I signaled Clark to join me. The APC must be far behind us, I thought. Then it hit me.

Clark and I ran back about thirty yards. About six inches of red clay seemed to have broken off the edge of the roadbed. We could hear voices in the woods below, but we saw nothing except a few flattened trees. Somewhere below us lay the APC with our colleagues.

Wearing heavy flak jackets and helmets, we jumped off the edge of the road and started down the steep incline. We were less than ten feet below the roadbed when two enormous explosions went off. Small-arms fire broke out around us. From below and above people cried out in French, "Mines! Get back on the road!" Grasping roots to pull ourselves up, we scrambled back onto the road.

The shooting continued. Far below in the distance lay villages with a clear line of fire. We had no idea whether they were Serb or Muslim. I ran back to our Humvee and asked the sergeant to turn it around in case we had to get back to the relative safety of the woods and the soccer field–helipad. We tried to set up our portable satellite dish to establish communications with the outside world, but the vertical rise of the mountain made contact impossible. Colonel Banky had disappeared.

Finally—it seemed like an eternity but was in fact less than ten minutes—a French corporal ran up to us. The missing APC, he said, was not immediately below us, as we had thought, but beyond the next hairpin turn.

At that moment we realized how bad the situation was. Until then we had expected to find our colleagues injured but, we hoped, not seriously. I had not allowed myself to think of any worse possibility.

Wes and I started running down the road, twenty pounds of extra weight cutting into our necks and chests. We rounded the hairpin turn and followed the road for almost a kilometer. Finally, we ran into a cluster of French vehicles on the road, including a medical vehicle that had, by chance, been coming up the road. They were grouped at the spot, we now realized, where the APC had *bounced over the road* and continued to somersault down the mountain. Below us trees had been flattened as if by a giant plow.

The shooting died down and rain began to fall. In addition to five Americans, four French soldiers—the driver and three other men who had been in the APC—were missing. We established a weak radio contact with the Embassy in Sarajevo through the Embassy radio net, but because we did not know exactly what had happened, we asked Sarajevo to hold off reporting anything to Washington. It was not quite 4:00 A.M. in Washington, and whatever had happened, there was nothing for them to do until we knew more.

Since I was the only person on the mountain who spoke both French and English, I stayed on the road to work with the French while Wes descended. We anchored a rope around a tree stump so that he could rappel toward the vehicle, which French and Bosnian soldiers had already reached. Huge plumes of smoke rose from somewhere below us. We could hear Clark yelling through his walkie-talkie that he needed a fire extinguisher urgently. I looked around frantically; there was none.

A French jeep drove up and stopped. A solitary figure was seated upright in the backseat, covered in blood and bandages. His face was unrecognizable. I asked him who he was. He mumbled something unintelligible. "Who?" I asked again. "Hargreaves . . . your . . . security . . . officer . . . sir," he said, very slowly, talking in a daze. I climbed into the jeep and asked him if he wanted to lie down. He said he didn't know if he could make it. He thought his back was broken. Two French soldiers helped me ease Hargreaves out of the jeep and lay him on a cot on the road. I got down on my knees next to him. He was having great difficulty speaking. I understood him to be saying that he should have saved people, that it was his fault, that his back was broken. I tried to calm him down. Desperate for information, I started asking him, one by one, about our team.

"Frasure. Where is Ambassador Frasure?" I almost shouted.

"Died." He could barely say the word.

I stood up. Three years as a civilian in Vietnam had exposed me to occasional combat and its awful consequences, but this was different. This was *my* team, and my deputy was apparently dead. But there was no time to grieve. Wes Clark was still far below us on the mountainside, and the only thing I knew was that Hargreaves believed that Bob Frasure was dead.

I got back on my knees. "Joe Kruzel," I said. "What about Kruzel?"

"Don't know. Think he made it."

"Nelson Drew?"

"Gone. Didn't make it." Hargreaves started to cry. "I tried . . ."

"It's not your fault," I said hopelessly. "There was nothing you could have done." It was a refrain we would repeat regularly to Hargreaves over the next three days. His first reaction—typical of a highly committed security officer—was guilt for his failure to protect those for whom he was responsible.

Clark struggled up the hillside, using the ropes. He looked ten years older. "It's the worst thing you've ever seen down there," he said. By the time he reached the APC, he said, it was already on fire, apparently from live ammunition it was carrying that had "cooked off" and exploded. Bosnian soldiers in the area had reached the APC first, and had taken two Americans, tentatively identified as Joe Kruzel and Dan Gerstein, to the nearest field hospital. Wes had seen charred remains of two other bodies, probably Bob and Nelson.

As we stood on the road absorbing this unbearable news, a jeep drove up and stopped. A tall, thin French officer stepped out, introduced himself as General René Bachelet, the commander of Sarajevo Sector, and began issuing instructions to his troops. Behind him came another French medical unit and the first Americans, three security officers from the embassy.

By now, journalists in Sarajevo had picked up some conversations about the accident on the internal radio network of the French military and had begun to report a confused and inaccurate version of the accident around the world. It was time to talk to Washington. Asking the American Embassy security unit to take their orders from General Clark, I left for Sarajevo with General Bachelet. On the road we passed the wreckage of several other vehicles that had been hit or had slid off the mountain; one had gone down only a week earlier, killing two British aid workers.

The American Embassy in Sarajevo had recently moved out of crowded and vulnerable rooms in the Holiday Inn. It now occupied a small villa next to the U.N. military headquarters. The communications equipment—secure telephone lines, radio links, and telegraph facilities—were crammed into one tiny, windowless room. It was from there that we now attempted to coordinate our activities. John Menzies, a brave young career diplomat from the United States Information Agency who was awaiting final Senate confirmation to become Ambassador to Bosnia, had already alerted Washington to the tragedy. Shortly after 2:00 P.M. in Sarajevo (8:00 A.M. in Washington) the State Department Operations Center—the indispensable nerve center that keeps all senior State Department and other officials around the world linked to one another twenty-four hours a day—set up, in its usual efficient manner, a conference call with the National Security Advisor, Tony Lake, and his deputy, Sandy Berger; Deputy Secretary of State Strobe Talbott; and the Chairman of the Joint Chiefs of Staff, General John Shalikashvili. (Both Secretary of State Christopher and Secretary of Defense William Perry were on vacation.) I described the scene, stressing that our information was incomplete and that General Clark was still on the mountain.

The Associated Press, Reuters, and UPI had all reported that the French APC had hit a Serb land mine. It was important to correct this as quickly as possible, in order to prevent runaway journalistic speculation and pressure for a military response. I asked Washington to include in its initial announcement a flat statement that the tragedy had been caused by a road accident. We agreed that the officials designated to tell Mrs. Frasure and Mrs. Drew the news prepare them for the worst, but not confirm their husbands' deaths yet. Finally, I asked that someone call my wife, Kati—we had been married for less than three months—and tell her the news personally, so that she would not hear an incomplete version when she woke up.

Clark soon arrived with a vivid description of his efforts to retrieve the remains of the two men, who he was now certain were Bob and Nelson. We called General Shalikashvili again to discuss arrangements for bringing the bodies and the injured home through the American Army hospital in Germany. As I was talking to Shalikashvili, Menzies came into the tiny communications room. "Kruzel is dead," he said quietly, his long arms hanging motionless at his side. "Didn't make it to the hospital. Massive head injuries."

This was, in some ways, the worst moment of the day for us. We had barely absorbed the terrible news about Bob and Nelson, but we thought Joe and Dan Gerstein had made it. Now all three of our senior colleagues were dead. And the thought of Joe—funny, sardonic, wise Joe—dying helplessly as he was driven to the field hospital was simply too much. I asked General Shalikashvili to tell the others in Washington and turned the telephone over to Clark.

A short time later President Clinton called from Jackson Hole, Wyoming, where he was taking a short vacation. I did not realize then that it was his forty-ninth birthday. "Mr. President," I began, rather formally, "we have the sad duty to report that three members of your negotiating team died this morning in a vehicle accident on Mount Igman . . ."

With Strobe Talbott listening in silently, the President made some comments about the terrible nature of the loss, both personally and for the nation. I told him that he could be especially proud of the actions of his fellow Arkansan, and put General Clark on. Wes gave the President a sense of what he had found at the site of the APC, and said it was "like the Boston Road" in Arkansas, a steep and dangerous route both men knew well.

The President asked what effect the tragedy would have on the negotiations, and when we would be ready to continue the mission. "You sent us here as a team, Mr. President," I replied, "and we want to come home as a team. Then we will be ready to resume our mission."

"That's fine," the President said. "Come home as soon as you can, but make it clear publicly that our commitment to the peace effort will continue and that you will lead it. And see Izetbegovic before you leave." Knowing we were focused on our loss, the President was thinking ahead for us. He wanted to show publicly that the tragedy would not stop the peace effort.

"All of us, including Bob and Joe and Nelson, would want to continue," I replied. The President, in reporting to the nation from Jackson Hole a few minutes later, said publicly, "What they would want us to do is to press ahead, and that is what we intend to do."

The next few hours were a blur of action that felt meaningless; we kept thinking of how the smallest changes might have prevented the accident, yet it was already permanently imprinted on our lives. We found Gerstein alive in the makeshift French hospital in the basement of the Sarajevo Post Office Building; he was banged up but in surprisingly good shape. He told us a little about the terrible scene inside the APC: how it had slowly started to slide over the edge, how no one had time to speak or get out, how he had grabbed a metal pole above his head and pressed his face hard against the outer walls of the APC as it tumbled—he estimated twenty to thirty times—four hundred meters down the mountain; how it had come to a stop and he had climbed out the top hatch, then, hearing Pete Hargreaves moaning, had gone back to help him escape.

Then, Gerstein said, he and Hargreaves went back to the APC one more time and pulled Joe Kruzel out through the hatch just before the ammunition exploded. He last saw Joe as the Bosnians took him to the field hospital. It was his impression that the others had been knocked unconscious in the violent initial bouncing and tumbling of the APC, and that they never had a chance. Hargreaves himself had survived by wedging himself under his seat, after almost being thrown out the back doors as the APC fell.

We wanted to leave Sarajevo with our fallen and injured comrades that evening. But the injured could travel only by air, and this produced an ironic result: the very permission to use the Sarajevo airfield that had previously been denied us by the Bosnian Serbs—and that could have prevented the accident—suddenly materialized, arranged swiftly by the French directly with Mladic. As we went through that dreadful day, the French and British arranged to send helicopters to the Sarajevo airport to take us out.

Menzies sent word to President Alija Izetbegovic that we still wanted to see him, but, given the circumstances, we asked him to call on us at the Embassy rather than receive us in the normal manner at his office. At precisely 6:00 P.M., Izetbegovic and Sacirbey strode up the steps of the American Embassy. Menzies, Clark, and I greeted them outside the front door in front of a large throng of journalists, and escorted them into a conference room, where General Bachelet joined us.

Several people in Washington had suggested that we conduct substantive conversations with Izetbegovic, but it was clear that the circumstances were not appropriate for a serious discussion. With the press listening, I thanked the French and the Bosnians for their help during the long day. The Bosnians, having lost so many people in the war, seemed relatively unmoved by three American dead. Finally, slightly annoyed with Izetbegovic, Menzies pointedly said that, while we fully recognized how many Bosnians had died, these were the first Americans to lose their lives in Bosnia. This seemed to impress Izetbegovic, and he offered some words of condolence.

The helicopters would be at the airfield shortly. Light was beginning to fade in Sarajevo and the weather was deteriorating. We started for the airport, where there was one more terrible task to perform: the formal identification of Joe Kruzel. Then, as we stood at attention in a light drizzle, a French honor guard escorted three simple wooden coffins, each draped in an American flag, onto a French helicopter. The rain intensified. It was almost dark, and the clouds seemed to be descending toward us, obscuring the mountains that ringed the airfield. The flight out would be hell.

I turned to General Clark. "We've had enough for one day," I said. "Let's try again tomorrow. We'll spend the night in Sarajevo."

We slept, but only briefly, on Army cots in the Ambassador's office. Endless phone calls to Washington, to family and colleagues, filled the evening and the night. Sacirbey, who was distantly related to Joe Kruzel through a cousin of his American wife, came over and stayed for hours. Too exhausted to think, we were unable to sleep until, well after midnight, we had drained ourselves of the event.

On Sunday, August 20, we set out once again for the Sarajevo airport. This time without an honor guard, we loaded the three coffins onto a French helicopter and the two injured men onto a British helicopter. Although I had spent hundreds of hours on helicopters in and since Vietnam without fear, that French helicopter suddenly, irrationally, scared me. I started toward the British chopper. Clark said, "We should go with the coffins all the way." Wes and I had not been separated for what seemed like days, and we boarded the French chopper together.

The helicopters rose noisily into the air. With my knees pressed into one of the coffins, we flew on to Split. To distract myself, I tried to read a John le Carré novel I had been carrying with me, *The Secret Pilgrim,* but could not focus on the page.

Rosemarie Pauli had taken over the arrangements in Split from a confused and chaotic combination of military and civilian personnel. She had worked for me in Germany as well as Washington, and I had complete confidence in her ability. We needed to transfer the two men and the three coffins from the helicopters to a special American military plane, carrying medical equipment and military doctors, that would fly us to Germany. I gave Rosemarie only one instruction: make sure that the movement of Gerstein and Hargreaves, who were both on stretchers and looked awful, was done far from the television cameras and with dignity. All this Rosemarie accomplished with her usual skill. Shattered by the loss of our three colleagues, and aware that she would have been in the APC if there had been room for one more person in the helicopter, she carried out her responsibilities calmly and efficiently until we reached Andrews Air Force Base the next day.

As we changed aircraft at Split, we spoke briefly to the press, telling them we would resume our shuttle diplomacy in about a week. I expressed particular outrage at a statement by the Bosnian Serb leader, Radovan Karadzic, that we had taken "an unnecessary risk" by using the Mount Igman road rather than crossing Bosnian Serb territory—a deliberately nasty reference to the Serb offer to use the Kiseljak road. I called the tragedy "an accident, but an accident of war."

Air Force doctors quickly examined Gerstein and Hargreaves as we flew to Ramstein Air Base in Germany. The Supreme Commander of NATO, General George Joulwan, an old friend from Vietnam, had flown to Ramstein from his headquarters in Belgium. He stepped forward, saluted as we disembarked, and embraced me. Then we stood at attention as the three coffins received the first of many official American salutes on their way to their final resting places.

I knew the American military hospital at Ramstein well from my time as Ambassador to Germany, most unforgettably from an afternoon spent visiting the Americans wounded in the ambush in Mogadishu, Somalia, in October 1993. The raw courage and patriotism of those young men, several of whom had lost their sight or limbs during the fighting, were still vivid in my mind. Now the same doctors treated Gerstein and Hargreaves as we took our first showers in two days and prepared to return home.

At 12:15 P.M. the next day, August 21, we landed at Andrews Air Force Base. As our large C-141 pulled slowly up to the spot where so many of America's triumphal and tragic returns have taken place, the injured men were taken off the plane separately, out of sight of the television cameras. Clark, Rosemarie, and I walked into a silent crowd of friends and family. I could see some of our closest colleagues—Warren Christopher, Bill Perry, Strobe Talbott, Madeleine Albright, Tony Lake, Sandy Berger, Peter Tarnoff, and others—sitting immobile in chairs behind a velvet rope. A place had been saved for me next to my wife, who silently squeezed my hand as I sat down.

We had brought our comrades home, and it was time for others to carry on with the heartbreaking but necessary rituals of remembrance and farewell. Suddenly, exhaustion hit us. As we squinted into the bright midday August sun at Andrews and an Air Force band played "Nearer, My God, to Thee," the coffins were unloaded and placed by an honor guard into three hearses.

Christopher, Lake, and Perry talked movingly about the men who had died. We embraced one another and sought out the wives and children of Bob, Joe, and Nelson. Then, for a few moments, we stood around in a daze, not sure what to do next. Peter Tarnoff, the Undersecretary of State, found me and said gently he would take Kati and me home. We drove into Washington together with Peter, a close friend for over thirty years, and Brooke Shearer, Strobe Talbott's wife. Dropping us off, Peter suggested we take the rest of the day off, and asked if I could come to the State Department the next morning to meet with Warren Christopher.

BOOK ONE

BOSNIA
AT WAR

Twelve months ago in Brussels, I
Heard the same wishful-thinking sigh
As round me, trembling on their beds,
Or taut with apprehensive dreads,
The sleepless guests of Europe lay
Wishing the centuries away,
And the low mutter of their vows
Went echoing through her haunted house,
As on the verge of happening
There crouched the presence of The Thing.
All formulas were tried to still
The scratching on the window-sill,
All bolts of custom made secure
Against the pressure on the door,
But up the staircase of events
Carrying his special instruments,
To every bedside all the same
The dreadful figure swiftly came.

—W. H. AUDEN, *New Year Letter* (1940)

CHAPTER 2

"The Greatest
Collective Failure . . ."

(1991–93)

America, eternally protected by the Atlantic, desired to satisfy her self-righteousness while disengaging her responsibility.
—HAROLD NICOLSON, *Peacemaking 1919*

We do not interfere in American affairs; we trust America will not interfere in European affairs.
—JACQUES DELORS, President of the European Community, 1991

Europe took part in [the war] as a witness, but we must ask ourselves: was it always a fully responsible witness?
—POPE JOHN PAUL II, speaking in Sarajevo, April 13, 1997

IN EARLY 1995, IN AN ARTICLE PUBLISHED IN *Foreign Affairs,* I referred to the former Yugoslavia as "the greatest collective security failure of the West since the 1930s."[1] Although the article had been approved through the formal State Department clearance process, the phrase was not universally welcomed in the Administration. While it was intended to apply to events between 1990 and the end of 1992, there was concern that some people might also apply it to events as late as 1994, halfway into the Clinton Administration's first term.

Yugoslavia undeniably represented a failure of historic dimensions. Why and how had it happened—and just at the moment of the West's great triumph over communism?

There was, of course, no single, or simple, answer. But five major factors helped explain the tragedy: first, a misreading of Balkan history; second, the end of the Cold War; third, the behavior of the Yugoslav leaders themselves; fourth, the inadequate American response to the crisis; and, finally, the mistaken belief of the Europeans that they could handle their first post–Cold War challenge on their own.

I. Bad History, or The Rebecca West Factor. Many books and articles about Yugoslavia have left the impression that the war was inevitable. The most famous of all English-language books on the region was Rebecca West's monumental travel book *Black Lamb and Grey Falcon,* first published in 1941 and continuously in print since then. West's openly pro-Serb attitudes and her view that the Muslims were racially inferior had influenced two generations of readers and policy makers. Some of her other themes were revisited in modern dress in Robert Kaplan's widely acclaimed 1993 best-seller, *Balkan Ghosts: A Journey Through History,* which left most of its readers with the sense that nothing could be done by outsiders in a region so steeped in ancient hatreds. According to numerous press reports, the book had a profound impact on President Clinton and other members of the Administration shortly after they came into office.*

Thus arose an idea that "ancient hatreds," a vague but useful term for history too complicated (or trivial) for outsiders to master, made it impossible (or pointless) for anyone outside the region to try to prevent the conflict. This theory trivialized and oversimplified the forces that tore Yugoslavia apart in the early 1990s. It was expressed by many officials and politicians over the course of the war, and is still widely accepted today in parts of Washington and Europe. Those who invoked it were, for the most part, trying to excuse their own reluctance or inability to deal with the problems in the region. Some of the most surprising renderings of this view came from Lawrence Eagleburger, the former American Ambassador to Yugoslavia, who succeeded James Baker as Secretary of State near the end of 1992. Eagleburger regularly expressed his frustration with those Americans who called for action in stark terms. In September 1992, for example, almost two months after journalists had first filmed

---

* Kaplan wrote of West, whose work he called "this century's greatest travel book": "I would rather have lost my passport and money than my heavily thumbed and annotated copy of *Black Lamb and Grey Falcon.*" For a perceptive analysis of the negative effects of West and her followers, see "Rebecca West's War," by Brian Hall, *The New Yorker,* April 15, 1996.

In his account of his years as editor of *Oslobodjenje,* the Sarajevo daily that published throughout the war, Kemal Kurspahic wrote: "At a time of crucial decisions [President Clinton] simply read the wrong book, or more precisely drew the wrong conclusions from *Balkan Ghosts* by Robert Kaplan, which led to the comforting thought that nothing much could be done in Bosnia 'until those folks got tired of killing each other' " (*As Long As Sarajevo Exists*).

Kaplan has repeatedly stated that he did not intend to have this effect. His book is primarily about Greece and Romania. It devotes less than four chapters out of seventeen to the former Yugoslavia, mentions Sarajevo only once and Mostar not at all, and has only twelve references to Bosnia. In his preface, Kaplan says that "nothing I write should be taken as a justification, however mild, for the war crimes committed by ethnic Serb troops in Bosnia, which I heartily condemn."

the atrocities being committed by Serbs against Muslims in prison camps in western Bosnia, he said:

> I have said this 38,000 times, and I have to say this to the people of this country as well. This tragedy is not something that can be settled from outside and it's about damn well time that everybody understood that. Until the Bosnians, Serbs, and Croats decide to stop killing each other, there is nothing the outside world can do about it.

It was, of course, undeniable that the ethnic groups within Yugoslavia nursed deep-seated grievances against one another. But in and of itself, ethnic friction, no matter how serious, did not make the tragedy inevitable—or the three ethnic groups equally guilty.* Of course, there was friction between ethnic groups in Yugoslavia, but this was true in many other parts of the world where racial hatred had *not* turned into ethnic cleansing and civil war. There had been periods of intense ethnic conflict in Yugoslavia, most recently in World War II. But the fighting between 1941 and 1945 was part of the larger killing field, triggered by Hitler's ambitions, into which all of Europe had turned. Though some Serbs nursed ancient enmities that could be traced back to their defeat by the Turks on Kosovo Field in 1389, the three groups had lived together for centuries. Serbs, Croats, and Muslims worked together in every walk of life. There was no noticeable physical or ethnic difference between them, and, in fact, considerable intermarriage. Many people told me that until the collapse of their country they did not know which of their friends were Serb and which were Muslim. Throughout the war, I heard frequent accounts of old friends sending each other personal messages and gifts and helping each other escape across the battle lines. As Noel Malcolm wrote in his 1994 *Bosnia: A Short History,* "Having travelled widely in Bosnia over fifteen years, and having stayed in Muslim, Croat, and Serb villages, I cannot believe the claim that the country was forever seething with ethnic hatreds."†

Yugoslavia's tragedy was not foreordained. It was the product of bad, even criminal, political leaders who encouraged ethnic confrontation for personal, political, and financial gain. Rather than tackle the concrete problems of governance in the post-Tito era, they led their people into a war. Observing how racial hatred was deliberately inflamed, Warren Zimmermann wrote in his memoir of his ambassadorship:

---

* As journalists reported at the time, the American government had concluded by the early summer of 1992 that the Serbs had carried out close to 90 percent of all the atrocities in Bosnia and Croatia.

† Page 252. Malcolm's *Bosnia: A Short History* was the first serious English-language history of Bosnia, and argued convincingly that Bosnia had its own history and continuing identity. Malcolm undermined the conventional wisdom that the war was the inevitable result of ancient hatreds. It is unfortunate it did not appear earlier.

Those who argue that "ancient Balkan hostilities" account for the violence that overtook and destroyed Yugoslavia forget the power of television in the hands of officially provoked racism. While history, particularly the carnage of World War Two, provided plenty of tinder for ethnic hatred in Yugoslavia, it took the institutional nationalism of Milosevic and Tudjman to supply the torch. . . . Yugoslavia may have a violent history, but it isn't unique. What we witnessed was violence-provoking nationalism from the top down, inculcated primarily through the medium of television. . . . Many people in the Balkans may be weak or even bigoted, but in Yugoslavia it is their leaders who have been criminal. The virus of television spread ethnic hatred like an epidemic throughout Yugoslavia. . . . An entire generation of Serbs, Croats, and Muslims were aroused by television images to hate their neighbors.[2]

Malcolm similarly observed:

Having watched Radio Television Belgrade in the period 1991–2, I can understand why simple Bosnian Serbs came to believe that they were under threat, from Ustasa hordes, fundamentalist jihads, or whatever. . . . It was as if all television in the USA had been taken over by the Ku Klux Klan.[3]

II. The End of the Cold War. Yugoslavia was cobbled together at the Versailles Conference in 1919–20 from parts of decaying, dying, and defeated empires. In the name of Wilsonian self-determination, the victors of World War I established a country that violated that principle, creating a time bomb that would later explode. Revealingly, its original name was the "Kingdom of the Serbs, Croats, and Slovenes," which was later changed to Yugoslavia, or Land of the South Slavs.

World War II changed everything once again. Against the backdrop of ethnic violence, especially between Croats and Serbs, a legendary communist leader, Josip Broz Tito—half Croat, half Slovene—came out of the remote mountains of Yugoslavia, seized power by fighting the Nazis, and held it for an astonishing thirty-five years. In 1948 came the event that defined Yugoslavia, Tito's historic break with the Soviet Union. From then on, the West was ready to overlook or minimize all other problems within Yugoslavia because of the strategic importance of supporting an anti-Soviet state, albeit a communist and undemocratic one, in such a vital area of Europe. Yugoslavia would receive special treatment from the West for the next forty years.

By the time Yugoslavia started its final agony in 1991, momentous events elsewhere obscured what was happening in the Balkans. The Berlin Wall had been torn down and Germany was unified; communism was dead or dying in Central Europe; the Soviet Union was breaking up into fifteen independent nations; and, in August 1990, Iraq invaded Kuwait, setting in motion the U.S.-led coalition that liberated Kuwait early the following year. Yugoslavia, hav-

The Former Yugoslavia

Serbia and Montenegro remain under a single Federal structure, and call themselves the Federal Republic of Yugoslavia; the other former Yugoslav Republics are all independent states.

ing lost its strategic importance in the eyes of most Western policy makers, fell
to its death almost ignored by the West.

III. The Internal Yugoslav Drama. It was famously said during Tito's
time that Yugoslavia had six republics, five nations, four languages, three reli-
gions, two alphabets, and one party. But after his death in 1980, the Communist Party weakened. Like many other autocratic leaders, Tito had not
permitted the development of a strong successor. An increasingly ineffectual
central presidency rotated annually among the six semi-autonomous Yugoslav
republics, and, for a time, the Albanian-dominated region of Kosovo.

In the rest of Central and Eastern Europe, democracy and democratic ideals
had been the strongest weapon in the struggle against communism. But in Yugoslavia, against a backdrop of mounting debt, spiraling inflation, and high
unemployment, it proved to be extreme nationalism. Thus racists and demagogues—often communists or former communists—rallied people on the
basis of ethnic consciousness. Those who wanted to retain a multiethnic state
or work out a peaceful new arrangement giving more autonomy to the republics were either driven out of the country or silenced—sometimes brutally.

The crisis began in Catholic, Western-oriented Slovenia, the smallest and
wealthiest of the six Yugoslav republics. In 1989, as the Berlin Wall came
down, Slovenia began a series of direct challenges to the central government.
Kosovo, an "autonomous" region in Serbia whose Albanian majority lived
under harsh Serb rule, teetered on the edge of secession and open revolt.

In Serbia, Slobodan Milosevic, the most agile Yugoslav leader, saw his opportunity. Renaming the Serbian Communist Party the Serbian Socialist Party,
Milosevic took up the cause of Serb nationalism. In 1989, on the six hundredth
anniversary of the Serb defeat by the Turks at Kosovo, Milosevic went to the
legendary battlefield and delivered an inflammatory speech before one million
Serbs. (When I asked Milosevic in 1995 about this famous speech, he heatedly
denied that it was racist, and charged Ambassador Zimmermann with organizing a Western diplomatic boycott of the speech and the Western press with distorting it. But his words and their consequences are indelibly on the record.)

IV. Post–Iraq American Fatigue. In the spring of 1991, the Yugoslav crisis became acute. The victory in the desert against Saddam Hussein had been
the result of superb coalition leadership by the Bush Administration, but dealing simultaneously with both Desert Storm and the death throes of the Soviet
Union had exhausted Washington. As Zimmermann noted dryly in his memoirs, "Even a great power has difficulty in dealing with more than one crisis at
a time."[4] In addition, the American presidential election was only a year away.
American policy makers did not wish to get involved in Yugoslavia, and many
considered the situation insoluble. In the words of David Gompert, a senior

National Security Council staff member at the time, the Bush Administration knew "a year before the fighting began that Yugoslavia was being led toward the abyss by a few demagogic politicians, [but] simply knew of no way to prevent this from occurring. . . . The Bush national security team that performed so well in other crises was divided and stumped."[5]

In June 1991, Secretary of State James Baker made his only visit to Belgrade, a day trip jammed between an important meeting with Soviet officials in Berlin and an emotional trip to Albania, where one million Albanians cheered him in the streets of the capital.

Baker's perception of the situation was reflected in his personal report from Belgrade to President Bush that night, which he quoted in his memoirs: "My gut feeling is that we won't produce a serious dialogue on the future of Yugoslavia until all parties have a greater sense of urgency and danger. We may not be able to impart that from the outside, but we and others should continue to push."[6]

This was a crucial misreading. The Yugoslavs knew exactly how urgent and dangerous the situation was. They had been waiting to see if the United States and its allies would intervene. Once they realized that the United States, at the height of its global influence, was disengaged, they proceeded rapidly on their descent into hell. Only four days after Baker left Belgrade, Croatia and Slovenia both declared their independence. Two days later, on June 27, the first (and shortest) of the Balkan wars—the Yugoslav invasion of Slovenia—began. Three more wars—between Croats and Serbs, Serbs and Bosnians, and Croats and Bosnians—were to follow, killing hundreds of thousands of people, displacing over two million more, and destroying not only the country of Yugoslavia, but hopes for what President Bush called a peaceful "new world order" in Europe. Long after he had left Belgrade, Ambassador Zimmermann reflected on the tragedy: "The refusal of the Bush Administration to commit American power early was our greatest mistake of the entire Yugoslav crisis. It made an unjust outcome inevitable and wasted the opportunity to save over a hundred thousand lives."[7]

The United States was now in the position of supporting something that no longer existed. Given their Yugoslav expertise, the key figures in shaping American policy should have been Eagleburger and National Security Advisor Brent Scowcroft, who had been a military attaché in Belgrade early in his Air Force career. Questioned about this in 1995, Scowcroft said, "Eagleburger and I were the most concerned here about Yugoslavia. The President and Baker were furthest on the other side. Baker would say 'We don't have a dog in this fight.' The President would say to me once a week 'Tell me again what this is all about.' "[8]

V. Atlantic Confusion and Euro–passivity. For the first time since World War II, Washington had turned a major security issue entirely over to the Europeans. In his memoirs, Secretary Baker explains this decision: "It was time to make the Europeans step up to the plate and show that they could act as a unified power. Yugoslavia was as good a first test as any."[9]

In fact, Yugoslavia was the worst possible place for a "first test" of a new American policy to "make the Europeans step up to the plate." To be sure, with the Soviet threat gone and Germany united, Europe had to assume a larger role in the Atlantic partnership, as they themselves wanted. But for over a half century Europe had been unable to "act as a unified power" without American leadership. The Bush Administration's stellar performance in 1989–90 on one of the last great Cold War issues, German unification, had been one of the brightest chapters in American foreign policy in the entire century; without Washington's steadfast and visionary support, it would not have happened, given the opposition of Britain and France. Yet only a year later the same officials who had made it possible turned their backs on the first post–Cold War challenge in Europe.

The Yugoslav crisis should have been handled by NATO, the Atlantic institution that mattered most, the one in which the United States was the core member. The best chance to prevent war would have been to present Yugoslavia with a clear warning that NATO airpower would be used against any party that tried to deal with ethnic tensions by force. The United States and the Europeans could then have worked with the Yugoslav parties to mediate peaceful (although certainly contentious and complicated) divorce agreements between the republics. But Washington did not see it that way. As David Gompert candidly observed of his own colleagues:

> The U.S. Government's handling of the Yugoslav crisis from 1990 to 1992 contradicted and undermined its declaratory policy regarding the centrality and purpose of NATO in post–Cold War Europe, [which] implied NATO responsibility to respond to precisely the sort of conflict by then raging in the Balkans. . . . Predictably, the attempt to hold the Yugoslav crisis at arm's length did not spare the United States the effects of, or responsibility for, the failure that followed.[10]

Europe's own miscalculation was equally grievous. It was encapsulated in a memorable statement by the Foreign Minister of Luxembourg, Jacques Poos, whose country then held the rotating presidency of the European Community (later renamed the European Union). "The hour of Europe," Poos declared, "has dawned."

The day after the war between "Yugoslavia" and Slovenia began, six days after Secretary Baker's June 1991 trip, Poos led a mission of the European Community "troika"—the Foreign Ministers of the previous, current, and next presidencies of the E.C.—to Belgrade. Poos did no better than Baker. But the process revealed the disarray between the United States and the Europeans.

So determined was Baker to keep the United States uninvolved that he flatly rejected a proposal from Assistant Secretary of State Thomas Niles to send an observer to the talks between the Yugoslav parties sponsored by the Europeans, fearing that even such a minor action might imply a possible American role.

In this sorry sequence, Europe and the United States proved to be equally misguided. Europe believed it could solve Yugoslavia without the United States; Washington believed that, with the Cold War over, it could leave Yugoslavia to Europe. Europe's hour had *not* dawned in Yugoslavia; Washington *had* a dog in this particular fight. It would take four years to undo these mistakes—four years before Washington belatedly and reluctantly, but ultimately decisively, stepped in and asserted leadership, with European support. But this did not happen until after even more severe strain within the Atlantic Alliance, and historic disasters in Bosnia.

The Yugoslav-Slovene war started on June 27. It was short and, by the standards of what was to come next, almost a lark. Within ten days, after light casualties on both sides, Milosevic ordered the Yugoslav Army to withdraw. A few days later, at a meeting on the Adriatic island of Brioni, Dutch Foreign Minister Hans van den Broek, the senior European representative, negotiated an agreement that effectively gave Slovenia its independence, but left the situation more explosive than ever. As Laura Silber and Allan Little put it, "The Brioni Agreement was hailed as a triumph of European diplomacy. It was nothing of the sort. It left every important item of contention unresolved. . . . The diplomatic triumph belonged to Milosevic and [Slovenian President Milan] Kucan, who had, between them, agreed on Slovenia's departure from the federation . . . and, in effect, destroyed federal Yugoslavia."[11]

The Kucan-Milosevic deal was a characteristic example of Milosevic's tactical flexibility and superb negotiating skills, and served his long-term purposes in ways not well understood at the time. Slovenia's departure from Yugoslavia made it easier for Milosevic to create a Yugoslavia dominated by the Serbs, since it removed from the country a republic with almost no Serbs.

Croatia, with hundreds of thousands of Serbs within its boundaries, was not ready to accept such an outcome. Croatian President Franjo Tudjman had long dreamed of establishing Croatia as an independent country. But the boundaries of his "country," drawn originally by Tito to define the republic within Yugoslavia, would contain areas in which Serbs had lived for centuries. In the brief war in Slovenia the Yugoslav Army seemed to be defending the territorial integrity of Yugoslavia; when that same army went to war only a few weeks later against Croatia, it had become a *Serb* army fighting for the Serbs inside Croatia.

The Croatian-Serbian war began with irregulars and local incidents, and escalated rapidly to full-scale fighting. In August 1991, an obscure Yugoslav Army lieutenant colonel named Ratko Mladic joined his regular forces with the local irregulars—groups of young racists and thugs who enjoyed beating up Croats—and launched an attack on Kijevo, an isolated Croat village in the Serb-controlled Krajina. There had been fighting prior to Kijevo, but this action, backed fully by Belgrade, "set the pattern for the rest of the war in Croatia: JNA [Yugoslav] artillery supporting an infantry that was part conscript and part locally-recruited Serb volunteers."[12] Within weeks, fighting had broken out across much of Croatia. The JNA began a vicious artillery assault on Vukovar, an important Croat mining town on the Serbian border. Vukovar and the region around it, known as eastern Slavonia, fell to the Serbs in mid-November, and Zagreb was threatened, sending Croatia into panic. (The peaceful return of eastern Slavonia to Croatia would become one of the central issues in our negotiations in 1995.)

After exhausting other options, the European Community asked the former British Foreign Secretary Lord Carrington to take on the task of bringing peace to Yugoslavia. Carrington, an urbane man of legendary integrity, told me later that he had never met such terrible liars in his life as the peoples of the Balkans. As the war in Croatia escalated and Vukovar crumbled under Serb shells, Carrington put forward a compromise plan to end the war.

Again the United States stayed away. No American negotiator entered the effort; Washington's support for the Carrington plan was confined to tepid public statements and low-level diplomatic messages. In mid-November, United Nations Secretary-General Boutros Boutros-Ghali appointed Cyrus Vance as the United Nations negotiator, and asked him to work closely with Carrington. Because Vance was a former Secretary of State, many people believed the United States was now somehow involved—an impression the Bush Administration did not discourage. But it was not true.

In 1991, the United Nations Security Council voted to impose an arms embargo on all of Yugoslavia. The United States supported this, and subsequent, resolutions. In practice, this seemingly neutral position was a gift to the Serbs, since almost all the armaments and weapons factories of Yugoslavia were located in Serbia. To the Croats and especially to the Muslims of Bosnia, this was a huge blow. Paul Wolfowitz, President Bush's Undersecretary of Defense, argued against this, later calling it "totally and disastrously one-sided in its effect,"* but to no avail. As the war worsened, Senators Dole, Biden, and Liberman would make repeated efforts to "lift" the embargo unilaterally, lead-

---

* *The National Interest,* Number 53, p. 102.

ing to some of the most emotional and contentious struggles of the Clinton Administration.

The appointment of Cy Vance quickened my own interest in Yugoslavia. I had worked for Vance twice—first in 1968, during the Paris peace negotiations with North Vietnam, and again when I was Assistant Secretary of State for East Asian and Pacific Affairs during the Carter Administration. We had been close allies in the Carter years, and I had great respect and affection for him and his family. Vance was a born mediator. Even in his mid-seventies, he still brought intensity and meticulousness to his work, with enough focused energy to outlast people half his age. Furthermore, Vance brought to the table something Carrington could not offer—the possibility of a U.N. peacekeeping force in Croatia if there was an agreement to end the fighting.

The Germans Recognize Croatia. As the Vance-Carrington effort commenced, the European Community addressed one of the most controversial decisions of the war: whether or not to recognize Croatia as an independent nation. For months Germany had been pressing the E.C. and the United States to recognize Croatia. Vance and Carrington opposed the German position vigorously. They both told me later that they had warned their old friend and colleague German Foreign Minister Hans Dietrich Genscher, in the strongest possible terms, that recognizing Croatia would trigger a chain reaction culminating in a war in Bosnia. They reasoned, correctly, that Bosnia would have to follow Croatia's lead and declare independence next. Once Bosnia did this, Vance and Carrington predicted, the substantial Serb minority within Bosnia would then rebel against living in a state dominated by Muslims. As one Yugoslav later put it, each ethnic group would ask, "Why should I be a minority in *your* state when *you* can be a minority in mine?" War would be inevitable.

Genscher, the senior Foreign Minister in Europe, ignored the warning of his old friends. Uncharacteristically flexing Germany's muscles during a critical Foreign Ministers meeting in Brussels in mid-December 1991, he told his colleagues that if they did not support him Germany would simply recognize Croatia unilaterally. Faced with a threat of a public break in European "unity" just when the historic Maastricht Treaty was proclaiming the dawn of a new, unified Europe—a treaty whose prime mover had been German Chancellor Helmut Kohl—the other Europeans yielded to Genscher.

The United States opposed the E.C. decision, but without noticeable vigor: as Baker admitted in his memoirs, "our central focus for months to come would be on managing the peaceful dissolution of the USSR."[13] Even the unfailingly polite and generous Warren Zimmermann was critical of his superiors on this point, later describing Washington's telegram of instructions on recognition "perfunctory, . . . enough to show we had done something, but not enough to produce results." The State Department's statement, Zimmermann wrote, was "weak and nuanced, [designed] mainly to avoid ruffling the Croatian community in the United States."[14] Washington itself would recognize Croatia a few months later.

In recent years, I have been asked repeatedly whether or not the German decision to recognize Croatia triggered the war in Bosnia. This question is complicated. On the one hand, I believe the German decision was a mistake. On the other, many other actions taken in 1991 by the outside powers proved to be more serious errors. In the end, while the German decision probably hastened the outbreak of war in Bosnia, the conflict would have occurred anyway once it was clear that the West would not intervene. To blame Bonn alone for causing the war in Bosnia evades the responsibility of many others. Germany was scapegoated for what happened in Bosnia by people seeking to deflect attention from their own failures.

Given Germany's history in the region—the Nazi associations with their puppet state in Croatia during World War II, and the death camps in Croatia, where both Jews and Serbs had died—Bonn's position also raised concern that Germany, united for the first time since 1945, was about to embark on a more activist, perhaps more aggressive, foreign policy in Central and Eastern Europe. But I see no evidence for the theory that German policy was derived from either its history in the region or a plan for new German assertiveness in Central Europe. During my ambassadorship in Germany, I came to know Genscher and many of his former Foreign Ministry associates well. They were among the most civilized and progressive people with whom I have ever worked. They understood the terrible history of their country under the Nazis, and were deeply committed to making a democratic Germany the key to a democratic and peaceful Europe. I felt—and so stated as Ambassador—that with the end of the Cold War it was desirable for Germany to develop a more active foreign policy, one that would be commensurate with its size and economic strength.

President Clinton, who had visited Germany several times as a student and had studied German, welcomed Germany's emergence as a major participant in shaping European policy. Better to work for the gradual re-emergence of Germany as a European power, this time prosperous and democratic, he felt, than to bottle it up and risk an abrupt reaction later.

Thus, while the German decision on Croatia was wrong, its importance should not be overstated. In fact, Alija Izetbegovic's remarkably bold statement to the Bosnian Parliament on February 27, 1991—almost ten months *before* Germany recognized Croatia—foreshadowed the problems to come: "I would sacrifice peace for a sovereign Bosnia-Herzegovina," he said, "but for that peace in Bosnia-Herzegovina I would not sacrifice sovereignty." As Silber and Little observe, "To the Serbs, this was a war cry."[15]

Vance got an agreement to stop the fighting in Croatia at the beginning of 1992. By February he had overcome resistance from the local Krajina Serbs, gained Milosevic's support, and formally recommended to the United Nations the deployment of 12,500 U.N. peacekeepers. Within days, the U.N. had voted to send to Croatia the second-largest international peacekeeping force ever deployed.

It was a substantial achievement, but there was a cost. Almost one third of Croatia now lay in areas supposedly protected by the United Nations but in fact controlled by the Serbs. Ethnic cleansing of the Croats from these "United Nations Safe Areas" by the Krajina Serbs—who contemptuously proclaimed an independent "republic" on the same terrain—proceeded under the passive eyes of a thirty-nation U.N. peacekeeping force. Vance and Carrington had stopped a war, but the feeble U.N. follow-up left a legacy of pent-up Croatian nationalism that would explode in the Krajina three years later, just as we were beginning our shuttle diplomacy.

CHAPTER 3

A Personal Prelude

(1992)

> With other men, perhaps, such things would not have been induce-
> ments; but as for me, I am tormented with an everlasting itch for
> things remote. I love to sail forbidden seas, and land on barbarous
> coasts.
>
> —HERMAN MELVILLE, *Moby-Dick*

A PRIVATE TRIP

ON MARCH 3, 1992, BOSNIA DECLARED ITSELF an independent nation. The
United States and the European Union recognized it on April 6. Backed by
Belgrade, the Bosnian Serbs demanded that Bosnia withdraw its declaration
of independence. Izetbegovic refused, and fighting began, first as local skir-
mishing. The war had finally come to Bosnia, and with such savagery that,
alerted by a few courageous journalists—notably Roy Gutman of *Newsday,*
Chuck Sudetic and John Burns of *The New York Times,* Kurt Schork of
Reuters, and Christiane Amanpour of CNN—the world woke up during the
summer of 1992 to the fact that an immense tragedy was taking place, as the
cliché went, "in Europe's backyard." An ugly new euphemism entered the English language, courtesy of the Serbs: "ethnic cleansing." It meant the killing,
rape, and forced removal of people from their homes on the basis of their ethnic background. Both Muslims and Croats were targets of Serb brutality. But
even with a new United Nations peacekeeping force that entered Bosnia in
1992 to assist in humanitarian relief, the catastrophe only worsened.

Almost by chance, I began to edge into an involvement in the region. In the
spring of 1992, I saw the Bosnian Ambassador to the United Nations,
Muhamed Sacirbey, on television calling on the world to save his nation. Impressed with his passion and eloquence, I phoned him, introducing myself as
an admirer of his cause, and offered my support. Sacirbey thus became my

first Bosnian friend, although neither of us imagined that someday we would be negotiating together for his country's future.

Sacirbey was one of the bright hopes of the fledgling Bosnian government. Married to an American, he was until 1992 as American as he was Bosnian; his enemies in Bosnia attacked him for speaking his native language with an American accent. But when the new nation needed an effective spokesman at the United Nations, Bosnia's founder-President, Alija Izetbegovic, chose Sacirbey, whose father, a distinguished doctor in suburban Washington, D.C., was his close friend.

It was an inspired choice. The terrible television pictures from Bosnia were deeply moving, but Americans needed to identify with an articulate Bosnian who could personalize his nation's cause. I was only one of many who, moved by his forceful public appearances, offered help. Unfortunately, he was less popular with government officials in both Washington and Europe, who regarded him as inexperienced, even immature, when it came to serious policy issues. He loved journalists and television cameras, and often gave dramatic sound bites without considering their consequences. But he was fun to work with, and enjoyed a teasing, almost fraternal relationship with many Americans, including myself once we began working together in 1994. By the time he was promoted to Foreign Minister in 1995, Sacirbey was one of the two most important Bosnians with whom we dealt on a regular basis. The other was his archrival, Prime Minister Haris Silajdzic.

In the summer of 1992 all that lay in an unimaginable future. I was still a private citizen when, in early August, I received a telephone call from my old friend and tennis partner Winston Lord, who had been the American Ambassador to China* and was now vice chairman of the International Rescue Committee, a private refugee organization on whose board I also served. Lord asked if I would be interested in joining an IRC fact-finding mission to Bosnia. Within a few minutes Robert deVecchi, president of the IRC, called: Would I be able to leave within a week?

THE FIRST TRIP

We left for Croatia on August 11, 1992. Our core group consisted of deVecchi; John Richardson, an Assistant Secretary of State in the Nixon and Ford Administrations; and Sheppie Abramowitz, an old friend and refugee expert whose husband, Morton Abramowitz, had served with great distinction as Ambassador to Thailand and Turkey and was now the president of the

---

* In 1993, Lord became Assistant Secretary of State for East Asian and Pacific Affairs, the same job I had held during the Carter Administration.

Carnegie Endowment for International Peace. The Abramowitzes and I had worked closely together on the Thai-Cambodian-Vietnamese "boat people" refugee crisis in 1979–80.

As we approached Zagreb, I started keeping a journal. Rereading it for the first time four years later, I was struck by how this trip shaped my subsequent understanding of the situation:*

> **August 12, 1992:** We are going blind into a war zone, since almost no one has yet seen much inside the area, and then only in the last few days. We are going to try to get into the death camps that have gotten so much publicity, but this may be hard; it seems unlikely that the Serbs will let us see anything that further damages their already horrible reputation. . . .
>
> ZAGREB: At first glance from a car, Zagreb looks like an ordinary Central European town, with an old section that evokes the Austrian imperial roots from which it came, and newer sections of ugly and banal buildings. At the Inter-Continental Hotel, we find the sort of scene that usually signals a story of high drama—an odd-looking collection of people congregating in the hotel lobby: a large man with a flowing mane of white hair; journalists; several Arabs or Iranians whispering to each other in a corner; military personnel in various uniforms.
>
> **August 13:** After a day of briefings in Zagreb, I can see that the situation is far more complicated and more difficult than other problems I have seen, even Cambodia. It is the peculiar three-sided nature of the struggle here that makes it so difficult. Everyone says that most people did not want this to happen. Yet it did. Everyone says it must stop. Yet it doesn't.
>
> The U.N. refugee briefing yesterday was depressing. Maps filled with the numbers of refugees in each sector lined the room. Our host, Tony Land, a bearded Englishman with a wry sense of humor and a keen sense of the impossibility of his task, gave us a fine explanation of the situation. But when we ask him about the prison camps, he surprises us. "We are absolutely amazed at the press and public reaction to all this," he says. "For six months we have seen Sarajevo systematically being destroyed without the world getting very upset. Now a few pictures of people being held behind barbed wire, and the world goes crazy. We have seen more deaths in Sarajevo than in the prisons . . ."
>
> This turns out to be a widely shared view among the international field-workers. On one hand, they are right—the war is deadlier than the camps. But to the extent that television pictures rouse the world to attention and action—they are, for example, the reason we are here—the pictures of the camps will help Land do his job. . . .
>
> Noon: The difficult trip to Banja Luka has begun. As I write this, we are sitting in a long line of cars and trucks at the Croatian border, about 60 kilometers from Banja Luka, on the edge of the "Serbian Republic of Krajina"—the Serb-controlled areas of western Croatia. The town just ahead of us has life in it, but

---

* The excerpts that follow are edited for repetition and digressions, but are otherwise unchanged.

an air of tension—little sound, no one raises their voices. A moment ago we heard machine gun fire, and smoke is rising in the near distance. Our driver has just nervously asked me to stop videotaping from our car window. The mood is subdued and edgy.

Five P.M.: We have arrived in Banja Luka after a trip across land wasted by war. There is no electricity in the town. Our rooms at the Hotel Bosna are small and hot. Heavy gunfire breaks out just outside the hotel. No one can see where it is coming from, and in the street people keep going, on bike or foot, as though nothing has happened.

Later: The afternoon begins with a scary incident—I am hauled out of my hotel room by Serb policemen because someone reported that I had illegally videotaped inside the U.N. warehouse. Stalling in my room for a moment, I quickly erase the offending footage and go with a young UNHCR employee to see a Serb security officer at the warehouse, Our interpreter-guide explains to the nasty-looking Serb security man that I am not a journalist, etc., and after an angry talk, everything seemed to be under control.

Our young guide illustrates the dilemma here. When I ask him what his background is, he says, "I don't know what I am." He goes on to explain that his immediate family (parents, in-laws, grandparents) is a mixture of Croatian, Serb, Armenian, Russian, Muslim, and Slovenian. "What can I do?" he asks. "I have three choices: to leave, to join the army, or to help people. I choose the third— for now. . . ."

August 14: An extraordinary day! It begins with loud noise and shooting outside our hotel rooms. We go outside to find armed Serbs conducting a "mild" form of ethnic cleansing right in front of journalists with television cameras. We tape the whole scene. At close to gunpoint, Muslims are signing papers giving up their personal property, either to neighbors or in exchange for the right to leave Bosnia. Then they are herded onto buses headed for the border, although they have no guarantee they will actually be able to leave the country. Some leave quietly, others crying. This is the end of their lives in an area their families have lived in for centuries.

After this terrible scene, which leaves us shaken and subdued, we pile into white UNHCR vehicles. A few miles north of Banja Luka, we begin to see terrible signs of war—houses destroyed all along the route. As we progress toward the front lines, the destruction increases. We encounter the occasional house left completely undamaged in a row of ruined ones—its occupant a Serb, not a Muslim. Such destruction is clearly not the result of fighting, but of a systematic and methodical pogrom in which Serbs fingered their Muslim neighbors. This is how it must have been in Central Europe and Russia a century ago, but now using modern weapons and communications.

We are guided through this horrorscape by a tiny and vivacious young Montenegrin from the UNHCR named Senja, who spent a year in Ft. Collins, Colorado, as an exchange student. Whenever we hit a roadblock, she firmly orders us to stay in the car and take no pictures. Then she hops out to talk our way past the awful-looking guards, lounging around with their weapons.

The men in this country act as if they would be impotent if they didn't carry guns. Weapons have empowered people who were until recently gas station mechanics or shopkeepers. I have never seen so many weapons on so many men, even in Vietnam and Cambodia.

We drive to Sanski Most, crossing a difficult checkpoint at a bridge. As we reach the local Red Cross offices, the most frightening incident of the day occurs: an angry-looking man in a sloppy uniform, wearing Reeboks and smoking a cigarette, starts yelling and waving a semi-automatic around wildly in our direction. He seems drunk. He wants to "borrow" our vehicle, then dump us at the edge of the town—or worse. After a heated argument, Senja insists we be taken to the local police station, where she tells us to stay outside while she goes in alone. For a tense hour we wait, watched with open hostility by the heavily armed men lounging in front of the police station. We worry about Senja, but finally she emerges from the police station, saying urgently, "We have to leave immediately. These people are very angry and very dangerous." And we take off rapidly for Zagreb, relieved but mystified. . . .

August 15: We have flown to Split. After checking in at a lovely resort hotel on the sea, we set out for a refugee holding area just across the Croatian border in Bosnia, climbing through a typical Mediterranean landscape, with steep rocky mountains, seaside houses, and small villages. The towns could be in Italy, just across the Adriatic, but the militia makes me think more of Lebanon.

We arrive in Posesje, a town just inside the Bosnian border. The refugee holding area is a dreadful mess. In a school and its grounds are about 3,000 Muslim refugees who have fled from Serb-controlled areas of Bosnia and were stopped by the Croatians from crossing the border into Croatia.

Under a broiling sun, with several women crying out their stories at the same time, the refugees tell us for hours of the ordeals they and their families have lived through. Women gather around to recount how their men are still missing, how they were taken away and never seen again. No young men around. It is overwhelmingly oppressive. We return, depleted, to Split.

For a change of pace, we go to the ancient Roman ruins, near the main street. At this time of year Split is usually filled with tourists, but now there are only a few, mostly German, who seem a dreadful, walking insult to the terrible events happening a few miles away. We visit Emperor Diocletian's palace, a small part of which has been converted into a church.

As we look around, an unforgettable scene takes place, in sharp contrast to the rest of the day. Two nuns appear and sit down at the organ. A young girl starts singing, rehearsing for a wedding. Her beautiful voice fills the little church, echoing off the ancient stones. We stop, transfixed. The horrors of Bosnia are both far away and yet right here. We cannot tear ourselves away. If these moments of love, family, and tradition could last longer, perhaps they could fill the space that war possesses in this self-destructive land.

August 16: Zagreb. Dinner is again at the buffet of the Inter-Continental, where we are joined by Steve Engelberg, an impressive *New York Times* correspondent. He offers some opinions: those who might replace Milosevic would probably be worse; Vance did a terrific job stopping the Croatian-Serbian war; there is a serious danger of a European Islamic radical movement if this war is not stopped soon.

NEW YORK: **August 23, 1992:** The trip is over. As always, New York's problems are so demanding that it is hard to get people to worry about misery thousands of miles away. But I do not agree with the argument that we cannot afford to deal with these faraway problems when we have difficulties at home. Such thinking leads to an unacceptable global triage. Our society is still rich enough to deal with the outside world, even after the end of the Cold War.

The trip had hooked me. Not since Vietnam had I seen a problem so difficult or compelling. I told Strobe Talbott, then a columnist at *Time,* that if there were a change in Administrations Bosnia would be "the worst kind of legacy imaginable—it would be George Bush and Larry Eagleburger's revenge if Clinton wins." Before the trip, *The Washington Post* and *Newsweek* had both asked me to write about my trip. I was now anxious to do so. The *Newsweek* article, in the issue of September 17, 1992, marked my first effort to propose a course of action in Bosnia:

> By its inadequate reaction so far, the United States and, to an even greater extent, the European Community may be undermining not only the dreams of a post–Cold War "common European House" but also laying the seeds for another era of tragedy in Europe.
>
> Not that such a dire future is inevitable. . . . If the Europeans and the United States act with boldness and strength, worst-case scenarios do not need to occur. . . . [But] if the war continues, and the Serbs succeed in permanently reducing the Muslims to a small state or "cantonment" within a Bosnia that has been divided between Croatia and Serbia, the immediate consequences will be terrible—and the long-term consequences even worse. In the short run, the Muslims will have been removed from areas in which they have lived for centuries, with countless thousands butchered, often by their longtime neighbors. Hundreds of thousands, perhaps over one million refugees will have been thrust into a world community already staggering under enormous refugee burdens in Africa, Southeast Asia, and South Asia. . . . Most observers believe that nothing is likely to deter the Serbs except actions that raise the costs of their genocidal policies to an unacceptable level.
>
> What might this mean in practice? First, international (presumably United Nations) observers should be deployed along the borders and in Kosovo and Macedonia immediately, *before* fighting spreads to these two critical regions. . . .
>
> Another possibility would be to change the rules of the present [arms] embargo on all combatants—which in practice heavily favors the Serbs, who control the old Yugoslav military-industrial complex—so that the Bosnians can obtain more weapons with which to defend themselves. . . .

Other actions, including bombing the bridges linking Serbia with Bosnia, and attacking Serb military facilities, must be considered. Such actions may well increase the level of violence in the short term. But since the West does not intend or wish to send its own troops into the war, it is unfair to deny the Muslims the means with which to defend themselves. . . .

Every day that the killing goes on the chances of preventing the long-term tragedy decrease. What would the West be doing now if the religious convictions of the combatants were reversed, and a Muslim force was now trying to destroy two million beleaguered Christians and/or Jews?

THE 1992 CAMPAIGN

In 1988, I had supported Senator Al Gore during the primaries, traveling with him from time to time. Although his campaign started late, it got off to an excellent start, but it ran into immense and, as it turned out, insurmountable obstacles when it hit the primaries in key northern states, especially New York, where I lived through some difficult days with him, his campaign team, and his close-knit family.

I told Gore I would support him again if he ran in 1992. When he decided not to run—in large part because of the aftereffects of an automobile accident that almost killed his young son—I was uncommitted until several close friends began to draw my attention to Governor Bill Clinton of Arkansas.

The first was Strobe Talbott, who had been Clinton's housemate at Oxford when they were both Rhodes scholars. Strobe, a friend since he had covered the State Department during the Carter Administration, could not get involved in the campaign since he was still at *Time*—but his wife, Brooke Shearer, went to work for Hillary Clinton, and traveled with her during much of the campaign. Another journalist I knew well, Joe Klein, then with *New York* magazine, later with *Newsweek* and *The New Yorker,* who had written a series of columns drawing national attention to Clinton, told me the Arkansas Governor was the most exciting Democrat in a generation. The third was Samuel Berger (universally known as Sandy), a partner in a leading Washington law firm and a former colleague in the Vance State Department.

I met Governor Clinton and his wife, Hillary, at several New York events in the early fall of 1991, and introduced him at one. After a breakfast meeting with a very smart and, it seemed to me, very young aide named George Stephanopoulos, I called Sandy Berger and told him I was ready to support Governor Clinton in any way I could.

Berger predicted that President Bush would try to portray Governor Clinton as inexperienced and unqualified to deal with national security issues—a technique that had worked well for Republicans in many recent campaigns, including Reagan's 1980 win over Jimmy Carter and Bush's defeat of Michael Dukakis in 1988. To prevent this, Sandy wanted to form a small group to work on national security issues early. The core group Berger had in mind would consist of the two of us and his old boss from the Vance State Department, Tony Lake. Sandy thought that Tony, who was teaching at Mount Holyoke, would have more time available than either of us, and, if he took leave in the fall, might be able to devote all his time to the campaign while we assisted him. Lake was at first reluctant: he was planning to write a book about the campaign, not participate in it. Sandy asked if I would call Tony and help persuade him to accept the challenge.

I was pleased to do so. Tony Lake and I had been close friends for a long time. We had entered the Foreign Service together in 1962, studied Vietnamese together, and served in Vietnam together. Twice in our careers, with his support, I had succeeded him, first as the aide to the Ambassador in Saigon, then as an assistant to the number-two person in the State Department, Nicholas Katzenbach, during the Johnson Administration. I had been the head of the search committee that had given him the job as the director of International Voluntary Services, a small private organization similar to the Peace Corps. He had made the arrangements for my wedding, in Saigon, in 1964; I was godfather to his second child. If we were no longer as close as we used to be—given the effects of time and diverging career paths after 1980—we had remained in constant touch and worked together for thirty years.

Shortly after our talk Tony went to Little Rock to meet the candidate. The meeting was a success, and Tony quickly got started.

The Clinton campaign message was, famously, focused on the economy. Still, it was not wise to leave Bush's leadership in foreign policy unchallenged—a mistake that had badly damaged Dukakis in 1988. To deal with this dilemma, the team proposed to Governor Clinton and Senator Gore a two-pronged approach on foreign policy. On the negative side, they would criticize the Bush record; we did not think it as invulnerable as was commonly believed. On the positive side, Governor Clinton would present positions that would show him as slightly more forward-looking than Bush. As this strategy took shape in the summer of 1992, the issue that presented itself most starkly—because it fit both parts of this strategy—was Bosnia.

The tragedy in the former Yugoslavia was suddenly emerging into world consciousness. About the same time that I made my first trip there in the summer of 1992, the world began to see shocking film of emaciated prisoners in northern Bosnia, looking at the unblinking camera through barbed-wire fences, scenes straight out of World War II—yet happening now.

Governor Clinton attacked. Criticizing the Bush Administration for "turning its back on violations of basic human rights" and "being slow on the uptake," he called on President Bush to show "real leadership" and urged air strikes, supported by the United States if necessary, against the Serbs if they continued to block the delivery of humanitarian goods to the people trapped in Sarajevo. President Bush fired back, attacking his opponent for a "reckless approach that indicates Clinton better do some homework." However, by early August, partly in response to the criticism, the Bush Administration had adjusted its policy, urging the United Nations Security Council to use force, if necessary, to deliver humanitarian aid to Bosnia. But Clinton pressed on in a speech in Los Angeles on August 14 (the same day, by coincidence, that I was in Banja Luka), promising he would "make the United States the catalyst for a collective stand against aggression." "In a world of change," he said, "security flows from initiative, not from inertia." None of this made much of an impact on the American electorate, but it got a lot of attention in Europe.

As I told Tony and Sandy, these were correct and brave positions, both morally and politically, and both men deserved praise for proposing them. There was only one concern, I said: Would *President* Clinton carry out what *candidate* Clinton proposed? Proud of getting Governor Clinton to take these positions, Lake said he was confident they would be part of the policy if Clinton was elected. With this in mind, after the trip, I wrote a memorandum to the candidates on August 23:

To: Governor Clinton, Senator Gore (through Tony Lake and Sandy
           Berger)
From: Richard Holbrooke
Subject: Former Yugoslavia

    . . . Whatever happens the rest of this year, the next Administration is certain to be confronted with a problem of staggering political, strategic, and humanitarian dimensions. I therefore want to bring the following points to your attention:

    1. The Bush Administration's reactions have been weak and inadequate. . . .

    2. The attention of the press, the efforts of the international relief community, and the belated response of European leaders and President Bush may have slowed down the more awful aspects of the situation, but only slightly. . . .

    3. Your public statements have made a real difference, especially in pushing the Bush Administration into doing more than they otherwise would have done. They have also been interpreted as a sign that, if elected, you will follow a more vigorous policy against Serb aggression, which is the right signal to be sending to all parties. . . .

    This is not a choice between Vietnam and doing nothing, as the Bush Administration has portrayed it. There are many actions that might be done now, including: dropping the arms embargo against the Bosnians, stationing U.N. observers along the Kosovo and Macedonia borders. . . . Doing nothing now risks a far greater and more costly involvement later.

In the weeks after Clinton's election victory, I heard little from my campaign colleagues; people with whom I had spent hours were now closeted in transition meetings in Little Rock or otherwise inaccessible. Asked by a Washington-based representative of the Presidential Transition Task Force what I hoped to do in the Clinton Administration, I replied that unless offered the position of Deputy Secretary of State, which was highly unlikely, I would prefer to remain a private citizen in New York and undertake special negotiating assignments for the Administration—a sort of troubleshooter role. Ever since my experience in Paris in 1968 as a junior member of the Vietnam negotiating team under Averell Harriman and Cyrus Vance, I had wanted to test myself against the most difficult negotiations in the world. At this time, I said, the toughest seemed to be Bosnia; I would be interested in becoming the American negotiator for that problem, a position that did not exist in the Bush Administration.

In those weeks Strobe Talbott and Brooke Shearer stayed in close touch. After Strobe turned down the ambassadorship to Russia for family reasons, the President-elect asked his former Oxford housemate to serve as a senior advisor on relations with the former Soviet Union.* It was a perfect job for him; he had unwittingly been preparing for it most of his life, studying Russian language and history, and writing a series of important books on U.S.-Soviet relations. I helped him draft terms of reference that would give him a larger role than that of previous senior advisors on Soviet affairs, a position that had existed in many earlier administrations, but always as a one-person shop. With the Soviet Union broken up into fifteen independent nations, the existing Bureau of European and Canadian Affairs could not handle the extra responsibility. We proposed creating a separate office to oversee relations with the former Soviet republics, closely linked to the old European Bureau. Despite some grumbling from the bureaucracy, it was put into effect over the next year under his leadership and with the backing of Secretary Christopher.†

CHRISTMAS IN CAMBODIA, NEW YEAR'S IN SARAJEVO

In mid-December, Tony Lake called to tell me that he was going to be the President's National Security Advisor. People who did not understand our

---

* Brooke Shearer was named Director of the prestigious White House Fellows Program, which she dramatically revitalized and revamped, making it more engaged in current events and more diverse in its selection process. In the second term, she became senior advisor to the Deputy Secretary of Interior.

† Because the United States had never accepted the incorporation of the three Baltic states, Estonia, Latvia, and Lithuania, into the Soviet Union, responsibility for them was left in the European Bureau.

complicated relationship had suggested that Tony and I were competitors for this position, but the truth was otherwise. As Tony and Sandy both knew, I had supported Tony for this job. His experience as Henry Kissinger's assistant in the Nixon White House—a position he resigned in 1970 to protest the invasion of Cambodia—had given him the perfect background for this demanding job. Besides, as I told Tony, I did not wish to compete with him; I wanted to work with him, as we so often had in the past, always with success.

Standing in the kitchen of a friend's house during a New York dinner party, I congratulated Tony and offered him whatever assistance he wanted. When he asked what would interest me, I repeated my conversation with the official from the transition team, and mentioned Bosnia. We ended by reminiscing about the long road that had led from Saigon to his new job—the job of his dreams—and Tony closed by promising he would keep in close touch.

Feeling detached from the excitement swirling around Washington, I decided to make a trip unusual for the holiday season, but fitting my mood. I spent Christmas Eve in Bangkok, floating down the river on a restaurant-boat with a group of Thai officials and Senator and Mrs. Sam Nunn. It was one of those strange cross-cultural experiences Asia offers Americans: we sang Christmas carols and listened to a Thai businessman demonstrate his love of the United States by reciting to us, word for word, President Kennedy's Inaugural Address. The next morning I flew to Phnom Penh, Cambodia's exhausted capital, to spend Christmas Day with Tim Carney, a Foreign Service officer who had been assigned to work on the U.N.-sponsored elections. During the day I talked at length with the senior U.N. representative in Cambodia, Yasushi Akashi, who had done a fine job in a nearly impossible situation. At the time these were simply interesting personal conversations with friends, but they later took on another, deeper meaning: when my diplomatic mission began in 1995, Akashi was the U.N. Secretary-General's senior representative in the former Yugoslavia, and our previous association proved valuable. And Carney, who became Ambassador to the Sudan, would later be part of our planning team for the final negotiations, advising us on how to supervise an election just after a war.

After another day in Southeast Asia, long one of my favorite parts of the world, I left for Zagreb, thinking that perhaps no one else on earth in 1992 would spend Christmas in Cambodia and New Year's in Bosnia. As my oldest son, David, said, "Who else could possibly want to do such a crazy thing?"

First Brush with the Krajina. On December 28, 1992, the afternoon I arrived in Zagreb, I was invited to meet the Foreign Minister of Croatia, Mate Granic. This was my first meeting with a man who was already a key figure in the negotiations, and with whom I would later spend many hours. Balding, immaculately dressed, charming, and polite, he greeted me and almost immediately began to explain why, if the United Nations did not fulfill its obligations under the Vance plan and restore the Krajina to its rightful owners, another war between Serbia and Croatia was inevitable.

Granic seated me on a sofa—"in the exact spot where Cy Vance sits," he said, with obvious pride—and took out a huge map of his country. Then, in a controlled but intense manner, Granic described how the Serbs had used the Vance Plan as cover to drive the Croats out of their lands in the Krajina. "Over twenty-five percent of our land is occupied by the Serbs," Granic said. "Before the war there were two hundred and ninety-five thousand Croats in the Krajina. Now there are only three thousand five hundred. This is our land. This is our country. The Serbs have cut our country almost in half. This is wholly unacceptable to us."

Granic's mild, almost deferential style was in sharp contrast to his words. If the Serbs did not return the Krajina peacefully, he said, his country would have to go to war again. As Granic's hands moved quickly over the large map in front of us, outlining Croatia's "lost territory," it occurred to me that this must have been how the French felt about Alsace-Lorraine, annexed by the Germans after the War of 1870–71, until they regained it after World War I; as Henry Kissinger had written, the effort "to regain that region had sustained French policy for half a century."[1]

Granic left the impression that a war to regain the Krajina would take place no later than the summer of 1993. In fact, it would be two and a half years before Tudjman attacked. I would never forget that conversation, however, which first alerted me to the absolute implacable determination of the Zagreb government to regain every inch of their territory.

A Wooden Statue. While in Zagreb, I visited several refugee camps, accompanied by Stephanie Frease, a dedicated young American refugee worker from Cleveland who spoke Croatian perfectly. One of her parents was Serb, the other Croat, and until the wars began, she had lived in Cleveland almost unaware of the enmity between the two peoples. We visited a refugee camp in Karlovac, about an hour from Zagreb, where we listened to chilling accounts of how the Serbs had carried out ethnic cleansing in Bosnia. Story after story reflected the confusion of the Muslims; they described how some of the Serbs with whom they had lived and worked for decades turned on them in the summer of 1992. Stephanie struggled through tears as she translated.

Among those we talked to was a young man who identified himself only as a baker from Sanski Most. Suddenly, he fished a plastic bag out from under a thin mattress, and handed me two carefully wrapped wooden figures. "I carved these with a piece of broken glass while I was at Manjaca prison camp," he said, "to show how we had to stand during the day, with our heads down and our hands tied behind our backs." The small figures seemed to burn in my hand with their pain and intensity. Mumbling something about their power and beauty, I started to hand them back. "No," he said. "Please take them back to your country, and show them to your people. Show the Americans how we have been treated. Tell America what is happening to us."

When I returned to New York a week later, I took the wooden statues with me to an interview on the Charlie Rose show, and showed them on camera. Within days, the editor of *The New York Times Magazine,* Jack Rosenthal, asked to print a full-page color photograph of one of the statues, along with a short description of how I had received it. In 1993, the IRC reproduced it on a bronze plaque, which they gave annually to someone who had made a contribution in the field of refugee relief. The baker got his wish—and in 1995, the IRC honored me with the award.

Sarajevo. After the visit to the refugee camp, Stephanie and I flew to Split, staying with the IRC field officer there, then set out, on December 30, for the interior of Bosnia. We spent the day driving through the steep and rocky ravines that had always made Yugoslavia such difficult terrain for military operations, stopping frequently to talk to international relief workers—an inspiring group of men and women from many lands—and listen to stories of families torn apart by the war.

As dusk fell, we drove on to Vitez, where we planned to spend the night, look at refugee operations, and return to the coast. Once again, however, chance changed my plans. When we arrived in Vitez, there was a telephone call waiting from Lionel Rosenblatt, who by coincidence was at that moment only one hour away in Zenica, and had discovered that we were headed in his direction. Lionel was traveling with Sylvana Foa, the press spokesperson for the UNHCR. They were going to try to get into Sarajevo the next day, and asked if we would like to join them. Of course, we said yes.

Rosenblatt, the most dynamic person I knew in the refugee field, had ranged across the globe over the previous two decades, going wherever the problems were greatest—Cambodia, the Turkish-Iraqi border, Somalia, and now Bosnia—trying to rally public attention and support for the plight of refugees. His small nonprofit humanitarian organization, Refugees International, had made a name for itself by pressuring—or, not to put too fine a point on it, harassing—governments around the world into doing more for their unwanted refugee populations.*

---

* Full disclosure: after leaving the government in 1995, I became chairman of the board of Refugees International.

In order to get to Sarajevo the next day, we had to drive to Zenica that night. Under a moonless sky, on a sharp curve on the road between Vitez and Zenica, our vehicle hit a sheet of ice, spun a full 360 degrees, and finally bumped up against a dirt embankment only inches short of a twenty-foot drop into an icy stream. Catching our breath, we drove on to Zenica, where we found Lionel and Sylvana dining at the grimy International Hotel, seated among assorted military personnel and civilian aid workers.

To get into Sarajevo, we would have to travel through Serb-controlled territory in United Nations armored personnel carriers. Under the agreement reached between the U.N. and the Serbs, who controlled the road, we needed U.N. accreditation papers. Everyone else in our group had such papers, but I did not.

With his usual ingenuity and bravado, Lionel solved the problem. From his bag, he fished out a motley collection of mug shots and, after some deliberation, picked one out. Lionel, it turned out, carried a collection of pictures for just such an occasion. "This ought to do the trick," he announced as I looked in astonishment at the photograph, which I did not think looked at all like me.

In the morning, Lionel obtained a blank U.N. identity pass from another one of his many friends—he seemed to know everyone—and created a U.N. identity card for me, using a cigarette lighter to seal some plastic he had found. Watching Lionel's performance with a combination of admiration and apprehension, I thought of Milo Minderbinder, the character in *Catch-22* who sold eggs to both sides during World War II.

Equipped with this highly dubious identification, we drove to Kiseljak in our own vehicle. This was as far as we could go without U.N. authorization; the final stage of the trip, which crossed Serb lines, would be in a U.N. armored personnel carrier. After buying food at a store near the U.N. base, with the thought of giving it away in Sarajevo, the four of us jammed into a Danish armored personnel carrier; I sat in front, under a huge helmet, trying to look invisible. Four or five times as we proceeded toward the Bosnian capital we were stopped at Serb checkpoints, where men and women—some heavily made up for New Year's Eve parties—poked rifles around the inside of the APC and inspected our IDs. It was only much later that I realized how dangerous the trip had been.

The Danes dropped us off at the Post Office Building in Sarajevo, where the press and most international aid workers worked. As we climbed out of the APC and blinked into the weak afternoon sun, a black limousine passed slowly by, followed closely by a U.N. tank, painted white, and hordes of journalists. Looking through the heavily tinted windows of the limousine, I saw, but only for a moment, a tired-looking Cy Vance staring straight ahead on one side of the car, and U.N. Secretary-General Boutros Boutros-Ghali on the other. Vance did not see me through the dark tinted glass, nor would he have recognized me, in my heavy flak jacket and helmet, bundled up against the biting cold and caked in dirt. It was a strange feeling to see my old boss behind the plate glass of an armored car just as I arrived in Sarajevo in an APC—so close, yet so far away.

Two days in that hellhole left impressions for a lifetime. That winter, people burned their books and furniture (usually starting with the closets and bookshelves) to keep warm. Some food was reaching Sarajevo, but it was poorly distributed, especially to the outlying areas. The cold was biting and debilitating. It sapped one's strength so quickly that every other activity, such as collecting food from a distribution center, was extremely difficult. The shooting (small arms, machine guns, mortars, snipers, artillery) was almost continuous, and had a destructive effect even on the extraordinarily brave people of Sarajevo. The international community of relief workers and journalists was huddled in three miserable locations—the Post Office Building, the shattered and grotesque Holiday Inn, and the airport, all of which were under frequent sniper fire. Every street was littered with destroyed vehicles, lying on their sides and blown apart, and I saw not a single building that was not damaged. There was no running water anywhere except at a few outside locations, some of which were sniper targets. The Serbs had destroyed several parts of town, the Muslims others; in some areas the two sides were separated by only a block.

In the midst of this inferno, the U.N. agencies, including the U.N. military (known as UNPROFOR, or United Nations Protection Force), negotiated the content and size of each relief convoy with the Bosnian Serbs, who permitted about half of what was needed to reach the city, just enough so that the world did not demand decisive military action. It was as if the U.N. were negotiating with the city's executioners as to whether Sarajevo's death would be by starvation or freezing, slow or fast. By allowing the Bosnian Serbs to determine what got in, the U.N. had, in effect, become an unintentional accomplice to Serb policy. In its press releases, the UNHCR boasted about the amount of food it had brought in, not the inadequacy of the system or the rising death toll.

From my journal:

1 A.M., January 1, 1993, Sarajevo—As this strangest New Year's Eve reaches its end, I am in an ice-cold room at the Holiday Inn, with no water, one small electric light that goes on and off without warning, listening to the sound of sniper fire (or is it celebrating?).

This Holiday Inn has to be one of the most peculiar hotels ever. Its cavernous lobby/atrium is freezing cold, dark, and dismal. The upper stories are shot to hell, with gaping holes to the outside world. The upper stories are closed to guests, since the fighting inside the Inn left them in shambles, and there is still blood all over the rooms.

No elevators or service, obviously. We carry our bags up to our freezing rooms. We eat in the hotel dining room with John Burns of *The New York Times,* the very essence of the old-time foreign correspondent. I first knew him in Asia. He is courageous, maybe even slightly crazy-courageous, and just the man for a New Year's Eve in Sarajevo. Other reporters pour in, and the room gradually fills with a noisy, smelly crowd of smokers, universally criticizing Boutros-Ghali for his press conference performance today. He actually said he could think of at least ten places on earth that were worse than Sarajevo—a very peculiar and ill-advised statement to make anywhere, but especially here.

After dinner, Burns invites us to go with him to a local New Year's Eve party. Thus ends 1992, in a crowded, noisy, and very smoky place called The Hole in the Wall—because to reach it one has to walk through a hole in a wall made by a mortar round. It is crammed with young people dancing, shouting, drinking, and trying to forget the nightmare around them. A mixture of reporters, U.N. people, and young Sarajevans who work with them or know them. They dance feverishly to the Rolling Stones, throw beer at each other at midnight, and hug each other continually. . . . The girls are beautiful, but the whole thing feels hopelessly melancholy. Was this how the Spanish Civil War felt, a romantic lost cause?

Midday, January 1, 1993—At 7:30 we rise, don't bother to dress since we slept fully clothed; don't bother to wash since there is no water; and go down for breakfast—an excellent cup of tea, some stale cheese and two awful slices of bologna. A big storm is forecast. I debate leaving early, can't make up my frozen mind, and, after checking out of the Holiday Inn (cash only), drive in an armored car to the PTT, where we can see children foraging through the debris and begging in the freezing cold. . . . Automatic weapon fire can be heard frequently as we cross the city. We pass the newspaper offices, once a proud tower, now reduced to almost total rubble. But from the basement people are still putting out a daily paper.* A man sits in the debris of the one of the public buses, holding his head in his hands, presumably drunk from the previous night.

In a "soft skin" (an unarmored vehicle) we race to the airport, weaving across the bridge where sniper fire has killed so many people, snaking through checkpoints, past overturned trucks and buses, and over icy roads.

2:30 P.M.: We are still at the Sarajevo airport, waiting amidst growing confusion and tension. In the last hour, the British and Canadian planes have been cancelled; a U.S. Air Force plane refused to take us out; there are reports that the Bosnians are massing in the hills around the airport, and that the UNHCR has ordered the evacuation of all of its personnel from Sarajevo immediately.

As in Vietnam, much of war is mindless waiting, but waiting in wartime is strangely paradoxical. One's senses are sharper because of the heightened sense of danger, but at the same time, there is an extraordinary waste of time and effort.

---

* The story of this brave newspaper, *Oslobodjenje,* is told by its former editor, Kemal Kurspahic, in *As Long As Sarajevo Exists.*

Zagreb, later: Weary almost beyond description, we get out of Sarajevo, just ahead of nightfall. Our Canadian plane crew, obviously in a great hurry to leave, shovels us aboard. The crewman in the belly of the C-130 yells at us, "O.K. Hold on. We're going to do a zoom takeoff!" and quickly buckles himself in. The plane leaves the ground quickly but does not rise at first, hovering about six feet off the ground until almost reaching the end of the runway. Then, with a tremendous thrust of power, it seems to go almost straight up in the air, soaring over the hills filled with Serb snipers and, perhaps, massing Bosnian troops.

Landing in Zagreb, we head directly for the Inter-Continental Hotel. Never had a shower seemed so wonderful. I turn on the television and hear CNN proclaiming the start of a major offensive.

I returned to New York full of a sense that something had to be done rapidly. I turned for advice, as I had done so often in the last twenty-five years, to my friend Les Gelb, then a columnist for *The New York Times,* who warned me that Clinton's team, in the midst of a delicate minuet over their own interrelationships, did not want to hear about Bosnia. Earlier, as I sat freezing at the Sarajevo airport, I had written in my journal: "If I don't make my views known to the new team, I will not have done enough to help the desperate people we have just seen; but if I push my views I will appear too aggressive. I feel trapped."

THE 1993 MEMORANDUM

On January 13, 1993, one week before they were to assume office, I sent a long memorandum to Warren Christopher and Tony Lake. It began:

> Bosnia will be the key test of American policy in Europe. We must therefore succeed in whatever we attempt. The Administration cannot afford to begin with either an international disaster or a quagmire. Despite the difficulties and risks involved, I believe that inaction or a continuation of the Bush policies in Bosnia by the Clinton Administration is the least desirable course. Continued inaction carries long-term risks which could be disruptive to U.S.-European relations, weaken NATO, increase tension in Greece and Turkey, and cause havoc with Moscow. . . .
>
> No one with whom I talked last August expected the Bosnians to last this long. . . . An important reason the Bosnian Muslims are surviving is that they are beginning to get significant weapons shipments from Islamic nations, apparently including Iran. These are coming through Croatia, *with Croatian complicity.** . . . Four key points about these *not-so-secret* secret shipments to the Muslims:

---

* All italics in the original memorandum.

—first, the Croats, who do not want to let the Muslims become too strong, have not allowed them to include heavy weapons or artillery;

—second, every weapons shipments has a Croatian "weapons tax"; that is, the Croats siphon off some of the weapons for their own army and for the HVO [the Bosnian Croats] in Bosnia-Herzegovina;

—third, there is now strong evidence that small but growing numbers of "freedom fighters" or mujahideen are joining the Bosnian forces, although, as one might expect, the strict fundamentalists from the Mideast and the loose, secular Muslims of Bosnia do not understand each other or mix well;

—finally, these shipments will continue—and they will increase.*

I suggested four objectives for the new Administration: first, "to save as many lives as possible in Bosnia"; second, "to make containment of the war a top priority"; third, "to punish the Serbs for their behavior . . . and to brand certain individuals war criminals"; fourth, "to use this crisis as an opportunity to strengthen the U.N. system." We should act, I added, "in concert with other nations," even creating "some sort of ad hoc military coalition, [but] avoid getting dragged into a ground war in the region."

At the time the incoming Administration was trying to decide whether to support peace proposals put forward by Cyrus Vance and David Owen, the former British Foreign Secretary who had replaced Lord Carrington as the European Union negotiator. The Vance-Owen plan proposed dividing Bosnia into ten "cantons," some of which would be Muslim-controlled, some Serb-controlled, and some Croat-controlled. It had been attacked by many American commentators as a sellout, another Munich, and a precursor to the breakup of Bosnia.

* When I wrote these paragraphs in January 1993, no one could have imagined that this matter would re-emerge four years later as the subject of numerous journalistic inquiries and six congressional investigations, and become a major issue again during Tony Lake's attempt to become CIA Director.

These investigations were premised on the theory that secret arms shipments to the Bosnians from Iran had *begun in 1994,* and that the Clinton Administration had somehow acted illegally in not stopping them. It is especially noteworthy, therefore, that the activities in question were already taking place two years earlier, during the Bush Administration, with the clear knowledge of American Embassy and U.N. officials in Zagreb, and were even mentioned in newspaper stories at the time.

The events that were investigated took place in April 1994, when I was still Ambassador to Germany, but in late 1996 I was asked to testify several times as to my subsequent knowledge. The United States had played no role in the covert assistance to the Bosnians and the Croatians, but when asked for his views by President Tudjman, Ambassador Galbraith, under instructions, had not objected. This was the correct policy decision, although it was sloppily executed. As I stated in sworn testimony before the Senate Intelligence Committee, the "covert" support given to the Bosnian Muslims by Islamic nations (including Iran) had helped keep the Sarajevo government alive at a time when its survival hung by a thread. For the United States to have continued to object to such assistance without providing something to replace it would in my opinion have been unconscionable.

There was already deep division within the new team about Bosnia. The Joint Chiefs of Staff, led by its formidable Chairman, Colin Powell, was especially opposed to American involvement. The Vance-Owen plan was flawed, but if the United States killed it without coming up with a plan of its own, the consequences would be far worse, so I recommended that Washington give qualified public support to their plan:

> If Vance-Owen leads to a temporary cessation of fighting and relief to the Muslims, and offers the new Administration some breathing room to put a [full-fledged] policy into place, it should be welcomed. It will not solve the problem, only perhaps let the world think it is solved for a while. If the Vance-Owen plan is rejected, we must face the fact that the negotiating track is effectively dead—and that using it as an excuse for inaction or insufficient action is no longer acceptable.

I ended the memorandum with a series of specific recommendations, actions that the United States should consider, especially if the Vance-Owen plan was either rejected or if it failed. This was the most provocative part of the paper:

> LIFTING THE ARMS EMBARGO TO BOSNIA: I favored lifting the arms embargo to the Bosnians before I visited the region, and am still in favor of it, if it can gain UN Security Council approval. But this might be difficult to obtain (and create strains with Moscow). . . .
>
> I would therefore [also] recommend consideration of something that I know will cause many people heartburn: that we allow covert arms supply to the Bosnian Muslims, *so that Bosnia's outside support no longer comes solely from the Islamic nations.* Such a policy requires sophistication within the USG, including Congress, and, if it involves the US directly, a legal finding. It would undoubtedly leak, as our support to the Afghan resistance leaked long before it was openly acknowledged. But this might be the best way to help the Bosnians *quickly* without provoking a new round of escalatory steps from the Serbs. It does, however, carry the serious drawback of showing the United States evading a Security Council resolution that it previously supported. This concern could be lessened if our actions were accompanied by public efforts at the UN to change the embargo, or if *we acted only through third parties,* as we did in Afghanistan.
>
> DIRECT USE OF FORCE AGAINST THE SERBS: Bombing the Bosnian Serbs and even Serbia proper if necessary would send the proper message. However, the actions must be effective, both militarily and politically! . . . If done only to show the world we are "doing something," minor bombing—like the enforcement of the no-fly zone—might be a quick public relations success, but it would be followed by a long-term disaster.

ESTABLISH AN AMERICAN DIPLOMATIC PRESENCE IN SARAJEVO: This would be a dramatic step to show the world where we stand. An American Embassy can be very small; symbolism counts.

KEEP UP THE PRESSURE ON THE WAR CRIMINAL ISSUE: This policy, while belated, is useful. Name more names. Set up a separate staff to create more pressure on this front.

As Gelb had warned, the memo was not welcome; in fact, I got no reply. Finally, some weeks after the Inauguration, I called Lake to ask if he had received it. Yes, he said, they had gotten it; it was "useful," but it contained some suggestions that would "undercut us at the U.N." We argued the issue briefly, but hopelessly. I told Tony again of my interest in special duty on Bosnia, but he did not respond; a few weeks later the Administration appointed Reginald Bartholomew, the former Ambassador to NATO, as special negotiator on Bosnia.

CHAPTER 4

Bonn to Washington

(1993–94)

Life is lived forward, but understood backward.
—SØREN KIERKEGAARD

AN UNEXPECTED ASSIGNMENT

MY PHONE RANG IN NEW YORK AT 6:45 in the morning. It was June 8, 1993. Since the Inauguration, I had kept in sporadic contact with various people in the Administration, but not on Bosnia, an issue that was placing great strain on the new foreign policy team. In January, Peter Tarnoff, calling on behalf of Christopher, had asked if I wished to be considered for Ambassador to Japan, a country to which I had made almost one hundred trips. I would be honored, I said, to let my name go forward. I heard nothing further on the matter for almost five months.

There had been one exception to my disengagement from Bosnia. In February, soon after Tarnoff called to discuss Tokyo, I asked for a private meeting with Tony Lake. I felt obliged, almost compelled, to offer some unsolicited thoughts on Bosnia.

Tony and I ate lunch, served by a Navy steward from the White House mess, alone in his office in the West Wing. I urged him to press for a greater American effort to stop the accelerating catastrophe in Bosnia. He protested, arguing that while people were still dying in large numbers, "you don't know how many more people would now be dead if it were not for our efforts." I replied that this was true but irrelevant. Even if, as Tony claimed, the situation was better than if the Bush Administration were still in office, it still fell far short of what it should be, and of what the world had been lead to expect by Governor Clinton's campaign rhetoric, which he was once so proud of having written. Agitated, Tony said he was doing his best and asked me to be patient. The meeting ended coolly and inconclusively.

A few weeks later, Warren Christopher went to London, Paris, and Bonn with a proposal to lift the arms embargo and conduct air strikes against the Bosnian Serbs—"lift and strike," as the idea was termed. The European reaction was, predictably, negative. The Administration began to reel, destabilized by this rebuff and troubled by the deteriorating situation on the ground. As the chances of American involvement visibly declined, the Serbs became bolder. Croat attacks on Muslims also increased. Soon a war-within-a-war between Bosnian Croats and Bosnian Muslims broke out at Mostar and other multiethnic towns. Meanwhile, the press was flaying the Administration for its weakness. Although no one wanted the United States to get involved in a ground war in Bosnia, public opinion was divided over what to do. Deeply frustrated, Christopher publicly referred to Bosnia as "the problem from hell."

After Tarnoff's call in February I heard nothing but rumors about the Embassy in Tokyo. A delay of several months on appointments was not uncommon in the Clinton Administration, but it was disconcerting, and increased the chances of leaks. In April, Walter F. Mondale turned down an offer to become Ambassador to Russia and indicated to the White House his interest in Tokyo. On June 4, with the issue still undecided, Elaine Sciolino wrote a front-page article in *The New York Times* describing the awkwardness of a situation in which "two old friends and allies," one of them a former Vice President of the United States, the other a former Assistant Secretary of State, had been cast as "reluctant warriors in an unseemly contest that pits political eminence against diplomatic experience." Mondale, one of the most decent people I ever worked for, called me immediately to let me know how much he regretted the whole business. He ended by saying, "We'll all get through this thing."

"I have good news and bad news." I was still half-asleep when Christopher began the conversation on June 8 with uncharacteristic mischievousness. "The bad news is that the President has asked Fritz Mondale to go to Tokyo. [Pause.] The good news is that he would like you to go to Germany."

To say I was stunned would be an understatement. The idea of serving in Germany had never entered my mind, and no one had ever mentioned it as a possibility. "I know this is rather sudden," Christopher said, "but we need your decision as quickly as possible." In tongue-tied astonishment, I was able to ask only one question: "Chris, how did the President reach this decision?"

"I have no idea," Christopher replied. Then, with apologies, saying he had to board a plane, he hung up.* Thus began a sequence of almost accidental

---

* More than three years later, while I was researching this book, Sandy Berger told me that when the *Times* article appeared, Sandy knew immediately that the long uncertainty over Tokyo was about to end with the choice of the former Vice President. Hoping to see both of us serve the new Administration, Sandy suggested to the President that he send me to Bonn, which was still open.

events that would lead me, via a convoluted and rocky path, back to the Bosnia assignment for which I had once volunteered.

Curiously, even though it was only one hour by plane to the war zone, Bosnia rarely came up during my year in Germany. The issue was handled entirely by Charles Redman, a senior Foreign Service officer who had replaced Ambassador Bartholomew as the Bosnia negotiator. Although I welcomed Redman each time he came to Bonn, I stayed away from the process, barely glancing at the endless telegrams on the situation in Bosnia. I now felt detached from the issue, knowing I could do nothing further about it, and was immersed in my fascinating new job.

But all was not well in Washington. Bosnia was beginning to damage American foreign policy throughout Europe. The press was merciless in its coverage of the Administration. The pressure reached into the highest levels of the government, and in the fall of 1993, to my great pleasure, Warren Christopher promoted Strobe Talbott to Deputy Secretary of State as part of a dramatic reorganization that greatly strengthened the State Department's senior management. At the same time, less happily, Les Aspin was forced out as Secretary of Defense, ending a brief and difficult tenure in the job that he had dreamed about for such a long time. Tragically, his forced departure from the Pentagon turned out to mark the end of his impressive career; he died less than two years later from a brain clot. As Frank Wisner wrote me from India, despite his enormous achievements, Aspin's life was unfinished. His many friends could not think of Les—his clothes always rumpled, his quick mind always asking questions, his cheerful mood masking deep uncertainty and loneliness—without an immense feeling of sadness.

By early 1994, stories were circulating widely in Washington about growing problems in the Bureau of European and Canadian Affairs. In the spring both Tarnoff and Talbott called and asked if I would consider leaving Bonn to take it over. I told them that, having served as Assistant Secretary of State for East Asian and Pacific Affairs fifteen years earlier, I was not interested in returning to Washington for a similar job; I loved my job in Germany and wanted to stay at least another year. But Peter and Strobe kept calling.

Finally, in May, Talbott played his ace: both the Secretary of State and the President wanted it to happen. This dramatically changed the nature of the request; I believed strongly that if the man who had given me the assignment on the Rhine wished to take it away, it was his prerogative; a presidential appointee owes the President his complete loyalty in such matters.

After a private meeting with Christopher in Rome, I agreed to take the job on one condition: that I could chose all my deputies. I asked to delay my return long enough to complete a full year in Germany and participate in President Clinton's trip to Bonn and Berlin.

. . .

Talbott and Tarnoff had listed three priorities for the new job: revitalizing the European Bureau, shaping a coherent policy on the enlargement of NATO, and Bosnia. I told Strobe I had one major concern. There were about thirty people in the State Department with the rank or equivalent rank of assistant secretary; this level of government no longer carried the authority it once had. But, in order to succeed on such contentious issues as Bosnia and NATO, I would have to operate in a rather assertive manner. If I were to operate in a routine manner, putting process ahead of substance, I might make fewer enemies but would have less chance of accomplishing their goals.

When I laid out this "lose-lose" dilemma to Strobe, he laughed. "We assume you will be aggressive," he said. "That's why we need you. We'll back you up." This time it was my turn to laugh. "How long have you been in Washington?" I asked, amused. "Anyway," Strobe said, "*I'll* back you up—and you'll finally be part of *our* team."

The President Visits Germany. Ambassadors dream of a presidential visit during their tenure. Although it is a logistical nightmare, the security requirements beyond any outsider's imagination, it can make a huge difference to policy. It is an unforgettable experience; ambassadors can dine out for the rest of their lives on tales of chaos and near disaster, their own brilliance in preventing some terrible calamity, and their moments with the President.

At the time of President Clinton's trip to Germany in July 1994 I was still in Germany, awaiting Senate confirmation hearings for my new post. The highlight of the trip—and one of the highlights of my government career— was President Clinton's visit to Berlin on July 12. He was the first U.S. President to visit Berlin since unification, and I proposed that he and Chancellor Kohl walk through the Brandenburg Gate from West to East as a symbol of the new Germany. Once inside what was once East Berlin, the two men would address as large a crowd as we could assemble.

The plan worked perfectly. On a nearly cloudless day, Clinton and Kohl and their wives walked together through the gate and into a roaring crowd of over one hundred thousand people, many waving small American flags, supplied for the occasion by local businesses. President Clinton's speech was short and eloquent. Gigantic video screens, something unimagined in Kennedy's day, carried his face as well as his words deep down Unter den Linden. I saw Germans, including two ministers, with tears in their eyes as the President spoke in his passable German. It was probably the last great American moment for the people of Berlin, a city with an open love affair with the United States, which had given us some of the most memorable moments of the last fifty years: the Berlin Airlift, the Wall, the confrontation between Soviet and American tanks at Checkpoint Charlie in 1961, Ronald Reagan's "Mr. Gorbachev, tear down this wall" speech, and above all, John F. Kennedy's "*Ich bin ein Berliner*" address in 1963.

As the speech ended, the President characteristically plunged into the crowd, but the security lines broke down and almost caused a friendly riot. The Secret Service went into high alert and tried to rush the President back to his car, where Mrs. Clinton was already waiting, but he was enjoying himself hugely. Once back in the car, he said that Berlin had been one of the best experiences of his presidency, "the second-largest crowd, after the Inauguration, since I became President."*

"Well, then you'll let me stay," I said jokingly.

"No way," he replied amicably. "We need you back home. Anyway, you can't top this."

During the drive from the airport to the hotel in Berlin, and again the next morning, I spoke directly to the President about my new assignment. He made the usual comments about doing well, but he added something no one else had mentioned. "When you come back, I want you to get out there with the press a lot," he said. "You're good at it, and we are in real trouble." Hillary Rodham Clinton later told me the same thing in even more explicit terms.

Driving to another meeting in Berlin that day, I mentioned my conversation with the President to Warren Christopher, who said he agreed completely. But despite Christopher's comment, I expected difficulties. No question was more sensitive in the government than how to deal with the press. It was, in a sense, another lose-lose situation: keeping a "low profile" was good policy within the bureaucracy, but without public support for a controversial policy it would fail, and public support required making oneself available to the press. The risk was of being accused of seeking personal publicity, sometimes by the same journalists who had sought the access.

The European Bureau. After a routine confirmation hearing, I was sworn in as Assistant Secretary of State for European and Canadian Affairs on September 13, 1994. I passed up the large ceremony and reception that normally goes with such an event in favor of a very small event in the large front office of the Secretary of State, with just a few friends and family, and went directly to work after the ceremony.

Selecting the right personnel is 50 percent of the decisions one makes in a job. Do it wrong, and you will pay for it for the rest of your tenure, in ways both tangible and invisible. By then I had chosen Bob Frasure. I had to make

---

* This number was later passed on a few occasions, most notably during his extraordinary trip to Ireland in December 1995.

one more important personnel decision: choosing a senior deputy. Since assistant secretaries have to spend a great deal of time on the road, the senior deputy has to have the confidence of the Secretary of State and his senior aides. After some thought, I offered the job to John Kornblum, then the State Department's senior European hand.

Kornblum became my indispensable alter ego, able to take over issues I did not have time for, and an articulate spokesman for the Bureau's point of view when I was out of the country. John steadily gained the respect of the Secretary and his inner team, and when I left the government in 1996, the President and Secretary Christopher selected him as my successor. Later, they appointed him Ambassador to Germany.

My first meeting after being sworn in was on Bosnia, as was my last, seventeen months later. In between I worked on many other problems, some of which—like NATO enlargement, the Baltic states, Albania, Cyprus, Turkey, Ireland, and the turmoil in Central Europe—were both interesting and important. But there was rarely a day when Bosnia did not overwhelm every other issue, never a day when we did not feel that we were, at best, only one more disaster from the abyss. At that first meeting, both Warren Christopher and Strobe Talbott had said that they felt we were heading into a terrible new phase of the Bosnia crisis. They were right.

CHAPTER 5

From Decline to Disaster

(September 1994–August 1995)

> We stand face-to-face with the terrible question of evil and do not
> even know what is before us, let alone what to pit against it.
>
> —CARL JUNG

THE NEXT ELEVEN MONTHS WERE EXTREMELY DIFFICULT. Even as we made
progress on a wide range of issues important to the shaping of America's
post–Cold War relations with Europe—notably NATO enlargement and relations with the former Soviet satellites of central Europe—Bosnia continued to
deteriorate, raising serious questions about the nature of America's post–Cold
War commitment to Europe.

My first few weeks in Washington were dominated by NATO enlargement.
After intense internal debate, we forged a position in nine weeks, just in time
for Christopher to present it at the Foreign Ministers meeting in Brussels at the
beginning of December 1994. We announced that NATO would begin a formal dialogue in 1995 with all potential NATO members and other nations affected by the decision, including Russia. Under our timetable, no nation
would be invited to join until 1997, with actual membership slated for 1999.
The process would be careful and methodical—too slow for those, like Zbig-
niew Brzezinski and Henry Kissinger, who wanted NATO to accept new
members immediately, and too fast for those, including George Kennan and
Sam Nunn, who feared the effect of enlargement on Russia, and did not believe NATO should expand at all. Despite such challenges to the policy from
both sides, the Administration stuck to its original schedule for the next three
years—a remarkably steady course in the face of difficulties and objections
from both sides. In May 1997, in Paris, President Yeltsin signed the NATO-
Russia Founding Act, which established a new relationship between Russia
and NATO. Six weeks later, NATO formally invited Poland, Hungary, and the
Czech Republic to join, and kept the door open for other members later.

There were other achievements during my first year in Washington, including American-sponsored solutions or breakthroughs on several second-tier is-

sues that could have escalated into first-class crises. These included a serious Greek-Albanian border dispute and quarrels over political prisoners, and problems between Hungary and its two neighbors Slovakia and Romania over the treatment of their Hungarian minorities. With American encouragement, the European Union approved a controversial but important Customs Union with Turkey in the spring of 1995 and moved Cyprus into the first tier of countries to be considered for future membership. And under President Clinton's skillful personal touch, relations with Russia and its temperamental President moved steadily forward despite a series of sharp challenges.

But these steps toward an undivided and secure Europe lay in an uncertain and troubled future in the fall of 1994, when America's policies were facing great difficulties and challenges. There could be no time for self-congratulation over NATO or any other issue in the desperate nine months between November 1994 and the end of July 1995, as Bosnia went from low point to lower point, culminating in the terrible events at Srebrenica. The value of the Administration's other achievements in Europe would be dependent, after all, on what happened in Bosnia.

Pinpricks. At the end of November, the Serbs attacked Croat and Muslim positions in western Bosnia, using warplanes based at a military airfield in Udbina, in the Serb-controlled part of Croatia. This was a remarkably bold escalation of the war: not only was the use of an aircraft itself a violation of United Nations "no-fly" provisions, but these planes had crossed an international border between Croatia and Bosnia. From London, where I was at the time of the incident, I urged Christopher to insist that NATO destroy the Serb planes and the Udbina air base. The next day, NATO released photographs of large holes made in the runway at Ubdina, and proudly announced that it had launched the largest air raid in Europe since the end of World War II. Twenty-four hours later it became apparent that the "massive attack" was simply a series of minor air strikes—later contemptuously but accurately labeled "pinpricks" by the press. The runway could be repaired within a day or two, and was. The United Nations, which had agreed to the NATO air strikes, reverted to its former passivity, and the Serbs prepared to wait out the winter before attacking again. It was a shameful moment that left Bob Frasure and me deeply distressed.

Sarajevo. In early January 1995, I visited Sarajevo and Zagreb. The trip gave me new insight into the political mess within Bosnia. The Federation—the Croat-Muslim entity that had been negotiated in Washington the previous March—existed only on paper, and friction between the Croats and the Muslims was enormous. Sarajevo itself was not under attack, thanks to a four-month winter cease-fire announced by former President Jimmy Carter after a hurried trip to Sarajevo and Pale in late December. But President Izetbegovic told me that the cease-fire had been agreed to by both sides only because of the difficulty of fighting in the winter. He predicted the war would resume with even greater intensity well before the four months ran out.

Izetbegovic presented an astonishing picture of determination in the face of his difficulties. Sitting in his unheated and ill-lit Presidential Palace, its *interior* walls pockmarked with bullet holes and broken plaster, its windows partially replaced by heavy plastic sheeting, he showed no sign that he would ever yield or move his capital to the safety of nearby Tuzla. That evening, Prime Minister Haris Silajdzic and I walked alone through the frozen streets of Sarajevo as he told me of his youth in a multiethnic city where, he said, he did not even know the religion or ethnic background of his friends. "That city I knew and loved is dying because the West has not stopped this war," he said bitterly.

In March 1995, Tudjman insisted that the Serbs give up control of the Krajina, the border sections of Croatia seized in 1991 and now "administered" by the United Nations—an international presence that had become a cover for continued Serb ethnic cleansing of a once-mixed Croat-Serb region. If the Krajina region was not returned to him peacefully, Tudjman warned, he would attack it soon, no matter what the risks. This was precisely what Croatian Foreign Minister Granic had warned me about in December 1992, during my first private trip.

American and British intelligence had long predicted that if the Croatians attacked in the Krajina, the Serbs would defeat them. Secretary of Defense Perry and General Shalikashvili gave this assessment directly to the Croatian Defense Minister, Gojko Susak, in a meeting I attended in Munich on February 4, 1995, telling him that the Serbs would defeat any Croatian attack, either with their own local resources or with support from the regular Yugoslav Army under Milosevic's control. Later, after the success of his own forces, Susak enjoyed teasing me about the Munich meeting.*

In March 1995, I flew to Zagreb to try to persuade Tudjman not to launch the attack. Tudjman not only agreed not to attack the Krajina Serbs, but said he would announce it publicly if he could meet with Vice President Gore the following week, when both men would be in Copenhagen for an international conference. A week later, on March 12, Tudjman and Vice President Gore met

---

* From my notes of the meeting in Munich with Susak: "A grim meeting. Perry told Susak that we continue to feel that his government was making a mistake. Perry suggested that his country was sliding toward war and it might not turn out well for them. General Shali warned him that the JCS assessment of the balance of forces was far more pessimistic than Zagreb's. My own instinct is that the Croatian gamble might pay off, although the risks are high."

in the chaotic atmosphere of a huge conference hall in Copenhagen. Logistics were a nightmare; at one point, as we moved from meeting to meeting, the Vice President almost bumped into Fidel Castro, whom he was trying to avoid. Gore told Tudjman that the United States strongly opposed the use of force to settle the problems in the Krajina, and Tudjman pledged that he would not attack—provided the region was returned to him peacefully. The Gore-Tudjman announcement was widely hailed as a step away from the abyss, and for the time being, war was averted. But in the end, the Croatian assault in the Krajina was only delayed, not prevented, and the American intelligence judgment as to what would happen if the Croatians attacked proved—fortunately—to be profoundly wrong.

The Frasure Mission. By March the "Carter cease-fire" had begun to crumble, each side blaming the other. Frasure was by now in the midst of intense negotiations with Milosevic, enthusiastically supported by the Europeans. Several times he came close to a compromise that would suspend the U.N. economic sanctions in return for a partial recognition of Bosnia. But each time Bob returned home empty-handed. Finally, in late May, Frasure recommended that we back off and allow the new European Union negotiator, former Swedish Prime Minister Carl Bildt, who had just replaced David Owen, to take the lead for a month or two, after which we would reassess the situation. No one imagined that this short period in which the new European negotiator took the lead would coincide with some of the most disastrous events of the war.

A Personal Interlude. This may not have seemed the best time to get married, but on Sunday, May 27, that is exactly what I did, marrying Kati Marton, an American writer and journalist, in her native Budapest. It was a wonderful wedding, beautifully arranged and hosted by Ambassador Donald Blinken and his Budapest-born wife, Vera. We held the ceremony and reception in the garden of the Ambassador's residence, a building that during the Cold War had symbolized America and freedom to Kati and her parents, brave journalists who escaped from Hungary in 1957, after having been jailed by the communists before the Revolution of 1956.

Our wedding preparations were shadowed by the drama in Bosnia. Two days before the ceremony, NATO bombed Bosnian Serb positions in retaliation for the increasingly blatant Serb shelling of Sarajevo and the other "U.N. Safe Areas," which were anything but safe. The air attacks were slightly heavier than the previous "pinpricks," but not by any standards serious or sustained. In response, the Bosnian Serbs raised the stakes dramatically: they seized more than 350 U.N. peacekeepers and, calling them "human shields" against further attacks, handcuffed them to trees and telephone poles. The world's press was invited to film these men standing miserably in the broiling sun. Images of French soldiers waving white flags of surrender were broadcast around the world, to the horror of the new French President, Jacques Chirac.

The television pictures were appalling. That the world's greatest powers would be brought to their knees by such thugs seemed to me inconceivable. As Kati and I prepared for the wedding, I kept in close touch with Washington. A high-level White House meeting was scheduled for early afternoon on May 27; I realized with a start that it would be taking place at exactly the same time as our wedding.

A few hours before the ceremony I made one final call from Budapest to Washington, and was connected by the Operations Center to Madeleine Albright, John Kornblum, and Tom Donilon, Christopher's chief of staff, who were preparing for the White House meeting. Giving advice to Europeans, whose personnel were at great risk, was difficult for the United States, which had no troops in the field. The nations with peacekeepers in exposed areas, including the British, the French, and the Dutch, feared that any retaliation against the Bosnian Serbs would result in the murder of hostages and other peacekeepers, and sought to negotiate their release, an approach I feared would weaken the U.N. and strengthen the Serbs. I argued that NATO should threaten new air strikes if the hostages were not released. I closed the conversation with my colleagues by asking that my views be presented at the meeting. "I recommend," I said, "that we give the Serbs forty-eight hours to release all the hostages unharmed, and tell them that if they don't, we will bomb Pale. And then do so if necessary. I recognize that the Europeans will oppose this because they fear reprisals, but not one U.N. soldier has been executed, and the Serbs cannot be permitted to defy the entire world community any longer. I am convinced that they will cave if the threat is credible." The silence on the other end of the line suggested that my colleagues in Washington thought that, with the wedding only a few minutes away, I had lost my mind. "I'm serious," I said, "but now I have to get married."

During our honeymoon, as Kati and I tried unsuccessfully to ignore the Balkans, the Bosnian Serbs released the peacekeepers unharmed. But there was substantial, if circumstantial, evidence of secret deals between the U.N. and the Bosnian Serbs. The release of the hostages came in stages after a secret meeting on June 4 at Zvornik between the top U.N. commander, French general Bernard Janvier, and the Bosnian Serb commander, General Ratko Mladic. It was not clear what assurances, if any, the Serbs got from the U.N. commanders, but a suspicion spread rapidly that the Serbs and the local U.N. commanders had made a deal never to use NATO airpower in Bosnia again.

While Milosevic and the Pale Serbs said publicly that they had received such assurances, French and U.N. officials denied it. To this day, Washington has never been sure of what actually was agreed to, but after the hostages were released, the intensity of the Bosnian Serb military effort increased dramatically, with no further U.N. or NATO air strikes.

The senior U.N. official in the former Yugoslavia, Yasushi Akashi, who had originally approved the air strikes, told his staff that the events of May had "finally shown" their "ineffectiveness." This was a repudiation of the British commander in Sarajevo, General Rupert Smith, who had tried to put a more muscular policy into effect. U.N. Secretary-General Boutros Boutros-Ghali removed from General Smith the authority to ask NATO for air strikes and said he would personally make all future decisions on an individual basis from New York, thus further reducing the chances of more air strikes.

A debate now broke out within the Western alliance over whether or not to stay in Bosnia. Some governments with troops in Bosnia, including Canada and Great Britain, began talking openly of withdrawing. On June 2, an American pilot, Captain Scott O'Grady, was shot down flying an F-16 over Bosnia. He survived, escaping a week later to become, briefly, an American hero.

While Prime Minister John Major supported the continuation of the British presence, a majority of his Cabinet favored withdrawal before the beginning of another harsh Balkan winter. In France, President Chirac took a more assertive position. His much older predecessor, François Mitterrand, had shown the pro-Serb sentiments of many Frenchmen of his generation, steeped in the history of Serb resistance to Germany in two world wars. Chirac was different, in both style and substance; he felt that the situation in Bosnia had reached a dead end, and that the Western powers either had to strengthen their forces and punish the Bosnian Serbs, or else withdraw. Under prodding from Chirac, the British, French, and Dutch announced on June 3 the creation of a new Rapid Reaction Force to strengthen the U.N. in Bosnia. But it was not clear, perhaps not even to its creators, whether the Rapid Reaction Force was designed to keep the U.N. in Bosnia or to help it get out quickly. The existing middle ground, Chirac correctly perceived, was indefensible, both politically and militarily. If the British withdrew, the French position would be impossible. To keep the British in Bosnia, Chirac judged that greater American involvement and support were essential. If this did not happen, Chirac would support withdrawal.

Chirac thus put the Administration in a tight bind, but one that was important in forcing us to start dealing with the reality—that one way or another, the United States could no longer stay uninvolved.

OpPlan 40–104. As it happened, there was a little-noticed, but critical, exception to American policy against sending troops to Bosnia: President Clinton had pledged that American troops would be used to support a U.N. withdrawal. As the situation in Bosnia deteriorated in the spring of 1995 and many countries began talking openly of withdrawing from the U.N. force, the Pentagon and NATO completed OpPlan 40-104, a highly classified planning document that covered every aspect of NATO's role in supporting a U.N. withdrawal, from bridge building to body bags.

Immediately upon returning from our honeymoon on June 8, I asked the Pentagon for a briefing on 40-104. At first they resisted, claiming the plan was a NATO document, but finally Lieutenant General Howell Estes, the chief Pentagon planner, came to my office and laid out before Kornblum, Frasure, and me a plan that left us stunned. As Estes, who was not its author, told us, it was bold and dangerous—and had already been formally approved by the NATO Council as a planning document, thus significantly reducing Washington's options. It used twenty thousand American troops, some of whom were assigned to carry out a risky nighttime U.S. heliborne extraction of U.N. troops from isolated enclaves, an operation likely to produce casualties. As soon as General Estes finished our briefing, I rushed to Christopher's office and insisted that he and his inner team get the same briefing. When he heard it, Christopher was equally amazed.

General Estes's briefing convinced me that it would no longer be possible to stay out of Bosnia. To assist in the U.N.'s withdrawal, which would be followed by an even greater disaster, made no sense at all. Using American ground troops to fight the war was equally out of the question. Something had to be done or else a Serb victory, and additional ethnic cleansing, were inevitable. It was a terrible set of choices, but there was no way Washington could avoid involvement much longer. I still favored air strikes, but there was fierce opposition to this in most parts of the government and throughout Europe.

When OpPlan 40-104 came to the attention of senior officials, there was some confusion as to its status. Although President Clinton had promised that U.S. troops would support a U.N. withdrawal, he had never formally approved (or been briefed on) OpPlan 40-104. But it had already been endorsed by the NATO Council. According to complicated Cold War procedures that had never been tested, if the NATO Council gave the order to assist the U.N.'s withdrawal, the planning document would become an operational order, adjusted for specific circumstances. Thus if the U.N. withdrew, OpPlan 40-104 would trigger the immediate deployment of twenty thousand American troops in the heart of the Balkans as part of the NATO force. The operation, which would have an American commander, would be impossible without the participation of Americans.

The President would still have to make the final decision to deploy U.S. troops, but his options had been drastically narrowed. If, in the event of a U.N.

withdrawal, he did not deploy American troops, the United States would be flouting, in its first test, the very NATO process it had created. The resulting recriminations could mean the end of NATO as an effective military alliance, as the British and French had already said to us privately. It was not an over-statement to say that America's post–World War II security role in Europe was at stake. Clearly, we had to find a policy that avoided a disastrous U.N. with-drawal. This meant a greater U.S. involvement.

M. Chirac Comes to Town. Jacques Chirac arrived in Washington on June 14 for his first presidential visit, demanding American action in Bosnia. It was not for nothing that he had acquired the nickname "Le Bulldozer." He was di-rect, intuitive, and blunt where his predecessor, François Mitterrand, had been opaque, intellectual, and elegant. The trip was supposed to be one in a series of semi-annual U.S.-E.U. summits, and Chirac was accompanied by Jacques Santer, the new President of the European Union. But it quickly turned into a Bosnia crisis session and the rest of the agenda—including economic, trade, law enforcement, and environmental issues—was swept away.

The day began with the "pre-brief," a normally routine session to prepare the President, but it quickly degenerated into an angry and contentious dis-cussion of Bosnia. The presentation given by members of the National Secu-rity Council staff was, in my view, misleading as to the situation, and especially the degree of American "automaticity" in assisting a U.N. with-drawal. When I started to offer a contrary view, the President, obviously dis-turbed that he was receiving contradictory information before an important visit, cut me off sharply. Then, as various people offered differing views, Christopher and I had to excuse ourselves in order to go to the French Em-bassy, where Chirac was expecting us for lunch. In the car, I expressed my as-tonishment at what had just happened. Christopher, much sobered by the meeting, agreed that we had to talk to the President again as soon as possible.

The rest of the day was chaotic. The President met alone with Chirac for well over an hour instead of the scheduled twenty minutes, while Vice Presi-dent Gore, Christopher, and half the American Cabinet milled around in the Cabinet Room, chatting with our perplexed European Union visitors. Clinton then sent Chirac on an impromptu trip to Capitol Hill to see Senate Majority Leader Bob Dole and Speaker Newt Gingrich, hoping that he would be able to persuade the Republican leaders to give the Administration greater support on Bosnia. Chirac's meetings, while cordial, changed nothing. Then he returned to the White House for a small dinner, which we spent, for the most part, in conversation about subjects other than Bosnia.

After Chirac left, I stood in the main entrance hall, in front of the North Por-tico, with Christopher, Berger, and Albright. The President and First Lady danced alone to the music of a Marine Band ensemble, which had played dur-

ing dinner, then walked over to us. It was a beautiful June evening, and the
White House exuded all its special magic. I looked at Christopher, concerned
that we would lose the moment. The President joined us and broke the ice.
"What about Bosnia?" he asked suddenly.

"I hate to ruin a wonderful evening, Mr. President," I began, "but we should
clarify something that came up during the day. Under existing NATO plans,
the United States is already committed to sending troops to Bosnia if the
U.N. decides to withdraw. I'm afraid we may not have that much flexibility
left."

The President looked at me with surprise. "What do you mean?" he asked.
"I'll decide the troop issue if and when the time comes."

There was silence for a moment. "Mr. President," I said, "NATO has already approved the withdrawal plan. While you have the power to stop it, it
has a high degree of automaticity built into it, especially since we have committed ourselves publicly to assisting NATO troops if the U.N. decides to
withdraw."

The President looked at Christopher. "Is this true?" he said. "I suggest that
we talk about it tomorrow," Christopher said. "We have a problem." Without
another word, the President walked off, holding his wife's hand.

I hoped that the day with Chirac would mark a turning point in the internal debate. The President continued the discussion the next day on the flight to Hal-
ifax, Nova Scotia, for the annual G-7 Summit, which Canada was hosting. He
began to press his advisors for better options; he understood how odd it would
be to send troops to Bosnia to implement a failure.

In late June, Tony Lake convened several meetings to consider the problem.
He did not invite me, but other participants kept me informed. Disturbed by
this exclusion, I consulted Vernon Jordan, one of the wisest men in Washington and a close friend of the President. I had promised Kati I would leave the
government within a year; now I told Jordan that I was considering departure
before the end of the summer. If Bosnia policy was going to be formulated
without my involvement, then there was little reason to stay. Jordan reacted
strongly, telling me that I could not "abandon Clinton" at such a moment of
crisis. Jordan then talked to various people in the Administration, including
the President and Christopher, and the situation eased slightly.

Meanwhile, events in Bosnia were moving faster than the policy-review
process in Washington. As the Administration deliberated, the Bosnian Serbs
attacked. This time their action would go down in history.

Srebrenica. Emboldened by his successes in intimidating the U.N. peacekeepers, General Mladic now focused pressure on the three isolated Muslim

enclaves in eastern Bosnia—Srebrenica, Zepa, and Gorazde—that had been completely surrounded by Serb forces since early in the war. They had been designated as "United Nations Safe Areas" by Security Council resolutions in 1993, but there was nothing safe about them. A small number of U.N. peace-keepers had been sent to each enclave, but they were bottled up, unable to re-lieve the siege conditions of the three towns. By the summer of 1995 all three towns were swollen with Muslim refugees from the surrounding areas. Mladic decided to eliminate the enclaves from the map in order to secure the entire eastern portion of Bosnia for the Serbs.

On July 6, 1995, Mladic's forces began shelling Srebrenica, allegedly in re-taliation for forays into Serb territory by Bosnian Muslim forces based in the enclave. Three days later, the Serbs took thirty Dutch peacekeepers hostage. On July 10, they took the town, and the rest of the Dutch soldiers, about 370 people, became hostages. The next day Mladic entered Srebrenica and an-nounced that he was "presenting this city to the Serbian people as a gift." He added, "Finally, after the rebellion of the Dahijas, the time has come to take revenge on the Turks in this region"—a reference to a Serb rebellion against the Ottomans that was brutally crushed in 1804. Mladic's identification of modern-day Bosnian Muslims with the Turks of 191 years earlier was reveal-ing of his dangerously warped mind-set.

Over the next week, the biggest single mass murder in Europe since World War II took place, while the outside world did nothing to stop the tragedy. Mladic's forces killed thousands of Muslims, most of them in cold-blooded executions after the town had surrendered. Precise details of what was hap-pening were not known at the time, but there was no question that something truly horrible was going on. By coincidence, I had an additional source be-yond the official reporting to confirm our worst suspicions about Srebrenica. My younger son, Anthony, who was then twenty-five, showed up in Tuzla to assist the State Department in interviewing refugees. He had been working in a refugee camp in Thailand when Refugees International president Lionel Rosenblatt asked him to rush to Bosnia to help with the emergency. Anthony and Lionel arrived in central Bosnia in late July, just as the first desperate sur-vivors from Srebrenica and Zepa reached the safety of the airfield outside Tuzla. They were soon joined by Assistant Secretary of State for Humanitar-ian Affairs John Shattuck.

With Anthony assisting, Shattuck interviewed shell-shocked survivors of Srebrenica—and heard the stories that were to horrify the world: how the Serbs, directed by General Mladic, had rounded up all the Muslims in the town and piled them onto buses; how most of the men were never seen again; how people were herded into a soccer field and killed in large numbers; how there were still men in the thousands trying to escape through the woods toward Tuzla. Then Shattuck and Oakley returned to Washington to press the government to greater action. Anthony stayed in Tuzla, calling me regularly with vivid stories of the continuing drama. Several times, in his characteristically blunt and passionate style, Anthony yelled into the phone that Washington had to do something, that I should "get my ass in gear." In fact, I had spent long hours unsuccessfully trying to find a way to stop the tragedy in Srebrenica and Zepa. My recommendation—to use airpower against the Bosnian Serbs in other parts of the country, as well as Srebrenica—had been rejected by the Western European nations that had troops at risk in Bosnia, and by the Pentagon. On July 13, the same day the Serbs began killing Muslims systematically in the soccer stadium, Chirac called President Clinton. He said that something had to be done, and proposed that American helicopters carry French troops into Srebrenica to relieve the town. This proposal had already been discussed through official French channels, and run into fierce opposition not only from the British and the Pentagon, but from Chirac's own generals. It had no chance of acceptance.

There was no more energy left in the international system. Everywhere one turned, there was a sense of confusion in the face of Bosnian Serb brutality. The first line of resistance to any action was the Dutch government, which, after initially considering action, refused to allow air strikes until all its soldiers were out of Bosnia. Through every channel available, in London, Paris, and NATO headquarters, we pressed for some response. It was useless. For a week I called our Ambassador in the Netherlands, Terry Dornbush, asking him to press the Dutch to allow air strikes, but to no avail. The other Europeans had reached their limits; with their own soldiers also at risk, they were not going to agree to any action that endangered the Dutch. (The British would pull their forces out of Gorazde within weeks.) The Serbs knew this, and held the bulk of the Dutch forces captive in the U.N. compound at the nearby village of Potocari until they had finished their dirty work at Srebrenica. According to the International Committee of the Red Cross, the death toll of Bosnian Muslims in Srebrenica between July 12 and July 16, 1995, was 7,079. Most of the victims were unarmed, and most died in ambushes and mass executions. For sheer intensity, nothing in the war had matched, or ever would match, Srebrenica. The name would become part of the language of the horrors of modern war, alongside Lidice, Oradour, Babi Yar, and the Katyn Forest.

The London Conference. The destruction of Srebrenica was an enormous shock to the Western alliance. But there was more in that terrible month. On July 19, emboldened by the events in eastern Bosnia, the Krajina Serbs attacked the Muslim enclave in the farthest corner of northwestern Bosnia, the Bihac pocket. Bihac, an agricultural area jutting deep into Croatia, had been cut off from Sarajevo throughout the war, but it was less than an hour by car from Zagreb, and its fall would have changed the balance in Croatia and made Croatian recapture of the Krajina much more difficult.

The war was escalating dangerously. In the east, the last two enclaves, Zepa and Gorazde, lay open to Mladic's rampaging forces. In the far northwest, Bihac seemed about to be cut in half. Tudjman was preparing to reopen the war in the Krajina, despite the agreement he had reached with Vice President Gore and me in March. Sarajevo was under renewed attack. Washington was still uncertain about what to do next. After judging Srebrenica the "worst humiliation for the Western democracies since the 1930s," Speaker Gingrich offered an unhelpful view. "There are twenty ways to solve this problem without involving a single American directly in this thing," he said. I agreed with his assessment of Srebrenica, but could not imagine any of the "twenty ways" that Gingrich said he had in mind.

Chirac complained publicly that France was "alone," and added, "We can't imagine that the U.N. force will remain only to observe, and to be, in a way, accomplices in the situation. If that is the case, it is better to withdraw." Chirac did not mention, of course, that the U.N. forces were commanded by a French general. Prime Minister John Major publicly rejected Chirac's continued proposals to relieve Srebrenica and reinforce Gorazde. Instead, Major unexpectedly proposed an international "crisis meeting" that he would chair in London on July 21.

Washington reacted with a flurry of activity. General Shalikashvili rushed to Europe to meet his NATO counterparts, and then joined Christopher and Perry in London for Major's conference. To my great frustration, I could not attend the London meeting because of a serious ear infection. Grounded by the chief State Department medical officer, I watched from Washington as Christopher and Perry struggled to give the U.N. force in Bosnia greater authority—indeed, to head off a U.N. withdrawal.

The London conference was one of those remarkable events in which something unexpectedly positive emerges from an initially unpromising idea. The British did not have a clear goal for the conference, nor did the United States when Christopher and Perry accepted the invitation. But in that dreadful month of July 1995, when the situation in Bosnia was at its low ebb, the very act of bringing together all the Foreign and Defense Ministers of NATO, as well as the Russians, produced its own result, which was to play an important role in the eleventh-hour revival of NATO.

The conclusions of the London conference were not drafted until Christopher was airborne. But by the time he landed in London, his team—Chief of Staff Tom Donilon, John Kornblum, Bob Frasure, and Policy Planning Director Jim Steinberg—had produced a document that proposed two important policy changes:

- First, NATO would draw "a line in the sand"—the evocation of President Bush's 1990–91 language on Iraq was deliberate—around the enclave of Gorazde.

- Second, the decision as to whether or not to use airpower, and how much, at Gorazde, would be made by NATO only, thus removing the U.N. from its dreadful "dual key" authority in regard to Gorazde—but not other parts of Bosnia.*

But in London, Christopher found initial reluctance on the part of the Europeans to such measures. In two private meetings with Prime Minister Major, he took a tough line. He found a partial ally in the new Foreign Secretary, Malcolm Rifkind, and the new Defense Minister, Michael Portillo, who overruled their subordinates and accepted Christopher's draft. Because it identified a place where NATO would finally make a stand, London was an important benchmark, a sort of bottoming out at the last possible moment. Bill Perry later put a framed photograph of himself, Christopher, and Shalikashvili taken during the conference in a place of honor in his office, and labeled it "Turning Point." But that could not be foreseen at the time. The results in London were understandably greeted with skepticism by a world just beginning to learn what had happened in Srebrenica and familiar with earlier Western assertions of resolve that had evaporated before the cruelty of the Bosnian Serbs.

London did not go as far as many, including myself, wanted. For one thing, it doomed Zepa, now directly in the path of the Bosnian Serb Army. In addition, neither Sarajevo nor Bihac was yet covered by the new tough language. (This was partially corrected by General Joulwan and our Ambassador to NATO, Robert Hunter, who, in a tumultuous all-night session a few days later, forced the NATO Council to broaden the terms of engagement to include Sarajevo.)

The Croatian Offensive. In early August, the Croatians launched a major offensive to retake the Krajina. It was a dramatic gamble by President Tudjman. When it finally took place—still against our advice—the offensive was a complete success. The Krajina Serbs unexpectedly gave up their "capital," Knin, without a fight. President Tudjman had won his bet: contrary to American and British predictions, Milosevic had not come to the aid of the Krajina Serbs. For the first time in four years, the Serbs had suffered a military setback.

The Croatian offensive proved to be a wedge issue that divided not only Americans and Europeans, but the top echelons of the American government

---

* "Dual key" was a system that required both the U.N. and NATO to "turn the key" to authorize NATO air strikes. In practice, the "dual key" was a "dual veto," used by the U.N. to prevent or minimize NATO action.

itself. Most officials saw these military thrusts as simply another chapter in the dreary story of fighting and bloodshed in the region. They felt that the duty of our diplomacy was to put a stop to the fighting, regardless of what was happening on the ground. For me, however, the success of the Croatian (and later the Bosnian-Croat Federation) offensive was a classic illustration of a fundamental fact: the shape of the diplomatic landscape will usually reflect the actual balance of forces on the ground. In concrete terms, this meant that as diplomats we could not expect the Serbs to be conciliatory at the negotiating table as long as they had experienced nothing but success on the battlefield.

Zagreb's almost uncontested victory began to change the balance of power in the region. And the abandonment of the Croatian Serbs by Milosevic eliminated one of our greatest fears—that Belgrade would re-enter the war.

Joe Kruzel reflected the general view of our team in his last message to Washington, sent the night before he died. "For the first time," he wrote, "I realize how much the Croatian offensive in the Krajina has profoundly changed the nature of the Balkan game and thus our diplomatic offensive."

Bob Frasure had also shared this view. At our lunch with President Tudjman in Zagreb on August 17, two days before the Mount Igman tragedy, one member of our team tried to persuade Tudjman that he should halt the offensive immediately, as Washington wanted. Frasure passed me a note written on his place card, which I saved and later gave to his wife, Katharina—it was the last note I ever got from him:

> Dick: We "hired" these guys to be our junkyard dogs because we were desperate. We need to try to "control" them. But this is no time to get squeamish about things. This is the first time the Serb wave has been reversed. That is essential for us to get stability, so we can get out.

This view was not accepted by most of our Washington colleagues, especially the military and the CIA, which still feared, and predicted, a military response from the regular Yugoslav Army. The true importance of the Croatian offensive was thus not taken into account during the policy review that occurred in Washington in early August, well before our shuttle began so tragically.

The Policy Review and the Seven–Point Initiative. In early August, the President chaired three meetings in three days on Bosnia. Christopher was in Asia, and I was traveling in the western states with Kati. Tarnoff and Talbott represented the State Department and kept me closely informed. Finally, the President decided on a two-stage strategy: First, Lake and Tarnoff would go to seven European nations, including Russia, as presidential emissaries, and present a framework for peace. Then I would begin a last-ditch, all-out negotiating effort.

The Lake-Tarnoff presentation was produced through the usual interagency drafting process. My absence from Washington was later to result in a flurry of press speculation that I had been cut out, but in fact I'd deliberately remained at a distance, not only because of my family commitments but because participating might have reduced my negotiating flexibility later.

The final product contained seven points, ranging from the general to the specific. It called for (1) a "comprehensive peace settlement"; (2) three-way recognition among Bosnia-Herzegovina, Croatia, and the Federal Republic of Yugoslavia (Serbia and Montenegro); (3) the full lifting of all economic sanctions against Yugoslavia if a settlement was reached, and an American-backed program to equip and train the Croat-Muslim Federation forces if there was a settlement; (4) the peaceful return to Croatia of eastern Slavonia—the tiny, oil-rich sliver of Croatian land on the Serbian border that had been seized by the Serbs; (5) an all-out effort to pursue a cease-fire or an end to all offensive operations; (6) a reaffirmation of support for the so-called Contact Group plan agreed to in June 1994 by the Foreign Ministers of the United States, Great Britain, France, Germany, and Russia—dividing Bosnia into two entities, 49 percent of the land going to the Bosnian Serbs, 51 percent to the Croat-Muslim Federation; and (7) a comprehensive program for regional economic reconstruction.

By sending his National Security Advisor, the President, who had been criticized for excessive detachment from Bosnia policy, was saying: this is it—the real, and perhaps last, American push for peace. I had little difficulty with the broad outlines of the initiative, but several specific aspects of the proposals troubled me. I decided to hold off on making my views known until after the completion of Lake's trip to Europe.

The "Handoff." Strobe and Peter had warned me to be prepared to cut my trip short, and on Saturday, August 12, after only a few days in Colorado, I returned to Washington, repacked my bags, and left for London, where Lake and his team were waiting. On August 14, I arrived in London for a "handoff" meeting in the American Embassy. For the first hour we met alone.

The meeting was quietly emotional. Tony and I had been linked by close personal and professional ties through five Administrations. "This is the kind of thing we dreamed of doing together thirty years ago when we started out in Vietnam," Tony began in a low, intense voice. "I'm going to be with you all the way. And if this thing fails, it's my ass more than yours."

Tony briefed me on his talks with the allies and the Russians, which had gone well. They were pleased that the President was engaged so deeply. I told him that the framework he had proposed in his tour of Europe was fine, with an important exception: I could support neither his proposal to give the Serbs a wider corridor of land at Posavina nor the suggestion that we abandon Gorazde. Both of these ideas had been part of an attempt to create "more viable borders" for the Federation by trading Muslim enclaves for Serb concessions elsewhere. The Pentagon insisted it would not defend enclaves and slivers of land if called upon later to implement a peace agreement. Nonetheless, I told Tony that the United States could not be party to such a proposal. "This would create another forty thousand or more refugees," I said, "and we cannot be a party to that, especially after Srebrenica." Tony asked if it was not true that Izetbegovic had once told me he knew that all three eastern enclaves were not viable and would have to be given up. Izetbegovic had, in fact, made such a statement to me in Sarajevo in January, but that was long before the loss and horrors of Srebrenica and Zepa. "A trade is no longer possible," I said. "After Srebrenica, we cannot propose such a thing."

After a larger meeting with the rest of our team and a call on several senior British officials, we shook hands warmly and parted, Tony and Sandy Vershbow heading west and home to Washington. Our team—General Clark, Rosemarie Pauli, Bob Frasure, Joe Kruzel, and Nelson Drew—flew to the Balkans to begin the negotiations that we hoped would end the war.

BOOK TWO

THE SHUTTLE

(August 22–October 31, 1995)

Tonight a scrambling decade ends,
And strangers, enemies and friends
Stand once more puzzled underneath
The signpost on the barren heath
Where the rough mountain track divides
To silent valleys on all sides,
Endeavouring to decipher what
Is written on it but cannot,
Nor guess in what direction lies
The overhanging precipice.
Far down below them whence they came
Still flickers feebly a red flame,
A tiny glow in the great void
Where an existence was destroyed;
And now and then a nature turns
To look where her whole system burns
And with a last defiant groan
Shudders her future into stone.

—W. H. AUDEN, *New Year Letter*

CHAPTER 6

Pale's Challenge

(August 22–28)

> The inscrutability of history remains the salvation of human freedom and of human responsibility. The failure of prediction permits us to act as if our choices make a difference. For no one can prove that they don't, and there is no other way that we can vindicate human dignity and contrive a moral existence.
>
> —ARTHUR SCHLESINGER, JR.[1]

AT 10:00 A.M. ON AUGUST 22, the day after our return from Sarajevo, Secretary Christopher convened his senior team to discuss Bosnia. As usual, we met in his working office, a small room directly behind his large, formal office on the seventh floor. When I first visited the State Department during a spring break from college in 1961—a trip that inspired me to join the Foreign Service the following year—Dean Rusk had used the large room as his office. But most recent secretaries of state preferred the more intimate surroundings of the back office, and Christopher used the ornate larger room almost entirely for formal meetings with foreign officials.

Although the State Department's unique bureaucratic culture has survived every one of its leaders (and defeated some), the personal style of each secretary deeply affects the way the Department reacts to events. Warren Christopher's style was methodical and cautious. He was, as the press often said, a lawyer's lawyer. He rarely talked about himself, but once offered a revealing comment to a journalist about his style: "I always thought that I would do things in a conservative way to maximize the progressiveness of my policy positions. . . . If you are courteous and prudent, you can advance causes and advance ideas that would be unacceptable for others."[2] Highly successful in his Los Angeles legal practice, he went to Washington in 1977 as Deputy Secretary of State to Cyrus Vance, and carried out a number of key assignments, most famously the complex negotiations over the release of the fifty-two American hostages in Tehran at the end of the Carter Administration. Unfailingly polite, adept at concealing any annoyance or impatience that he might be feeling, Christopher preferred to let others take the lead in recommending a course of action, while he focused on the risks it entailed. As a result, those advising him often divided into two groups: advocates of action, and "doubting Thomases" who argued the dangers of the proposed policy.

Christopher formed his positions only after careful deliberations, which included not only the substantive officials responsible for the issue, but a core group of trusted senior aides who sat in on almost every discussion. He would listen quietly, ask a few clarifying questions, more in the style of a judge than an advocate, and generally withhold his views until the end of the discussion. When he took a strong stand on an issue, he carried great weight within the government.

That morning, August 22, Christopher's core team crowded into the meeting. Peter Tarnoff, Chief of Staff Tom Donilon, and Director of Policy Planning James Steinberg squeezed side by side on the sofa; others, including Strobe Talbott, Wendy Sherman, who held the critical position of Assistant Secretary for Legislative Affairs, and my senior deputy, John Kornblum, took seats on the chairs scattered around the small room. Latecomers sat on a narrow bench under a window that overlooked the Potomac and the Lincoln Memorial. Christopher sat, as always, behind his desk in the corner, sometimes leaning back against the bookcases, but usually taking careful notes on a legal pad. I sat in the chair closest to Christopher's desk, which was by custom saved for the primary action officer in the meeting.

The mood was understandably subdued. Our first need was to assemble a new team. I said that Christopher Hill, the brilliant, fearless, and argumentative country director for the Balkans, was ready to take the place of his good friend Bob Frasure, as we had planned before the accident. We left the designation of the NSC and Defense representatives to Lake and Perry.

Christopher noted that we lacked the legal expertise that would be essential if the negotiations got serious. He suggested adding to the team Roberts Owen, a distinguished Washington lawyer. Bob Owen, whom I had known since he had served as the Legal Advisor to the State Department during the Carter Administration, was calm, witty, and always cheerfully ready for the most demanding tasks, though he was almost seventy. Everyone marveled at his eternal youthfulness; he looked at least ten years younger than his age. Christopher's inspired idea gave our team something it was to need continually: an experienced and wise international lawyer.

Our meeting broke up quickly, and we left for the Fort Myer Memorial Chapel at Arlington National Cemetery to begin the painful ceremonies that would remain engraved on our consciousness for the rest of the Bosnian peace mission.

The wives of all three men had chosen Arlington for the final resting place of their husbands. The first of the services was for Bob Frasure. Even though all were painful, Bob's funeral was made particularly heart-wrenching by the eloquent yet unreachable anguish of his sixteen-year-old daughter, Sarah.

"One question I will always ask myself is 'Why?' " she said, speaking, in a voice breaking with pain, from the altar above her father's casket. "I took him for granted. I never told him how much I loved him, and I never showed him how much I cared about him. Now I will never wake to hear him making pancakes on a Sunday morning."

The mourners in the chapel could hardly breathe. We filed out in silence broken only by the sounds of soft crying, and slowly followed Bob's casket to a grave site high on the hill above Washington, where, in an eerie and disquieting hush, it was blessed by a priest. I placed a flower on top of Bob's casket, said good-bye, and turned back toward Washington for another meeting.

The Principals' Committee began its meeting an hour after we had left Arlington on August 22. These meetings—somewhat misleadingly named because the real principals, the President and Vice President, rarely attended them—were supposed to be the primary decision-making forum in the Executive Branch. In theory, the views of senior officials, including any disagreements, were then brought to the President for final policy decisions. In fact, if a clear consensus was not reached at these meetings, the decision-making process would often come to a temporary halt, which was followed by a slow, laborious process of telephoning and private deal making. People hated to take their disagreements to the President; it was as though a failure to agree somehow reflected badly on each of them, and consensus, rather than clarity, was often the highest goal of the process.

During my first ten months as Assistant Secretary, most high-level meetings on Bosnia had a dispirited, inconclusive quality that often left Bob Frasure and me depressed and frustrated. Although no one could ignore the crisis, there was little enthusiasm for any proposal of action, no matter what it was. The result was often inaction or half-measures instead of a clear strategy.

This was not the case, however, immediately following the tragedy. The loss of three friends infused our meetings with a somber sense that there was no turning back. In addition, the President was now imparting to everyone his own sense of urgency. Not for the first time, I observed the value of—indeed, the necessity for—direct, personal presidential involvement to overcome bureaucratic stalemates or inertia and give policy direction and strategic purpose.

We met in the Situation Room, the windowless basement room in the West Wing of the White House that has been the scene of so many historic crisis meetings over the last thirty years. First-time visitors were usually surprised at how unimpressive the room was. Movies always made the room seem larger and fancier, but the real thing was small, with low ceilings, three plain wood-paneled walls, and the fourth partially covered with a dreadful gray curtain. The end wall held clocks showing the time in various parts of the world, and above another wall floated a television screen, through which officials could participate on a secure U.S. government network. The table was small, with seats for only about ten people.

As chairman of the Principals' Committee, Tony Lake sat at the head of the table, with the Secretary of State and the Secretary of Defense flanking him. The rest of the principals arrayed themselves along the table according to rank, and second-tier personnel took seats along the walls. The room was usually overcrowded, giving a physical sense of intimacy rarely reflected in the tone of the meetings themselves. When she could not get to Washington from New York for the meeting, Ambassador Albright hovered above us on the television screen, a disembodied but effective participant. She told me once that when she attended the meeting by television she had the sense of observing and participating simultaneously, thus affording her a degree of detachment that made her comments seem more perspicacious and convincing.

Completing the Team. Tony ran through a review of the issues in preparation for the next day, when the President planned to meet with us after a special memorial service at Arlington. As we broke up, Tony pulled me aside and said he wanted to assign Brigadier General Donald Kerrick to our team as Nelson Drew's replacement. Kerrick, whom I knew slightly, seemed an excellent choice.

We now lacked only a new civilian Defense Department representative. Perry said he was thinking of letting General Clark represent both the civilian and the uniformed sides of the Pentagon. I disagreed, saying it was vital to have a representative of the civilian side of the Defense Department in whom the Secretary had personal confidence.

In pressing this seemingly minor point, I was influenced by my experience as a junior member of the American negotiating team that met with the North Vietnamese in Paris in 1968–69. Despite an extraordinary delegation—Averell Harriman as leader, Cyrus Vance as his co-head, and Philip C. Habib, the outstanding career Foreign Service officer of his generation, as number three—the team in Paris never had full backing from Washington. The military representatives on the negotiating team fought with Harriman and Vance, and sent frequent "back-channel" messages to the Pentagon that undermined the negotiators. Although Secretary of Defense Clark Clifford and Deputy Secretary of State Nicholas Katzenbach supported Harriman and Vance, they were mistrusted by Secretary of State Dean Rusk, National Security Advisor Walt Rostow, and our Ambassador in Saigon, Ellsworth Bunker.

Watching that episode in Paris as a twenty-seven-year-old junior Foreign Service officer had been unforgettable, but not enjoyable; I had seen Governor Harriman, a historic figure who had negotiated directly with Stalin and Churchill, reduced to fury and frustration by what he considered the excessive detail of his instructions from Washington, and by internal intrigues with the military and with Bunker. No other experience was more important to me in preparing for the Bosnian mission; I would not tolerate any similar internal divisions within our team, and the negotiating flexibility we needed could come only with the full backing of all the key members of the Principals' Committee.

Perry, himself a veteran of the Vietnam era at the Pentagon, was sympathetic to my concern and chose James Pardew, who as director of the Balkan Task Force at the Pentagon had been Joe Kruzel's closest aide on Bosnia. I did not know Pardew, a retired Army officer, but said we would be delighted with anyone in whom the Secretary of Defense had confidence.

So our seven-person core team was set: myself, General Wes Clark, Bob Owen, Chris Hill, General Don Kerrick, Jim Pardew, and Rosemarie Pauli. It would remain unchanged through the next six months, although many other people became vital parts of the effort as we gathered momentum—and the support of Washington was at all times critical. As I was soon to discover under conditions of the highest stress, I could not have wished for a stronger team to replace our fallen colleagues.

The Europeans. The next day, August 23, Peter Tarnoff and I met in the Secretary's Conference Room with representatives of the European nations who had come to Washington to pay tribute to our three comrades.

Dealing with the Europeans was delicate and nettlesome throughout the Bosnia crisis, and put an unprecedented strain on NATO and the Atlantic Alliance just when the Cold War ties that had held us together had also disappeared. Our steadfast allies, who had looked to the United States for leadership during the Cold War, were ambivalent about the American role in post–Cold War Europe, and especially Bosnia. They had long called for greater American involvement but at the same time, they feared that they would be publicly humiliated if the United States took the lead. Our colleagues in the Contact Group—France, Germany, Great Britain, and Russia—were disturbed that we planned to negotiate first and consult them later, reversing the previous procedure, in which the five nations tried to work out a common position *before* taking it to the parties in the Balkans—a system that was cumbersome and unworkable.

Alain Dejammet, Political Director at the French Foreign Ministry, mentioned that Izetbegovic would be visiting Paris early the next week, and proposed a Contact Group meeting at that time. The French could be famously difficult, but among the Europeans they now had the strongest, most assertive foreign policy. They had paid for their involvement in Bosnia with the heaviest casualty toll, over fifty killed. We needed French support to succeed, and I was convinced we could handle any problems that might arise if we met in Paris. If we meant our high-minded rhetoric about partnership, we had to find ways to work with the French. So, despite the aversion of some American officials to any event held in France, I agreed immediately to Dejammet's suggestion.

Keeping the Atlantic Alliance, the main pillar of American foreign policy for over half a century, from coming apart over Bosnia was one of our greatest policy challenges. After a year as Ambassador to Germany, I was especially committed to repairing the strains that Bosnia had caused. We needed to work in partnership with the Alliance on a large number of other issues—the enlargement of NATO, a common policy toward the former Soviet Union, the Mideast, and Iran, terrorism, human rights, the environment, and organized crime—but Bosnia had begun to adversely affect everything. I addressed this problem in a blunt personal note to Christopher on August 23:

> The Contact Group presents us with a constant conundrum. We can't live without it, we can't live with it. If we don't meet with them and tell them what we are doing, they complain publicly. If we tell them, they disagree and often leak—and worse.
>
> In the end, we must keep the Contact Group together, especially since we will need it later to endorse and legitimize any agreement. . . . On August 20, [one member of the Contact Group] told me in confidence that [his government] now believes that "at least one member" of the Contact Group is passing details of the Contact Group meetings directly to Belgrade. . . .*
>
> Any temporary Euro-annoyance with less information can be managed. It must be outweighed by our need for speed and security. . . . But we must never forget that we will need them *all* if there is ever a settlement—the E.U. for economic assistance, our NATO allies for the new post-U.N. peacekeeping force, the U.N. for legitimizing resolutions, the Islamic Conference for additional aid, and the Russians and Greeks for their influence (however limited) on Belgrade.

* This was a reference to Russia.

The Memorial Service. Our edgy meeting with the Europeans provided a sharp reminder of the unsentimental world to which we would soon return. But first there were more sad ceremonies at the Fort Myer Memorial Chapel. The next was a service in honor of all three men. There would be only one speaker: the President.

Any gathering with a President, even a tragic one, has a distinctive quality. The Fort Myer chapel was now infused with a combination of mourning and anticipation. Numerous security personnel, seemingly oblivious to the purpose for which we were gathered, added to the strange feeling, so different from the previous day's despair.

Four hundred people crowded into the nondenominational chapel. The President awarded each man the President's Citizen Medal, and then met privately with their families. He was masterful in such meetings, and afterward Katharina Frasure told me that he had comforted them and shared their loss in a very personal way.

Emerging from the chapel, the President spoke directly and movingly to the widows and children, saying the three men had "made reason their weapon, freedom their cause, and peace their goal." Praising them as "quiet American heroes," the President said that "Bob, Joe, and Nelson were in Bosnia because they were moved by the terrible injustice and suffering there."

When the President finished speaking, the audience stood in total silence as he came down from the podium and went up to the families, briefly holding hands with each of the three wives and six children. Then his senior advisors and the negotiating team followed him down a narrow corridor and into a small room with white cinder-block walls and shelves of inspirational books.

The meeting at Fort Myer proved to be an important benchmark. Although scheduled almost as an afterthought to the memorial service, this casual, quietly emotional meeting with the President was exactly what the Administration needed to restart the process and pull itself back together.

Pulling up chairs haphazardly, we gathered in a circle. The formality of meetings in the White House, with every seat carefully assigned by rank, was abandoned. Some people, having crowded into the room only to find that there were no more seats, stood against the walls.

The President asked me to review the status of each of the seven points Lake and Tarnoff had presented on their European trip two weeks earlier. We moved quickly past the more general points to focus on several more problematic issues.

Lake had told the Western Europeans that we "would pursue cease-fires or an end to offensive operations on the ground." This was, of course, contrary to the emerging view of the negotiating team, which I explained: the Croatian offensive, while brutal (as is all war), was valuable to the negotiating process. The time would come when a cease-fire was desirable, but right now the trend on the battlefield was, for the first time, unfavorable to the Serbs. Unless given specific instructions to the contrary, I said, we would not seek a cease-fire yet. To my relief, no one took issue with this.

Lake had also said that the United States was ready to update the Contact Group map to "incorporate more viable borders and distribution of territory," consider proposals to widen the Posavina Corridor, and provide the Serbs "de jure control over the eastern enclaves" in return for the Bosnians and Bosnian Croats receiving more area around Sarajevo and other territory in central and western Bosnia that would create a more compact and coherent Federation territory. Finally, Lake had told our European allies that because the beleaguered enclave of Gorazde would be difficult to defend and would add to the difficulty of peace-plan implementation, we would seek to steer both parties toward solutions that would "trade Gorazde for other substantial Serb concessions." I had already told Lake, in London, that I would not support this, but my position was still unknown in Washington.

I outlined why we should not press Sarajevo to trade away Gorazde or recommend a widening of the Posavina Corridor. The Bosnian government would never voluntarily give up Gorazde following the massacres at Srebrenica and Zepa, nor should we put ourselves in the position of advocating the creation of tens of thousands of new refugees. The Pentagon representatives in the room, who had previously been adamant on this point, said nothing. Breathing another sigh of relief, I quickly moved on.

Finally, we came to the last point in Lake's original presentation, the comprehensive program for regional economic reconstruction. This provoked the first real discussion of the meeting, one that we would often remember later.

The issue went far beyond Bosnia. Everyone in Washington recognized the sea change that had come over congressional attitudes toward foreign assistance. Traditionally hostile to foreign aid, Congress had been especially brutal since control of both houses had passed to the Republicans seven months earlier.

A huge economic reconstruction program was essential to any Bosnia settlement. Some people treated this as little more than rhetoric, but lasting peace in the region required rebuilding the interdependent economy that, until four years earlier, had existed in a single Yugoslavia, with a single economic infrastructure—railroads, highways, industry, etc. This would require not just rhetoric, but significant American leadership and resources.

However, because of the congressional repercussions of any new budgetary obligations, Lake and Tarnoff had not been allowed to indicate the size of

America's eventual contribution to a civilian reconstruction effort in Bosnia. Our obvious inconsistency on this issue was troubling. On the one hand, the United States wanted to remain the world's leading power; on the other, the Administration was reluctant to ask Congress for the resources to ensure that leadership—and Congress was even more parsimonious. This was wrong; even in an era of budget constraints and huge deficits, the nation could afford expenditures it considered vital to its national interests.

I suggested that an appropriate amount for the first year might be $500 million. My comments provoked a stirring among some of my colleagues. Perry said that an even higher figure—perhaps $1 billion for the first year—would be appropriate.

"If we can get peace, we should be prepared to put up a billion dollars," the President said emphatically.

Cautionary notes from several sides of the room came from people who had been bruised in budget battles with the new Congress. One person warned that since we were having difficulty getting "even $10 million for Ecuador," huge sums for Bosnia would be virtually impossible. The President turned to the White House Chief of Staff, Leon Panetta, a former Director of the Office of Management and Budget, who outlined the immense problem any supplemental request would confront. Panetta saw—and accurately predicted—the extraordinary budget crisis that was to erupt between the Gingrich Republicans and the Executive Branch later in the year, a confrontation so severe that it would ultimately close down most of the U.S. government for over a month.

I made one last attempt to underline the importance of the reconstruction effort, but a consensus had formed, as it often does in such meetings. It was clear that the amount of American assistance would be far less than desirable.

This exchange ended the meeting. The President asked us to return to the region quickly, and keep going until we had achieved something. Then, after greeting each new member of the team personally, he clapped me on the shoulder, pulled me aside for a moment to say he was counting on us, and was on his way back to Wyoming.

Leon Fuerth and the Sanctions Issue. On the morning of August 24, we said good-bye to Nelson Drew, and in the afternoon we walked in silence behind the horse-drawn casket of Joe Kruzel. By this time we had been to Arlington four times in three days; the week had turned into a blur. I asked the negotiating team to meet at the Officers' Club at Arlington between the two funerals so that we could begin planning our trip, which was only three days away. Because the United Nations sanctions against Serbia were always a central issue, Leon Fuerth joined us.

Fuerth, Vice President Gore's National Security Advisor, was one of those powerful but rarely seen people who play major roles behind the scene in Washington. Originally an arms-control expert, he had been a respected member of the national security community before he joined the staff of a young Tennessee Congressman named Al Gore in 1982. In 1993 the Administration gave Fuerth an important responsibility in addition to his duties as the Vice President's closest foreign policy advisor—implementing American policy worldwide on economic sanctions.* It was unprecedented to give such an assignment to a member of the Vice President's staff. But when sanctions against Bosnia became a critical issue in 1993, the Principals' Committee took responsibility away from State, apparently because of a failure to manage it properly, and gave it to Fuerth—an old friend with whom I had worked closely during Senator Gore's 1988 presidential campaign.

For months sanctions had been the subject of a heated dispute within the Contact Group, with the United States and Germany on one side, and Britain, France, and Russia on the other. Milosevic hated the sanctions. They really hurt his country, and he wanted them lifted. This gave us a potential lever over him, but by the fall of 1994, London, Paris, and Moscow wanted to lift all or most of the sanctions in return for almost nothing. Washington had a different view, although it was not held unanimously. Some officials believed we should offer Milosevic a small incentive, in the form of some sanctions relief, to "jump-start" the process; others, like Fuerth and Madeleine Albright, opposed any softening of our position without a significant reciprocal action by Milosevic. Although we had some tactical differences, I also opposed giving Milosevic relief without getting something tangible in return.

Since the end of the Cold War few issues have caused greater tension with our major European allies and Russia than sanctions. But to the credit of Vice President Gore, Leon Fuerth, and Madeleine Albright, the decision to take a hard line on sanctions proved correct; had we not done so, we would have begun the negotiations with almost no bargaining chips.

Friday, August 25, was my last day in Washington before the resumption of the shuttle. I spent it in endless meetings with foreign ambassadors and colleagues in the Department. But there was one more essential act of mourning and rebuilding. The tragedy on Mount Igman was deeply personal for the European Bureau, which had lost a truly beloved colleague. It needed to pull itself together. So, in the early afternoon, I invited the entire Bureau to join

---

* Fuerth's mandate, while focused heavily on Bosnia, also covered sanctions against other countries, including Iran and Iraq.

Strobe Talbott and me in the Dean Acheson Auditorium on the ground floor of the Department to decide how we were going to cope with the tragedy. I described the accident in detail, hoping to dispel some of the misunderstandings or rumors so endemic in such a situation. I asked everyone in the Bureau to give John Kornblum full support, and said that we would not replace Bob at this point. We would simply do the best we could; history would judge us by our results.

Several people asked how Bob's family was coping. Strobe told them of the extraordinary strength that Katharina Frasure was demonstrating, and described how the previous day she had visited Pete Hargreaves in the hospital, to tell him that she realized he could not have saved her husband. (Strobe, who had visited Hargreaves with her, said it was one of the most inspiring moments of his life.) Finally, I asked my colleagues to consider what permanent memorial we should set up for Bob. Then, after asking everyone to stand for a moment of silence for Bob, Joe, and Nelson, we went back to work.*

I flew to Long Island to spend the weekend with Kati. We had been married less than two months. The author of a recent book on extremists in the Middle East, she was concerned that rejectionist Bosnian Serbs—the "Hamas wing of the Serbs," as she put it—would try to kill us, especially if we were making progress toward peace. The risk was real, but we had no choice; the negotiations could not succeed unless we went to Sarajevo.

We were scheduled to leave for Europe on Sunday, August 27, but before we left, there was one last television interview, with NBC's *Meet the Press.* All through the week, the Bosnian Serbs had continued to make provocative statements, and had even exchanged fire with U.N. troops. This interview provided an opportunity to issue a clear warning that there were limits to American forbearance. Such a statement, however, required coordination within the government. On Saturday afternoon, therefore, I called Tom Donilon, Warren Christopher's chief of staff, for advice. He suggested that, while carefully avoiding a specific commitment that might be repudiated by others, I send a strong signal that we would no longer ignore hostile actions by the Bosnian Serbs. He volunteered to "protect" me within the government if anyone objected later.

Donilon, the only senior official at State with real political experience, brought a needed focus and crispness to the decision-making process. A proud "working-class kid" from Providence, Rhode Island, Tom joined the Carter White House in 1977 at the age of twenty-two, one of the youngest and bright-

---

* In 1996, the State Department established the Robert C. Frasure Memorial Award to "honor an individual who exemplifies a commitment to peace."

est of a group of outstanding political operatives assembled by Vice President Mondale's chief of staff, James A. Johnson.* In 1993, Donilon, who was then a partner in the Washington office of Warren Christopher's law firm, went to State as an aide to Christopher and emerged, somewhat unexpectedly, as the new Secretary of State's closest advisor. Although almost unknown to the public, Donilon was widely respected by the press and within the government; he was literally indispensable to the smooth functioning of the State Department.

At 6:00 A.M. on Sunday morning, an NBC crew arrived to set up their equipment in the sitting room of our weekend house in Bridgehampton. My new family stumbled sleepily over wires and watched in dismay as the crew turned the house into a makeshift television studio. The interview covered many issues that would be critical in the next few months. With Brian Williams moderating, the conservative columnist Robert Novak challenged the heavy emphasis we put on the fact that the leaders of the Bosnian Serbs, their "president," Radovan Karadzic, and General Ratko Mladic, had been indicted as war criminals by the International War Crimes Tribunal. "Do you think it's helpful to call [Karadzic] a war criminal?" Novak asked in his famous baiting style, as always on the attack. "Do you think it's helpful in the negotiations?" I replied:

> It's not a question of what I call him or what you call him. There's an international tribunal going on. And let me be clear on something. At Srebrenica a month ago, people were taken into a stadium, lined up, and massacred. It was a crime against humanity of the sort that we have rarely seen in Europe, and not since the days of Himmler and Stalin, and that's simply a fact and it has to be dealt with. I'm not going to cut a deal that absolves the people responsible for this.

Doyle McManus of the *Los Angeles Times* asked the question we had prepared for: "What leverage do you have on [the Bosnian Serbs]?" I answered:

> I'd rather not go into the diplomatic details. I think secret negotiations have a right to remain somewhat secret. But I do want to make one thing clear. If this peace initiative does not get moving, dramatically moving, in the next week or two, the consequences will be very adverse to the Serbian goals. One way or another NATO will be heavily involved, and the Serbs don't want that.

---

* In 1981, Johnson and I formed a consulting firm, which we sold to Lehman Brothers in 1985. Jim later became chairman and CEO of Fannie Mae and chairman of the John F. Kennedy Center for the Performing Arts.

I spent the rest of the interview trying to avoid saying what this meant—was I threatening NATO air strikes? What were the criteria for success? Under what circumstances would we send in ground troops?

Most newspapers covered the interview positively the next day. *The New York Times* ran a front-page article under the headline "U.S. Officials Say Bosnian Serbs Face NATO Attack If Talks Fail"—a headline justified by neither my interview nor the text of the story, but useful in creating the impression of a tougher policy than in fact existed. The *International Herald Tribune,* a newspaper to which we attached special importance since it was available in the Balkans, ran a similar headline: "U.S. Warns of Air Strikes Unless Serbs Negotiate."

With the interview completed, I spent the rest of the day trying to relax, even finding time to go to the local horse show, where my stepdaughter, Elizabeth, was competing. Good luck calls from Gore, Christopher, Lake, and Albright brightened the day. Some friends came over in the early evening for a long-planned housewarming party, in the middle of which, with most of the guests still there, I left for the Islip airport, where the Air Force plane carrying our new team stopped to refuel and pick me up. Boarding the C-20—the military equivalent of the Gulfstream III—we settled into our seats with nervous jokes and tried to get some sleep before Paris.

The Final Outrage. At 8:00 A.M., we landed at the military airport outside Paris. Waiting on the tarmac was our Ambassador to France, Pamela Harriman. It was typical of her that she would meet us, even at such an early hour, as a sign of support and in order to brief us immediately on the French point of view; some Ambassadors never made such an effort, no matter what the circumstances. We drove into Paris through heavy traffic, as she outlined a complicated schedule involving meetings with the French, the Contact Group representatives, and President Izetbegovic, who had asked to see us late that evening. I had time for a brief nap before our first meeting, a courtesy call on French Foreign Minister Hervé de Charette. As I woke up, I turned on CNN and heard terrible news: a Bosnian Serb mortar shell had killed at least thirty-five people in a marketplace in Sarajevo. It was the second-worst incident of the war against civilians in Sarajevo. Watching the small screen fill with scenes of new carnage, I wondered if this was a deliberate response to my public warnings of the day before, which had been widely reported in Bosnia. It seemed possible and, as I noted at the time, "I felt doubly awful."

Public reaction came quickly. From Pale the Bosnian Serbs accused the Bosnian Muslims of staging the incident to draw NATO into the war. The Muslim leadership called for the suspension of the American peace initiative "unless the obligations and role of NATO are clarified." United Nations Secretary-General Boutros-Ghali issued a statement that, typically, meant almost exactly the opposite of what it seemed to say: he "unreservedly condemned the shelling" and ordered his military commanders to "investigate this attack immediately and take appropriate action without delay." In fact, this was a device to avoid taking action.

None of this mattered much. What counted was whether the United States would act decisively and persuade its NATO allies to join in the sort of massive air campaign that we had so often talked about but never even come close to undertaking. Would our threats and warnings, including my own on *Meet the Press* the previous day, finally be backed up with action?

Even before we knew the exact casualty toll—thirty-eight killed and more than eighty-five wounded—I felt this was the final test for the West. Was this a deliberate Bosnian Serb attempt to show the world that our threats were empty? Or was it simply a single mortar fired by a single angry person? And the key question: what would we do in response?

Within a short time, Strobe Talbott, who was acting Secretary of State, called. He felt that a military response to the latest outrage was "essential," and wanted to know if the negotiating team agreed. He asked a key question: what effect might retaliatory air strikes have on the negotiations? "Your advice could be decisive," he said. "There's a lot of disagreement here."

I did not need to think about my reply. The brutal stupidity of the Bosnian Serbs had given us an unexpected last chance to do what should have been done three years earlier. I told him to start NATO air strikes against the Bosnian Serbs—not minor retaliatory "pinpricks," but a serious and, if possible, sustained air campaign, which was now authorized by the "London rules." It would be better to risk failure in the negotiations than let the Serbs get away with another criminal act. This was the most important test of American leadership since the end of the Cold War, I said, not only in Bosnia, but in Europe.

Our telephone conversation was about how to respond to the newest Bosnian Serb atrocity, but it was also part of a controversy that had gone on for thirty years about the relationship between diplomacy and airpower. This issue had haunted American decision makers since 1965, when the use of airpower against North Vietnam had been one of the most controversial aspects of that most controversial of all American wars.

Vietnam was, of course, the seminal event of our generation. By 1995, its shadows were lengthening, but they had marked almost every contemporary official and politician in Washington—some as student radicals, others as Vietnam veterans; some as doves, others as hawks. There was irony in my support of air strikes. As a young Foreign Service officer working on Vietnam,

I had disagreed with the air campaign against North Vietnam. To many of those opposing the use of airpower in Bosnia the lesson of Vietnam and Kuwait was that airpower would be ineffective unless backed up by ground troops—a political impossibility in Bosnia. But the comparison was dangerously misleading: Bosnia was different, and so were our objectives. While we had to learn from Vietnam, we could not be imprisoned by it. Bosnia was not Vietnam, the Bosnian Serbs were not the Vietcong, and Belgrade was not Hanoi. The Bosnian Serbs, poorly trained bullies and criminals, would not stand up to NATO air strikes the way the seasoned and indoctrinated Vietcong and North Vietnamese had. And, as we had seen in the Krajina, Belgrade was not going to back the Bosnian Serbs the way Hanoi had backed the Vietcong.

The August 28 mortar attack was hardly the first challenge to Western policy, nor the worst incident of the war; it was only the latest. But it was different because of its timing: coming immediately after the launching of our diplomatic shuttle and the tragedy on Igman, it appeared not only as an act of terror against innocent people in Sarajevo, but as the first direct affront to the United States. As we sleepwalked through a busy schedule in Paris, my mind drifted back over the many failures of Western leadership over the last few years, and I hoped—prayed—that this time it would be different.

CHAPTER 7

Bombing and Breakthrough

(August 28–31)

> The time will come when those few hours will say much about war and peace in Bosnia, the role that the United States played in the outcome, the real importance of France, and perhaps the world order that will reflect it.
>
> —BERNARD-HENRI LÉVY, *Le Lys et la Cendre*

Paris, August 28, 1995. With the Administration facing some of the most important decisions since it took office, the "Principals," including the President and Vice President, were all on vacation. As the hours and the days blurred into one continuous crisis session, the deputies were in charge—so much so that they began teasing each other about it. "We joked," Strobe Talbott, who was acting Secretary of State, recalled later, "that it was 'deputy dogs' day,' and how we felt like the kid in *Home Alone.*"

There was, of course, no joking about the issue at hand. It would prove to be one of the decisive weeks of the war, indeed a seminal week in the shaping of America's post–Cold War foreign policy. Led by Sandy Berger, who was acting National Security Advisor, the team included John White (acting Secretary of Defense), Admiral Bill Owens (acting Chairman of the Joint Chiefs of Staff), George Tenet (acting Director of the CIA), Undersecretary of Defense Walter Slocombe, and Undersecretary of State Peter Tarnoff. The only Cabinet-level official not on vacation was Madeleine Albright, who shuttled feverishly between Washington and New York trying to overcome the reluctance of U.N. officials to take action. The rest of the team spent much of its time hunched over the oak table in the White House Situation Room, eating cold pizzas and trying to forge a united front with our NATO allies and the U.N.

Pamela Harriman. We delayed our departure for Belgrade a day while we pressed Washington for air strikes, and set up makeshift offices at Ambassador Harriman's magnificent official residence on Rue du Faubourg St.-Honoré. Less than two hundred yards from the Élysée Palace, where the French President lived, the huge eighteenth-century *hôtel particulier* and large gardens would have been a powerful weapon for any diplomat; Pamela Harriman knew how to use it especially well.

Pamela Harriman was no ordinary custodian. Her nearly legendary life was endlessly revisited by breathless journalists, but the gossip obscured the fact that she had done a superb job in Paris. The French, initially impressed only with her glamorous background, which had included many years in Paris in the late 1940s and early 1950s, came to realize that she was a huge asset. Believing France the key to Europe—an ironic position for a person who had spent most of her life as a British citizen and who, moreover, was the daughter-in-law of Winston Churchill—and using her ability to reach almost anyone in Washington by phone, she gained greater access for French officials to important members of the U.S. government than ever before.

She had married Averell Harriman in 1970, after both her second husband, the celebrated Broadway producer Leland Heyward, and Harriman's wife, Marie, had died. It was famously part of this story that Pamela Digby Churchill and W. Averell Harriman had had a prior relationship during World War II, when she was still married to Randolph Churchill and Harriman was President Roosevelt's personal representative in London. Almost eighty when they were reunited, Harriman was rejuvenated by his marriage to Pam, who was then fifty. During the fifteen remaining years of Harriman's life, Pam created a wonderful final act to his long and storied career. One day, near the end, as we sat in his house in the Westchester hills near New York City, I asked my old boss if there was anything he regretted in his life. Harriman, rarely given to introspection, snapped back without a moment's hesitation, "Not marrying her the first time."

As Harriman aged slowly but inexorably, Pam began to play a more prominent role. When he died in 1986, Pam continued their joint efforts on her own. A number of articles and, finally, two books portrayed her in an unflattering light, as cold and ambitious, but, although upset by the books, she pushed on, ignoring her critics.

We remained close friends and political allies throughout this period, both before and after Governor Harriman's death. Now the meeting with Izetbegovic in Paris had given us a chance, after more than twenty years of friendship, to work together during a crisis. Even in the midst of such an intense day, I could not help but take a moment to ask her if it had occurred to her how extraordinary this was. "Of course," she said. "And Averell would have been so proud of both of us."

·   ·   ·

During the day, on August 28, I met twice with Izetbegovic and Sacirbey, once at the Hôtel Crillon, the second time at the great house on the Rue du Faubourg St.-Honoré. At the first session, Izetbegovic was still in the suit he had worn to his official meetings with his French hosts, but for the second meeting, he changed into a sort of paramilitary outfit, complete with loose khakis, a scarf, and a beret bearing a Bosnian insignia. I watched with amusement as his car drove across the courtyard of the residence, where our Ambassador awaited him at the front door, dressed in one of her trademark Courrèges dresses. Each was rendered momentarily speechless by the sight of the other—Pam, towering like a Parisian landmark over the diminutive Bosnian, not realizing for an instant that this strange person, dressed like an aging Left Bank revolutionary, was his country's President; and Izetbegovic, having one day earlier left a shattered city under siege, looking up at this astounding vision in silk.

When we finally settled down, Izetbegovic demanded that NATO launch strikes against the Bosnian Serbs immediately. Sacirbey went further, saying his President would not see us again until NATO began bombing, a position he repeated in a telephone call to Strobe Talbott. I told Sacirbey that while Strobe and I supported his desire for bombing, such threats were unacceptable.

What Do the Bosnians Want? To determine our negotiating goals, we needed to know what Izetbegovic and his government wanted. This proved far more difficult than we had expected, and began a debate that would continue for years, one that went to the heart of the matter—the shape of a postwar Bosnia-Herzegovina, and whether it would be one country, or two, or three.

That evening, for the first time, I posed to Izetbegovic and his colleagues the most important question that would need to be addressed: do you want us to negotiate a single Bosnian state, which would necessarily have a relatively weak central government, or would you prefer to let Bosnia be divided, leaving you in firm control of a much smaller country?

We would return to this issue repeatedly—and after the end of the war it would take center stage as people debated whether or not the attempt to create a single multiethnic country was realistic. Many in the West believed—and still believe—that the best course would have been to negotiate a partition of Bosnia. At the outset we were ready to consider this approach, even though it ran against the stated policy goal of both the United States and the Contact Group—but only if it were the desire of *all three ethnic groups.* Most Bosnian Serbs would want to secede from Bosnia and join Serbia itself—this was after all the issue that had led to war. Similarly, most of the Croats who lived along the strip of land in the east bordering Croatia would, given a free choice, seek to join Croatia. But there were also many Serbs and Croats in towns and villages that were ethnically mixed or isolated who could not survive in anything other than a multiethnic state. There was no easy answer to this crucial question: to divide Bosnia-Herzegovina into two independent parts would legitimize Serb aggression and ethnic cleansing, and lands that had been Muslim or Croat for centuries would be lost forever to their rightful inhabitants. On the other hand, trying to force Serbs, Croats, and Muslims to live together after the ravages and brutality of the war, after what they had done to one another, would be extraordinarily difficult.

The key voice in this decision had to be the primary victims of the war. But Izetbegovic was not prepared to discuss the future shape of Bosnia when I first brought it up in Paris on August 28. He was focused on the necessity for immediate NATO bombing, and wary of negotiations, which had thus far resolved nothing and resulted only in broken promises. Furthermore, the Bosnians had not resolved this question among themselves. Having put all their effort into survival, they had never functioned as a government in the normal sense of the word, nor clearly defined their postwar aims. Yet despite his obvious ambivalence and confusion, even in his first response, he gave an indication of where he wanted to go: Bosnia should remain a single country, he said, but he would accept a high degree of autonomy for the Serb portion.

Prime Minister Haris Silajdzic, with whom we had a similar discussion a few days later in Zagreb, had the same overall goal in mind, but a far different structure. He wanted a stronger multiethnic central government, with, not surprisingly, a powerful prime minister. Silajdzic spoke with passion about the need to re-create a multiethnic country, although he referred to the Croats with such animosity that I did not see how he could ever cooperate with them. This internal disagreement between the Bosnian President and Prime Minister was disturbing, and was to repeat itself often in the coming months.

At the center of this tangle was the remarkable figure of Alija Izetbegovic. He had kept the "idea" of Bosnia alive for years under the most difficult circumstances. It was an extraordinary achievement, a tribute to his courage and determination. At the age of seventy, after surviving eight years in Tito's jails and four years of Serb attacks, he saw politics as a perpetual struggle. He had probably never thought seriously about what it might mean to run a real country in peacetime. Even minor gestures of reconciliation to those Serbs who were ready to re-establish some form of multiethnic community were not easy for Izetbegovic. His eyes had a cold and distant gaze; after so much suffering, they seemed dead to anyone else's pain. He was a devout Muslim, although not the Bosnian ayatollah that his enemies portrayed. Yet though he paid lip service to the principles of a multiethnic state, he was not the democrat that some supporters in the West saw. He reminded me a bit of Mao Zedong and other radical Chinese communist leaders—good at revolution, poor at governance. But without him Bosnia would never have survived.

Three Signals from Pale. Tuesday, August 29, dawned with press reports from Washington that the Clinton Administration was urging NATO and the U.N. to respond militarily. In an editorial, *The New York Times* objected. "Diplomacy is clearly the better course," it wrote. "Mr. Holbrooke risks becoming the latest intermediary to fail at Balkan diplomacy, but he is right to try."

In Pale, the Bosnian Serbs seemed to realize they had blundered badly by shelling the marketplace. Trying to reduce the chances of air strikes, they took three revealing steps. First, they issued a statement welcoming the American peace initiative. This meant nothing, but it was a sign that Pale felt isolated and overexposed.

The second signal came directly from Karadzic, who in a fax asked former President Jimmy Carter to return to Pale to negotiate an immediate cease-fire and start peace negotiations. In public, the Administration was properly polite about Carter's role. Nicholas Burns, the State Department spokesman, said the letter to Carter "contains some potentially positive elements which we are examining carefully." In fact, however, we saw the letter as a clever attempt to lure the United States back into direct negotiations with Pale, something we had flirted with and rejected six months earlier as dangerously unproductive. Bob Frasure had been the primary architect of the strategy of negotiating solely with Milosevic; although it had not yet borne fruit, I was persuaded, as were my Washington colleagues, that it was the correct approach. While we did not want to elevate Milosevic to statesman status, we planned to negotiate only with him and, at the same time, hold him strictly accountable for the behavior of the Bosnian Serbs.

Fortunately, Carter's main contact with Washington on Bosnia was Harry Barnes, a respected former Ambassador to India, Chile, and Romania with whom my colleagues and I had worked for many years. Barnes understood that opening a direct channel to Pale at such a critical moment would undermine our strategy. After talking to Tarnoff and me, Barnes drafted a reply from President Carter to Karadzic that kept him at arm's length and ended this channel for the time being.

Pale's third and oddest effort to make direct contact came through Mike Wallace, who called me in Paris. He told me that he was in Pale, where he was taping a profile of Karadzic for *60 Minutes*. He said that they had been watching CNN together—the thought made me laugh—when an interview with me appeared and Karadzic told Wallace he would like to meet me. When Mike told him we were old friends, he asked Wallace to try to arrange a meeting the following day in Belgrade to discuss peace.

One of the toughest people in television, Wallace was trying to promote a good story, an exclusive. I laughed and told him that I would love to help him win another award, but that we would no longer meet with Karadzic unless he were part of a delegation headed by Belgrade. Mike repeated our position to Karadzic, sending a useful signal through an unexpected channel.

In view of what was about to happen, it was more than fortunate that we rejected these three probes from Pale. Had we opened any of these doors, the course of the next three months would have been significantly different.

Dîner Chez Harriman. In New York, Ambassador Albright continued her vigorous campaign with those United Nations officials she could round up; fortunately, Secretary-General Boutros-Ghali was unreachable on a commercial aircraft, so she dealt instead with his best deputy, Kofi Annan, who was in charge of peacekeeping operations. At 11:45 A.M., New York time, came a big break: Annan informed Talbott and Albright that he had instructed the U.N.'s civilian officials and military commanders to relinquish for a limited period of time their authority to veto air strikes in Bosnia. For the first time in the war, the decision on the air strikes was solely in the hands of NATO—primarily two American officers, NATO's Supreme Commander, General George Joulwan, and Admiral Leighton Smith, the commander of NATO's southern forces and all U.S. naval forces in Europe.

I asked our Ambassador in London, Admiral William Crowe, who had been Chairman of the JCS under Presidents Reagan and Bush, to make the case to his senior British counterparts for bombing, while at NATO Ambassador Robert Hunter and General Joulwan carried the case forward with our allies. We also gained vital support from the NATO Secretary-General, Willy Claes. This mattered: Claes, the former Foreign Minister of Belgium, was relatively new to his job, and this was a major decision for him; he was, after all, now advocating the biggest military action in the forty-five-year history of NATO, amidst a notable lack of enthusiasm from most of his fellow Europeans. Claes made one of those bureaucratic decisions whose importance is lost to most outside observers. Instead of calling for another formal meeting of the NATO Council to make a decision, Claes simply *informed* the other members of NATO that he had authorized General Joulwan and Admiral Leighton Smith, the commander of all NATO forces in the Mediterranean, to take military action if it was deemed appropriate. As it turned out, Claes's bureaucratic maneuver was vital; despite the decision of the London conference in July, the NATO Council would have either delayed or denied air strikes.

Izetbegovic would be busy with official events until after a dinner speech, so, to fill our evening, Ambassador Harriman put together a last-minute dinner for the delegation and a few French and Bosnian officials, including Sacirbey, who brought with him several friends, one of whom was the popular French *philosophe* and writer Bernard-Henri Lévy.

Although dinner was served, as always, in the impeccable manner that was Pamela Harriman's hallmark, it quickly degenerated into what must have been one of the most disjointed soirées ever held at the residence on the Rue du Faubourg St.-Honoré. The telephone never stopped ringing, and Wes Clark and I were constantly called from the table to discuss with Washington, Brussels, or New York some new problem in the effort to start the bombing. Finally, just as Lévy was leaving, he noticed an unannounced visitor in khakis and a paramilitary beret sitting quietly in a corner in one of the grand reception rooms.

With a keen and cynical Gallic eye, Lévy described the dinner in his bestseller *Le Lys et la Cendre,* published a year later. Because Lévy was one of only two or three outsiders who ever saw the negotiating team in action, his journal notes are worth quoting in some detail—although I hope that Lévy, whom we found engaging as well as engagé, later understood that we were not, in fact, as crazy as we seemed to him that frantic evening:

> Sacirbey and I both went to the residence of the American Ambassador, the lovely Pamela Harriman. I knew Pamela Harriman slightly. . . . I had had an opportunity to appreciate her pleasant intellect, her attentiveness to others, her way of feigning ignorance to force you to talk and reveal yourself to her. And her charm. Her strange beauty that evaded the attacks of age.
>
> At my table were two people whom, I must say, I couldn't place right away. Facing me, stuffed into an olive-green uniform dripping with decorations that seemed to have come from the wardrobe department of *Platoon* or *Full Metal Jacket,* was General Wesley Clark. . . . On my left was a civilian in his fifties, jovial, athletically built, with wire-framed eyeglasses. . . . He called Mohammed "Mo" and Sacirbey, in turn, unfailingly called him "Dick." At first I found him rather rude, since he was constantly leaving the table to go and answer the phone. This was Richard Holbrooke himself, the head of the peace mission, the "bulldozer diplomat," who, it was said, might be in the process of stopping the war in the Balkans. . . .
>
> After Holbrooke had gotten up for the eighth or ninth time to answer telephone calls . . . I remember saying to myself, "What is going on here anyway? Does he have St. Vitus' dance? And who is he trying to impress, getting up eight times in a row in the middle of dinner?" . . .
>
> It was now midnight. Pamela Harriman, who up to now had been the perfect host, began to look pointedly at her watch, as if she were suddenly in a hurry for us to leave. . . . We let ourselves be swept along in the commotion, almost a rush for the door, the reason for which we had absolutely no idea. . . . And whom did we find, lost in the immense [formal living room] that was even more imposing because it was otherwise empty? Over there, under the Renoir, perched casually

on the arm of a chair, talking on the phone in a low voice—a small scrawny guy, wearing a sort of loose-fitting jacket that looked from a distance like a painter's smock or a pajama top . . . was Bosnian President Izetbegovic. . . .

The Ambassador came over, utterly embarrassed. She let us talk for two or three minutes more . . . and then took him gently by the arm and led him over to join Holbrooke, Clark and the others. . . . My last image was of Pamela Harriman, very dignified, strangely earnest, followed in silence by Izetbegovic in his quasi pajamas and the American diplomats, all of them seemingly in awe, bathed in a wan light that made them look like conspirators caught in the act.

Of course, the next day, I had the key to this strange scene. I then realized that the Bosnian president had left the [official French] dinner, dropped by his hotel to shower and change, and then had come to join the other main actors as the major air strikes against the Serbs were launched.

I then understood that this was what Holbrooke had had on his mind during dinner, while we had been somewhat annoyed at what we perceived to be his self-importance . . . when in fact he was probably in the process of settling the last details of choreography. . . .

The time will come when those few hours will say much about war and peace in Bosnia, the role that the United States played in the outcome, the real importance of France, and perhaps the world order that will reflect it.[1]

Lévy was almost correct. The final decision to start the bombing had not yet been made, but was fast approaching—hence the drama and tension of the evening. After Lévy left, Clark spread out on the floor of the residence huge maps of Bosnia. Under Harriman's van Gogh and Picassos, Izetbegovic wandered aimlessly over the maps, trying to orient himself, while Clark's aides tried to keep the corners of the map panels aligned. The mere sight of maps, as Jim Pardew put it, "energized" the Bosnians into a deeply emotional state. Izetbegovic told us that the territorial issues—"the map"—would be far more difficult to resolve than the constitutional issues. At the time, I did not fully appreciate what he meant, but when we finally got down to serious map discussions more than two months later he was proved all too correct.

Just after midnight, after another telephone call from Washington, I pulled Izetbegovic aside. "Mr. President," I said, "we have some good news. Acting Secretary Talbott asked me to inform you that NATO planes will begin air strikes in Bosnia in less than two hours." I shook his hand warmly, but either because he was exhausted or because he had seen previous NATO bombing "campaigns" turn out to be meaningless pinpricks, he just smiled his strange smile, and slipped out into the Paris night.

The Bombs of August. Operation Deliberate Force began on August 30 at 2:00 A.M. local time. More than sixty aircraft, flying from bases in Italy and the aircraft carrier *Theodore Roosevelt* in the Adriatic, pounded Bosnian Serb positions around Sarajevo. It was the largest military action in NATO history. French and British artillery from the Rapid Reaction Force joined in, targeting Lukavica barracks southwest of Sarajevo. Unlike earlier air strikes, when the U.N. and NATO had restricted themselves to hitting individual Serb surface-to-air missile sites or single tanks, these strikes were massive. Planned by Admiral Smith and his brilliant Air Force commander, Lieutenant General Michael E. Ryan, the targets had been picked months in advance. General Ryan had prepared his forces for a possible bombing campaign for several years. I had examined the bulky photoreconnaissance books during a visit to Smith's headquarters high in the hills above Naples over a year earlier, and knew that NATO had photographs of thousands of targets, ranging from tiny bunkers to the new, sophisticated Serb surface-to-air system that had significantly increased the danger to NATO pilots in recent months. When the assignment came, he and Smith carried out the mission with great skill and astonishing success.

Press and public reaction was highly positive. Izetbegovic, his doubts temporarily erased, said, "The world has finally done what it should have done a long, long time ago." Senator Dole, calling the attacks "long overdue," backed them fully. Roger Cohen, *The New York Times*'s Sarajevo bureau chief, began his article: "After 40 months of awkward hesitation, NATO today stepped squarely into the midst of the Bosnian war." *The Wall Street Journal* began its news story: "The U.S. and its NATO allies, after four years of disagreement and feckless intervention . . ." The *Financial Times,* whose coverage of Bosnia had been unsurpassed, editorialized that "Western policy would not have had a shred of credibility left if there had not been a tough response." Rethinking its editorial policy overnight, *The New York Times* decided that the bombing was "a risk worth taking in this particular situation and for the purpose of sustaining the specific diplomatic initiative now under way." A *Times* article by Steven Greenhouse especially caught my eye, since it attributed to unnamed senior Washington policy makers a view at variance with mine: that "it would not be the smartest thing [for Mr. Holbrooke] . . . to show up in Belgrade this week to meet with President Slobodan Milosevic of Serbia right after NATO planes bombed his Bosnian Serb brothers . . . [because] the large-scale bombing might cause Serbian nationalists to pressure Mr. Milosevic to tell Mr. Holbrooke to go away—and derail the peace initiative."

The most insightful commentary came from the Paris-based American columnist William Pfaff. He saw instantly what it would take others months to discern: that the NATO bombing marked a historic development in post–Cold War relations between Europe and the United States. "The humiliation of Europe in what may prove the Yugoslav endgame has yet to be fully appreciated in Europe's capitals," he wrote on September 1 in the *International Herald-*

Tribune. "The United States today is again Europe's leader; there is no other. Both the Bush and Clinton administrations tried, and failed, to convince the European governments to take over Europe's leadership."

Operation Deliberate Force came after a magnificent effort, quarterbacked by Berger, Talbott, and Albright on the civilian side, and Admiral Owens, John White, and Walt Slocombe for the Pentagon. When it was all over and we could assess who had been most helpful, my Washington colleagues usually singled out Kofi Annan at the United Nations, and Willy Claes and General Joulwan at NATO. Annan's gutsy performance in those twenty-four hours was to play a central role in Washington's strong support for him a year later as the successor to Boutros Boutros-Ghali as Secretary-General of the United Nations. Indeed, in a sense Annan won the job on that day.

The President, who was still in Wyoming, did not make any telephone calls himself, but he made it clear that he wanted a military response. He told Sandy and Strobe that he wanted "to hit them hard," and was ready to make calls if necessary. This evidence of the President's own determination was vital in persuading the Europeans and the U.N. that action was unavoidable.

After all the years of minimal steps, the historic decision to "hit them hard" had been made remarkably quickly. What, therefore, had caused such a sudden and dramatic change of heart, after months in which there had been no NATO action, even in response to the horrors of Srebrenica and Zepa?

Different vantage points may produce different answers to this question. When I asked my colleagues later, they cited four factors: the sense that we had reached the absolute end of the line, and simply could not let this latest outrage stand; the grim, emotional reaction of Washington after losing three close and treasured colleagues on Mount Igman; the President's own determination; and the strong recommendation of our negotiating team that bombing should take place regardless of its effect on the negotiations.

From the vantage point of the Europeans, the issue undoubtedly looked different. They had opposed massive bombing in the past because they feared their soldiers would be taken hostage by the Serbs, and because they saw the stakes in Bosnia differently. The last British troops had been removed from the Gorazde enclave just before the bombing began, thus extracting the most vulnerable forces from positions where they could be taken hostage. But because many other U.N. peacekeepers remained vulnerable, there was still great concern about, even opposition to, the bombing as it began. Despite the rule changes for bombing that came out of the London conference, I have no doubt the Europeans would have blocked or minimized the bombing were it not for Washington's new resolve. We knew from the moment the bombing started, therefore, that there would be a continued disagreement with our

NATO allies and the U.N. over its duration and its scope—and that the United States would have to keep pressing.

History is often made of seemingly disparate events whose true relationship to one another becomes apparent only after the fact. This was true of the last two weeks of August. As our negotiations gathered momentum in the weeks following the bombing, almost everyone came to believe that the bombing had been part of a master plan. But in fact in none of the discussions prior to our mission had we considered bombing as part of a negotiating strategy. Lake himself never mentioned it during his trip to Europe, and in private he had shown great ambivalence toward it. The military was more than skeptical; most were opposed. Later, the Administration was praised for—or accused of—having planned what the Chinese might have called a policy of "talk-talk, bomb-bomb." In fact, this would not have been a bad idea—both Frasure and I had long favored it—but it simply did not happen that way. It took an outrageous Bosnian Serb action to trigger Operation Deliberate Force. But once launched, it made a huge difference.

By 3:00 A.M., with the bombing under way for almost an hour, I tried to get some sleep, but General Clark came to my room with a distressing piece of news: the U.S. Air Force did not want us to travel to Belgrade because of the danger of flying in or near the war zone. Clark explained that the Air Force was especially worried that we might be shot down by Serb missiles.

This was absurd, I told Clark, and asked him to ensure that, one way or another, we got to Belgrade in the morning, even if we had to fly around the combat zone. We simply had to get there immediately to see the effect of the bombing on Milosevic and the Pale Serbs.

I rose at 7:00 A.M. on August 30 to find that during the night Clark—who seemed to operate on even less sleep than the rest of us—had persuaded the Air Force to take us to Belgrade. After a one-hour delay to coordinate a new flight path with NATO, I told him that we should start for Belgrade without confirmation that we would be able to land, and divert to Zagreb if necessary. The flight east toward the Serbian capital was very tense, even after we received word that we would be cleared to land. We spent the journey trying to figure out a response to every possible contingency we might face in Belgrade. Would Milosevic refuse to see us? Keep us waiting for a day or more? See us but refuse to discuss anything except the cessation of the bombing? Negotiate more intensively? We covered every possibility—except the one that actually occurred.

One historical analogy, however inexact, came to mind: the gamble Nixon and Kissinger had taken when they mined the harbor of Haiphong just before the May 1972 Moscow summit. Even though they felt they were putting the summit, the centerpiece of their global diplomatic strategy, on the line, they decided to proceed with the attacks on North Vietnam. While I did not agree with the action, I respected the cool calculation involved in taking such a risk, and the fact that it had succeeded—that is, it did not wreck the U.S.-Soviet summit. Without overdramatizing the comparison, I mentioned it to my colleagues as our plane began to descend toward the military airport outside Belgrade.

Rudy Perina was waiting for us. As we drove into the city, he said there were no signs of public reaction to the bombing, which had now been going on for almost eight hours. The meeting was on, but Rudy had no idea what to expect. As we drove to the Presidential Palace, I could feel my stomach muscles tightening, as they often did before a high-risk, high-stakes meeting.

The Patriarch Paper. We had not been in Belgrade since Mount Igman, and Milosevic opened our August 30 meeting with words of sympathy about our three lost comrades. He spoke, in particular, about Bob Frasure, whom he knew better than Joe and Nelson. I was startled to hear Milosevic talk in detail about Bob's family, his farm, and his dreams for the future, and I realized, for the first time, that he and Bob must have spent a lot of time discussing personal matters.

Then, abruptly, he shifted gears. "I've been a busy man while you were away," he said, and, reaching into his breast pocket, he pulled out two sheets of paper.

"I have listened carefully to your public statements," he continued. "I have been meeting with the Bosnian Serb leaders—Karadzic, Mladic, Krajisnik, Buha, all of them—all weekend and again yesterday. This is the result." He handed me the document. Not being able to read it—it was in Serbian—I handed it right back.

"This paper creates a joint Yugoslav–Republika Srpska delegation for all future peace talks," Milosevic said, using their own name for the Bosnian Serbs. "I will be the head of the joint delegation. And this document has been witnessed by Patriarch Pavle, the leader of the Serb Orthodox Church. Look here." Milosevic pointed to a single signature centered below two vertical rows of signatures, at the bottom of the second page of the document. Below the signature was the Eastern Orthodox cross.

For a moment I did not dare to believe it. For sixteen months, the Contact Group had argued fruitlessly with Milosevic over how to get the Bosnian Serbs to participate in negotiations under the Contact Group plan. Now we had the answer to the question we had asked for those sixteen months: who would speak for Pale? And the answer was: Slobodan Milosevic. Washington's decision to negotiate with Belgrade and try to isolate Pale had produced its first success—only a procedural one, to be sure, but a real breakthrough. Genuine negotiations were about to begin.

The document—which we afterward referred to as the Patriarch Paper, as if it were the title of a Robert Ludlum thriller—gave Milosevic virtually total power over the fate of the Bosnian Serbs. They agreed to the establishment of a six-person negotiating team, with three people from Yugoslavia and three from Pale. Milosevic proudly pointed to the most important clause in the Patriarch Paper: in the event of a tie vote on any issue, the head of the delegation would make the decision. And who was the head of the joint delegation, Milosevic asked rhetorically? We already knew the answer to this—Slobodan Milosevic!

As Milosevic explained this remarkable document, I whispered to Chris Hill, "If only Bob Frasure could have seen this." Chris told me later he'd had the same thought at exactly the same moment.

Milosevic was now at his most charming. Lighting up a huge Monte Cristo cigar, he proposed that I convene an international peace conference immediately, where he could meet Izetbegovic and Tudjman and "settle everything." Such a conference was, in fact, what Washington wanted, but our talks in Paris had made it evident that the Muslims were not ready. Besides, the bombing had just begun. "We will have a conference sooner or later," I said, "but not yet."

I questioned the positions of the Bosnian Serbs. "How do you know that your friends from Pale will—"

Milosevic showed momentary anger—real or feigned, I could not tell. "They are not my friends. They are not my colleagues. It is awful just to be in the same room with them for so long. They are shit." Milosevic pronounced the last word with an Eastern European accent, so it sounded like "sheet," but I was impressed with his undiplomatic command of the English idiom.

For the next eight hours, we discussed almost every issue that we would later negotiate to a conclusion in Dayton. For the first time, everything was on the table, including several issues that had never been discussed before as part of the peace process.

War Criminals . . . and the Bombing. Not until we had talked for almost two hours did Milosevic finally bring up the bombing in Bosnia. I was struck by his lack of emotion on the subject, in contrast, for example, to his passion on the subject of lifting the economic sanctions against Serbia.

If we stopped the bombing, Milosevic said, Mladic would stop the shelling of Sarajevo. Such an offer would be favorably received in the U.N. and most

NATO capitals, and by the military; they had little enthusiasm for the bombing, and had already lost a Mirage fighter jet: two French pilots were missing and presumed captured.

I told Milosevic that if he could guarantee an end to the siege of Sarajevo, I would consider "recommending" a *suspension* of the bombing. Milosevic, repeating his performance of ten days earlier, immediately asked his faithful aide, Goran, to contact Mladic. We ate while waiting for Mladic's reply. The meal was, as usual, several different preparations of lamb, accompanied by potatoes and vegetables, and, for variety, some pork.

As we ate, Goran returned with an answer from Mladic. Milosevic read it aloud: "Mladic says that he promises to stop actions against the Muslims in Sarajevo if both NATO and the Muslims stop actions against his forces."

Typically, Mladic had tried to slip in a condition: the Bosnian Muslims would have to cease their own military activities throughout the country. This they would not do, as Milosevic well knew. He made no effort to argue Mladic's case, but turned back to a discussion of other matters. I decided to bring up, for the first time, a critical issue.

"Mr. President," I began, "there is one matter I must raise with you now, so that there is no misunderstanding later. That is the question of the International War Crimes Tribunal."

Milosevic started to object, but I pressed on. "Mr. President, two of the men who signed the Patriarch agreement are indicted war criminals—Radovan Karadzic and Ratko Mladic. They cannot participate in an international peace conference of any sort. Under international law they will be arrested if they set foot on the soil of the United States or of any member of the E.U." I also stressed that what had happened at Srebrenica and Zepa would have to be investigated.

Milosevic argued about the events surrounding the fall of the two eastern enclaves; he continued to deny any involvement in or prior knowledge of the attack. I told him we knew that Mladic, who considered himself an officer of the Yugoslav Army, had received support from their units situated just across the Serbian border from Srebrenica, from an army under Milosevic's command. "I want to be sure, since this is the beginning a serious negotiation with you as the head of a united Yugoslav-Srpska delegation," I said, "that you understand that we will not, and cannot, compromise on the question of the war-crimes tribunal."

"But you need Karadzic and Mladic to make peace," he replied.

"That is your problem. Karadzic and Mladic cannot go to an international conference. They will be arrested if they set foot in any European country. In fact, if they come to the United States, I would gladly meet them at the airport and assist in their arrest. You have just shown us a piece of paper giving you the power to negotiate for them. It's your problem."

Milosevic continued to object to the exclusion of Karadzic and Mladic from the peace process. "We should not decide this now," he finally concluded wearily. "As for Srebrenica, I repeat: I had nothing to do with it, and I didn't know it was going to happen." Then he said he would agree to allow international investigators to travel to the enclaves to gather on-site information on what had happened—a significant concession if he meant it.

We needed a break to alert Washington to the Patriarch Paper, which Milosevic wanted to make public. As I left to call Washington, I sought to dampen the upbeat mood, which had been fueled by a certain amount of scotch, wine, and plum brandy. "We'll be back soon, Mr. President," I said, "but remember, NATO planes are in the air over Bosnia as we speak."

"Yes, Mr. Holbrooke," he replied. "And you have the power to stop them."

The Press. When we arrived at the Presidential Palace in the morning, a large number of journalists were waiting outside. This had not happened before Mount Igman, before the bombing. I made a short, impromptu statement, saying that "President Clinton has sent us on a mission of peace in a moment of war." An even larger group of journalists was waiting when we left the presidency building eight hours later. We realized that a big and aggressive press corps would henceforth be following our efforts—a significant development that we would have to take into account.

By this time Milosevic had released the Patriarch Paper, and it was necessary to make some public comment about it. Deliberately seeking to downplay its significance, I said the document was "an important procedural breakthrough, but only a procedural one." In our effort to prevent optimism, we were almost too successful; John Pomfret of *The Washington Post* got it just about right, describing it as "a conciliatory move" and a "significant advance," but *The New York Times* did not even mention the document for several days.

We asked Washington not to sound too upbeat. Bosnia was not a good place for the conventional Washington "spin," that natural American style of making everything look as good as possible. I believed it was best to underplay signs of progress and minimize optimism, while simultaneously seeking to establish a sense of new American commitment and engagement. If the glass was filling up, I would prefer that we said it was still almost empty.

Thus, our original plan to maintain "radio silence" and let Washington speak for us fell by the wayside. We did not even have a press officer with us—unprecedented for a major negotiating team. But as the pace picked up, the need for carefully calibrated nuance that was more likely to be understood by journalists in the region than Washington-based reporters required a major change in our approach to the press. The six-hour time difference created a special problem; our day was half over before most Washington officials got to the office, and they would often be asked to react early in the day to incomplete early-morning accounts of our activities on radio and television, before they could coordinate with, or sometimes even find, us. Considering this unexpected problem, Tom Donilon, Nick Burns, and White House Press Secretary Mike McCurry asked us to take the lead with the press. We continued to travel without a press officer, and, on over two hundred different flights, allowed a journalist on our small plane only twice. Relations with the press were admirably handled by Rosemarie Pauli and by the USIA press officers in the local Embassies. I encouraged every member of our small team to talk directly to journalists whenever they wanted to, provided they worked from a single script. The change in the way we dealt with the press would have far-ranging and positive consequences. The system worked well, a remarkable tribute to the dedication and discipline of our small group. With only a few relatively minor exceptions, the coverage of our efforts by the press based in the region was accurate and fair.

We returned to the Hyatt Hotel from Milosevic's office late in the evening. The sense that real negotiations had begun at last had given us a huge lift, and we stayed up half the night, reviewing our options and calling Washington and Brussels. In a handwritten note Jim Pardew captured our mood. "I've now put down the hammer I was using to beat down my own optimism," he said. "This may work."

The scene at the hotel that evening also had its comic aspects. In an effort to prevent our hosts from eavesdropping on our private conversations, General Clark had brought into the hotel a bizarre setup designed, in theory, to allow us to discuss highly sensitive matters inside our hotel rooms. Clark's team set up a small military tent inside a hotel room. Inside the tent they installed an air blower that emitted a continuous loud noise designed to "defeat" anyone trying to listen to our conversations. So, one by one, we huddled inside the tent inside the hotel room making secure telephone calls to Washington over an antiquated telephone system. But the noise from the air blower was so loud, and the secure telephone circuits often so weak, that we had to shout to be heard on the phone, thus making it easy for any listening devices (or anyone in the general vicinity) to pick us up.

The military's second device will remain forever enshrined in our memories, and we teased Wes about it endlessly long after we had abandoned it as unusable. This was a collection of bulky plastic "nose and mouth cones," which we placed over our faces so we could speak to each other in privacy. The cones smelled of old rubber, and worked only intermittently. Placed next to one another at our small conference table, they were linked by messy wires that ran like spaghetti across the table. Sitting at the table, elbow to elbow, we talked to each other through these smelly devices, which we held over our faces. At two in the morning, after a day that was ending with a diplomatic breakthrough in Belgrade nineteen hours after its uncertain and tense beginning in Paris, these smelly, ineffective devices broke the tension. As we joked and took ceremonial photographs of everyone wearing his cone, Rosemarie came in and told us that we were yelling so loud that everyone in the hotel corridors could hear our supposedly classified conversations.

The next morning, August 31, we met briefly with the Belgrade representatives of the British, French, German, and Russian governments. The British representative, Ivor Roberts, was erudite and charming, and I respected him for his intellect and his knowledge, although he seemed excessively pro-Serb. He was impressed by the Patriarch Paper, but cautioned me, in an eloquent letter, never to forget that the Serbs felt that history had victimized them. Don't put them in a corner, Roberts urged, or they will lash back. The clear subtext was that the bombing was a mistake. I thanked Roberts for his views, and thought again of Rebecca West. The Serb view of history was their problem, I told Roberts later; ours was to end the war.

After breakfast we flew to Zagreb to give briefings to President Tudjman and Muhamed Sacirbey on the talks in Belgrade. Tudjman immediately saw the full implications of the Patriarch Paper. "Sanctions worked," he noted, "and we should keep up the military pressure."

NATO was doing just that. August 31 was, in fact, the busiest day of military action in NATO history, with planes ranging across all of northern and western Bosnia. The bombing was spreading into areas far beyond Sarajevo, areas that had nothing to do with the mortar attack. The Bosnian Serbs were stunned. I knew there would be great pressure from the U.N.

Although we clearly were not ready for a full-scale international peace conference, I wondered about some intermediate step, one that would show progress. What about a short meeting, under American auspices, of the three Foreign Ministers—something that had not taken place in over two years?

I asked both Tudjman and Sacirbey what they thought of the idea. Without hesitation, Tudjman said he would send Foreign Minister Granic to Geneva whenever we wanted. Sacirbey also agreed to go, although he expressed skepticism that anything could be accomplished without Milosevic present.

The idea of convening a meeting of the three Foreign Ministers provoked a serious debate within our delegation as we flew back to Belgrade that evening. Not everyone on our delegation supported the idea. Our designated skeptic, Bob Owen, was—well, the most skeptical. "What will we accomplish?" he asked. "We have no position papers, no idea of what the parties will agree to. I'm not sure we are ready for this yet."

But the Patriarch agreement and the bombing had greatly strengthened our hand. It was time to see how much we could get from a preliminary meeting. We would be able to observe how the delegations interacted with one another and internally—good practice for the full-scale conference that still lay in the uncertain future. I asked Owen to start drafting the outlines of an interim, or partial, agreement. We did not consult or inform Washington.

A great deal of any good negotiation is improvisation within the framework of a general goal. After the tumultuous events of the last three days, a concept of how we should negotiate had begun to form in my mind. Although Washington wanted us to get the three Balkan Presidents together as quickly as possible, it was far too early to do this. But it was worth trying to reduce the huge differences between the parties with a series of limited interim agreements, which we could attempt to negotiate through shuttle diplomacy, then unveil in a series of quick one-day meetings at the Foreign Minister level. This might create a sense of momentum toward peace, and narrow the differences to the point where we could bring the three Presidents together.

Our negotiating team had already developed an internal dynamic that combined bantering, fierce but friendly argument, and tight internal discipline. Complete trust and openness among all seven of us were essential if we were to avoid energy-consuming factional intrigues and back channels to Washington. This presented difficulties for representatives of those agencies—the NSC, the JCS, the Office of the Secretary of Defense—that often distrusted or competed with one another and whose representatives normally sent private reports back to their home offices each day. (While Harriman and Vance could not solve this problem in 1968, Kissinger had famously solved it later by cutting everyone else out of the process, producing dramatic results in the short term and great animosity later.) We succeeded in avoiding this problem, in part because our team was so small, and in part because we shared all our information internally and developed close, even intense personal relationships. I told my colleagues that if we could not come up with a single position, each member of the team could make his viewpoint known to Washington directly—provided only that he shared his dissent with the rest of us. This system worked, and was a key ingredient in the success of our small team.

CHAPTER 8

The Longest Weekend

(September 1–4)

> The historian must . . . constantly put himself at a point in the past
> at which the known factors will seem to permit different outcomes.
> If he speaks of Salamis, then it must be as if the Persians might still
> win; if he speaks of the coup d'état of Brumaire, then it must re-
> main to be seen if Bonaparte will be ignominiously repulsed.
>
> —JOHAN HUIZINGA

OUR DIPLOMATIC SHUTTLE REACHED NEW INTENSITY. With a travel schedule that changed every few hours, we moved so unpredictably across Europe
that Washington often did not know where we were. Driven by the bombing
and by the sense that it was now all or nothing, we felt ready to take on almost
any challenge—so much so that in the midst of the Bosnia shuttle, we took on
an additional, related problem: the two-year-old crisis between Greece and the
former Yugoslav Republic of Macedonia, where five hundred American
troops were deployed to prevent hostilities.

It hardly dawned on us that the Labor Day holiday was starting in the
United States. Our own weekend would take us to Belgrade, Bonn, Brussels,
Geneva, Zagreb, Belgrade, Athens, Skopje (the capital of Macedonia),
Ankara, and back for a third time to Belgrade. During those four days we
would:

- arrange and announce the first high-level meeting among the three
  warring parties in two years;

- meet our Contact Group colleagues (and a half-dozen Central European heads of government) in Bonn;

- spend most of a night at NATO headquarters in Brussels arguing for
  the resumption of the bombing;

- meet representatives of the Organization of the Islamic Conference in
  Geneva to get Muslim support for our efforts;

- negotiate a draft agreement with Milosevic and Izetbegovic for the high-level meeting—the first such agreement that would ever hold;

- resolve the dangerous situation between Greece and the former Yugoslav Republic of Macedonia;

- plead for the resumption of the bombing, while holding off another invitation to Jimmy Carter to step into the negotiations.

FRIDAY, SEPTEMBER 1

NATO suspended its bombing in Bosnia at 5:00 A.M. on Friday, September 1. I had told Washington we would support a short halt so that the U.N. commander, General Bernard Janvier, could negotiate with Mladic—but only if the pause would end promptly if the Bosnian Serbs did not agree to lift the siege of Sarajevo. With considerable prescience, Hill and Pardew warned that my position could cause a serious problem: it would be hard to resume the bombing once it was stopped, they feared, because the U.N. and some Europeans would try to prevent its resumption no matter what the circumstances. As if to prove Hill and Pardew right, U.N. headquarters in Zagreb, hiding its own desire for a total bombing halt behind our highly conditional support for a brief pause, told the press that the pause was at our request, a line that prompted a strong criticism of us by *New York Times* columnist William Safire.

The afternoon before the bombing halt began, we met General Janvier in his headquarters in Zagreb. Janvier, a small, unhappy-looking man, gave the impression that he wished he were somewhere else, and politely offered evasive nonresponses. He was clearly waiting for us to disappear, as had so many other negotiators in the previous three years, so that he could get on with his work. His demeanor suggested that he thought he could negotiate successfully with Mladic if only we would leave him alone.

Milosevic received us at Dobanovci, one of the many hunting lodges Tito had maintained around the country. About thirty minutes from downtown Belgrade, it was a collection of modest buildings set among large fields and forests, on the edge of a lake, not as fancy as Tito's more fabled retreats. We sat at a long table outside the main house, eating and drinking almost continually. Milosevic had added to his entourage Nikola Koljevic, a short, plump, and hard-drinking Shakespeare scholar who had taught English literature in Michigan. Koljevic held the title of "Vice President of Republika Srpska," but he was not trusted by the hard mountain men of Pale, the leaders of the Bosnian Serb movement, who viewed him as a Milosevic stooge. Koljevic liked to quote the Bard selectively to support his positions, frequently making statements like "The quality of mercy is not strained" or "The fault, dear Brutus . . ." Trying to keep even in the Shakespeare contest, I would offer up half-remembered phrases such as "Cry havoc, and let slip the dogs of war" or "There is a tide in the affairs of men."

The meeting at the hunting lodge rambled on for twelve hours, with a break during which we returned to our hotel for a short press conference. Milosevic had changed the venue in order to create a more relaxed atmosphere. There was heavy drinking for much of the day, which clearly affected Koljevic, but I saw no evidence—then or later—that the alcohol affected Milosevic's judgments. The Americans drank little, and I began a policy of accepting Milosevic's frequent offers of drinks only when we reached agreements.

Jim Pardew later called it the day of "bonding with the godfather." Milosevic could switch moods with astonishing speed, perhaps to keep others off balance. He could range from charm to brutality, from emotional outbursts to calm discussions of legal minutiae. When he was angry, his face wrinkled up, but he could regain control of himself instantly.

Near the beginning of the meeting, I suggested that we take a walk, accompanied only by General Clark. As he led us through the woods and fields behind the hunting lodge, he talked with nostalgia about his trips to New York as a banker—"I want to smell that wonderful New York air again," he said, and he seemed to be serious. He described his career as a successful Yugoslav businessman during the late Tito era, and, for the first time, he talked to us about the need for regional economic cooperation, ignoring his own central role in the destruction of Yugoslavia. When we returned to the villa, we asked him about his famous 1989 speech at Kosovo that ignited Serb extremism. He vigorously denied that this was his intent, and repeated his accusation that Ambassador Zimmermann had sought to turn international opinion against him by organizing a diplomatic boycott of the speech. But Milosevic made an interesting admission: "I was wrong not to meet with Ambassador Zimmermann for so long," he said. "I was angry at him, but I should not have waited a year." Chris Hill, who knew the history in detail, defended Zimmermann and reminded Milosevic that the speech had been inflammatory by any standards.

Over the lunch table, I proposed that the three Foreign Ministers meet in a week to start the peace process. Milosevic agreed instantly, and asked only that the United States, not the full Contact Group, be in charge. He would leave all details of location and timing to us. He criticized the Russians, saying that they presumed to a far greater influence in Serbia, based on historic Slav-Serb ties, than was justified. He was scornful of Moscow's attempts to pressure or bribe the Serbs with aid—"tons of rotten meat, and crap like that," he said. Since the Russians were his strongest supporters within the Contact Group, this was obviously said, at least in part, to have an effect on us.

Using a secure telephone system Clark had set up on the veranda of the lodge, I called Talbott and told him that we had a "little surprise" for Washington: all three countries had agreed to send their Foreign Ministers to Geneva in about a week for a U.S.-sponsored meeting. It would be the first meeting at such a high level in over two years. We asked him to get the British, French, Germans, and Russians on board immediately so that the meeting could be announced in four hours. Strobe was completely supportive, and said he would call us back as soon as he could.

Four hours is normally far too little time to coordinate such a complicated matter. But Strobe and John Kornblum, working frantically, accomplished it on schedule. Calling dozens of other Washington officials and the many foreign leaders, they gained rapid agreement from London, Paris, Moscow, Bonn, and the E.U.'s Carl Bildt for the Geneva meeting. Just over two hours later, as we sat anxiously on the patio outside Belgrade, Strobe called back with a characteristic opening line: "All set, pal. Everyone is on board." His dedicated executive assistant, Victoria Nuland, later told me it was the most satisfying day she had ever spent in public service, "because we worked together as a team and everything went off like clockwork on a big issue."

I had told Strobe that the Geneva meeting should be chaired by Secretary of State Christopher. He had discussed this with both Christopher and Donilon before calling back. Their reply surprised me. "The Secretary wants you to run the Geneva meeting," he said. "He has other matters to take care of. Besides, if he comes, the other Contact Group Foreign Ministers will insist on participating, and with all the grandstanding it could become hard to focus on the main event."

Government offers small moments like this, whose full import one realizes only later. Few Secretaries of State would have given up the chance to chair such a meeting. But it was characteristic of Warren Christopher, who firmly believed in delegating both authority and responsibility downward to key subordinates, provided they operated within established policy guidelines.

Nick Burns made the first announcement in Washington. A few minutes later, we made a short press appearance at the Hyatt in Belgrade. Our greatest regret, I began, was that Bob, Joe, and Nelson, to whom we had dedicated our shuttle effort, could not be with us for this announcement.

After the press conference, we returned to the villa. Milosevic's Foreign Minister, Milan Milutinovic, was openly fearful about the Geneva meeting. Pulling me aside during one of our many breaks, Milutinovic—smooth, affable, beautifully dressed, at ease in the language and style of international diplomacy, with its elaborate circumlocutions and nonconfrontational evasions—had just become Foreign Minister, and said he could lose his job ("Even my head," he joked weakly) if anything went wrong. Everything, he said, had to be "one hundred percent" agreed upon before we got to Geneva;

once there he would have no authority or flexibility. "The Master," he said, gesturing toward Milosevic, "will pull all the strings."

SATURDAY, SEPTEMBER 2

We flew to Bonn in the morning for a Contact Group meeting and an international conference on the future of Central Europe. The meeting and the conference both took place in Germany's state guest house at Petersburg, high on a hill above the Rhine overlooking the German capital, in the same rooms in which I had first met Chancellor Kohl.*

The Europeans. Carl Bildt was enthusiastic about the idea of the Geneva meeting, which he would co-chair. Although the selection of a Swede as the chief European negotiator, replacing Lord David Owen, carried no special meaning to most Americans, in Bildt's native land there was high symbolism in the selection of one of their countrymen (especially a former Prime Minister) to represent the European Union only a few months after Sweden had formally ended over 150 years of determined neutrality by joining the E.U. Bildt's selection had been the result, in large part, of our suggestions; even during our frequent arguments, a result of the pressures we faced, Bildt and I remained close friends. Tall, elegant, and witty, Bildt was to play an important role over the next two years before returning to Swedish politics. We had an unusual relationship for two diplomats—quite the reverse of the normal pattern in international diplomacy of outward cordiality masking animosity: we argued often but remained good friends, and made a productive team.

Everyone supported the Geneva meeting, but some of the Europeans were irritated because we had acted first and informed them later. This was particularly true of Pauline Neville-Jones of Great Britain, one of the most forceful people in the Contact Group. Strong-willed and dedicated to her work, she placed enormous importance on proper procedures, and vividly expressed her unhappiness that we had arranged the Foreign Ministers meeting without getting prior approval from the Contact Group. She and her German and French counterparts also said the meeting should be held in a U.N. building, rather than at the American Mission in Geneva. However, the Russian Contact Group representative, Deputy Foreign Minister Igor Ivanov, accepted an American venue immediately—on the condition that the next meeting be hosted by his government.

---

* I also met privately with leaders from Hungary, Poland, the Czech Republic, and Slovakia on NATO enlargement. The most difficult session was with the authoritarian Prime Minister of Slovakia, Vladimir Meciar. Two years later, Poland, the Czech Republic, and Hungary were invited to join NATO, but Slovakia was left behind because it still restricted internal freedoms.

Such arguments over the location and "hosting" of meetings may seem comical, but they were a constant and time-consuming subplot of the negotiations. In fact, disagreements over substance were rarely as intense as those concerning procedure and protocol. These minidramas had relatively little to do with Bosnia, but were a manifestation of the confusion within the European Union over how to forge a common foreign policy position. From a procedural point of view, Pauline Neville-Jones certainly had a point. However, as I had written Christopher ten days earlier, if we consulted the Contact Group prior to each action, it would be impossible for the negotiations to proceed, let alone succeed. Now that the United States was finally engaged in Bosnia, we could not allow internal Contact Group squabbles to deflect us.

The Russians. That day, Foreign Minister Andrei Kozyrev demanded publicly that Russia be made the third co-chair of the Geneva meeting. If Moscow secured an active role in the negotiations, it could cause a serious problem, given its pro-Serb attitude. But we felt that Moscow's primary goal was neither to run nor to wreck the negotiations. Rather, what it wanted most was to restore a sense, however symbolic, that they still mattered in the world. Strobe Talbott sometimes called this "the Rodney Dangerfield syndrome"; the Russians felt they "got no respect" anymore, and looked for ways to be seen as one of the "big boys." We felt that, despite occasional mischief making, Moscow would be easier to deal with if we gave it a place co-equal with the E.U. and the United States as a co-chair of the Geneva meeting than if we tried to downgrade it.

Meshing overall policy toward Russia with the search for peace in Bosnia was never simple. We spent much time calibrating and recalibrating our activities to promote both objectives simultaneously. In the end the effort succeeded, and produced, among other things, a historic arrangement that put Russian soldiers under an American commander in Bosnia.*

Behind our efforts to include Russia in the Bosnia negotiating process lay a fundamental belief on the part of the Clinton Administration that it was essential to find the proper place for Russia in Europe's security structure, something it had not been part of since 1914. There was a constant power struggle in Moscow between old-style officials who had served the communists—the so-called *nomenklatura*—and a newer, post-Soviet leadership that was just starting to emerge. The United States sought to encourage the latter. Sticking to this policy in the face of the 1993 coup attempt, the war in Chechnya, Boris Yeltsin's uncertain health, and officially sanctioned corruption took patience and determination, particularly because of constant attacks on the policy by

* See chapters 14 and 15.

American conservatives, who unfairly attacked the Administration, and especially Strobe Talbott, for being "soft on Russians."

As we left Bonn, a remarkable but invisible drama was playing itself out over whether or not to resume the bombing. Some U.N. and NATO commanders hoped to avoid resumption no matter what the outcome of the Mladic-Janvier talks. This was particularly true of General Janvier himself and, surprisingly, Admiral Leighton Smith, the commander of NATO's southern forces and Commander in Chief of all United States naval forces in Europe. Even though he carried out his assignment with precision and skill, Smith did not like the bombing; using the same phrase that Secretary of State James Baker had made famous four years earlier, Smith told me he did not have a "dog in this fight."

General Clark, on the other hand, believed the bombing should resume. This put him in a difficult position. For a three-star general to make unwelcome suggestions to men with four stars on their shoulders was not normally a wise career move, but after Mount Igman Clark was committed. As the personal representative of the Chairman of the JCS, he had the authority to make suggestions—but only suggestions—to senior officers, and report directly to General Shalikashvili. This awkward situation came to a head on Saturday afternoon, September 2, in an Embassy car on the Cologne airfield as Clark and I were about to board our plane to Brussels. As Clark explained to Smith why the bombing might have to resume, I could tell by the noises emanating from Clark's cell phone that he was being scolded by a very angry, very senior American naval commander. Genuinely worried about Clark's future, I grabbed the phone from his hands and told Smith that if Mladic did not comply with our demands on Sarajevo within the next few hours, I would insist on the resumption of the bombing. Smith, fuming at Clark, remained unconvinced.

In my view, Smith was edging into an area of political judgments that should have been reserved for civilian leaders. But Smith saw it differently: he told me that he was "solely responsible" for the safety and well-being of his forces, and he would make his decision, under authority delegated to him by the NATO Council, based on his own judgment. In fact, he pointed out, he did not even work for the United States; as a NATO commander he took orders from Brussels.

Clark and Smith never got along well after that telephone call. To ensure that no damage would be done to Clark's career, Strobe, Sandy Berger, and I all talked to General Shalikashvili. When, a year later, Clark received his fourth star and became Commander in Chief of the United States Southern Command in Panama, General Shalikashvili told me that Clark's performance in Bosnia had, in the end, been the key factor in his promotion. In 1997, Clark was chosen as Supreme Commander of NATO, succeeding General Joulwan. Ironically, the very thing that had once threatened his career, his service with the negotiating team, proved to be crucial to the assignment of a lifetime.

Problems such as these are not uncommon between the military and civilians in the government. I disagreed with Smith on this issue, but, as the person directly responsible for the safety of the NATO forces, his position was entirely rational. One must never forget in such circumstances what is at stake: the lives of young men and women. The wrong decision could send his men to their death or capture, as had happened in Somalia less than two years earlier. On the other hand, other lives were also at stake: those of the United Nations peacekeepers, over one hundred of whom had already been killed, and countless civilians on all sides. If negotiations failed, the war would continue—and even more United Nations troops might die while American leadership in Europe continued to decline.

At the NATO Council. With the friction between our delegation and Admiral Smith rising, we moved on to NATO headquarters in Brussels. As we arrived, confusion reigned: People milled around Secretary-General Claes's offices as he talked by phone to his military commanders, trying to find out how General Janvier's talks with General Mladic had gone. General Joulwan had been ready to support a resumption of the bombing, but had been pulled up short by Admiral Smith, who had already called to complain about Clark.

The bombing pause was now thirty-six hours old. I felt that the bombing should resume after no more than seventy-two hours unless Mladic accepted every detail of the conditions for the relief of Sarajevo, which was unlikely. But at NATO headquarters, many Ambassadors did not wish to resume the bombing.

By chance, the NATO Council was about to debate the issue when we arrived. Claes and Joulwan asked me to delay our departure in order to convey our views directly to them. We agreed immediately.

The Council convened in the early evening. After Ambassador Hunter made some introductory remarks, I said we confronted in its purest form "a classic dilemma in political-military relations, one we faced but never solved in Vietnam: the relationship between the use of force and diplomacy. The NATO decision to bomb was necessary, given the provocation. It is now essential to establish that we are negotiating from a position of strength. . . . If the air strikes resume and hurt the negotiations, so be it."

The questioning from the NATO Ambassadors continued for hours. As the clock passed midnight, Clark and I moved to a conference room and talked first to Admiral Smith, then at length with the White House, where Talbott, Berger, Admiral Owens, Sandy Vershbow (the NSC's senior European hand),

and Slocombe were tracking both the NATO debate and the talks between Janvier and Mladic. The news from Bosnia was shocking, but not surprising: Janvier had received an insolent proposal from Mladic—and publicly deemed it acceptable. He was immediately supported by Admiral Smith. "Our dilemma," Berger said, "is that Janvier and Smith have accepted a bad proposal from Mladic. He has played them for fools." We told Washington that while Smith did not want to resume the bombing, he would if ordered to by NATO. Berger and Talbott called Joulwan, Smith, and Claes to press for action.

With the NATO Ambassadors locked in a hopeless bureaucratic deadlock, NATO Secretary-General Willy Claes came through for the second time in a week, ruling on his own authority that a new NATO Council decision was not needed to resume the bombing. Claes's contribution during this week was hardly recognized at the time, and virtually forgotten within weeks, as he faced a personal scandal that forced him from the top NATO job. A Flemish Socialist and former Belgian Foreign Minister, Claes was best known as an amateur orchestra leader, a pursuit his critics used as a metaphor for his reputation as a weak man given to searching for a consensus at all costs. Our Ambassador in Belgium, Allan Blinken, had assured us this was not true, and predicted that Claes would surprise us. Blinken was right. Before Claes was forced to resign as NATO Secretary-General because of charges that he and his party had received bribes from a helicopter company—allegations that, two years later, had still not received a full and proper judicial hearing—he made a major contribution to a historic new policy.

SUNDAY, SEPTEMBER 3

Our team split up. Sending most of my colleagues to Zagreb to see Tudjman, I flew to Geneva to meet with the Organization of the Islamic Conference, which had long felt its pro-Bosnian positions had been ignored by the West. We met at the American Mission to the United Nations in Geneva, where our Ambassador, Daniel Spiegel, deftly led me through the meetings. The presence of the Ambassador from Iran, whom I ignored, made the meeting somewhat strained, but I was pleased to hear strong support from several nations, notably our NATO ally Turkey, Pakistan, and Malaysia. I had complete trust in Spiegel, who had been an assistant to Secretary of State Cyrus Vance during the Carter years and had then become a lawyer in Washington, and turned over to him the delicate task of arranging the logistics for the Foreign Ministers meeting, which was only five days away.

Early Sunday morning, Vice President Gore called Izetbegovic to say that the United States did not believe that the pause should continue. His call was designed to reassure an increasingly disturbed Izetbegovic that we were not abandoning him, while we continued to fight for a resumption of the bombing. Meanwhile, I flew from Geneva to Belgrade, where my colleagues had already begun a meeting with Milosevic. Owen and Hill had produced a short set of "Joint Agreed Principles" for Geneva. We used as our starting point the Contact Group plan of 1994, which divided the country into two "entities," giving the Croat-Muslim Federation 51 percent and the Serbs 49 percent of the land. Our long negotiating session, accompanied by a meal consisting of various kinds of lamb and sausages, ended with partial agreement on a draft we would discuss with Izetbegovic, who was visiting Turkey, the next day. By the time we returned to our hotel, called Washington, and went to sleep it was 4:00 A.M. Our colleagues in Washington were still struggling to get the bombing resumed.

Jimmy Carter. Early Sunday morning in Washington, at about the same time as my meeting in Geneva with the Islamic representatives, Talbott received a call from Jimmy Carter. In an effort to head off a resumption of the bombing, Radovan Karadzic had reached out again to Carter. Using as his channel a Serbian-American plastic surgeon from Beverly Hills who knew the Carters well, Karadzic said that he would stop the attacks on Sarajevo in return for a United Nations guarantee of the safety of the Bosnian Serb Army. It was a difficult situation for Strobe, one of the most polite people in Washington, and always respectful of the former President, whose administration he had covered as a journalist. But, determined to protect the negotiations, he told Carter that the Karadzic channel had to be shut down at least until our efforts were given a fair test. The Administration, Strobe told Carter, would not accept any offer from Karadzic, no matter what it was. Carter was not happy; a CNN camera crew was already standing by outside his office, and he had hoped to announce that he had reached an agreement with Karadzic. After several difficult talks with Strobe, he agreed to hold off.

MONDAY, SEPTEMBER 4: THE MACEDONIAN QUESTION

It was Labor Day in America, and we were starting the longest day of the entire shuttle. The battle over resumption of the bombing was still unresolved. We did not have an agreed text for Geneva yet, and to discuss it with Izetbegovic we had to follow him to Ankara, Turkey, where he was making an official visit. But on our way to Turkey we decided to take a side trip to Athens and Skopje to tackle the bitter dispute between Greece and the former Yugoslav Republic of Macedonia (FYROM) over the name of the country and its national flag.

The world's press tended to treat this as a comic issue. But to the two countries, the name and the flag of the new country were serious, and Washington and Western Europe feared that the tiny landlocked country would be the next flash point in the Balkans.

FYROM had explosive problems with all its neighbors—almost 30 percent of its population was Albanian, its language was virtually identical to Bulgarian, and, since it was supporting the economic sanctions against Serbia, relations along that border were also tense. The most threatening situation was to its south, with Athens, which felt that the new country posed a direct threat to Greece's very identity by attempting to co-opt Hellenic culture and a sacred name. Greece felt that by calling itself the "Republic of Macedonia," the government in Skopje was trying to create the basis for a future annexation not only of Greek culture and history but perhaps even parts of Greece's northernmost province, which had always been known as Macedonia. To the people of the former Yugoslav Republic of Macedonia, however, the name and the flag defined the identity of a new state carved—like Slovenia, Croatia, and Bosnia-Herzegovina—out of the old Yugoslavia. The new country added to the tensions by adopting an ancient Greek symbol, the sixteen-point Star of Vergina on the tomb of Philip of Macedon (the father of Alexander the Great), as the central motif of its national flag.

In February 1994, Greece imposed an economic blockade on the new country to its north, crippling its economy, which had already been hurt by its support for the sanctions against Serbia. The situation was so explosive that the United States made its only exception to the policy of not sending troops to the region, and sent 550 American soldiers to FYROM on a United Nations peacekeeping mission in order to prevent the war in Bosnia from spreading to the south and igniting a general Balkan conflict.

For more than two years, two tenacious negotiators had worked side by side to resolve the dispute: Cyrus Vance, representing the United Nations, and Matthew Nimetz, a New York lawyer who had served as Counselor to Secretary Vance during the Carter Administration, as the American negotiator. Inching through the maze of complex issues, they had come within sight of ending the dispute several times, only to see one or both sides back away from the final concessions required for settlement.

The idea that we try to settle this issue came from Chris Hill and Marshall Adair, the Deputy Assistant Secretary of State who covered Greece and Turkey. They suggested that we fly to Athens and Skopje to see if we could use the momentum of the Bosnian shuttle to end the dispute. We were greatly encouraged in this risky venture by the advice of Greece's Ambassador in Washington, Loucas Tsilas, who urged us to try for a breakthrough.

Hill and Pardew flew to Skopje in secret on September 1 to see President Kiro Gligorov. They returned with an upbeat report. "When I learned that you were coming today, I decided that now is the right time for an agreement," President Gligorov told them. He said he was ready to drop his long-standing insistence that the Greeks agree to end the embargo before the two sides sat down for a final agreement.

Greece was the member of NATO and the E.U. with the most positive feelings toward Belgrade—primarily because of a common religious heritage—and Milosevic had been careful not to alienate Athens by recognizing Macedonia. He predicted that no agreement between Athens and Skopje was possible in the foreseeable future. As he spoke, I privately hoped we would stun him with a breakthrough. We did not tell him we were going to Skopje.

We landed in Athens late on the morning of September 4. As our cars maneuvered through the crowded streets with the help of a sizable police escort, Chris Hill and the acting Ambassador, Tom Miller, wrote out by hand a short announcement that we hoped the two sides would make later that day. At the Greek Foreign Ministry, our first stop, an unruly group of journalists knocked one another down, shoved tape recorders into our faces, and backed into glass doors as we entered. Once behind closed doors, we found Greek Foreign Minister Karolas Papoulias openly hostile to any movement. He neither believed that Gligorov was ready to make a move, nor did he care. "You can never trust those people," he said. "Never."

Discouraged, we drove to the so-called Pink Villa, the luxurious new home of Prime Minister Andreas Papandreou in the suburbs north of Athens. The gardens were still unfinished, and the house had provoked controversy because of its opulence, but Papandreou did not care: he had built it as a present for his young new wife, Dimitra, whom he had married in 1989 after a long public affair that had led to a bitter breakup with his American wife, Margaret.

Papandreou was nowhere to be seen when we arrived. Instead, we were met by Mrs. Papandreou, who was wearing an almost transparent silk pajama suit that barely concealed important parts of her impressive anatomy. Greeting us warmly, she apologized for her husband's delay, and promised he would see us shortly. Mrs. Papandreou had a reputation as a sort of Greek Imelda Marcos. Whatever the truth about her past, I had previously observed the genuine tenderness that existed between her and her aged, frail husband. I knew she would not sit in on the meeting itself, but would have great influence on him. Taking her aside, I said we were carrying a message from Gligorov that offered her husband a unique opportunity to make history. If we achieved a breakthrough, it would greatly enhance the chances for peace in Bosnia. The new Mrs. Papandreou was highly controversial, and given her costume it was easy to see why, but I felt that she had her husband's best interests at heart and understood my message. She showed no interest in the details of the issue, but seemed focused on her husband's welfare and his place in history.

The word "legendary" is much overused, but it certainly applies to the seventy-six-year-old Andreas Papandreou, whose life had encompassed so much Greek-American history. As a Greek-born American citizen, he earned a doctorate in economics from Harvard, served in the United States Navy during World War II, and then taught at Harvard, the University of Minnesota, and Berkeley (where he was chairman of the economics department). He was part of Adlai Stevenson's advisory team during his two runs for the presidency. Then he returned to Greece and fought his way into power, surviving a long period in the political wilderness after right-wing pressure forced the resignation of his father, Georgios Papandreou, in 1965, two years before the military coup. He won the prime ministership fifteen years after his father had been forced out of it, and then lost it following a series of corruption scandals—only to make another astonishing comeback, regaining it again in 1993. To conservative Americans, he was anathema, an American turncoat. To Greeks, both those who followed him and those who hated him, he was the dominant political figure of the era.

He emerged from a back room, frail and moving slowly. His hands were thin, and his handshake all bones. But his mind was alert and he was cordial as he ushered us into his study. His wife plumped up some pillows behind his head, whispered something to him, and left us alone with him, his Foreign Minister, and his diplomatic advisor, Dimitrius Karaitides.

We outlined Gligorov's new position. Unlike his Foreign Minister, Papandreou was immediately interested. But Papoulias objected. First he said that it would require the approval of the entire Cabinet. This was a phony issue, and I said so, noting that the Prime Minister seemed to agree. Finally, Papoulis turned to Hill with a gleam in his eye. "When did you last see Gligorov?" he asked. "Because if it was more than twenty-four hours ago"—Papoulias knew it had been three days earlier—"his word is worthless."

The deal we were offering did no damage to Greece's basic interests. On the contrary, it gave Athens what it wanted on the flag; removed the economic embargo, which was hurting both nations; and left open the issue of the country's name—an issue that negotiators could continue to discuss without prejudice to the position of either side.

As the Foreign Minister argued, Papandreou began to tire. Time was running out. We still had to see Gligorov in Skopje, and then meet Izetbegovic in Ankara. Papandreou seemed unable to decide. He appeared sympathetic, but no longer possessed the strength with which he had for so long dominated the Greek scene. I decided to make one last effort, addressing in highly personal terms this proud man's long and complex love-hate relationship with the United States.

"Mr. Prime Minister, you and I have something in common," I began. "We both began our involvement in American politics working for Adlai Stevenson in 1952—only I was an eleven-year-old distributing bumper stickers, and you were a senior member of Stevenson's economic team. We both grew up despising Nixon. But we must admit that it took a Nixon to go to China, and it took a Sadat to go to Jerusalem. History will remember their courage and vision. Today, Mr. Prime Minister, you can do the same thing—and at no cost to your nation's interests, only benefit. And you can start us on the road to peace in Bosnia, on the eve of the Geneva meetings. But only you can do it."

The Foreign Minister glared at us, and spoke in Greek. Trying to convey a sense of urgency, I tried one more idea that had come to mind as Papoulias warned that Gligorov's word was worthless.

"Mr. Prime Minister, your Foreign Minister does not believe you can accept the word of the leaders in Skopje. But let the United States act as the guarantor of Skopje's pledge. Let us hold Gligorov's pledge 'in escrow.' "

Papandreou looked puzzled. "You do not have to accept Gligorov's word for anything," I explained. "We will fly to Skopje now, hear Gligorov out, and call you from his office to tell you whether or not he has given his word, and whether the Americans think it is reliable. You do not need to accept anything directly from him, only from the United States."

There was a long pause. Then, in a very frail voice, the old man said, "I like you. I want to do something to help peace in Bosnia, and to help you and your country. I will trust you. Call me from Skopje, from Gligorov's office."

It was time to leave. It was clear Papandreou would try to undo our progress as soon as we left, so I asked Tom Miller to be present at the Pink Villa when we called from Skopje. Then I bade good-bye to the old man whose life had reflected every up and down in the stormy drama of U.S.-Greek relations since World War II. I saw him last standing at the door of the Pink Villa, waving weakly.

We flew to Skopje to lock up the deal, hoping to rush through the meeting and go to Ankara. But Gligorov had other ideas. Even though he had given Hill and Pardew his new offer three days earlier, now he wanted to make us sweat awhile. We were learning that reneging on earlier offers was a basic style in the Balkans. These old men—Gligorov, like Papandreou, was in his seventies—were stubborn, but they would yield to pressure from the United States, if applied at the right moment.

Gligorov went over every detail of his earlier discussions with Hill and Pardew. Once Tito's Finance Minister, Gligorov had almost literally invented his country in late 1991 and early 1992. He wanted the embargo lifted, but would rather let his people suffer than betray what he viewed as his sacred mission to protect his nation's identity. Finally, he yielded, and I rose hurriedly to call Papandreou. But Gligorov wanted to stretch out the process, and demanded that we eat first. A large meal of meats and Lake Okhrid trout, a famous local fish, materialized. As we ate, I excused myself and called Tom Miller at the Pink Villa. Papandreou, he said, was so excited that he had not taken his afternoon nap, and was pacing up and down anxiously waiting for the call. I told Papandreou that the deal was done, and suggested we announce it simultaneously in Washington, Athens, and Skopje. He agreed, asking only that the Americans make the announcement in all three capitals.

I called Strobe and Sandy, who were in the Situation Room, totally preoccupied with the struggle over the resumption of the NATO bombing. They hardly had time for the breakthrough on Macedonia, but suggested that I call George Stephanopoulos, the President's senior advisor, who was also the key Administration connection to the Greek-American community. When he heard the news, George's voice—normally flat, unemotional, and analytical—broke for a moment. He said he would immediately call key members of the Greek-American community, starting with Senator Paul Sarbanes of Maryland. I also asked him to call Papandreou directly on behalf of the President. As we ended the conversation, his voice broke again, just for a moment, and he said, "God bless you and your team. This is truly wonderful."

Nick Burns made the announcement from the State Department, while Macedonian Foreign Minister Stevo Crevenkovski and I held a short press conference outside the Presidential Palace in Skopje. At Papandreou's request, Tom Miller made a similar announcement in Athens—more evidence of the deep desire in the region to let the United States take the lead in forcing solutions to long-standing problems. We stressed the special role of Vance and Nimetz, who had labored so long on the problem. The main newspapers caught the importance of the agreement; *The New York Times,* for example, reported the end of "a four-year dispute that had threatened to break into war." There were still some unpleasant scenes a week later when the two negotiators in New York both threatened to walk away from the September 4 agreement, but the two sides signed a formal agreement resolving the flag issue and lifting the embargo. Negotiations on the name of the new country continued, but the danger of a war on Greece's northern border had disappeared.

It is often said that timing is everything. It was only later that we realized just how true this was in regard to the Greece-FYROM question. Papandreou was hospitalized in November, resigned the prime ministership in January 1996, and died on June 22. Gligorov was nearly killed in an assassination attempt on October 3, 1995. The window had closed; the deal could not have been made even a few weeks later.* Had we not made our side trip when we did, the issue, a flash point in one of the most unstable regions of the world, might still be unsettled today. Yet as a result of the breakthrough, tensions dropped dramatically, and the economies of both countries benefited substantially. By 1998 Greece was the largest investor in Macedonia, and its second-largest trading partner.

Our intervention had demonstrated anew two central truths of the region: the United States was the only country that could force all the parties to a solution; but to do so, we had to be assertive.

By the time we reached Ankara it was 9:00 P.M., too late to meet with President Suleyman Demirel, Prime Minister Tansu Ciller, or Izetbegovic, who were already at an official dinner. We repaired to the residence of the American Ambassador, Marc Grossman, for a meal with some leading Turkish officials and businessmen. Grossman, one of the most outstanding career diplomats then serving in Europe, had foreseen the problem, and arranged for us to meet with Izetbegovic and Sacirbey after their state dinner. This meant that the long day would be even longer, but we had no choice; the negotiations for Geneva had to be completed in Ankara or we would run out of time, making a catastrophe likely.

Meanwhile, the drama had grown over the resumption of the bombing. Throughout Labor Day officials in Washington and New York kept the telephone lines going nonstop to Brussels, Naples, Zagreb, Sarajevo, and the other Contact Group capitals. As we called Washington repeatedly, our delegation became increasingly concerned. Knowing the high regard in which General Kerrick was held by his colleagues at the NSC, I asked him to speak directly to Berger to emphasize the urgency of the situation.

At NATO, both General Joulwan and the stalwart Willy Claes had received the erroneous impression from Janvier and Smith that Mladic had made important concessions. This astonished us and Joulwan. In fact, Janvier had been rudely treated by Mladic, but the French general, still trying to avoid resumption of the bombing, tried to portray his discussions as "progress." Joulwan joined us in pressing for action.

As Washington, Brussels, New York, Zagreb, and the major NATO capitals argued over the bombing, two dramatically different documents arrived from the Bosnian Serbs—one seemingly conciliatory, the other blatantly provocative. The first struck me from the outset as a phony, but it almost derailed our efforts to get the bombing resumed; the second made the decision to resume easier.

---

* Gligorov made an amazing recovery and resumed the presidency within a few months, but by that time Papandreou was no longer functioning in Athens.

The first was a strange, short letter from "Vice President" Koljevic. Writing to Yasushi Akashi, the civilian chief of United Nations operations in the Balkans, Koljevic said that he was prepared to "accept conditions" of General Janvier's letter. That was all. In a telephone call to Washington as we waited for Izetbegovic at the Ambassador's residence in Ankara, I argued that this letter was meaningless on at least two levels. First, Koljevic, a creature of Milosevic's, had no authority in Pale. Second, the omission of any definite or indefinite article preceding the word "conditions" was, I argued, a dead giveaway. Where was a word like "all" or even "the" preceding the word "conditions"? I pointed out that the author of the letter was a Shakespeare scholar, and knew perfectly well the exact meaning of words in English. We were startled that anyone in the United Nations or Washington was taking this silly letter seriously.

The second letter of the day was from General Mladic—and it was chilling. Addressed to General Janvier, Mladic's letter was five pages of single-spaced ranting that suggested its author was out of control. He accused Janvier of reneging on the "long hours of agreeable talks in Zvornik" a few days earlier, of which, he said, "there are TV and phone records." In a remarkable passage, Mladic charged that the NATO bombing was "more brutal" than that of the Nazis against Belgrade on April 6, 1941, a famous date in Yugoslav history. "Hitler stopped the bombing on April 7 and 8 to allow the burial of victims after the Christian custom," Mladic wrote, "while NATO deliberately targeted our churches and cemeteries during the burial of the killed." The letter continued with a series of wild threats against U.N. personnel.

Mladic followed his threats with a ludicrous peace offering. "I assure you," he wrote, "that Sarajevo is running no danger from the Republika Srpska Army." Mladic called for "an urgent meeting between the warring sides' Commanders to sign an agreement on complete, lasting, and unconditional cessation of hostilities in the former Bosnia-Herzegovina. Until this meeting I declare a one-sided cessation of hostilities in the Sarajevo region."

When we saw Mladic's letter, we assumed it resolved any questions about resuming the bombing. What answer other than a resumption of the bombing was appropriate under the circumstances?

But Mladic's combination of peace offering and threats gave Janvier and other U.N. officials pause. The French general, who had spent an almost sleepless night and morning in meetings with Mladic, had come away from the meetings publicly expressing the view that "there could be room for negotiation with the Bosnian Serbs." A U.N. spokesman in Zagreb described Mladic's letter "as the first step toward full compliance."

Our reaction to these signs that the U.N. was looking for an excuse to avoid resumption can easily be imagined. But as Clark, Kerrick, Pardew, and I called Washington to express our outrage, Izetbegovic and Sacirbey arrived at Grossman's residence. It was already after 11:00 P.M. Temporarily leaving the drama over the resumption of bombing aside, we turned again to the draft document for the Geneva meeting.

The scene that now unfolded in Grossman's living room was memorable. Everyone was tired, especially the seventy-year-old Bosnian President, but we had important issues to discuss. As we talked, the telephones were constantly in use, as Clark or one of the other members of the delegation spoke to Washington, Naples, or Brussels about the bombing or, on several occasions, aspects of the Athens-Skopje deal, which was just beginning to get public attention.

The central issue that evening concerned names—the name of the country, and the name of each of the entities. Having spent the day in Athens and Skopje discussing the name and flag of another former Yugoslav republic, we were especially sensitive to, and increasingly weary of, the obsession the leaders in this region had with words and names. An outright military victory was no longer possible for either side, but the leaders of all three sides were willing to let their people die while they argued.

I watched Izetbegovic carefully. He and Sacirbey sat next to each other in the middle of the room. They studied carefully the draft that we had negotiated in Belgrade, entitled "Joint Agreed Statement of Political Principles." They were not happy with it. Despite the late hour, Izetbegovic had replaced his normal vagueness with a tougher, more focused attitude. He squinted and stared at the drafts Bob Owen had given him as if searching for verbal tricks that might destroy his country. He repeated phrases slowly in English while Sacirbey translated them, arguing heatedly over what they might mean.

Well after midnight, we had narrowed the discussion down almost entirely to two sentences—but they were critical to the future of Bosnia. The previous day in Belgrade we had obtained substantial concessions from Milosevic in a sentence that recognized for the first time that Bosnia would "continue its legal existence with its present borders and continuing international recognition."

In these twelve words, Owen and Hill had obtained three key concessions from Milosevic that had been unattainable for years:

- First, by accepting the words *"continue its legal existence,"* Milosevic agreed that the state of Bosnia had a legal existence—moreover, an existence that was deemed to "continue," thus clearly implying a retroactive acceptance of Bosnia's claim of independence, denied by the Serbs throughout the war. This was the first time that the Bosnian

Serbs had explicitly conceded Bosnia's right to exist as an independent country.

- Second, *"with its present borders."* Speaking for both Serbia and the Bosnian Serbs, Milosevic had accepted the existing boundaries of Bosnia, thereby officially ending territorial claims on Bosnia by Serbia, and rejecting the separatist goals of Pale.

- Third, *"continuing international recognition."* Had Milosevic only acknowledged international recognition, there might have been uncertainty as to what was being recognized. But the use of the word "continuing" eliminated a possible ambiguity; "Bosnia" would be the same country that had been recognized by many nations and sat in the United Nations. We felt that this phrase represented a huge breakthrough, amounting to de facto recognition of Bosnia by the Serbs.

But there were also some problems with the draft:

- First, Milosevic had opposed allowing the country to keep the name "Republic of Bosnia and Herzegovina." He demanded "Union" or perhaps "Confederation," names we knew Izetbegovic would reject.

- Second, Milosevic insisted that the Serb portion of the country be referred to as "Republika Srpska (R.S.)." The use of the name that Karadzic and the Pale Serbs had given themselves was certain to be a big problem for Sarajevo.

As Izetbegovic stared at the paper in front of him, he did not acknowledge the unprecedented concessions we had wrested from Milosevic. But as we expected, he was unhappy at Milosevic's attempt to change the name of the country, and strongly opposed to the use of the phrase "Republika Srpska."

I reassured Izetbegovic that the United States would never agree to Milosevic's desire to use "union" or "confederation." We urged Izetbegovic to let us propose to Milosevic that the country be called, simply, "Bosnia and Herzegovina." Izetbegovic objected. We argued that many countries, including Japan, did not have "republic" or "kingdom" or some other description of their political structure before their name. "Giving up the word 'republic' is giving up nothing, especially compared to the fact that Milosevic has now effectively recognized your country within its present boundaries," Owen told Izetbegovic.

The second point was more difficult. "That name [Republika Srpska] is like the Nazi name," Izetbegovic said. We replied that the name meant nothing, and that the governing—the overriding—sentence was the preceding one that recognized Bosnia and Herzegovina as a country "with its present borders"—

that is, a single country, of which R.S. was a part. "In our country," Owen noted, "some states, including Texas and Massachusetts, call themselves 'republics' or 'commonwealths.' It doesn't matter, as long as they acknowledge that they are part of one country, and are so recognized by the rest of the world."

Izetbegovic continued to object for over an hour. From time to time, I left the room to speak to the White House about the bombing. It helped that Izetbegovic saw that I was fighting hard for something he desperately wanted—the resumption of bombing. But it was still difficult for him to agree to a document that contained the name Republika Srpska.

It was one in the morning. "We understand your problems with this," I told the President, "but it is the best we can do with Milosevic at this time. We do not believe that the name Republika Srpska, awful though it is, means much as long as you get everything else—international recognition, defined borders, acceptance of your legal status. You had none of this before. We can't get 'Republika Srpska' out of the draft. I'm sorry, but this is as much as we can do."

A long pause. Some discussion among the Bosnians. Finally, the answer from Sacirbey, while Izetbegovic sat silent and unhappy. "This is bad for my President, but we will try to accept it. It will be very difficult for him to explain to his people."

When Izetbegovic and Sacirbey left Ambassador Grossman's residence, it was well after 1:00 A.M. We turned back to Washington for one last, extraordinary series of telephone calls. One by one, Kerrick, Pardew, and Clark told their superiors in Washington why the bombing should be resumed. Then I had my last shot at my friends. Berger, Talbott, Slocombe, Owens, and Vershbow were still in the White House Situation Room. I had a mental picture of the group, eating pizzas and hero sandwiches, huddled together all day—still Labor Day!—while we had raced across Serbia, Greece, Macedonia, and Turkey. In fact, they had been at it now for three straight days, missing almost all of their long-planned Labor Day weekends with their families. (Berger and Talbott had canceled their plans to attend the wedding of Madeleine Albright's daughter.)

Yet no decision had been made, and within the Situation Room we sensed several different views. I later learned that Talbott and Berger, who both supported the bombing, had thought earlier in the day that its resumption would be relatively easy, but that as the day progressed, opposition from various quarters, including the U.N. field commanders and the French, made the situation far less certain. In Ankara, we were unaware of the impact that CNN was having: one of its star correspondents, Peter Arnett, had been taken by the Bosnian Serbs to positions outside Sarajevo, where he had filmed scenes he was told were the beginning of the withdrawal of heavy weapons from the area around Sarajevo, as Mladic had promised in his ranting letter. This was a standard Bosnian Serb tactic: showing unilateral and phony "compliance" in an effort to head off NATO action—but it had worked for years.

"Let me be clear," I said. "It is very late here now, and we are perhaps overly tired, but we have an absolutely unanimous point of view: the bombing must be resumed. If it is not, we will do our best, but our chances for success in the negotiations will be seriously reduced. The Bosnians are barely on board with our Geneva draft, and when we see Izetbegovic again in the morning for a last review of the draft, the bombing must have resumed."

I wanted to end on a high historical note, unusual for this sort of conversation. "If we do not resume the bombing, it will have lasted less than forty-eight hours. It will be another catastrophe. NATO will again look like a paper tiger. The Bosnian Serbs will return to their blackmailing ways." There was a short silence at the other end of the phone. Don Kerrick, who was listening in on an extension, looked at me, smiled, and gave me thumbs-up sign. I concluded: "I know how difficult this is, and what I am about to say may sound melodramatic, but history could well hang in the balance tonight. I truly believe that you may never take any decision as public officials more important than this one. Give us bombs for peace. Give us a resumption of the bombing by morning."

CHAPTER 9

Geneva

(September 5–8)

> There is no process by which the cross-hatched complexity of acted history can be reproduced faithfully in the written word.
> —C. V. WEDGWOOD, *History and Hope*

WHEN WE AWOKE IN ANKARA ON TUESDAY, September 5, we still had no idea if the bombing would resume. Calls to NATO headquarters were uninformative, and it was too early to call Washington, even Strobe Talbott, who was notorious for rising at an ungodly hour. With uncertainty hanging over our heads, we drove to the residence of Turkish Prime Minister Tansu Ciller for a meeting that Izetbegovic would join. Then we planned to fly to Belgrade to close the Geneva agreement with Milosevic.

Turkey had once shared a common history with Bosnia. Even today, when Serbs and Croats speak disparagingly of the Bosnian Muslims, they call them "Turki," in memory of the distant time when the Ottoman conquerors had come to the southern Balkans. Izetbegovic respected the Turkish leaders, especially President Demirel, and their support for any postsettlement activities in Bosnia, such as improving the quality of the Bosnia-Croat Federation military forces, would be important.

En route to Ankara the previous evening, we had discussed Cyprus, the long-running problem that had caused so much tension between Greece and Turkey, especially since the 1974 Turkish invasion. The image of Cyprus, its two hostile ethnic groups divided for twenty-one years by an ugly wall that cut the island in half, would haunt us during the entire Bosnia peace effort. Was this how Bosnia would look after we were done, even if we succeeded in ending the war? It would be better than war, but it would hardly be a real peace. Haris Silajdzic and some of the better-informed journalists often raised this specter with us. Aware of the problem, our team talked frequently about the need to avoid letting Bosnia become another Cyprus—that is, allowing a temporary cease-fire line to harden into a permanent partition line.

． ． ．

When Izetbegovic arrived, we held an unusual trilateral session with Ciller—not a normal grouping, but one that helped reduce the edge from the previous night's difficult meeting. Izetbegovic was clearly troubled, and seemed unsure whether to go forward with the text he had accepted the previous night. He was deeply annoyed that the bombing had not yet been resumed, and linked his final acceptance of the draft for Geneva to the resumption of bombing. Waiting for word from NATO, I thought this an entirely reasonable position.

After the meeting, Sacirbey and I headed for the Ankara Hilton, where we were scheduled to hold a joint press conference. As we drove through the streets, Strobe called. Reluctant to discuss sensitive matters over an open cellular telephone yet anxious to give us some much-needed good news, he talked in an improvised code: "The Smith Brothers and our jolly friend have made a new decision that makes our conversations of last night OBE."

What did he mean? It took a moment to understand that he was trying to tell me that the two (unrelated) Smiths, Admiral Leighton and General Rupert, and General Joulwan ("our jolly friend") had agreed to resume the bombing, and thus our discussions of the previous evening were now "OBE" (overtaken by events).

The persistent efforts of officials like Willy Claes and General Joulwan in Brussels, and Berger, Talbott, and Admiral Owens in Washington had paid off. Once again, the Bosnian Serbs had brought down upon themselves something that they could have prevented—fortunately for us. It is impossible, of course, to say with certainty what effect a failure to resume the bombing would have had on our efforts. After the peace settlement, some European officials argued that the negotiations would have achieved the same results with or without the bombing. I am glad that we did not have to test this proposition.

On the plane from Ankara to Belgrade, Hill and Owen predicted that Milosevic would not accept several of the key provisions in our Geneva draft. With three days to go before Geneva, they said, we faced a stalemate. We had pushed Izetbegovic as far as he could go, and could not go back to Sarajevo, literally or figuratively, to ask for changes. But would Milosevic agree to the document we had hammered out in Ankara? The views of Chris and Bob, who had done most of the negotiating with Milosevic on this issue, worried me. On the plane, anticipating a contentious meeting, we agreed that I should see Milosevic alone—my first private meeting with him.

Leaving our colleagues in the main sitting room, he and I went into the room next door as soon as I arrived. We sat side by side on a sofa. "This is what we agreed to with Izetbegovic," I said, handing him the Ankara draft. "We cannot change it."

Milosevic, who prided himself on his legal training and ability to read and absorb highly technical material with great speed, scanned the document rapidly. Even Bob Owen, a great lawyer and a demanding taskmaster, had been impressed with how quickly Milosevic assimilated every nuance of documents written in English. This skill made Milosevic all the more dangerous as a negotiator; he would regularly try to slip into documents words or phrases that seemed innocuous, but contained potentially deadly traps.

Milosevic objected to several phrases. He wanted the country to be called either the "Union of Bosnia-Herzegovina" or, perhaps, the "United States of Bosnia-Herzegovina." I countered that we should drop the use of "Republika Srpska," a suggestion Milosevic termed "absolutely impossible." He retreated gradually from his initial demands, and, after thirty minutes of argument, accepted the document without any changes.

I walked with Milosevic back into the main room, where my colleagues had been listening to the Serb Foreign Minister lament his fate in having to go to Geneva. Handing the document to Owen, I said, "We have an agreement." He looked astonished, and gave me a thumbs-up sign.

Were I allowed to revisit the negotiations, this is where I would probably start. In its entirety the document represented significant gains for Sarajevo, as both Milosevic and Izetbegovic knew. But I regret that we did not make a stronger effort to drop the name Republika Srpska. We underestimated the value to Pale of retaining their blood-soaked name. We may also have underestimated the strength of our negotiating hand on that day, when the bombing had resumed. In retrospect, I think we should have pushed Milosevic harder to change the name of the Bosnian Serb entity. Even if the effort failed, as Owen and Hill predicted, it would have been worth trying.

Geneva was still four days away. Leaks could be fatal, since they would trigger public pressure in Sarajevo to ask for more. To maintain maximum secrecy, we faxed a copy of the agreement to Talbott's office in Washington and asked him to hand-deliver it to a few senior officials; it was a sad truth of modern Washington that no reporting sent through normal State Department channels—no matter how it was "slugged" for distribution—was safe from the risks of uncontrolled distribution and leaks.

We spent the night in Belgrade, then headed for Zagreb, where we reviewed Geneva with a decidedly uninterested Tudjman. He had only one thing on his mind: regaining eastern Slavonia from the Serbs. Repeating our warnings not to use force, we promised to include eastern Slavonia in any international negotiation. Tudjman welcomed this, but refused to eschew public threats.

We had an agreement. But before Geneva, we had to pull together our allies and the Contact Group, which had little idea of what we were up to. Clark and Pardew headed for Brussels to help NATO plan for deploying a force in Bosnia if we achieved a peace agreement. Hill flew to Paris to join Peter Tarnoff, who was briefing senior French, British, and German officials. I drew what appeared to be a pleasant assignment: at the urging of Tony Lake and Ambassador Bartholomew, a visit to Rome to calm down some very unhappy Italians.

My first stop in Rome was a call on an old friend, Foreign Minister Susanna Agnelli. Universally known as Sunni, she had been appointed to the post by the government of Lamberto Dini in part because of her personal stature. A former mayor and senator, the sister of Italy's most famous businessman, Gianni Agnelli, and the author of a best-selling memoir with the delightful title *We Always Wore Sailor Suits,* Sunni Agnelli combined aristocratic bearing with casual informality. Her giant white mane of hair and her imposing height added to her presence. She approached her job as she had probably approached almost everything else: with a relaxed confidence in her own intuition. She conveyed an impression of great amusement at the passing parade of overly intense men formulating policy. We had known each other for years, but only socially. I liked her, and expected, as did Bartholomew, a friendly call between old friends that would resolve a relatively minor problem—Italian pique at their exclusion from the Contact Group, which, as I had repeatedly tried to explain, was not our fault.

It was no social call. Flanked by her staff, one of whom glared at me through thick glasses, she lit into the United States for failing to keep her country adequately informed or involved. Reading from notes prepared by her staff, she said that we had reneged on Lake's commitment to get Italy into the Contact Group. Pleased that she was venting their frustration, her staff occasionally fueled the fire with short comments.

Only a few hours earlier, I had been in the ugliness of Belgrade and Zagreb, trying to end a war that threatened the stability of Europe. Now, in one of the most beautiful cities on earth, the capital of the only NATO nation with a common border with the war zone, a Foreign Minister whom I liked and knew as a friend was reading us the riot act. Bartholomew, one of America's most accomplished ambassadors, was as astonished as I was. He had said that my trip would mollify the Italians, but it seemed only to inflame them.

We explained that Lake had made no commitment to bring the Italians into the Contact Group, something that was beyond our capability. Her aides insisted that he had made a promise. Perhaps there had been a misunderstanding, we suggested gently: it was not Washington that objected to Italy's membership in the Contact Group, it was the European Union members of the

Contact Group. We stressed that the United States wanted Italy, the only NATO nation bordering the war zone, to play a greater role in the region. Tony had said only that we would seek to convene a larger group (the "Contact Group Plus") from time to time.

This was nothing less than the truth. Britain, France, and Germany liked the prominence that came from being senior members of a prestigious international negotiating group. (Never mind its ineffectiveness.) To allow Italy to join, they felt, would not only dilute it but create pressure to add Spain, the Netherlands, and other nations with troops in Bosnia. We later learned that senior diplomats from Paris, London, and Bonn had met privately and decided not only to keep Italy out of the Contact Group, but to tell Rome that Washington was the culprit.

I could not solve Italy's Contact Group problem, but, trying to ease the tension, I suggested we hold a special meeting of an "expanded Contact Group" in Rome in October, provided that we could get the rest of the Contact Group to agree to meet in Rome. She accepted immediately. When we had finished, Bartholomew and I met with Prime Minister Dini, who presented a position identical to Agnelli's. Recognizing by now that there was little we could do in the face of this profound misunderstanding by our Italian friends, I repeated our offer to hold a special meeting in Rome, stressed how important Italy was to the United States, and left.

Exhausted by our continuous shuttle, now in its eleventh straight day, I returned to the graceful ambassadorial residence in Rome for a quiet dinner with the Bartholomews. The visit had not been the pleasant, relaxed stop among friends in the Eternal City that we had expected. But in the end, the trip had been useful, since it would lead to more involvement by the Italians in the Bosnian peace effort. In fact, the Italians did end up hosting several key meetings in Rome, including a dramatic Balkan summit in February 1996. In 1997 they finally became members of the Contact Group. None of this would have happened if we had not taken such a strong pro-Italian position.

GENEVA

We arrived in Geneva on Thursday, September 7, and drove with Ambassador Spiegel directly to the U.S. Mission. I was impressed. In four days, he had somehow arranged everything and produced a room and table that fit our needs so well that we copied it exactly for all subsequent meetings, including the final negotiations.

In diplomacy, details matter. During the 1968 peace talks with the North Vietnamese in Paris, we had famously wasted more than two months arguing over the shape of the negotiating table, while the war continued. I had watched as two great American diplomats, Averell Harriman and Cyrus Vance, were humiliated and furious; I was determined not to let such an event happen to us. With this in mind, I had asked Spiegel to construct a round table large enough to seat no more than nine people—one representative from each of the five Contact Group nations, plus a seat for Co-chairman Carl Bildt, and one seat for each of the three Balkan countries. The chairs had to be close enough to one another so that there would be no room at the table for the Bosnian Serbs or anyone else. I asked for nameplates without country names, and the national flags of only the five Contact Group nations and the European Union. I was struck by the parallel with 1968: Hanoi's insistence that the Vietcong get a seat at the table separate from the North Vietnamese had been the reason for the argument over the table shape in Paris.

On the day before the meeting, NATO intensified the bombing, hitting the Lukavica barracks southwest of Sarajevo, and bombing ammunition dumps, communications equipment, and other facilities. I was pleased to see a column in *The Washington Post* by Charles Krauthammer, a constant critic of American policy, concluding that "U.S. policy on Bosnia is finally on track." In a phrase more perceptive than he may have realized, Krauthammer wrote that the bombing should continue until "(a) the Serbs have made concessions at the bargaining table . . . or (b) we run out of targets."

There was great tension that night in Geneva. So far, we had achieved nothing except the deal between Greece and the former Yugoslav Republic of Macedonia. Now, for the first time, everything was on the line. I called on Milutinovic and Sacirbey separately. The Yugoslav Foreign Minister was, as always, the essence of a smooth, affable diplomat. But when I asked him about the Bosnian Serb delegation, he waved his hand dismissively and said that they were staying at another hotel. He did not care to deal with them. Sacirbey was much more troubled. The agreement was not good for his country, he told me, and his President was taking "a lot of heat" for it back home.

September 8. We thought everything was agreed to; the agreement had been accepted by everyone two days earlier. We planned to meet, approve the agreement formally, discuss the future informally, and then meet the press. But nothing goes according to plan in the Balkans—and, for a day, the U.S. Mission in Geneva turned into part of the war zone. The troubles began fifteen minutes before our Contact Group colleagues were due to arrive, when Sacirbey called to say that he would not come to the meeting unless his government could retain the name "Republic of Bosnia-Herzegovina." They were getting heavily criticized in Sarajevo, Sacirbey said, and needed this last-minute change.

This was the first instance of a recurring pattern in the negotiations—second thoughts or changes in position by Sarajevo after it had agreed to something. I could sympathize with it, but Izetbegovic had made an agreement in Ankara, and if we tried to renegotiate it in Geneva, Yugoslav Foreign Minister Milutinovic would refuse; as he had repeatedly told us, he had no authority and could make no decisions.

In no uncertain terms, I told Sacirbey that if he precipitated a failure in Geneva, the United States would hold him responsible, and only the Serbs would benefit. It was a harsh conversation—the most difficult I had had with Sacirbey—and it was overheard by several other people. Later on, after it was leaked to the press in an exaggerated form, it became part of negotiating folklore that the chief American negotiator was a "bully" who had yelled at everyone. But in fact, such emotional exchanges were extremely rare, and usually deliberate. Whatever my tone, Sacirbey was convinced that it was in his interests to appear at the conference on time. But to protect the process, I later asked Warren Christopher to call Izetbegovic and Silajdzic in Sarajevo to calm them down. He did so immediately, explaining to both men that the first sentence of the Geneva agreement represented a "powerful recognition" of Bosnia's status that more than made up for their concessions on the names.

Shortly after 10:00 A.M., the delegates convened around Dan Spiegel's small round table. Carl Bildt sat to my right, and Russia's Deputy Foreign Minister Igor Ivanov to my left. Directly across from us sat the three Foreign Ministers, and behind them hundreds of journalists. Without warning, I rose and walked around the table to the three Foreign Ministers. "Would you all join me in a handshake for the world?" I asked. Astonished but unable to avoid it, Sacirbey, Granic, and Milutinovic rose and posed awkwardly for the photograph that would be seen around the world as a sign of momentum toward peace. Then we asked the press to leave and settled down to business.

As soon as I gaveled the session to order, we ran into a problem. The leader of the Bosnian Serb delegation, Republika Srpska "Vice President" Nikolai Koljevic, rose from his seat behind the table. "I protest this arrangement," he said. "My delegation should be seated at the table, and we will not participate in this meeting if we are denied our rights." This was precisely what the seating arrangements were designed to prevent. I was thankful that there was no room for Koljevic at the table. I replied that, according to the Patriarch Paper, Foreign Minister Milan Milutinovic spoke for the Bosnian Serbs. Koljevic angrily persisted, and when I looked at Milutinovic, expecting him to silence Koljevic, he looked away. I immediately called for a recess.

We had set aside a set of small rooms just off the main conference room for private meetings. Taking Milutinovic into one of them alone, I asked him whether this was a game that he and Koljevic had devised. If it was, I said, the meeting would break up and the consequences would be serious. "If not," I said, "you must get your 'friends' under control."

Nervous and unhappy, Milutinovic said he could not control the little Bosnian Serb. "Only my Master can do that," he added. Then he made a suggestion that surprised me. "I think if you talk to him firmly he will understand."

I asked Koljevic and his colleague, "Foreign Minister" Aleksi Buha, to join us in the tiny room. With Milutinovic watching in silence, I told them that if they continued their protest they would deal themselves completely out of the process. "Walk out if you want to," I told the astonished Serbs. "But if you do, we will continue without you, and Bosnian Serb influence in this process will be eliminated. I doubt President Milosevic will be pleased, but it's up to you."

Koljevic seemed to deflate in front of our eyes. Suddenly he was everyone's friend, a man of peace who wanted only to be allowed to quote a few lines of his beloved Shakespeare before fading away. He proposed that he be allowed to rise one last time from his seat behind the table, concede that Milutinovic spoke for him and his colleagues, and then remain silent.

I said we would agree to his request, provided he said nothing substantive, and that Sacirbey and the Croatian Foreign Minister, Mate Granic, both agreed in advance. The confrontation had been intense, but it was over in less than thirty minutes. When we resumed, Koljevic followed his script, pathetically quoting the Bard and "relinquishing" his right to speak, after which we finally started the meeting.

The rest of the meeting was routine. Each person at the table made a speech; as is usual on such occasions, they were of little consequence. Given the chance to perform before an audience—even without journalists present— the three Foreign Ministers reverted to sterile and accusatory rhetoric.

That afternoon, at the InterContinental Hotel, flanked by Carl Bildt, Igor Ivanov, Pauline Neville-Jones, Jacques Blot, and Wolfgang Ischinger, my colleagues and I faced over four hundred journalists, with live broadcasts on CNN and several European networks. We did not invite the three Balkan Foreign Ministers to the press conference, knowing that their natural proclivity to argue would divert attention from the Joint Agreed Principles. Before reading the agreement, I made a personal statement:

> Our first thought this morning when we walked into the room and found that the Foreign Ministers of Bosnia, Croatia, and Serbia were in the room for the first time in so many months, that they were willing to shake hands and reach a common agreement which, though limited, moves us toward peace . . . our first thought—all of us—was: if only Nelson, Joe, and Bob Frasure could have seen this day.

I faltered for a moment, and Carl Bildt graciously picked up the same theme, saying of Frasure that "his excellence, knowledge, and humor made a lot of this possible."

The Joint Agreed Principles of September 8 were only a first step toward peace, and we did not want to oversell it. The bombing and the war were still going on. I stressed the limitations of the agreement:

> The statement takes us an important step closer to peace. Yet, important as it is, this statement does not constitute the end of the tragedy in the Balkans. Far from it. . . . The hardest work still lies ahead. The [two] entities have yet to develop a design for a central connecting structure. . . . In addition, the parties need to define their internal borders within Bosnia in accordance with the 51–49 principle. We should be under no illusions that these will be easy tasks.

After the press conference, I asked every member of our team to meet with journalists individually or in small groups organized by the European Bureau's energetic press officer, Aric Schwan, who had flown to Geneva to assist with the media. We wanted to be sure that the story was properly reported; most especially, we wanted to be sure that everyone understood that the next step was to fix the major omission in the Geneva agreement—the lack of any agreement on a central government. Without this, the agreement could easily be construed as having partitioned Bosnia, when the exact opposite was our goal.

We were through the first phase of the negotiations, and the world was taking notice. Yet, despite some overly optimistic reporting, we were still far from our goals. We planned to resume the shuttle within a week, but as we headed home we had no clear plan as to how to proceed.

CHAPTER 10

The Siege of Sarajevo Ends

(September 9–14)

In one of his many public statements, the leader of the Bosnian Serbs, Montenegrin Radovan Karadzic, said that the Serbs in the past period, when everyone was on their side, had been subjected to "genocidal extermination," whereas now, over the last year, when so many are against them, they are suffering the least.

Of all the innumerable absurdities and untruths that have been uttered, this statement truly takes the cake. For more than forty years Bosnia was inhabited by Bosnians, and we did not distinguish between Serbs, Muslim, and Croats, or at least such distinctions were not paramount in their mutual relations. Throughout that period, to the best of the Yugoslav and world public's knowledge, there were no detention camps for Serbs in Bosnia, no brothels for Serb women, no Serbian children had their throats cut. . . . But according to Karadzic, the Serbs were somehow unhappy then. And now, in the war, with so many dead, . . . now, according to their leader, the time has come when they are suffering the least. . . . Ethnically pure states are an impossibility in today's world, and it is ridiculous to try to create and maintain such a state, even when there is just one nation.

—MIRA MARKOVIC (Mrs. Slobodan Milosevic),
in her newspaper column, January 20, 1993[1]

AFTER THIRTEEN DAYS ON THE ROAD—the longest of all our shuttle trips—we planned to spend at least a week in Washington. There were personal reasons for this, but, with major policy issues to be decided, we also needed a few days to develop a consensus on some key issues.

Events in Bosnia, however, were moving too fast for a coherent policy review, and after only one working day in Washington we were on our way back to the region. This time we would negotiate the end of the three-year siege of Sarajevo—and unexpectedly meet with the world's two most wanted indicted war criminals, Radovan Karadzic and Ratko Mladic.

On Sunday, September 10, even as we regrouped in Washington, Janvier met again with Mladic in the border town of Mali Zvornik. The meeting had been arranged by Presidents Chirac and Milosevic, both of whom wanted another bombing pause as soon as possible. Chirac was anxious for the release of the two French pilots who had been captured during the bombing. Janvier went to the meeting expecting Mladic to offer the withdrawal of Bosnian Serb heavy weapons from the hills around Sarajevo. But once again the meeting did not go according to the U.N. plan. Instead, Mladic threatened to attack the remaining "safe areas," and refused to negotiate until after the bombing had ended.

Mladic's behavior opened the door for two of the most unexpected and important tactical decisions of the NATO air campaign—to attack vital military targets near the largest Serb city in Bosnia, Banja Luka; and to use Tomahawk cruise missiles. Thirteen of these expensive radar-guided missiles were launched against important Bosnian Serb military centers in western Bosnia, far from Sarajevo and Gorazde. Although a few seven-hundred-pound warheads were hardly as powerful as the hundreds of two-thousand-pound bombs that were being dropped by planes, the psychological effect of such sophisticated weapons, previously used only in the Gulf War, was enormous. The damage, however, was more than psychological: one of the missiles knocked out the main communications center for the Bosnian Serb Army in the west, with devastating consequences.

Karadzic seemed increasingly desperate. In a letter addressed to Presidents Clinton, Yeltsin, and Chirac, he combined pleading, outrage, and threats, calling the attacks against Banja Luka "bizarre" and "barbaric." If they continued, he said, the Bosnian Serbs would "reconsider participation in further peace talks." NATO, he went on, "has declared war against the Republic of Srpska. . . . Time is rapidly running out."

Although Karadzic's letter seemed to me to confirm the effectiveness of the Tomahawks, the strikes added to the tension within NATO. On September 11, at a special meeting of the NATO Council, France, Spain, Canada, and Greece criticized the attacks in western Bosnia, claiming that they represented an unauthorized escalation.

There was also a wintry blast from Moscow. Even before the Tomahawks, Yeltsin had written President Clinton on September 7 to express concern about the bombing. Now, the use of cruise missiles, the quintessential Cold War weapon, rattled the Russians deeply. They could not, they announced angrily, "be indifferent to the fate of the children of our fellow-Slavs." (The Pentagon immediately denied that any children had been killed in the air strikes.) Russian diplomats threatened to withdraw from the Contact Group. Defense Minister Pavel Grachev called Bill Perry to warn that the strikes could lead Moscow to reconsider its military cooperation agreements with NATO, and even threatened "to help the Serbs in a unilateral way" if the bombing continued. The next day, Russia proposed a U.N. Security Council resolution to condemn the bombing, but Ambassador Albright swiftly headed it off.

This strong Russian reaction to the bombing could not be entirely ignored. Perry and Grachev had already begun discussions about Russian participation in a post–peace agreement force in Bosnia. Beyond the Balkans lay the larger issue of Russia's relations with NATO, a volatile issue ever since President Clinton had announced our intention to enlarge the Atlantic Alliance. With tensions mounting, the President and Christopher sent Strobe Talbott to Moscow immediately for "quiet consultations." His trip proved timely and effective. After his forceful explanation that the bombing was consistent with NATO's authority and essential to the negotiations, the Russian concerns, while not eliminated, abated considerably—thus clearing the path for the continuation of the Perry-Grachev negotiations.

As the bombing continued, Croat and Bosnian Muslim military forces enjoyed their best week since the war began, even though there was still no military coordination between them. In the week after Geneva, the Croats took the town of Donji Vakuf, thus opening up a large area in western Bosnia. Karadzic charged that the NATO air strikes had assisted the offensive. But while the air strikes had undeniably aided the Federation, there was no truth to Karadzic's charge; in fact, such coordination was the ultimate nightmare of many NATO officers, the "slippery slope" toward the deep military involvement they feared and opposed. The truth remained as simple as it was ironic: the air strikes would never have occurred if Pale had not made a historic misreading of President Clinton and the United States.

We were approaching circuit overload when the Principals' Committee met at the White House on the afternoon of September 11. The President attended part of the meeting, and his presence made a huge difference, giving our discussion focus and enabling us to reach some important conclusions quickly.

Tony Lake wanted us to convene an international peace conference right away. Others began to support him, but I resisted; we needed to allow the Federation offensive to continue, and the gap among the three sides was still too great for face-to-face meetings of the three presidents. Our next diplomatic goal, I said, had to be to fix "the major flaw in the Geneva principles"—the lack of "connective tissue between the two entities."

"Has the NATO bombing reached the point of diminishing returns?" the President asked.

The question was an indication of the heavy pressure the President was under to end the bombing. "No, Mr. President," I replied. "There may come a time when continued bombing would hurt the peace efforts, but we're not there yet. The negotiating team believes we should tough it out. Our leadership position is getting stronger. We should use it or we will lose it. It is hurting the Bosnian Serbs, and helping us. As for Milosevic, he is not making a big point of it."

Christopher agreed. "The bombing should continue," he said. "It would be a mistake to back off now."

"Okay," the President said. "But I am frustrated that the air campaign is not better coordinated with the diplomatic effort."

This was an astute observation. The same point troubled me deeply; there was no mechanism or structure within the Administration capable of such coordination. It was, in fact, the role of the NSC to coordinate such interagency issues. I wanted to tell the President that this problem required immediate attention. But relations among the NSC, State, and Defense were not something an Assistant Secretary of State could fix. In fact, we later learned that Admiral Smith had ordered Lieutenant General Ryan, who was in charge of the bombing, to have no contact with the negotiating team.

Unexpectedly, Bill Perry suggested we consider another unilateral bombing pause. This caught Warren Christopher and me slightly off guard. Why would the Secretary of Defense propose a bombing halt just when his forces were dramatically expanding the scope of the bombing? To people not familiar with the ways of the Pentagon it may have appeared inexplicable. But the huge military establishment often operates at several different levels at once. Correctly understood, the Pentagon's behavior was less surprising. The military did not like putting its pilots at risk in pursuit of a limited political objective, hence their desire to end the bombing as soon as possible. At the same time, if asked to continue the bombing, they would seek to make it as effective as possible. Thus their desire to use Tomahawk missiles and F-117s, the airplane least detectable by radar. In addition, the Navy and the Air Force both wanted to publicize, especially to Congress, the value of their new weaponry. For the Navy, this meant the Tomahawks, which were launched from naval vessels in the Adriatic. For the Air Force, it meant the expensive and controversial F-117, whose value had been questioned by some Pentagon critics.

Warren Christopher objected first. Because he was normally so soft-spoken, Christopher was especially effective when he raised his voice or showed emotion. "We must carry on the bombing until it has achieved real effectiveness," he said firmly. "The Serbs must be impressed with our willingness to bomb on a continuous basis if necessary." Christopher was supported by Lake, Albright, and myself.

Almost immediately a more serious problem arose. Admiral Owens, the Vice Chairman of the JCS, made a remark that surprised Christopher and me. In his calm, methodical, and authoritative style, Owens said NATO would run out of new authorized "Option Two" targets within two or three days. Of course, Owens said, the bombing could be continued by hitting old Option One and Two targets again. However, this would have diminishing value, and put the pilots at continually greater risk as the Bosnian Serb anti-aircraft gunners became more proficient. To attack Option Three targets, a much broader group that included Serb troop concentrations and equipment throughout Bosnia, we would need to return to both the NATO Council and the U.N. Security Council for permission. But everyone in the room knew that the chances of getting approval from our NATO allies to attack Option Three targets was close to zero.

On the drive back to the State Department after the meeting, Christopher told me that he doubted that the military had really exhausted all its authorized Option Two targets. But there was no way to question the military within its own area of responsibility—the military controlled the information and independent verification was virtually impossible.

Only moments earlier the President had observed that the bombing should be calibrated for political and diplomatic purposes, but in fact the opposite was suddenly the case; the military had rewritten our negotiating timetable. My immediate concern was that if the information became public, as so often happened after White House meetings, it would weaken our negotiating hand. If the air campaign was really going to end within a few days, we had to continue the bombing long enough to negotiate something in return. "If NATO runs out of targets before we resume our talks with Belgrade, we won't have a chance to get anything in return for the bombing," I said. "Let's not stop it for free." Christopher agreed. "Let's be sure the negotiating team has the benefit of the leverage of military force for as long as possible," he said.

Confronting this new time pressure, Christopher asked that the negotiating team leave for Belgrade the next day, four days ahead of schedule.

Before leaving the next day, I called Admiral Smith in Naples to ask how much longer he would be willing to continue the bombing. Smith replied that, assuming routine weather, he thought he had about three more days of new targets, after which he could keep the bombing going only by returning to targets that had already been hit—or, as Smith put it in his best salty old sea dog style, "cleaning up a few stray cats and dogs." The meaning behind the message was clear: Smith did not wish to let the bombing be "used" by the negotiators, and would decide when to stop based on his own judgment. This was hardly the best way to integrate diplomacy and military pressure, but we had no choice in the matter.

· · ·

We slept little as we flew to Belgrade on the night of September 12–13. As we prepared for the meetings, I raised a sensitive issue: What should we do if asked to meet the two indicted war criminals who led the Bosnian Serbs, Radovan Karadzic and Ratko Mladic? Should we meet with them at all, and, if so, how should we deal with them? It was one of those rare questions that combined political and tactical considerations with questions of morality.

There was a history here. Karadzic and Mladic had met in the past with Western negotiators, including Vance, Owen, and Lord Carrington. Jimmy Carter had spent a great deal of time with Karadzic only seven months earlier, and remained in regular contact with him by phone and fax.

Nonetheless, I felt deeply uncomfortable about the prospect of sitting down with indicted war criminals. But in the end I decided it was justifiable under these circumstances. In reaching this conclusion, I was deeply influenced by the stories of Raoul Wallenberg and Folke Bernadotte, two legendary Swedes—both the subject of biographies by my wife, Kati—who had negotiated, respectively, with Adolf Eichmann and Heinrich Himmler in 1944–1945. Each man had decided to deal with a mass murderer in order to save lives. History had shown the correctness of their decisions, which had resulted in the rescue of tens of thousands of Jews before the two men themselves were killed—Wallenberg in a Soviet prison, Bernadotte at the hands of Israeli terrorists in Jerusalem in 1948.

We concluded that it was similarly acceptable to meet with Karadzic and Mladic if it would help the negotiations. As our plane descended toward the military airport in Belgrade, we decided we would not ask to meet the two men, but would see them if Milosevic suggested it. However, we would set certain conditions. We would not meet with any Bosnian Serbs—indicted or unindicted—if they presented themselves as a separate delegation or tried to negotiate on their own. At the same time, I said each member of the team could decide whether to participate if either man showed up, and whether to shake hands with them.

We landed in Belgrade in the late morning on September 13. Two hours later we were back at Milosevic's villa outside Belgrade. He was anxious to get started. An ABC television crew, led by correspondent Sheila McVicker, filmed the opening moments of our meeting for a *Nightline* special they were producing, and then retreated to the garden. As soon as they left, Milosevic complained about the expanded bombing. "Your planes are giving close air support to the Muslims and Croats," he said. I told him that he was misinformed on this point, but I readily agreed—in fact, with a certain pleasure—that the bombing, even though it was not coordinated with Federation ground troops, had the effect of helping the Muslims and Croats. "The Serbs brought it down upon themselves," I said.

Milosevic said the situation on the ground needed "calming." He thought he could get the Bosnian Serbs to agree to a cease-fire throughout the country in return for a cessation of the bombing. Then, he said, we should convene an international conference as quickly as possible to end the war.

Milosevic's proposal for a nationwide cease-fire was new. I knew this was what Washington wanted, but it was premature as long as the offensive was progressing. "A general cease-fire is out of the question at this point," I said. "But we can talk about one for the Sarajevo area."

We were struck by the change in his tone. Clearly, the Croat-Muslim offensive in the west and the bombing were having a major effect on the Bosnian Serbs. Milosevic seemed in a rush. Unfortunately, so were many people in the West. Not for the first time, I thought: the chances for a viable peace will improve if the bombing and the offensive continue, at least for a while.

At about 5:00 P.M., Milosevic unveiled his big surprise. "Karadzic and Mladic are in another villa, about two hundred meters away," he said. "They can be here in ten minutes. Why don't we ask them to join us so you can negotiate directly with them?"

I was grateful we had prepared ourselves for this moment. At that instant, however, I felt a jolt go through my body. It is not an exaggeration to say that I simply hated the two men for what they had done—including, indirectly, causing the deaths of our three colleagues.

"Let's talk awhile first," I said, trying not to appear anxious. "Are you sure that we can accomplish anything? Why don't you see them first while we wait here?"

Milosevic said he was sure we could make progress if we used his "technology"—by which he meant the theatrical style with which he loved to dazzle and outmaneuver other politicians in the Balkans.

"Mr. President, in that case, we are ready to meet with them, but with two conditions. First, they must be part of your delegation, you must lead the discussions, and you must control them. Second, they must not give us a lot of historical bullshit, as they have with everyone else. They must be ready for serious discussions."

"They will agree," Milosevic said. "No bullshit. Let me get them." He told an aide to send for the Bosnian Serbs. We asked the ABC crew waiting outside to leave, without telling them why. Then we had drinks on the patio and waited for the men from Pale. The lawns blended into trees not far away. In the early August evening there was still plenty of natural light.

After about twenty minutes a couple of Mercedes sedans pulled up in the driveway. Two men stepped out of the first car, trailed by others. As they approached us through the trees in the fading summer light, their unmistakable silhouettes jolted me again: one, in a suit, tall with a wild shock of hair; the other, short and burly, in combat fatigues, walking as though through a muddy field.

Before the Bosnian Serbs could reach us, I turned to Milosevic and said, "We'll take a walk while you explain the ground rules. We'll return when you can assure us they have agreed." We retreated into the woods about one hundred yards behind the main house, where we waited nervously and reviewed our strategy. Ten minutes later an aide came running up to us and said Milosevic and his guests were ready.

I did not shake hands, although both Karadzic and Mladic tried to. Some of our team did, others did not; it was their choice. We sat down at a long table on the patio facing each other, and began to talk. Arrayed next to Karadzic were other Bosnian Serbs whose names were familiar to us, including Momcilo Krajisnik, the Speaker of the Bosnian Serb Assembly. Karadzic, speaking partly in English, began complaining immediately about how unfair the bombing was. He said he was ready for a nationwide cessation of hostilities, but only if the Federation agreed not to "take advantage of it." I said the United States supported a general cease-fire in principle, but not at this time. We were here only to discuss the situation around Sarajevo.

As Karadzic replied, I looked at Mladic. Hollywood could not have found a more convincing war villain. He glowered—there was no better word for it— and engaged each of the Americans in what seemed to us, when we compared notes later, as staring contests. Nonetheless, he had a compelling presence; it was not hard to understand why his troops revered him; he was, I thought, one of those lethal combinations that history thrusts up occasionally—a charismatic murderer.

Despite his size, Karadzic was not an imposing figure at this meeting. He had a sad face, with heavy jowls, a soft chin, and surprisingly gentle eyes. He had studied psychiatry in New York and understood English well. He was quick to launch into a self-pitying diatribe against NATO and the Muslims, whom he accused of mortaring their own marketplace on August 28 in order to lure NATO into the war. He referred several times to the "humiliation the Serbs are suffering."

After a few minutes of Karadzic's harangue, I turned to Milosevic. "Mr. President," I said, "you assured us that this would not happen. If it continues, we are prepared to leave immediately." Karadzic responded emotionally. "If we can't get anything done here, I will call President Carter," he said. "I am in regular contact with him." We already knew, of course, that Karadzic had invited the former President to get involved again. Karadzic started to rise, as if to make a telephone call.

For the only time in the evening, I spoke directly to him. "Let me tell you something," I said, my voice rising. "President Carter appointed me as Assistant Secretary of State. I worked for him for four years. Like most Americans, I have great admiration for him. But he is now a private citizen. We work only for President Clinton. We take orders only from President Clinton. That is all there is to it."

Karadzic sat down abruptly, and Milosevic said something to him in Serbian. For the rest of the meeting, Karadzic was on his best behavior. As Pardew noted later, Karadzic played the "facilitator who kept the Bosnian Serbs on track"—something we assumed his psychiatric training had prepared him for. He showed no sign of the qualities that had led even a cautious observer like Ambassador Zimmermann to label him the "Himmler of his generation."[2]

Karadzic calmly proposed that the Americans produce a draft agreement. I asked Clark, Owen, Hill, and Pardew to work on a document that would end the siege of Sarajevo. As my colleagues hunched over pads of paper, Milosevic and I walked around the garden and talked about other matters. "You know, that was smart," he said, "what you said about Jimmy Carter. Those guys"—he meant the Bosnian Serbs—"are so cut off from the world they think Carter still determines American policy."

Dusk had fallen by the time my colleagues produced a first draft. Seated on a low brick wall about seventy-five feet away, Milosevic and I watched as General Clark began to read his draft to the Serbs, pausing regularly for translation. We could not make out his exact words, but the deep, booming voice of the Serbian interpreter drifted toward us. The scene was unforgettable: Clark standing under the tall lamp, reading from his draft, the Serbs clustered around, listening intently, the familiar shapes of the two main Serb protagonists outlined in the shadows. Occasionally we could hear other Serb voices getting louder.

As Milosevic and I chatted, Milutinovic ran over to us and said something to Milosevic. "We better join them," Milosevic said. "They're in trouble." Everyone was standing, but Milosevic pulled up a chair and sat down. After a moment's hesitation, I did the same in order to establish some rough equality between us.

Karadzic, clearly angry, said that our draft proposal was unacceptable. Suddenly Mladic erupted. Pushing to the center of the circle, he began a long, emotional diatribe. "The situation is explosive, worse than at any time since the war began," he said. "There is no justification for the bombing. NATO is supporting the regular Croatian Army inside our nation. It's worse than the Nazis. But they cannot destroy the spirit of the Serb people. Neither can the United States. The bombing is a criminal act." Then, a memorable phrase: "No one can be allowed to give away a meter of our sacred Serb soil."

This was the intimidating style he had used with the Dutch commander at Srebrenica, with Janvier, and with so many others. He gave off the scent of danger. It was not hard to see how frightening this man might be, especially on his own home ground. I did not know if his rage was real or feigned, but this was the genuine Mladic, the one who could unleash a murderous rampage.

Turning my back on Mladic and Karadzic, I rose from my chair and looked down at Milosevic. "Mr. President," I said, "we had an agreement. This behavior is clearly not consistent with it. If your 'friends' "—I said the word with as much sarcasm as I could—"do not wish to have a serious discussion, we will leave now."

Milosevic paused for a moment, perhaps to gauge if this was a bluff. Perhaps he sensed that it wasn't. NATO planes were bombing Bosnian Serb territory as we spoke. It was our moment of maximum leverage, and I was not bluffing about leaving, although we were acutely conscious of the fact that we might lose our best negotiating chip, the bombing, within two or three days.

Milosevic spoke sharply in Serbian to his colleagues, and they began to argue. Motioning my colleagues to follow, I walked to the other end of the patio, where we waited, listening to the sounds of an increasingly angry debate under the lamps.

It was over in a few minutes. Milosevic came over to us, asked us to rejoin him, and said that the Bosnian Serbs were ready to negotiate on the basis of our draft.

Our draft began with a Bosnian Serb commitment to "cease all offensive operations" in the Sarajevo area and remove all heavy weapons from the same area within a week. They also had to open two land routes out of Sarajevo, one the Kiseljak road, to unimpeded humanitarian road traffic. The Sarajevo airport had to reopen within twenty-four hours. In return, NATO would stand down its bombing for seventy-two hours, but resume the bombing if there was no compliance.

I left most of the negotiating to my colleagues, intervening only when necessary to break an impasse. I did not wish to diminish my role by spending too much time with Karadzic and Mladic, and I trusted my colleagues completely. I called Christopher and Tarnoff to describe the remarkable scene unfolding at the villa, and wandered around with Milosevic, talking about next steps in the peace process. Food was set out on a table on the patio, and Milosevic invited me to eat dinner with him and Mladic. I sat with the two men briefly, but left without eating, returning only after Mladic had left. Commenting on this later, Milosevic said I had insulted Mladic by not shaking his hand or eating with him, and this would not make the negotiations any easier. "If that is true, so be it," I replied, and repeated an earlier theme of our meetings: "We expect you to make this process work."

The Bosnian Serbs argued over almost every word, but sometime after midnight we had what we wanted: after four years, the siege of Sarajevo would be lifted. There was still one important procedural matter to resolve. The Serbs insisted I sign or witness the document. I refused, explaining that we had no formal authority to reach any agreement concerning the activities of NATO or the U.N. We wanted a document with only Serb signatures—and Milosevic and Milutinovic as its witnesses. This was something of a diplomatic innovation—a document drafted by us but signed only by the Serbs as a unilateral undertaking. None of us was aware of diplomatic precedent for it, but it fit our needs perfectly. After it was signed and witnessed, I explained, we would deliver it to Janvier with a "recommendation" that NATO and the U.N. suspend the bombing. The Bosnian Serbs protested vigorously, but they had no choice, and after another long debate, they agreed to the format we had proposed.

At 2:15 on the morning of September 14, after more than ten hours of negotiations, the Serbs signed the document we had written. We watched as one by one they affixed their signatures to the paper—first Karadzic, who signed without hesitating; then the "Vice President of Republika Srpska," Nikola Koljevic, followed by Krajisnik. Mladic signed last. He had long since stopped participating in the negotiations, and sat slumped on a couch on the far side of the room away from his colleagues. One of Milosevic's aides carried the agreement to him. He reached out for the pen, scrawled his name on it without looking at it, and sank back into the sofa. He looked utterly spent.

Finally, Milosevic and his Foreign Minister signed the document as witnesses. We got up to leave, carrying the precious original with us. If it held, the long siege of Sarajevo would be over. Karadzic came over to me and grabbed my hand. "We are ready for peace," he said in English. "Why did you bomb us?"

"I think you know," I said.

I was beginning to get a sense of the Pale Serbs: headstrong, given to empty theatrical statements, but in the end, essentially bullies when their bluff was called. The Western mistake over the previous four years had been to treat the Serbs as rational people with whom one could argue, negotiate, compromise, and agree. In fact, they respected only force or an unambiguous and credible threat to use it.

CHAPTER 11

The Western Offensive

(September 14–20)

It's farewell to the drawing-room's civilised cry,
The professor's sensible whereto and why,
The frock-coated diplomat's social aplomb,
Now matters are settled with gas and with bomb.

—W. H. AUDEN, "Danse Macabre"

WE BELIEVED WE HAD MADE THE BEST possible deal in Belgrade, though I still wonder what might have been accomplished had we been able to continue the bombing for another two weeks. There were few second thoughts in Washington, however, where the reaction was astonishing. Buoyed by enthusiastic expressions of support during a long night of telephone conversations with Washington, we left Belgrade for Zagreb just after dawn on September 14 to deliver the Serb agreement to General Janvier. The United Nations command were sticklers for proper procedures, and we did not have formal authority to conduct a negotiation on their behalf. To minimize the U.N.'s sense of injured pride, we told Janvier that we were simply transmitting a "unilateral undertaking" by the Bosnian Serbs concerning Sarajevo, along with a recommendation that the U.N. suspend the bombing. But we asked him to wait until after we had talked to Izetbegovic, whom we planned to meet in Mostar that afternoon.

Janvier, whose own negotiations with Mladic had been a well-publicized disaster, seemed stunned by our success. But he recovered gracefully, thanked us, and said he would request a twelve-hour bombing "pause" and await the outcome of our talks with Izetbegovic. In military terminology a pause is different from a suspension—it is a brief period when planes are not flying, while the operational orders for the bombing are still in place.

From U.N. headquarters, we raced across town to brief Tudjman, who showed no interest in the Sarajevo agreement. He was focused entirely on the military offensive in western Bosnia. The Bosnian Serb Army was in disarray, and there were reports that some Serb soldiers had shot their own officers. At least one hundred thousand Serb refugees were pouring into Banja Luka or heading further east to escape the Federation advance.

Anger in Mostar. Bracing ourselves for a difficult encounter with Izetbegovic, we flew to Split and drove for three hours through the mountains to the medieval city of Mostar to meet Izetbegovic. We knew the Bosnians would be unhappy; from their point of view, stopping the bombing after only a few weeks in return for ending a four-year siege was a poor bargain.

One of my most vivid memories from my trip to Yugoslavia in 1960 was the beautiful sixteenth-century bridge linking the two parts of Mostar. It was perhaps Yugoslavia's most famous symbol of multiethnic harmony. When I last saw the high-arched bridge in 1992, it was crumbling under continuous shelling by the Croats, pathetically protected by automobile tires hung over its sides on ropes. Two years later, in September of 1994, when I visited Mostar with General Charles Boyd, the Deputy Commander in Chief of U.S. Forces in Europe, the bridge was gone, replaced by a narrow, swaying metal footbridge hundreds of feet above the Neretva River, which Boyd and I cautiously crossed, stepping over gaping holes in the steel planking.

When our negotiating team arrived on the afternoon of September 14, the fighting between the Croats and the Muslims in Mostar had been over for more than a year, as a result of intense efforts by Warren Christopher and U.S. negotiator Charles Redman. Their creation, the Federation, existed—but only on paper. As Silajdzic put it, the Federation was "a house with only a roof, a roof full of holes." The damage from that Croat-Muslim war was still palpable in Mostar, where the multiethnic city had become a cauldron of hate.

With Croat and Bosnian forces advancing against the Serbs in western Bosnia, there should have been a marked improvement in the situation in Mostar, far to the south. But there wasn't. Along the line dividing the two halves of Mostar, there were only rubble and tension. The hostility of the people was evident from their stares and gestures. The Croat portion of the city was held by organized gangsters. Each part of the city was patrolled by heavily armed men in police and paramilitary uniforms. When we had toured the "confrontation line" in 1994, Boyd and I had walked between armed Croats and Muslims men only ten or fifteen feet apart who drank and talked to one another, joked, and even played cards—but with the safeties off their weapons. It was one of the saddest and most tense walks of my life.

Now, a year later, little had changed. As our heavily armed convoy weaved through the streets, around wrecked vehicles and barricades, to reach the Muslim sector, where our meeting would be held, I was again appalled by the senselessness of the war.

. . .

The meeting with Izetbegovic was even worse than we expected. Christopher had called Izetbegovic earlier in the day, urging him to support the agreement, but the Bosnian President told the Secretary he wanted to withhold judgment until he saw us in Mostar. He showed no appreciation that the long siege of his capital city was over. He would prefer to let the people of Sarajevo live under Serb guns for a while longer if it also meant that the NATO bombing would continue.

Haris Silajdzic showed even greater fury. For the first time I saw in the normally urbane Prime Minister a tendency to explode that would re-emerge, sometimes disastrously, at tense moments in the negotiations. Calling the cease-fire "totally unacceptable," Silajdzic demanded that the bombing continue. As Silajdzic continued to complain vigorously, Izetbegovic signaled me to leave the room with him. Once alone, he told me he understood why the United States had taken its position, and would reluctantly support us. But, he said, he could not publicly endorse a bombing suspension yet. (There was a large press corps assembled outside our meeting place.) First, he would have to return to Sarajevo and, as he put it, "work with my people." He would have to show them that he had forced us to produce something "better" than the present agreement. In other words, he wanted us to return to Belgrade and "strengthen" the agreement.

I said that I sympathized with his dilemma. I told him, in confidence, that the bombing would have ended within days anyway and that his choices, like mine, were therefore limited. We returned to the larger meeting, where Silajdzic demanded several changes in the agreement. I agreed to negotiate all of these with Milosevic as soon as I returned to Belgrade, after a Contact Group meeting scheduled for the next day in Geneva. We parted amid confusion, in a mud-filled alley surrounded by journalists using long "boom" microphones to try to pick up our farewell comments. True to their promise, the Bosnians were reserved in their public comments, but they did not go so far as to attack the agreement.

Geneva. The next morning, I asked Bob Owen and Chris Hill to drive to Sarajevo with Silajdzic to reassure him and begin discussion of a postwar constitution. For both Americans it was their first trip over Mount Igman, and when they reached the scene of the accident, they got out for a moment to pay tribute to their fallen comrades and, as Hill told me later, take a look at that "godforsaken and worthless place."

The rest of us flew to Geneva for another round of Contact Group ritual. With the pace of negotiations so intense, I wanted to postpone the meeting, but we were locked in because we had agreed to let the Russians host it in lieu of a meeting in Moscow. The meeting was large and messy, but it received heavy publicity, which was all the Russians cared about. Igor Ivanov, the Russian Deputy Foreign Minister, chaired the meeting. Usually affable, Ivanov occasionally exploded in anger, but regained his composure quickly. The German Contact Group representative, Wolfgang Ischinger, helped smooth things over.

All four nations pressed us to convene an international peace conference. I replied that the differences between the sides were still too great, but we would get there eventually. Instead, I suggested we invite the three Foreign Ministers to another meeting, similar to the one in Geneva, to be held during the United Nations General Assembly session in New York near the end of September. We needed an agreement on the creation of central governmental institutions—the "connective tissue" between the Serbs and the Federation—that had eluded us at Geneva. If we could achieve that, we could begin to plan "the big one"—a full-fledged peace conference with the three presidents.

Belgrade. We flew back to Belgrade on the afternoon of September 16 to convince Milosevic to accept changes in the cease-fire agreement. The bombing had been suspended since 10:00 A.M. on September 14, but we made it clear to Milosevic that it could resume. President Clinton had made a strong and simple public statement, at our request, to underline this threat: "Let me emphasize that if the Bosnian Serbs do not comply with their commitments, the air strikes will resume."

Milosevic asked General Momcilo Perisic, the Yugoslav Army chief of staff, to join the meeting. Perisic was a sullen chain-smoker who looked like a living Cold War relic. Milosevic said that Mladic was in the hospital for removal of kidney stones. I silently hoped that they would be the kind of medical problem that Chinese and Soviet leaders sometimes discovered in their political opponents, stones from which there is no recovery. Perhaps reading my thoughts, Milosevic offered to let us visit Mladic in the hospital to prove he really was sick. I declined.*

We presented to Milosevic and Perisic the requirements for continuing the halt in the bombing: first, we wanted the French Rapid Reaction Force to protect the roads into Sarajevo; second, "humanitarian" goods would henceforth mean *all* civilian goods, including cement, glass, shoes, and radios, which the Serbs had previously prevented from reaching the Bosnian capital; third, we

---

* We were never sure of the truth about Mladic's illness, although we did confirm that he had been hospitalized. One theory, widely held around Belgrade, was that Mladic did not want to withdraw the heavy weapons from around Sarajevo, and was sent to the hospital so that he'd be sidelined while the deal was made. In any case, Mladic soon returned to the field to rally his troops.

needed assurance that a drafting error made during the long night of September 12–13 concerning the size of artillery that must be removed would be corrected. This mistake, the result of fatigue by a member of our military support group, had already been reported around the world as a "major concession" by the American negotiators. Finally, we told the Serbs that henceforth the United States and NATO, not the U.N., would decide if they were in compliance.

Throughout this long discussion, I shuttled between the smoke-filled dining room in the villa and an American military field telephone on the patio, through which we had opened a continuous line to Sarajevo and General Rupert Smith, the British commander of all U.N. forces inside Bosnia.* Milosevic and Perisic argued over some of our demands, but eventually they agreed to all of them. Still, the same issue that had undermined so many previous cease-fires remained: making sure the orders agreed to at one level were carried out at another. The Serbs had become expert at pretending that they could not control their field commanders.

To prevent this, we demanded the name of a Serb field commander in the Sarajevo area with whom General Rupert Smith could negotiate starting the next morning in Sarajevo. Perisic offered the name of General Dragomir Milosevic (no relation to the Serbian President), who, he promised, would appear for discussions in Sarajevo the next morning. From Sarajevo, over a poor telephone connection, Smith told me dryly that he doubted he would ever see the Serb general.

Smith and I spent over an hour speaking on the ancient field telephone that night, and Wes Clark took over whenever I had to return to the villa. The obsolete military telephone system—there were no direct telephone lines between Belgrade and Sarajevo—was difficult to use, and several times the system got so overheated that we had to wait in silence while it cooled down. From Sarajevo, General Smith impatiently questioned our negotiations. I understood why he might mistrust Serb promises—so did we—but, like Janvier, Smith seemed slow to realize that this new situation offered a unique opportunity to break the Serb siege of Sarajevo.

We had been with Milosevic for almost seven hours. As Owen and Hill waited for me to conclude my conversation with General Smith, they tried to talk to Milosevic about constitutional issues. But no matter how hard the polite but persistent Owen tried, Milosevic avoided the subject. Finally, Milutinovic pulled me into a corner of the dining room. "Listen," he told me, "tell your colleagues that my President will not discuss these issues in front of

---

* Smith reported to Janvier, whose command in Zagreb covered all U.N. military activities in the former Yugoslavia, including Bosnia, Croatia, and Macedonia.

General Perisic. Hold off, and he will talk about them later." Such deep distrust among close compatriots was as common as plum brandy in the Balkans.

When Milosevic accepted all of our demands that evening, NATO's bombing was truly over. Although it could have started again if the Serbs challenged the agreement, the threat of resumption kept the Serbs in line. We got our first proof of this the very next day: to General Smith's surprise, General Milosevic appeared on schedule, and the withdrawal of Serb heavy weapons from the Sarajevo area began shortly thereafter.

The following day, to dramatize the end of the siege of Sarajevo, we did something that had not been attempted during the war: we visited all three Balkan capitals and met all three Presidents on a single day. This was more than a stunt; we were entering a new phase of the negotiations, where the ability to visit all three capitals in a single day was essential.

Our first stop on Sunday morning was Zagreb, where the topic was the gathering momentum of the Federation offensive—although, of course, the Federation was never mentioned; as far as the Croatians were concerned, this was their operation. Two more important towns had fallen: Bosanski Petrovac and Jajce. The Bosnian Serb communications network in the west remained out of commission, although the Serbs were struggling to repair it.

With many of the roads toward the Serb strongholds lying open before his forces, Tudjman had to decide: should he continue the offensive, and, if so, how far should he go? His government was receiving mixed signals from the United States, and he was confused.

Tudjman's confusion about the American view was understandable. Two days before I returned to Zagreb, Galbraith had presented to Defense Minister Susak a formal message—a démarche, in State Department jargon—asking the Croatians to halt the military campaign. Galbraith, who did not agree with the démarche, had asked for a revision, but his appeal was overruled by Washington, and he unhappily delivered it. At almost the same time, in separate meetings with Croatian Foreign Minister Mate Granic in Washington on September 12, Lake and Christopher recommended that the advance stop as soon as the confrontation lines were "stabilized."

I did not agree, as John Kornblum told Washington. Simply stated, after four years of Serb aggression, the Federation forces were finally gaining territory lost at the beginning of the war. As a matter of both simple justice and high strategy, we should not oppose the offensive unless it either ran into trouble or went too far.

Like so many issues, the policy dispute began with a flawed intelligence assessment. Almost every morning's "daily intelligence report" brought to top Washington officials new warnings of the dangers posed by the offensive. The "experts" predicted that the more successful the Croatian-Bosnian offensive, the greater the chance that the regular Yugoslav Army would re-enter the war. These opinions were based not on secret intelligence of Yugoslav plans, but on a long-standing belief in the intelligence community about the military superiority of the Serbs and their cohesiveness.

By mid-September, having spent more time with the Serbian leadership than any other Americans, we had come to a different opinion. We concluded that Milosevic had virtually written off the Bosnian Serbs—as he had the Krajina Serbs—and would not intervene militarily to save them. In our opinion, there was only one move that might bring Yugoslav troops back into Bosnia: closing the narrow five-kilometer-long corridor at Brcko, an action that would physically cut off the majority of the Bosnian Serb population from Serbia.

Washington's desire to stop the offensive became public just as we met privately with Tudjman. In a front-page article in *The New York Times* filed from Belgrade—an article which, significantly, quoted Washington officials—Chris Hedges wrote,

> United Nations and American officials said they feared that the assault could draw Serbia directly into the war. . . . "All the lights have been red, irrevocably red," the [Washington] official said. "It risks blowing the whole thing out of the water." The message from Washington, this official said, was "quit while you're ahead."

The next day, White House Press Secretary Mike McCurry put the same message on the record. "There's fighting going on in western Bosnia," he said. "We wish they would suspend that fighting and turn their attention to the discussions that Ambassador Holbrooke has been conducting." I would have preferred a different message from the White House, but McCurry, a highly skilled press secretary, would not have made these remarks without guidance from the NSC.

While Washington wanted the offensive to stop, we never had a clear instruction, only the general sense of our senior colleagues, who left to us the exact calibration of the signal. Remembering again how Harriman and Vance had been "overinstructed" during their negotiations with the North Vietnamese in 1968, I was grateful that Washington was giving us such flexibility and support. Later, Tom Donilon told me that most of the credit for protecting our flexibility was owed to Warren Christopher, who, despite his own views, argued that Washington should back its negotiators.

Galbraith and I saw Tudjman on September 14. Tudjman wanted clarification of the American position. He bluntly asked for my *personal* views. I indicated my general support for the offensive, but delayed a more detailed exchange for a second meeting so that I could discuss it with my colleagues and Washington.

Galbraith and I met Tudjman alone again on September 17. At the same time, by prearrangement, Clark, Hill, Kerrick, and Pardew met with Susak. Peter and I sat side by side on an ornate sofa, embroidered with gold trim, while Tudjman sat at my right in a Louis Quinze armchair.

I told Tudjman the offensive had great value to the negotiations. It would be much easier to retain at the table what had been won on the battlefield than to get the Serbs to give up territory they had controlled for several years. I urged Tudjman to take Sanski Most, Prijedor, and Bosanski Novi—all important towns that had become worldwide symbols of ethnic cleansing. If they were captured before we opened negotiations on territory, they would remain under Federation control—otherwise it would be difficult to regain them in a negotiation.

Banja Luka, I said, was a different matter. As we spoke the road to this largest Bosnian Serb city appeared to lie open to the Croatian offensive, although it was not at all certain that the city could be taken. We knew that Susak wanted to go for it as quickly as possible. On the other hand, I told Tudjman, the city was unquestionably within the Serb portion of Bosnia. Even if it were captured, the Federation would have to return it to the Serbs in any peace negotiation. Finally, capturing Banja Luka would generate over two hundred thousand additional refugees. I did not think the United States should encourage an action that would create so many more refugees. I concluded my comments with a blunt statement: "Mr. President, I urge you to go as far as you can, but not to take Banja Luka."

Since we were encouraging military action in three specific areas while objecting to it in Banja Luka, I was conscious, of course, that we could be accused of applying a double standard. But these three towns were smaller and less charged with emotional and historical baggage, and they could be retained in a negotiation. And the number of refugees that would be created weighed heavily on my mind.

Even while encouraging the offensive, Galbraith and I expressed great concern over the many refugees already displaced. We told Tudjman that there was no excuse for the brutal treatment of Serbs that followed most Croatian military successes. The abuse of Serb civilians, most of whom had lived in the area for generations, was wrong. Using a provocative phrase normally applied only to the Serbs, I told Tudjman that current Croatian behavior might be viewed as a milder form of ethnic cleansing. Tudjman reacted strongly, but did not quite deny it; if our information was correct, he said, he

The Western Offensive, August–September 1995

SLOV.

Zagreb

Karlovac

HUNGARY

SERBIA

CROATIA

EASTERN SLAVONIA

Vukovar

KRAJINA

Bihac Pocket

Bosanski Novi

Prijedor

Bosanski Samac

Omarska

Sanski Most

Banja Luka

Doboj

Brcko

Bosanski Petrovac

BOSNIA-HERZEGOVINA

Udbina

Mali Zvornik

Tuzla

Jajce

Srebrenica

Knin

Kiseljak

Zepa

Sarajevo

Pale

Rogatica

Mt. Igman

Gorazde

Split

Foca

Mostar

MONTE-NEGRO

Dubrovnik

Podgorica

0   20 miles

0   20 kilometers

Direction of
Croat-Muslim
Offensive

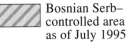

Bosnian Serb–
controlled area
as of July 1995

Croat-Muslim
Federation–
controlled area
as of July 1995

would put an immediate stop to it. On the critical question of whether or not to take Banja Luka, Tudjman was noncommittal, although he made a strange and troubling proposal—that we "trade" Banja Luka for Tuzla, the most Muslim city in Bosnia. Galbraith leaned over to me and whispered, "This is one of his obsessions. No one else agrees with it." I told him it was inconceivable, and it was never revived—but it had provided a momentary glimpse into his heart.

Tudjman's proposal reflected his deep hatred of the Muslims and his dream to unite all Croats in one country, under one flag—under his leadership. He knew he could not rearrange international boundaries while the war continued, but he was testing the idea of a substantial land swap that would restructure the entire region. Under this scheme, Zagreb would gain de facto control of much of western Bosnia, which was closer physically and economically to Zagreb than to Sarajevo, while the Serbs would control much of eastern Bosnia, leaving the Muslims with a landlocked ministate around Sarajevo. We called this the "Stalin-Hitler" scenario, recalling the division of Poland in August 1939. We had repeatedly asked Tudjman to repudiate rumors of such a deal—one version of which had received wide publicity after he had discussed it informally at a dinner in London in May 1995.

Tensions were growing again between the Croats and Muslims. That same day we received alarming news: after taking the town of Bosanski Petrovac, the two sides had turned on each other, and three Croats had been killed by Muslim soldiers. Something had to be done immediately.

I asked Tudjman if he would agree to meet with Izetbegovic under American auspices to forge a common position. Sacirbey had previously suggested that we convene such a meeting, but the idea of an American Assistant Secretary of State convening two heads of state, who already knew each other well and met regularly, seemed both presumptuous and odd. The alarming incident at Bosanski Petrovac changed that: the explosive situation could undo everything that the Federation offensive had gained.

Return to Sarajevo. On this three-country day, we wanted to take our small jet into Sarajevo to show our confidence in the cease-fire. But the U.S. Air Force felt it was too dangerous, so, from Zagreb, we flew to the American air base in Aviano, Italy, and switched to a C-130 military cargo plane. For this flight, the Air Force was taking no chances: the crew captain, a colonel from Germany, made us don flak jackets and helmets as we crossed the coastline, and the pilot discharged chaff to confuse hostile radar as we descended into the Sarajevo valley. I sat in the cockpit with the pilots, looking for the spot on Igman where the APC had plunged off the road, and soon spied a barely discernable vertical slash of flattened trees descending from the road. We stared at it in silence for a moment before we bounced onto the runway.

I cannot describe my feelings as we returned to the very spot from which we had lifted off with the bodies of our three colleagues exactly four weeks earlier. This time the sun was out, and so was a very large press contingent, behind a rope. I said a few words and quickly moved on. On the way into the city in our armored cars, past the overturned buses and shattered buildings, we saw streets with pedestrians for the first time in months. A few people waved at the American Embassy vehicles. By the time we reached the presidency building, several hundred people had gathered across the street. As we got out of our cars, they applauded, and a few waved small American flags. The siege of Sarajevo was over.

Inside the building there was no cheering. Izetbegovic was sour and Silajdzic visibly unhappy. When I tried to discuss rebuilding Sarajevo, they ignored me. They did not believe the Bosnian Serbs would actually withdraw their heavy weapons; after all, they had not done so before. I was not pleased with this response. "You are concentrating only on the small picture," I said to Izetbegovic. "If the Serbs violate, we will resume the bombing. But if they comply, you must be ready to move forward toward peace and reconstruction."

The situation had changed too fast for these brave but isolated men to recognize how much progress had been made. Further pressure would only cause further problems. I dropped the rest of our agenda, and we parted grumpily. As we walked out, Sacirbey told me I was spending too much time with the Serbs—a standard Muslim refrain.

Our delegation went to see General Rupert Smith to encourage him to take a firm line with the Bosnian Serbs. We had a chance to break them in the Sarajevo area right then if Smith would take an uncompromising approach to implementing the agreement reached two days earlier. "This is the time to challenge the Serbs," I said. "We finally have a written arrangement and a mechanism with which we can go back to Milosevic and force compliance. We can hold the threat of resumed bombing over their heads." Smith was well known for being more aggressive than Janvier, but he hesitated. He did not want to be held responsible for what he felt was excessively rigorous enforcement.

"We must do things our way," Smith said stiffly. "Perhaps you do not understand." He went to the map and began a lengthy explanation of the battlefield situation. He still feared retaliation. "And of course we have the usual troubles communicating our instructions to all the troops," he said. By this he meant that the various nationalities serving under him reacted unpredictably to instructions. "They are conditioned to do things a certain way," he said dryly. What he meant was: some U.N. troops do not follow my orders.

As we were leaving, Smith pulled me aside, suddenly much friendlier. "Let me be clear," he said in a voice so low no one else could hear. "I cannot control the French commander of Sarajevo Sector.* He gets his guidance directly from Janvier, and you know what that means."

We returned to Belgrade, again via Italy. If anyone was counting, observed Chris Hill, we had been in four different countries (and in Italy and Serbia twice) during the day. But we still had another three hours of talks with Milosevic ahead of us, accompanied by another heavy dinner. Milosevic seemed unconcerned about the general military situation. When Pardew and Clark told him that the Bosnian Serb forces in the west had fallen apart, he did not argue. Instead, he urged us again to convene an international peace conference in the United States as quickly as possible.

Milosevic was proud of his knowledge of America, and particularly admired the motorcycle daredevil Evel Knievel. Referring to one of Knievel's most famous (and unsuccessful) stunts, I responded, "You can't leap the Grand Canyon in two jumps. It's too early for a conference. The gap between the sides is still too great to bring you together." Milosevic shrugged; he would keep trying.

The House with Only a Roof. The next morning, September 19, we convened the Tudjman-Izetbegovic meeting in Zagreb. In the two days since we had arranged the gathering, its urgency had increased because of an unexpected military setback for the Croatians. Regular units of the Croatian Army had encountered heavy Serb resistance and high water while trying to cross the Una River on the Croatian-Bosnian border. For the first time since the offensive began, Croatian casualties had been significant, some twenty-five killed and fifty still trapped on the opposite bank. The Danish battalion in UNPROFOR, caught in the middle of the fighting, had suffered two killed and eight wounded. Furious at this violation of an international border by the Croatian Army, General Rupert Smith called to tell me that he was considering a request for NATO air strikes *against the Croatians*—more a proof of his understandable rage than a real possibility.

This first serious military setback visibly changed the Croatian mood. The aggressiveness two days earlier had been replaced with a more cautious attitude. In addition, the Bosnian Serb Army had begun to stabilize its lines, encouraged by Mladic's return to the front from his Belgrade hospital bed. Intelligence reports said Mladic was digging in east of Banja Luka with heavy artillery—ironically, weapons redeployed after being withdrawn from the

* Ironically, the man he was referring to was General Bachelet, who had been so helpful to us on Mount Igman.

Sarajevo area in accordance with our agreement. Banja Luka, swollen with refugees, still lay near the Croatian front lines, but already it seemed less open to a quick strike. The Federation would have to fight for it, which meant a big artillery battle; the Croatians, having prevented the Muslims from obtaining heavy artillery throughout the war, had the only long guns. Thus the decision on Banja Luka lay almost entirely with Tudjman.

The September 19 meeting between the two Presidents, held in a large conference room in Tudjman's palace, began badly. Izetbegovic was three hours late from Sarajevo, and this left Tudjman fuming, though the reason for the delay—bad weather, bad roads—seemed understandable enough. Except for Galbraith, none of us had ever seen the two men together before, and their intense personal animosity was worse than we had imagined.

Tudjman began aggressively. His appetite for conquest had diminished since his troops had been trapped on the river, but his anger at his Bosnian allies was ugly. "*We* have suffered the casualties, and we liberated eighty percent of this territory ourselves," he shouted contemptuously across the table at the diminutive Bosnian President, as forty people listened in astonishment. "Now you demand we turn over to you towns that belong to Croatia, that Croatians freed. You insist we capture areas and then turn them over to you. This is simply unacceptable." Izetbegovic shrank back into his chair, saying nothing. I watched in horror, listening through earphones to a frantic simultaneous translation. As Galbraith observed later, "It was like observing a therapy session through a one-way mirror."

Sacirbey, seated next to me, whispered urgently, "You've got to stop this. Take over before it's too late." I asked permission to make a comment, and both Presidents abruptly turned toward me. It was suddenly clear that they wanted the United States to tell them what to do—a strange moment, which we often recalled later. An aspect of the Balkan character was revealed anew: once enraged, these leaders needed outside supervision to stop themselves from self-destruction.

I began by reminding them that the main purpose of this meeting was to bring the two parts of the Federation back together. With the recent territorial gains, there was a real chance for success—but only if the Federation worked. Fighting between Croats and Muslims at Bosanski Petrovac, and the tensions over who would control each newly recaptured area, benefited only the Serbs. We could not go to a peace conference with a divided Federation.

I repeated my objections to the capture of Banja Luka, stressing that I was talking *only* about Banja Luka, and not about the rest of the offensive. Izetbegovic said nothing. This was Tudjman's decision. Listening for a moment, Tudjman turned to Izetbegovic, and asked, quite calmly, "Shall we agree with Ambassador Holbrooke?" With a shrug, Izetbegovic agreed.

Surprised at the speed with which the issue had been resolved—and the equally rapid change in Tudjman's mood—I proposed we make a joint announcement immediately after the meeting. Tudjman suggested that we make the announcement ourselves, and not in the presence of either Izetbegovic or himself. As usual, the leaders wanted to leave the impression that the Americans had pressured them to do what they probably would have done anyway.

As we left the meeting, I pulled Defense Minister Susak aside. "Gojko, I want to be absolutely clear," I said. "Nothing we said today should be construed to mean that we want you to stop the rest of the offensive, other than Banja Luka. Speed is important. We can't say so publicly, but please take Sanski Most, Prijedor, and Bosanski Novi. And do it quickly, before the Serbs regroup!"

The press was waiting outside the Presidential Palace. I told them that the two Presidents had asked the United States to announce that the offensive would not be aimed at Banja Luka. I pointedly made no mention of any other targets. However, most news stories that day left the impression that we had forced the Bosnians and Croats to "halt their victorious sweep through western and central Bosnia."* Normally we would have tried to correct these stories, but since they sent the public message Washington wanted, we left them uncorrected.

Months later, Roger Cohen would write in *The New York Times Magazine* that preventing an attack on Banja Luka was "an act of consummate Realpolitik" on our part, since letting the Federation take the city would have "derailed" the peace process.

Cohen, one of the most knowledgeable journalists to cover the war, misunderstood our motives in opposing an attack on Banja Luka. A true practitioner of Realpolitik would have encouraged the attack regardless of its human consequences. In fact, humanitarian concerns decided the case for me. Given the harsh behavior of Federation troops during the offensive, it seemed certain that the fall of Banja Luka would lead to forced evictions and random murders. I did not think the United States should contribute to the creation of new refugees and more human suffering in order to take a city that would have to be returned later. Revenge might be a central part of the ethos of the Balkans, but American policy could not be party to it. Our responsibility was to implement the American national interest, as best as we could determine it. But I am no longer certain we were right to oppose an attack on Banja Luka. Had we known then that the Bosnian Serbs would have been able to defy or ignore so many of

* *The Washington Post,* September 20, 1995, p. A1. One exception was Stephen Kinzer of *The New York Times,* who got it right.

the key political provisions of the peace agreement in 1996 and 1997, the negotiating team might not have opposed such an attack. However, even with American encouragement, it is by no means certain that an attack would have taken place—or, if it had, that it would have been successful. Tudjman would have had to carry the burden of the attack, and the Serb lines were already stiffening. The Croatian Army had just taken heavy casualties on the Una. Furthermore, if it fell, Banja Luka would either have gone to the Muslims or been returned later to the Serbs, thus making it of dubious value to Tudjman.

There was another intriguing factor in the equation—one of the few things that Milosevic and Izetbegovic had agreed on. Banja Luka, they both said, was the center of moderate, anti-Pale sentiment within the Bosnian Serb community, and should be built up in importance as a center of opposition to Pale. Izetbegovic himself was ambivalent about taking the city. This view was, it turned out, accurate.

After meeting in Zagreb in the late afternoon with British Foreign Secretary Malcolm Rifkind, who was touring the region, we flew back to Belgrade that night for dinner and one more session with Milosevic before returning to Washington. It was still September 19. We needed Milosevic's agreement on a framework for the New York Foreign Ministers meeting, which we planned to hold September 26. Milosevic said that he would like to see us again before the New York meeting, and requested that I either return to Belgrade, or send Owen and Hill to discuss the draft agreement.

By the time our meeting with Milosevic ended, Rifkind had reached Belgrade, and, after midnight, I went to the British Embassy to brief him again on our talks. I was so tired I fell asleep while we were talking, but Rifkind graciously pretended not to notice. I even dozed off while answering a question.

Strobe Talbott had suggested that before I return to Washington, I send Warren Christopher a personal assessment of the negotiations—a "scene setter" for the meeting of the three Balkan Foreign Ministers on September 26 in New York. Christopher intended to make New York the scene of his first personal involvement in the negotiations, and Strobe particularly wanted me to explain why the military offensive was helping the peace process; there was, he said, a growing disagreement between us and Washington on this critical point. In another example of his intellectual honesty, Strobe included himself and Christopher in the group that "needed convincing." My informal handwritten note, sent by fax on September 20, was my first written message from the shuttle, after more than a month on the road:

> I suspect that the most dramatic phase of the offensive is coming to an end,
> and that the recent fluidity of the front lines will gradually be replaced by a re-

turn to a relatively stable front line. . . . Contrary to many press reports and other impressions, the Federation military offensive has so far helped the peace process. This basic truth is perhaps not something we can say publicly right now. . . . In fact, the map negotiation, which always seemed to me to be our most daunting challenge, is taking place right now on the battlefield, and so far, in a manner beneficial to the map. In only a few weeks, the famous 70%–30% division of the country has gone to around 50–50, obviously making our task easier. . . .

We recognize that two potential targets should be ruled off limits: Banja Luka and eastern Slavonia. On Tuesday [September 19] in Zagreb we succeeded in getting both Tudjman and Izzy to say to us simultaneously that they would not go to Banja Luka. Both used "the American peace plan" as the excuse for this sudden burst of restraint, even though it seems likely that they did not want to go for it anyway. . . .

After these two "prohibited zones," the issue of how far is enough [for the offensive] gets murkier. In the past we weakened our credibility by flashing so many "red lights" that no one knew which ones we meant. . . . If they take Sanski Most or Prijedor, both of which are in Federation hands in the Contact Group map but which Milosevic has said he will not yield in a negotiation, it would make our job easier. . . .

Finally, a word about our support. It has been superb all the way, the best I have ever seen in an important negotiation. While I resent some of the blind quotes of a personal nature in several recent articles, I know they do not come from the core team that is supporting us. You, Strobe, Peter, Tom [Donilon], John [Kornblum], Nick [Burns], and now Beth Jones* have been magnificent. Many thanks from all of us. See you in Washington.

---

* Elizabeth Jones, a career diplomat later appointed as Ambassador to Kazakhstan, had been added to our Washington backup team for a few months.

CHAPTER 12

Drama in New York

(September 18–26)

> "I like the Walrus best," said Alice: "because he was a *little* sorry for the poor oysters." "He ate more than the Carpenter, though," said Tweedledee. . . . "Well!" [said Alice] "They were *both* very unpleasant characters."
>
> —LEWIS CARROLL, *Through the Looking-Glass*

WE WERE DETERMINED TO AVOID REPEATING in New York the chaos of Geneva. Yet, partly because of my own error of judgment, the New York Foreign Ministers meeting was nearly a complete disaster.

The drama surrounding New York would have surprised most journalists and outside observers, who had begun to impart a sense of inevitability to the negotiations. Their optimism was fueled by Administration officials who believed that when they talked to the press it was always necessary to emphasize the positive—which inevitably meant *over*emphasize the positive. Still, overstated or not, there was good news for the first time in four years. The city of Sarajevo was coming back to life. The aura of invincibility that surrounded the Serbs had been shattered. Milosevic, who had started the war because Bosnia had declared its independence from "Yugoslavia," had formally conceded in Geneva that Bosnia was an independent country, and had accepted its existing international boundaries.

Under these circumstances, Izetbegovic and his colleagues should have looked forward to New York as a chance to take another step forward. But they were disorganized and unfocused.

Meanwhile, Milosevic's first priority was the lifting of economic sanctions against his country. He favored an early international conference at which the three Presidents would sign an agreement of "no more than two or three pages" and freeze the contending armies in place. He wanted to keep the political provisions of any peace agreement ambiguous and limited, and restrict the functions and authority of a central government. His goal was to create a situation similar to Cyprus or the two Koreas—a land in which a temporary dividing line becomes a seemingly permanent one.

This was not what we had in mind; if and when we invited the three Balkan Presidents to a conference, it would be with the clear intention of reaching a comprehensive peace agreement, not another weak, meaningless set of general principles that would be forgotten or ignored as soon as the conference adjourned.

Not for the first or the last time, Tudjman was the critical variable. He had a clear sense of what he wanted: first, to regain eastern Slavonia; second, to create an ethnically pure Croatia; and third, to maintain maximum influence, if not control, over the Croat portion of Bosnia. The Croatian President disliked both Milosevic and Izetbegovic, but his leverage over Sarajevo was substantial; the Croats in Izetbegovic's government, including the most important, Federation President Kresimir Zubak, usually followed "guidance" from Zagreb. The veteran British journalist Misha Glenny, who had covered the Balkans for years, was one of the first to recognize publicly the importance of Zagreb. In a perceptive article for the *New York Times* op-ed page published just before the New York meeting, entitled, "And the Winner Is . . . Croatia," Glenny praised our negotiating efforts but noted that, under any peace settlement, "Sarajevo will be utterly dependent on Croatia economically." He concluded: "The champagne corks can be opened in Zagreb—nowhere else."

Washington: The Bureaucratic Game. We had spent only one working day in Washington in the last three weeks. When we returned, we found that interest in our activities had increased substantially. Agencies and individuals that had paid us little attention now wanted to be part of the process. For example, the Agency for International Development (AID), asserting that it would have to carry out the reconstruction program, sought a major role in the negotiations. Some agencies or bureaus wanted to place representatives on the delegation; we fended them off on the grounds that our plane was too small. Tony Lake talked about creating a committee, under NSC direction, to oversee our efforts.

We were concerned that if the unprecedented degree of flexibility and autonomy we had been given by Washington were reduced, and we were subjected to the normal Washington decision-making process, the negotiations would become bogged down. At the same time, our small team was tired and understaffed. With only five days left until the New York meetings, we needed help, but I did not want to increase the size of the core team or relinquish our autonomy.

Faced with similar challenges in earlier crises, some administrations had created secret bypass mechanisms that kept information and authority within a small group—but also deceived or cut out everyone else. Most famously, when Kissinger was National Security Advisor, he had frequently ignored the entire State Department—once making a secret trip to Moscow without the knowledge of the American Ambassador, and regularly withholding almost all information about his secret discussions with China from the Secretary of State. We did not want to arouse the kind of distrust and intrigue that, as a result, had marred the Nixon-Kissinger period—an atmosphere Kissinger told me that in retrospect he regretted.

To avoid this classic bureaucratic dilemma, John Kornblum set up a small, informal team to support our efforts. As we envisioned it, the group would be, in effect, an extension of the negotiating team, but located in Washington. We drew on people outside the European Bureau, but insisted they work solely for Kornblum on this particular project. This meant that its participants, with the prior agreement of their superiors, would have to agree *not* to process drafts through the regular interagency "clearance process," which, while essential to the normal functioning of government, was too cumbersome and time-consuming for a fast-moving negotiation.

What Kornblum and I proposed was highly unusual, and could be derailed by forceful objections from a number of people. But Warren Christopher, with the strong encouragement of Talbott and Donilon, protected us. Christopher believed firmly in backing his negotiators, even if he did not agree with all their positions; this was fundamental to the man and shaped his attitude toward his role as the captain of the State Department. He, Strobe, and Tom regularly held off efforts by others to get involved in too many details. Without their support, the process would probably have resembled the one that had taught me such a strong negative lesson in Paris in 1968.

Sandy Berger also protected the negotiations. Several times a week, he chaired Deputies' Committee meetings on Bosnia. At every meeting, Kornblum would bring the national security apparatus up to date on our activities, while keeping at arm's length efforts to interfere in them. Sandy handled this deftly, keeping everyone sufficiently involved so that the Kissingerian problem—cutting people out—was avoided.

Kornblum's core group consisted primarily of lawyers: Jim O'Brien, who was part of Madeleine Albright's Washington office; Tim Ramish, the legal adviser for Europe; Miriam Sapiro, a lawyer on Jim Steinberg's Policy Planning staff; John Burley, a lawyer in the European Bureau; Laurel Miller, a lawyer in Bob Owen's firm who worked pro bono; and Lloyd Cutler, the former Counsel to both Presidents Carter and Clinton, who gave the group the perspective of a senior outsider with decades of experience.

Kornblum ran this backstop operation with skill. He had long been the Foreign Service's most experienced German hand, and was widely respected for his intellect. But in the Foreign Service "brilliant" is often a subtle code word for "arrogant," and, with his sharp wit and fierce advocacy, John had made some powerful bureaucratic enemies during his long career. Because he had gone without a promotion for a lengthy period, under State Department regulations he was within a year of being forced into early retirement—a result not of any career problems, but of a State Department budget so sharply reduced by Congress that promotions at higher levels had virtually ceased. This strange regulation had originally been designed to force deadwood out of the senior Foreign Service, and was now driving out some of the country's most qualified diplomats simply because they had been promoted early and then run into a general promotion slowdown caused by budgetary constraints.

From the beginning, we worked as a seamless team; I could turn a problem or a meeting over to him in midsentence and he would pick it up without a moment's pause. I felt a strong intellectual kinship with him, and greatly respected his superior knowledge of Europe.

On September 21, the day after we returned from the region, Tony Lake convened a meeting in the White House. He said that the "red lights" that Washington had conveyed to Zagreb and Sarajevo to end the offensive were extremely important and should continue to be emphasized. I wondered if Lake was aware of our conversations with Tudjman and Izetbegovic about continuing the offensive. Kerrick, Clark, and Pardew had kept their home offices informed, and my message to Christopher and Talbott the previous day had discussed the subject in detail.

"I want to be frank in the privacy of this room," I replied. "We asked them not to take Banja Luka, but we did not give the Croatians and the Bosnians any other 'red lights.' On the contrary, our team made no effort to discourage them from taking Prijedor and Sanski Most and other terrain that is theirs on the Contact Group map. The map negotiations are taking place on the battlefield right now, and that is one of the reasons we have not delayed our territorial discussions. It would help the negotiations greatly if these towns fell."

"I am very concerned that we will be blamed publicly for encouraging more fighting and more bloodshed," Tony said. "We should emphasize peace. This may not be your view, but you should say it in a way that doesn't exacerbate differences on other fronts, like with the Russians."

Christopher said he agreed with Tony as far as public statements went. I had no problem with that; the negotiating team had been careful in public, so much so that journalists in the region continued to think, and report, that we were trying to stop the entire offensive. But I refused to try to stop the offensive.

I was puzzled by Tony's comments. Was he objecting to the position we had taken in Zagreb, or was he simply worrying that it might leak? It was never clear, either to me or to my colleagues, including Christopher, who told me later that his only concern was that we not seem publicly to be encouraging the offensive.

After the meeting, Christopher, Lake, and I spoke briefly by telephone with the President, who was traveling in California. "I want you to make an all-out effort for peace," the President said. He asked me to return to Bosnia as soon as the New York meeting ended. Late that evening, in a radio call-in show with Larry King, the President was asked about Bosnia. "I feel better than I have in a long time," he said. "I feel good about the process, but I want to caution the American people that this is Bosnia and we have a long way to go."

Congress. The Hill can never be taken for granted. Without its support, it is virtually impossible to construct and carry out policy on a controversial issue—and nothing is more controversial than placing American troops in harm's way. Now that there was a real possibility of deploying American troops to Bosnia, Congress wanted to be heard. Bob Dole had made Bosnia his personal project, but he was relatively quiet at this point; since he had long attacked the Administration for weakness, he was not in a position to oppose a stronger policy. Other critics of the policy, like Senator Joe Lieberman and Senator Joe Biden, who were both Democrats, held their fire, waiting to see what would happen next.

The first warning shot came on the same day as the White House meeting, September 21, during what was supposed to be a routine hearing by the Senate Armed Services Committee to approve a second tour of duty for General Shalikashvili as Chairman of the Joint Chiefs of Staff. It was fortunate for the Administration that the first person to testify on American troop deployments was Shalikashvili, rather than a civilian; his low-key style and ramrod bearing, combined with his unquestionable patriotism and integrity, made him the most credible witness we could have.

Leading the skeptics were three of the Senate's most independent-minded Republicans: John McCain of Arizona, John Warner of Virginia, and William Cohen of Maine.* "Administration officials," reported *The New York Times* the next day, "were surprised by the breadth of Republican opposition to their intentions." The *Times* noted that Shalikashvili "seemed momentarily taken aback by the criticism," but he responded to it vigorously. "We cannot come in and out of the alliance and choose to lead when it's to our benefit, and let them take the lead when we don't wish to," he said. "Absent America's leadership role, things still don't get put together right."

The Senators kept Shalikashvili under polite but persistent pressure. "Why can't the Europeans carry out these peacekeeping duties themselves?" asked McCain, a former Vietnam prisoner of war whose courage and integrity were

* Cohen became Secretary of Defense during President Clinton's second term.

unsurpassed in the Senate. Cohen worried about "the consequences to NATO itself if U.S. forces are caught in a cross fire and American public opinion turns against the operation." These and similar questions gave clear warning that an intense effort on the Hill would be necessary.

Just before our team returned from the region, Kornblum had invited French and Russian officials separately to Washington to discuss a postsettlement military and civilian structure. The British also began discussions with us on the same subject. From the outset, there was agreement that the senior military commander on the ground would have to be an American, or else Congress would not approve U.S. troop deployments.

But what about the chief civilian in Bosnia, the person who would have the difficult task of implementing whatever settlement was reached? Not surprisingly, the Europeans wanted this position for one of their own. There were good arguments on both sides of this issue, but it was not decided on its merits, or on the basis of Bosnia itself. The critical variable would be who paid for the civilian effort.

Here domestic politics collided with Bosnia policy, and the timing could not have been worse. As Leon Panetta had predicted exactly a month earlier during the discussion at Fort Myer, the Administration and Congress were heading into the biggest budget confrontation between the two branches in this century—one so serious that by November it would lead to a shutdown of most of the U.S. government. The President's domestic advisors warned that getting *any* funds approved for Bosnia would be extraordinarily difficult. The only exception to this would be the military budget. The Europeans, members of Congress told us, must pay for reconstruction in Bosnia.

Under these circumstances, Berger and the Deputies' Committee decided that the chief civilian had to be a European. In taking this decision, they recognized that we would significantly reduce our control over one of the most important aspects of the effort. But there was really little choice. Reluctantly—because civilian implementation would be just as important as the military effort—I agreed with Sandy's conclusion. We informed the Europeans, who began to look for the right person to head the civilian effort.

The situation also gave U.N. Secretary-General Boutros-Ghali a chance to start the U.N.'s disengagement from Bosnia, something he had long wanted to do. After a few meetings with him, I concluded that this elegant and subtle Egyptian, whose Coptic family could trace its origins back over centuries,*

---

* See *Egypt's Road to Jerusalem: A Diplomat's Story of the Struggle for Peace in the Middle East,* by Boutros Boutros-Ghali, which contains frequent references to "my own awareness of my family's long tradition," and "its many generations [of] rich tradition of service to the country" (pp. 6, 7, et al.).

had disdain for the fractious and dirty peoples of the Balkans. Put bluntly, he never liked the place. In 1992, during his only visit to Sarajevo, he made the comment that had shocked the journalists on the day I arrived in the beleaguered capital: "Bosnia is a rich man's war. I understand your frustration, but you have a situation here that is better than ten other places in the world. . . . I can give you a list." He complained many times that Bosnia was eating up his budget, diverting him from other priorities, and threatening the entire U.N. system. "Bosnia has created a distortion in the work of the U.N.," he said just before Srebrenica. Sensing that our diplomatic efforts offered an opportunity to disengage, he informed the Security Council on September 18 that he would be ready to end the U.N. role in the former Yugoslavia, and allow all key aspects of implementation to be placed with others. Two days later, he told Madeleine Albright that the Contact Group should create its own mechanisms for implementation—thus volunteering to reduce the U.N.'s role at a critical moment. Ironically, his weakness simplified our task considerably.

Countdown to New York. On September 22, I met for almost three hours with our backstop team to review the planning for the New York Foreign Ministers meeting. I asked them to try for a huge leap beyond Geneva—an agreement on the framework of a central government for Bosnia that both the Bosnian Serbs and the Federation would accept as the sole sovereign entity. Owen and Hill, with support from Jim O'Brien and Miriam Sapiro, had produced a draft agreement, which established many essential institutions: a division of responsibilities between the central government and the two entities, the Federation and Republika Srpska; elections for both the presidency and the national assembly; and the creation of a constitutional court. I explained our strategy to a reporter at the time: "If we can get a cease-fire, we'll take that. If we can get some more constitutional principles, we'll take them. If we can settle Sarajevo, we'll do it. We're inventing peace as we go."

Our plan was first to negotiate with Foreign Minister Muhamed Sacirbey in Washington, then to turn back to Belgrade. As at Geneva, nothing could be left unresolved prior to the meeting itself. Sacirbey wanted a strong presidency, with every detail of the final political structure spelled out in New York, whereas I continued to follow a step-by-step approach: find areas of agreement, lock them in with a public announcement, and then return to the region for another round of negotiations to narrow the differences further.

It was increasingly obvious that Sacirbey's distaste for Silajdzic was coloring his own behavior. After a day of contentious discussions with Owen and Hill, during which tempers flared repeatedly and Sacirbey threatened several times to "go public," the two men warned me that the Bosnian Foreign Minister would try to go around the delegation and get other American officials—

particularly Strobe, Madeleine, or Tony—to change our positions. Sacirbey also worked the Congress vigorously, often criticizing the Administration in conversations with Senators, some of whom promptly told us. As Strobe put it, "He goes public anyway, and he can't get around you."

Sacirbey's behavior irritated American officials during this trip. Many of his points had merit, but he left people uncertain of his goal. It was not entirely clear what drove Sacirbey: was he was trying to show his colleagues (and enemies) back home that he was a true Bosnian patriot despite having spent most of the war in New York? Was he positioning Izetbegovic for the struggle back home, or was he simply freelancing for the media?

As Sacirbey worked the town, Strobe Talbott was with his main Russian counterpart, Deputy Foreign Minister Georgi Mamedov, a witty and sophisticated man. The Talbott-Mamedov channel, low profile at the time, was the modern version of the special channel between Washington and Moscow that had existed from 1941 through the end of the Cold War, and now constituted the main vehicle for negotiating important issues between the two countries, including NATO enlargement, economic assistance, presidential summits, and sensitive political issues.*

Bosnia was a central part of "The Channel" as we entered the second month of our shuttle. On Friday, September 22, hoping to reduce the tensions between the Russians and the Bosnians, Strobe invited Sacirbey to meet Mamedov privately in his office.

Strobe began with an imaginative attempt to lighten the tension and create a bond between the two men. "You have something in common," he told them. "You both have Muslim heritage and the same name!" (Mamedov was a slavicized version of Muhamed, Sacirbey's first name.) Sacirbey was surprised. "So, you're one of us?" he asked. Mamedov, of part-Azeri background, laughed. "Well, by way of Baku," he replied.

Unfortunately, the rest of the meeting did not live up to this promising start. Each man had a position to defend, and, while pleasant, the conversation did not produce any breakthrough on either side.

During our last meeting in Belgrade, Milosevic had suggested that someone from the delegation return to Belgrade before the New York session to put direct pressure on the Bosnian Serbs—part, he said, of his "technology." Although it was Milosevic's responsibility to deliver the Pale Serbs, there was value to his suggestion. I asked Owen, Hill, Pardew, and John Burley from State's Balkan desk to return to Belgrade after only two days in Washington.

---

* Although it had existed in other forms for decades, Henry Kissinger gave "The Channel" its name when it was conducted by him and Soviet Ambassador Anatoly Dobrynin. See *White House Years,* by Henry Kissinger, p. 141.

The three men reached Belgrade on Saturday, September 23. Milosevic, upset by some of the changes Sacirbey had proposed, asked them to meet with Karadzic and Krajisnik. This was the "technology" that Milosevic so enjoyed. But, as the discussion progressed, the Americans realized that the Pale Serbs had not really accepted the central concession to which Milosevic had committed them at Geneva—that Bosnia would remain a single state. Karadzic demanded the right to vote for secession, and, showing an unexpected flair for metaphor, said that a single Bosnia would be "a wooden oven which would burn itself up the first time it was used." He attacked every provision of Owen's draft designed to create national structures. He objected to the election provisions, refused to discuss the "competency" of the central government, and insisted that the Bosnian Serbs have a separate foreign policy and their own embassies. A meeting that was supposed to be mere "technology" turned into another marathon sixteen-hour negotiation, during which the American team rejected every Karadzic effort to legitimize a divided Bosnia.

Reaching an impasse on Sunday afternoon, Owen and Hill asked Milosevic, who had left the Americans alone with the Bosnian Serbs, to return. While the Americans waited in the gardens, Milosevic engaged in his usual routine of outmaneuvering and intimidating the rest of the Serbs. He then summoned the Americans back into the room, and produced an agreement close to the one we had negotiated with Sacirbey. Owen and Hill agreed, however, to drop the word "direct" in the clause describing elections for the presidency and the national assembly. They also agreed to soften the language on the functions of the central government.

Calling just before they left Belgrade on Sunday, September 24, Owen and Hill told us that despite some "minor changes" the basic elements of the Further Agreed Principles were intact. I congratulated them and requested that they fax us the new draft right away. By this time, I was at the Waldorf-Astoria in New York to meet foreign ministers from other countries, accompanied by Rosemarie and Christopher Hoh, who worked for Chris Hill. Anticipating a day of intense communications with the field, I asked Philip S. Goldberg to go to the State Department early Sunday morning to handle telephone calls, then come to New York later in the day. Goldberg and Hoh were two of the best younger American diplomats: candid in private, reliable, and dedicated.

Sacirbey remained in Washington that Sunday morning for a meeting with Lake, Tarnoff, Fuerth, Kerrick, and Sandy Vershbow. Sacirbey said the draft agreement he had negotiated in Washington was fine, but he warned that Izetbegovic was upset about the Owen-Hill-Pardew trip to Belgrade. "The negotiating team has been contaminated by the Belgrade air," Sacirbey said. He was not joking. "My President is not going to tolerate your people going to Belgrade all the time. The optics are bad. You must spend more time in Sarajevo." He was not moved when Tarnoff noted that Owen and Hill had spent two days with Silajdzic in Sarajevo on the document, as well as an entire day with Sacirbey himself in Washington.

Peter called immediately to alert me to the problem, but it still seemed just another Balkan bluff; I did not see how serious it was. By this time, Owen, Hill, and Pardew had started home in their small military jet. But as the negotiators flew west over Europe, Izetbegovic announced that Sacirbey "has been instructed not to attend" the meeting in New York, less than forty-eight hours away. "The Serbian side has demanded wholesale changes which radically alter the agreement," Sacirbey told the press waiting outside the White House. A White House press spokeswoman, Mary Ellen Glynn, skillfully downplayed the difficulty, calling it "part of the ups and downs of shuttle diplomacy." As far as I could tell, however, this was all "downs."

More bad news followed immediately, in the form of a fax from Belgrade with the revised draft agreement. As soon as he saw the changes, Phil Goldberg warned that, while not substantial, they would be treated as "big" in Sarajevo. Later, we learned that Sacirbey had never sent the changes he made in Washington on September 22 to Sarajevo for approval. I felt the New York meeting slipping out of control.

In diplomacy process can often be as important as substance. This is especially true early on, when longtime adversaries are prone to maximize differences rather than reach out for agreements. Such was the case at that moment; we had been sloppy in not planning a stop in Sarajevo for Owen, Hill, and Pardew. Now we were paying the price. I blamed myself for three basic errors. First, I should have asked our team to reject any changes, no matter how small, in Belgrade. Second, even though we saw far more of the Muslims than the Serbs, many of our meetings were outside Sarajevo, and we had unintentionally left a public impression that we were spending more time with Milosevic than Izetbegovic; our team should have gone to Sarajevo. We also erred in thinking that Sacirbey could speak for the entire Bosnian government.

We needed to find a way to get the Sarajevo government back on track quickly, or the New York meeting would collapse, unleashing a cycle of disagreements and perhaps even a re-escalation of the war.

I had a desperate idea. Could we turn the Owen-Hill-Pardew team around in midair, and get them to Sarajevo in time to save the New York session? Goldberg and I realized our colleagues had not yet reached their refueling stop in Ireland. Goldberg gave the Operations Center and the National Military Command Center an urgent task: find the plane, get us in touch with it, turn it around.

We were in luck; Goldberg and the OpsCenter found the Irish official who ran the VIP room at Shannon; he knew us well from our frequent stopovers. The plane had just landed, and the official soon located our colleagues.

As we talked, Hill and Owen, unshaven and ragged, huddled around a green "Dial Your Relatives in America" shamrock-shaped pay phone, located next to the "Ladies' Toilet."

"Chris," I said, "you have to go back to Sarajevo. You have to go back. We will lose the agreement unless you get Izetbegovic back on board." They were halfway home, utterly exhausted. Now they were being asked to turn around in the middle of the night. It was not hard to sense Hill's fatigue and unhappiness. "Chris," I said, "let me talk to Bob."

I could hear Hill ask Owen if he wanted to talk to me, and, more faintly, Owen's dry, dignified voice saying, "Not much." Then he came on the phone. Anticipating his first question, I told him I had already talked to the Secretary of State and he shared my view. This provoked audible snorting at the other end of the phone, and a comment that they had allowed only "minor changes" in Belgrade. "Bob," I shouted into the phone, "there is no such thing as 'minor changes' in the Balkans!"

Although exhausted, they turned around and headed back across Europe, stopping in Ramstein, Germany, to switch to a C-130 flight to Sarajevo. After a sleepless wait, they were told that the only available transport plane was in Italy. After more difficulties at the Italian air base, they boarded a British C-130 and headed for Sarajevo at 7:30 A.M. Before leaving Ancona, Hill called Goldberg and me through the OpsCenter. It was 2:30 in the morning in New York, and both Phil and I sleepily understood that the call's primary reason was to make us share their exhaustion. "Do you realize how difficult this is for us?" Hill asked.

Hill said later he would never forget my answer. Just as I had visualized him at the shamrock-shaped pay phone in Shannon, he imagined me in a fancy suite at the Waldorf. "Look," I said, "you're in Ancona and I'm up at 2:30 A.M. We're all inconvenienced. We're having a difficult time here too. Now go get the Bosnians on board."

Owen, Hill, and Pardew finally arrived in Sarajevo on Monday morning, September 25. The meetings highlighted the widening split within the Bosnian government. An angry Haris Silajdzic immediately chastised them for dealing only with Sacirbey. "Do not believe," the Prime Minister said, "that you can reach an agreement without me."

The Bosnian government's opposition was caused not by the language changes in Belgrade but by a change of heart on the part of Silajdzic. After thinking further about the draft language he had approved on September 15, Haris told Owen and Hill that he now felt it was "too American"; the presidency was too powerful. He now favored a more "European" system; that is, one with a strong prime minister and a weak presidency. Silajdzic's annoyance was directed at Sacirbey, not the Serbs; he felt that the draft approved by the Foreign Minister, Izetbegovic's political ally, had been designed to weaken him. So deep was Silajdzic's anger that he insisted on a separate meeting with the three Americans, and refused to participate in their session with Izetbegovic.

To solve this impasse, Owen and Hill redrafted the New York document in such a way as to gain the support of both Bosnian factions and still be acceptable to the Serbs. They fell back on our standard approach of deferring the most difficult issues and focusing instead on general principles embraced by all, which could be made more specific later. As soon as we heard from Owen that the Bosnians had accepted the revised draft, Christopher called Izetbegovic to thank him. Izetbegovic assured him that Sacirbey would now attend the New York meeting.

But once unleashed, the cycle of demands for changes in the agreement could not easily be stopped. As soon as he read the revised election language from Sarajevo, Phil Goldberg said, "The Serbs will never accept this." He was right again. Hill sensed this as well; as he changed planes in Ancona on his way back to New York, he called the OpsCenter and left a short message: "Tell Holbrooke to call Milosevic over the elections provisions. They are going to cause a big problem."

It was now midday on Monday, September 25, and everyone was converging on New York. With concern in Washington rising, Christopher and I went to the teleconference room of the U.S. Mission to the United Nations, along with Madeleine Albright, to brief the President and the rest of the principals. Then Christopher, Albright, and I met with the three Balkan Foreign Ministers for a courtesy call. The meeting was short and perfunctory. To the press, Christopher was upbeat; but once they had left, the meeting became tense, with Christopher urging agreement, and then closing down the meeting before the three Foreign Ministers could start arguing with one another.

Working from my Waldorf hotel suite, Don Kerrick, Phil Goldberg, and I spent most of the next six hours on the telephone, alternating between Milosevic and Izetbegovic. Milosevic argued that he had reached an agreement in good faith with Owen, Hill, and Pardew and that he could not change it again. Milosevic was most adamant on the question of "direct" elections; having gotten it out of the draft, he did not want it to reappear. He also objected to elections by "popular vote," another clause that had been reinserted in Sarajevo.

Between phone calls, I saw Sacirbey. The meeting came closer to physical violence than any other during our long negotiations. I asked him if, for the sake of overall progress, he and his government could drop the "direct" clause for presidential elections. Even the United States, I pointed out, did not elect its president directly. Sacirbey said that without the precise word the Serbs could create "sham elections."

"That's nonsense, Mo," I said. "The Geneva principles guarantee international supervision of the elections. This is not the defining test of a democracy." Nothing in the draft precluded direct elections, I told Sacirbey; if we did not get them now, we would insist on them in the next round.

Sacirbey asked to call his President. We gave him some privacy, and he talked with Izetbegovic. When we resumed, he was angry and immovable. Without the direct-elections clause, there could be no agreement.

The atmosphere in the room grew tense. Sacirbey enjoyed a spirited, rowdy relationship with many of us, and we often expressed ourselves in rather rough-and-tumble terms. But this time the mood slipped over the edge, and the exchange became ugly. Without warning, Sacirbey slammed his jacket down on the sofa, stood up, and started for the door, yelling that the United States was betraying his country. "If you leave in this way, you will do your country immense damage," I responded, following him. He was in a rage, and for a moment it seemed to Goldberg and Kerrick that he was going to hit me. Kerrick stepped quickly between us, then moved smoothly into the hotel corridor to block Sacirbey's departure. As Sacirbey started out the door, he saw two dumbfounded journalists in the corridor watching this amazing scene. The sight of the journalists, and Kerrick's physical presence, seemed to calm Sacirbey slightly, and Don eased him back into the room. We shut the door again and managed to finish the meeting on relatively civil terms, but without any progress.

I called Izetbegovic as soon as Sacirbey had left. "Mr. President," I said, "we are on the brink of a disaster. You will gain a great deal from this agreement, and we will negotiate later to get direct elections. You are giving up nothing." He said he had to have the direct-elections clause. It was already after midnight in Sarajevo, and Izetbegovic disliked working at night. I gave up, ending with the hope that we could make progress in the morning.

Milosevic was, in this area as in so many others, the exact opposite of Izetbegovic. He enjoyed late-night drama, perhaps in part because his stamina and ability to hold liquor often gave him an additional edge over others at that time. Seeing we were in a hole, he stuck to his guns on the elimination of the direct-elections clause.

Kerrick, Goldberg, and I were drained. I called Christopher and asked if he would make a last-ditch call to Izetbegovic with me very early the next morning.

Tuesday, September 26. I arrived in our staff room at the Waldorf at 5:30 A.M. and was joined by Goldberg. It took almost an hour to reach Izetbegovic. When we finally connected, Christopher and I asked him to defer the question of direct elections, provided Milosevic would give up the reference that appeared to limit the role of the central government. After a few minutes of discussion, Izetbegovic agreed. We thought we were out of the woods.

The meeting of the Balkan Foreign Ministers was scheduled to start at 10:00 A.M. in the twelfth-floor conference room of the United States Mission to the United Nations on First Avenue, facing U.N. headquarters. The room, although less imposing, had been set up to resemble the one in Geneva. Fearing a repetition of Sacirbey's last-minute dramatics in Geneva, I sent Phil Goldberg to the Bosnian's offices to make sure that Sacirbey showed up on time. At 9:30 A.M., as our European colleagues were arriving at the twelfth floor, he called. "We've got a big problem," he said, speaking in a low voice. "Mo isn't going to agree. You'd better speak to him."

Sacirbey came on the line. He would attend the meeting, but he could not accept the agreement. I told him that there had to be a misunderstanding; the Secretary of State had just talked to his President, and everything was all set. No, said Sacirbey, "*I've* just talked to *my* President, and he told me not to agree."

It was Geneva all over again—a last-minute problem with the Bosnians. Racing down one flight of stairs to Albright's office, where Christopher had set up headquarters for the morning, I told him, Madeleine, and Tom Donilon what had happened. Moments later Goldberg arrived with Sacirbey and brought him directly to Albright's office.

Warren Christopher was famously a polite man who almost never raised his voice or showed personal discourtesy of any sort. But we were about to see an amazing sight. Sacirbey walked in smiling, said, "Hello, Chris," and stretched out his hand. Christopher ignored it, holding his own arms stiffly at his side. "What the hell is going on here?" he said in a voice just barely containing his fury. "I made an agreement with your President just two hours ago."

Taken aback by Christopher's anger, Sacirbey tried to explain that the Bosnian government had overruled Izetbegovic, but the more he talked, the more resistant Christopher became. "This cannot stand," he told Sacirbey. Albright, whose close relationship with Sacirbey dated from his U.N. ambassadorship, tried to reason with him, but to no avail. After fifteen minutes of useless argument, I pointed out that over one hundred journalists and officials from five nations were waiting for us upstairs. We had to join them.

Warren Christopher opened the meeting with brief remarks urging the parties to seize "this moment in history [to] end the fighting and end it for good." The photographers clicked away, and the press was ushered out. Immediately, to the surprise of nearly everyone in the room, I adjourned the meeting, whispered to Granic and Milutinovic that we had a problem with Sarajevo—this brought a gleam of real pleasure to the Serbian's eye—and asked the Contact Group to join us downstairs. We gave each of the Foreign Ministers a private "holding" room on the same floor.

Still furious, Christopher left for meetings across the street at the United Nations. Before he departed, he told Sacirbey that the situation would have to be cleared up right away if Sarajevo wanted to avoid serious consequences to its relations with the United States. I met with Carl Bildt and the four Contact Group representatives, who were distressed at having been shunted around. Apologizing, I invited them to talk to Sacirbey, but their efforts to move him got nowhere.

Sacirbey was scheduled to deliver his speech to the U.N. at 11:30. I asked him not to reveal to the press that we were in a state of crisis. He promised— and walked out onto First Avenue into a sea of journalists, whom he promptly told that he would not accept any agreement that did not provide for "direct elections."

The Contact Group waited, eating sandwiches in the office of Madeleine Albright's deputy, Edward "Skip" Gnehm. When Sacirbey returned, he seemed buoyed up by his public appearance at the General Assembly. Speaking in the great hall had taken some of the edge out of him. He now presented himself as the person who could solve the problem. Christopher returned from his other meetings to rejoin the fray. After coordinating with Tony Lake, we told Sacirbey that President Clinton would speak to the nation at 3:00 P.M. He would either announce the agreement and praise the Bosnians, or he would state publicly that New York had failed because of Sarajevo's stubbornness.

Asking for a private room, Sacirbey called Izetbegovic to relay our ultimatum. For a long time we waited. Then he emerged. "If President Clinton will say in his statement that he strongly opposes partition," he said, "we will agree." Since this was an existing American position, we assented on the spot. We also promised to pursue the cause of direct elections in the future. We went back upstairs to hold a brief formal meeting with the Croatian and Serbian Foreign Ministers, who had been waiting for four hours, and adjourned.

At 3:50 P.M. on September 26, the President announced the agreement from the White House pressroom. "There is no guarantee of success," he said, "but today's agreement moves us closer to the ultimate goal, and it makes clear that Bosnia will remain a single internationally recognized state. America will strongly oppose the partition of Bosnia."

As soon as the President finished his short statement, we met with the press. We could finally show the skeptics that we were building a central government, at least on paper. We had agreed on a three-person presidency, a parliament, a constitutional court, and other important attributes of a national government. A great bridge had been crossed—but with more difficulty than we had expected, revealing even more clearly than before the troubling divisions within the Bosnian government.

We announced our return to the region in two days to resume the shuttle. To journalists who asked if we were now going to get a cease-fire agreement, I was noncommittal. The truth was, we didn't know.

Cease–fire

(September 27–October 5)

> When the people vote on war, nobody reckons
> On his own death; it is too soon; he thinks
> Some other man will meet that wretched fate.
> But if death faced him when he cast his vote,
> Hellas would never perish from battle-madness.
> And yet we men all know which of two words
> Is better, and can weigh the good and the bad
> They bring; how much better is peace than war!
>
> —EURIPIDES, *Suppliant Women*

Your Place or Ours? No one wanted to relive the near disaster in New York. But despite the drama and difficulties, the September 26 agreement, with its unprecedented provisions for a central governmental structure, went a long way toward answering those who had criticized the Geneva agreement as a partition deal.

As we embarked on the evening of September 28 on our fourth trip to the Balkans, shuttle diplomacy had begun to lose its momentum. The three Balkan Presidents would soon have to be brought together in an all-or-nothing, high-risk negotiation. But none of the three key issues for such a meeting had been determined: its timing, its connection to a cease-fire, and where the peace talks would be held. Washington would leave the first two issues to us, but the third required a presidential decision, and our team had a serious disagreement with most of Washington.

Before we left for the region, there was the usual round of meetings with Foreign Ministers and other officials. The most important session was with French Foreign Minister Hervé de Charette in his suite at the United Nations Plaza Hotel in New York. De Charette did not share President Chirac's friendly, open style, or his admiration for American culture. He was a classic high French official, elegant, aloof, always sensitive to real or imagined insults toward himself or France—a distinction that he did not seem to acknowledge.

Yet even though his mission was to show that France still stood at the pinnacle of influence in Europe, on the day before our meeting he said to a group of reporters: "As President Reagan once remarked, 'America is back.' " De Charette was under pressure from his colleagues to show that the Foreign Ministry still mattered. To the annoyance of many professional French diplomats, we had been handling sensitive issues directly with Chirac's small but efficient staff at the Élysée Palace, headed by Jean-David Levitte, a brilliant young diplomat who served as Chirac's national security advisor.

My meeting with de Charette was a microcosm of the complicated relationship between the United States and France. De Charette began with a complaint. "The French press," he said, "is saying that the United States had taken over the negotiations and left France standing on the sidelines." He expressed suspicion that we were already secretly arranging a peace conference in the United States. "It must be held in France," he said. "If not Paris, then in Évian on the Lake of Geneva. We can seal the resort hotels off from the press, and provide a calm and controlled atmosphere." He added that the European Union had agreed that France should host the peace talks—something both Germany and Britain firmly denied when asked a few days later.

I assured a skeptical de Charette that no decision had been made on the location or timing of the talks, but told him frankly that I favored an American site. De Charette proposed that we start the talks in the United States and move them to France after a predetermined time, say, two weeks. I said I did not think this would work, but added that perhaps we could consider a formal signing ceremony in France. As we left his hotel suite, de Charette took my arm and said, "This is very important to me and to France."

The issue of where the talks should be held had become the subject of a fierce internal dispute within the Administration. Our team's unanimous preference was for the United States, but this was a distinctly minority view in Washington. Most of our colleagues, with the exception of Tony Lake, wanted to hold the talks in Europe, preferably in Geneva, a city that symbolized to me unproductive diplomacy from the Indochina conference of 1954 to the endless rounds of Mideast and Cold War diplomacy. If we had to end up in Europe, my preference was for Stockholm, where Carl Bildt would be our host. At my request, Bildt started planning, in complete secret, for a conference at a resort hotel on Saltsjöbaden, an island not far from the Swedish capital.

The final decision would have to go to the President. Worried that the battle was already almost lost, I decided to appeal directly to Vice President Gore, who did not interfere casually in the normal processes of government. Gore returned my call while I was in a car on the way to La Guardia Airport. For security reasons, he asked that we talk on a land line, and so, from a pay phone at the airport, I made my case. Gore, who seemed surprised by my intensity on this issue, said he would consider it favorably. But, as we headed for Europe, the likelihood of a U.S. site seemed low.

The C-130 lumbered into Sarajevo from Italy at 8:00 A.M. on September 29. In the twelve days since our last trip there had been a visible improvement in the city. In the shadows of the shattered buildings the city streets were animated, even crowded. Streetcars were functioning, and barricades of wrecked cars were being dismantled. It is an unusual experience for a government official to see a direct and immediate connection between his efforts and the lives of ordinary people, but as we drove through the city we felt that our negotiations had already begun to make a difference.

For the first time, we raised the possibility of a cease-fire—without advocating it. Izetbegovic said he was not ready yet: the military trend in western Bosnia was still running in his favor. In fact, we agreed with him.

The U.N. Dilemma. In the first thirteen days after the lifting of the siege, General Rupert Smith had not opened either of the main roads leading out of Sarajevo, though this was one of the guarantees we had obtained from the Serbs on September 14. One of the roads ran through a Serb portion of Sarajevo that had been closed throughout the war, forcing all traffic to detour through a tiny, winding, and dangerous street. The Bosnian government publicly criticized the U.N. for leaving it dependent on what Silajdzic called "that notorious street."

The Bosnians were right. Frustrated, General Clark and I went to Smith's office after the meeting with Izetbegovic and urged him to open the main roads and dismantle all checkpoints. "General," I said, "you have a written commitment from the Serbs that these roads will be opened. If they resist, you can use force—but I don't think that will be necessary."

It was a replay of our last meeting. Smith, while far tougher than either Janvier or his predecessor, General Sir Michael Rose, did not appreciate our unsolicited advice, and responded forcefully. He was ready to run his own vehicles out of Sarajevo, but the U.N. had long been doing that. The risks, he said, would be his—not ours. He told us, as he had before, that he did not really control the French forces in Sarajevo Sector who would have to open the road. There were mines everywhere. He needed backing from Zagreb and U.N. headquarters in New York, both of which were passive or negative. Fighting was certain to break out. It would take time. And so on. As for the checkpoints, Smith thought eliminating them was impossible. "Bosnia is a country," he said with a dry laugh, "where every boy grows up with the dream that someday he will own his own checkpoint."

We understood Smith's predicament (and forevermore quoted his memorable line about checkpoints), but even Clark, who had great respect for his fellow general, was disheartened. If we failed to implement the September 14 agreement, its value would quickly be eroded by Serb encroachments and U.N. passivity.

To demonstrate America's determination to uphold that agreement, I asked John Menzies to send his Embassy staff on daily road trips from Sarajevo to Kiseljak. This was not, of course, a real test of the agreement, since the Serbs would not fire on a vehicle with an American flag and U.S. Embassy license plates, but at least it would show that the United States, for the first time in years, was using these roads.

The "Menzies patrols" produced several minor confrontations and small gains that demonstrated anew the necessity of applying continual pressure on the Serbs. Embassy staffers reported that the Serbs still maintained an armed checkpoint just outside Sarajevo. After a vigorous protest to Milosevic, who at first did not believe we cared about "such chickenshit," the checkpoint was opened and the barrier raised. This was an example of the new American approach. We would stand firm on every point, no matter how small.

Most American officials viewed Prime Minister Haris Silajdzic as the Bosnian leader with the broadest vision—an eloquent advocate of a multiethnic state. But his power struggles with Izetbegovic and Sacirbey and other members of the Bosnian government often isolated him. His colleagues complained that he was difficult to work with. He carried a serious additional burden: Tudjman and Milosevic distrusted him. Nevertheless, Silajdzic was one of the two most popular Muslim politicians in Bosnia, along with Izetbegovic.

My own feelings about Silajdzic shifted frequently. There was something touching about his intensity and energy, and his constant desire to improve himself intellectually. Although always busy, he seemed alone—his wife and son lived in Turkey. Silajdzic was the only Bosnian official who seemed genuinely to care about economic reconstruction of his ravaged land. His unpredictable moods worried us, but his support would be essential for any peace agreement. Chris Hill got it right: "If we have Haris's backing, we'll still have problems with Sarajevo," he said, "but they will be much reduced."

John Shattuck and Human Rights. The next morning, September 30, we flew to Belgrade, stopping first at the Zagreb airport for a short meeting with Ambassador Galbraith and John Shattuck, the Assistant Secretary of State for Democracy, Human Rights, and Labor. Wedging themselves into the plane's cabin, they gave us a vivid description of their trip the previous day to the Krajina in Croatia, and to Bosanski Petrovac and Kljuc, two towns in western Bosnia that had fallen to Federation forces. They had passed "end-less" streams of Serb refugees fleeing eastward to escape the advancing forces of the Federation. At Kljuc, two miles from the front, with the sound of big guns in the distance, they had visited a mass grave site, the first to which any Americans were given access. Shattuck had given a press conference criticizing Zagreb for creating a new refugee flow, this one composed of Serbs driven out of *their* ancestral homes in the Krajina. His press conference infuriated Tudjman.

The Human Rights Bureau faced a long tradition of resistance from the regional branches of the State Department on bureaucratic grounds. It was not surprising, therefore, that some people initially opposed Shattuck's involvement in Bosnia. But I disagreed: his trips could focus public attention on ethnic cleansing and other war crimes, and increase the pressure on Milosevic to stop these practices. After much discussion, Christopher had agreed to let Shattuck travel in the region under our direction, an arrangement that prevented the creation of overlapping negotiating channels.

Shattuck masked his determination with a dispassionate manner. He had taught at Harvard Law School and served on the board of Amnesty International, and he understood the media, to whom he made himself easily accessible. In the end even the skeptics in the European Bureau, who initially argued that human rights should be handled by the Embassies in the region, saw the value of John Shattuck's highly publicized, highly focused efforts.

John and I intentionally did not travel together. But in my meetings with Milosevic we added a new demand: that Shattuck be allowed to visit war-crimes sites and towns. Shattuck's trips would be a constant public reminder that even as we sought peace, we were not abandoning the quest for justice. When Milosevic saw we were serious, he agreed.

Arkan. Shattuck and I were particularly concerned with the activities of Zeljko Raznatovic, popularly known as Arkan, one of the most notorious men in the Balkans. Even in the former Yugoslavia, Arkan was something special, a freelance murderer who roamed across Bosnia and eastern Slavonia with his black-shirted men, terrorizing Muslims and Croats. To the rest of the world Arkan was a racist fanatic run amok, but many Serbs regarded him as a hero. His private army, the Tigers, had committed some of the war's worst atrocities, carrying out summary executions and virtually inventing ethnic cleansing in 1991–92. Western intelligence was convinced he worked, or had worked, for the Yugoslav secret police.[1]

The only mechanism for dealing with such problems was imperfect but vital: the International War Crimes Tribunal, located at The Hague. When it was established by the United Nations Security Council in 1993, the tribunal was widely viewed as little more than a public relations device. It got off to a slow start despite the appointment of a forceful and eloquent jurist, Richard Goldstone of South Africa, as its chief. Credit for pumping up its role in those early days went to Madeleine Albright and John Shattuck, who fought for its status and funding. Other nations, especially its Dutch hosts and the Germans, also gave it substantial support. During our negotiations, the tribunal emerged as a valuable instrument of policy that allowed us, for example, to bar Karadzic and all other indicted war criminals from public office. Yet no mechanism existed for the arrest of indicted war criminals.

Although the tribunal had handed down over fifty indictments by October 1995, these did not include Arkan. I pressed Goldstone on this matter several times, but because a strict wall separated the tribunal's internal deliberations from the American government, he would not tell us why Arkan had not been indicted. This was especially puzzling given Goldstone's stature and his public criticisms of the international peacekeeping forces for not arresting any of the indicted war criminals.* Whenever I mentioned Arkan's name to Milosevic, he seemed annoyed; he frowned and his eyes narrowed. He did not mind criticism of Karadzic or Mladic, but Arkan—who lived in Belgrade, ran a popular restaurant, and was married to a rock star—was a different matter. Milosevic dismissed Arkan as a "peanut issue," and claimed he had no influence over him. But Arkan's activities in western Bosnia decreased immediately after my complaints. This was hardly a victory, however, because Arkan at large remained a dangerous force and a powerful signal that one could still get away with murder—literally—in Bosnia.

Belgrade and Zagreb. Our Zagreb airport meeting with Shattuck and Galbraith completed, we were back in the familiar sitting room in Belgrade by late afternoon on September 30. "The time for a cease-fire is now," Milosevic said. Like Izetbegovic, he insisted that any peace conference be held in the United States.

When we returned to Zagreb early the next morning, October 1, Tudjman lashed out against Shattuck's criticisms of his government. "This is not correct behavior between nations who are partners and friends," he said bitterly. I replied simply that Shattuck had an obligation to tell the story the way he saw it, and we would not muzzle him. Besides, Serbs who had lived for generations in the Krajina and western Bosnia should be allowed to remain in their homes in peace.

---

* The first military action against an indicted war criminal did not come until June 10, 1997, when British troops in Prijedor captured one Bosnian Serb and killed another who had been named in sealed indictments by Goldstone's successor, the Canadian judge Louise Arbour.

With pressure for a cease-fire building, we urged Tudjman to do as much as possible militarily "in the next week or so." Again we focused on three key towns in the west: Sanski Most, Prijedor, and Bosanski Novi. This might be the Federation's last chance to capture them before we started negotiating. I urged joint operations with the Bosnians. "The Bosnians can't take territory on their own," Tudjman said, as he so often did. He was right, of course, but part of the reason for this was that throughout the war the Croatians had denied the Bosnians access to heavy artillery.

Tudjman also wanted the conference to be held in the United States. At least there was one issue on which all three Presidents seemed to agree. But would Washington agree to an American site?

Sofia Side Trip. We were moving toward a cease-fire for which we were not prepared, and a peace conference whose location and structure were still undecided. Hoping to slow down the process, we decided to take a long-delayed side trip on October 1 to Bulgaria, a neglected part of the region. I had promised the Bulgarian Prime Minister during a meeting in New York a week earlier that we would visit his isolated nation to show that we recognized and appreciated the cost of its support for the embargo against Serbia.

The visit excited the Bulgarians. Finally someone from Washington was paying attention to them. Because we ran late in Zagreb, our meeting in Sofia with President Zhelyu Zhelev did not start until after 8:30 in the evening. Finally, at 10:00 P.M., he gave an enormous dinner in our honor, with leaders of about twenty political parties. When we expressed astonishment at the number of parties represented, Zhelev, a former dissident, said that these were only the leading factions, out of a total of over two hundred parties.

The dinner ended about midnight. We returned to our Stalin-era VIP hotel, now a Sheraton, for a surprise birthday party for my overworked assistant, Rosemarie Pauli, arranged by her fellow travelers and Bill Montgomery, our Ambassador in Sofia. Although we were exhausted, as usual, it was good to be away from the intensity of the three Balkan capitals and Washington.

The October 2 Cable. It was after 1:00 A.M. when I settled into my room, a huge, ill-designed suite, to call Strobe Talbott. I told him that with the Bosnian Serb military in the west stiffening, the front lines seemed to be less fluid. If the offensive ran out of gas, it would be time for a cease-fire. But, I told Strobe, we could not announce a cease-fire without announcing the location of the peace conference at the same time.

This linkage was not self-evident, Strobe said. Could we separate the three issues—cease-fire, peace conference, and location? I told him that we would then find ourselves in contentious and time-wasting negotiations within the

Contact Group. We had to bypass this step with a package announcement. Strobe said that Washington was still opposed to holding the talks in the United States. If they failed, the costs would be too high for the Administration. "It's about nine to one against you," Strobe said dryly, "and I'm afraid right now I'm one of the nine." He said that Lake was still the only person in the senior team supporting an American venue. A White House meeting was scheduled for the next day to make a recommendation to the President. "Strobe," I said, "let me make our case by phone."

"Look," he replied, "I don't think it makes sense for you to participate by phone; as a practical matter, it won't work well, and you won't be at your best in that format. But I have a suggestion: send us a careful, reasoned telegram stating your case. I will ensure it gets a fair hearing at the meeting." The suggestion was characteristic of Strobe: generous and fair-minded. He believed in settling tough issues openly, and he was willing to encourage a message whose content he did not support—in contrast to many officials who made deviousness, even with close colleagues, a way of life and rationalized such behavior as "necessary to get the job done."

So I sat down in the high-ceilinged sitting room to draft the cable. For the rest of the night, I wrote and rewrote, calling Donilon at 4:15 A.M. and Kornblum thirty minutes later to get a better understanding of the arguments against our position. When we boarded the plane early in the morning, I asked my colleagues to review my draft and took a much-needed nap.

By the time we landed in Sarajevo on the morning of October 2, we had distilled a sharp, focused, and unanimous message from my draft. This message would be our best shot at an issue we felt was absolutely critical. Unfortunately, because of concern about protecting the President's deliberative process, the White House would not permit direct quotation in this book from the message we sent that morning—a message that Strobe later called "the most effective cable sent so far in this Administration in terms of changing people's minds."

In our message we argued that we had already invested so much national prestige in the effort that our priority had to be to maximize success, rather than to reduce the cost of failure. A meeting site in the United States would give us physical and psychological control of the process; any other site would reduce our leverage dramatically. To those who claimed that failure on American soil would be more costly politically—the case most frequently advanced against us—we argued that the Administration's prestige was already fully on the line in the eyes both of the American public and of the world, and that failure would be no more costly in New Jersey than in New Caledonia. Failure, although quite possible, was not something we could worry about now.

The American peace initiative, which had already brought a lifting of the siege of Sarajevo and other benefits, had been a powerful signal that, as de Charette had said in New York, "America is back." The choice of venue would be *the* key indicator of how serious and committed we were. We ended by predicting that the Europeans would complain about an American site, but that they would respect our wishes and come along, and that—contrary to fears being expressed in Washington—it would not have an effect on the fundamental relationships we had with the Europeans and Russia.

A few hours later, Lake called Kerrick to report that while the White House meeting had "moved the ball forward," it had been ultimately inconclusive. Some officials still worried that a U.S.-based conference might somehow draw in the President against his will. But there was also good news: on the basis of the telegram and a talk with Bob Owen, Christopher had decided to support an American venue. So did Perry. Tony ended the phone call by asking Don to gather more arguments in favor of our position before the next meeting.

Meanwhile, on the Front. The best time to hit a serve is when the ball is suspended in the air, neither rising nor falling. We felt this equilibrium had arrived, or was about to, on the battlefield. On the trip from Sofia to Sarajevo, after an intense discussion, we decided to shift from "exploration" of a cease-fire to its advocacy. We feared that the Croat-Muslim offensive would soon run out of steam. General Mladic was highly visible again and trying to rally his forces. And we were concerned by the growing friction between Zagreb and Sarajevo, which had caused Zagreb to halt its advance and threatened what had already been achieved. John Pomfret reflected our concern in *The Washington Post* on October 3, reporting that "Croatian forces [have] stopped fighting, allowing the Serbs to concentrate their formidable firepower on the Bosnian army."

When we met Izetbegovic on October 2, he was buoyed by encouraging reports from his generals, and was even more resistant to a cease-fire than he had been three days earlier. The Croatians remained ambivalent, even unenthusiastic, about continued fighting, which they felt would gain ground only for the ungrateful and uncooperative Bosnians. Galbraith, Clark, and I continued to urge Susak to take as much territory as he could, especially Sanski Most and Prijedor.

October 3 ended with the astonishing news that President Kiro Gligorov of Macedonia had barely survived an assassination attempt in Skopje; he was in intensive care after hours of neurosurgery to remove shrapnel lodged in his head from a car bomb. Gligorov's driver had been killed, and it was not certain Gligorov would survive. We sent Gligorov wishes for speedy recovery and asked Washington to send him an emergency medical team.

October 4, Sarajevo. The United States Senate confirmed John Menzies as Ambassador to Bosnia-Herzegovina. Ambassadors normally take their oath of office in the State Department, but since Menzies was already in Sarajevo, we decided to swear him in immediately and to turn the swearing in into a high-profile event that would reaffirm our commitment to Bosnia.

The event was held in a building that resonated with history, the Konak House, where Archduke Franz Ferdinand and his wife, Sophia, lay in state after they were shot on June 28, 1914. The handsome nineteenth-century mansion, with its polished parquet floors and plaster molding, had not been used since the war began but it had survived in surprisingly good condition, with only a few mortar hits on its upper floor. Ghosts seemed to hang in the air of the old building, and as we walked up its elegant stairway, I was moved by the continuity of history. "This is where the twentieth century began to disintegrate," I whispered to Joe Klein, who was following us for *Newsweek*. Government officials, foreign Ambassadors, generals, Muslim mullahs, Serb Orthodox priests, Catholic prelates, and members of the fast-disappearing Jewish community in Sarajevo had assembled for the first genuine multiethnic ceremony in four years. Jammed into the elegant ballroom, many wearing ethnic or religious costumes, they reminded me of the famous photograph, taken minutes before the assassination, of the doomed royal couple descending the stairs outside the City Hall, flanked by costumed dignitaries.

After the short formal ceremony, Izetbegovic made a speech welcoming Menzies, and John spoke briefly. I closed my remarks by saying that Konak House's "historic failures impose a special obligation on all of us who are gathered here today." There was a warm mood among the guests, mingling as if in prewar Yugoslavia. This, I thought, was the perfect moment and place to raise the question of the cease-fire—better than the grim and grimy Bosnian presidency building, where we were scheduled to meet that afternoon. I suggested to Izetbegovic and Sacirbey that we meet in one of the private side rooms at once. The other guests, still drinking and talking, watched in amazement as we closed the doors and disappeared.

Only General Kerrick joined this meeting. I chose Don in order to emphasize the role of the White House, which he represented. We sat on four small gilded chairs in the corner of a large room, our knees almost touching. Stressing that Don was one of our nation's top military intelligence officers, I asked him to give President Izetbegovic and Foreign Minister Sacirbey an intelligence assessment of the military situation.

Kerrick and I had not discussed this meeting in advance. But he played his part perfectly. Quietly and authoritatively, he said that the Federation had probably reached its point of maximum conquest. He said he was concerned Tudjman would not support further territorial gains, lest they go mostly to the

Bosnians. Finally, Don reminded the Bosnian president that in all wars there were times for advance and times for consolidation, and in our opinion this was a time for consolidation.

Izetbegovic listened carefully and uncomfortably. His generals, he said, were still reporting advances in the west. "Your generals may be reporting advances that have not happened," Don said. "Our own information is quite different. According to our best intelligence, the Federation now controls around fifty percent of the land. You would be risking a great deal if the Serbs took back some of your recent gains."

"Mr. President," I said, "this is a crucial moment. Our advice is given to you in friendship and sincerity. I hope you are right and we are wrong. But if you are wrong the price to your country will be enormous. If you want to let the fighting go on, that is your right, but Washington does not want you to expect the United States to be your air force. If you continue the war, you will be shooting craps with your nation's destiny."

Sacirbey mumbled something to Izetbegovic—a translation, we learned later, of the phrase "shooting craps with destiny." Izetbegovic said he would consider the issue immediately with his senior military and civilian colleagues. Would we meet him at the presidency building at 2:00 P.M. to get his answer?

While we waited, Christopher and Lake called to report on the results of a short early-morning meeting at the White House. Tony was upbeat: he had successfully "precooked" the issue of where the conference would be held, and resolved all remaining internal differences. The President would formally approve—and the Bosnia peace conference would be held in the United States.

Nothing could have recharged our depleted energies as much as Washington's last-minute reversal. All the pieces were now in place for the final push to stop the fighting and bring the parties together.

Accompanied by Carl Bildt and Igor Ivanov, we reconvened at the Bosnian presidency building at 2:00 P.M. to discuss the draft constitution and the elections. Such discussions would not resolve the major issues, but they were useful in making the Bosnians contemplate what their government would look like in case of peace. Bildt and Ivanov then left for other meetings, leaving us alone with Izetbegovic and his colleagues.

Izetbegovic was flanked by his military and civilian advisors, and it was clear that they had been arguing up to the moment we arrived. "My military leaders don't want me to stop," Izetbegovic began, looking directly at Kerrick. "They don't agree with your judgment of the situation. But I will agree to a cease-fire if the Serbs meet certain conditions." First, he said he would not agree to a cease-fire for at least another five days. Second, he would accept the cease-fire only if the gas and electricity were turned on in Sarajevo, and the road to Gorazde opened before the start of a peace conference.

One had to admire his conditions. They skillfully straddled the distance between our position and that of his hard-line generals. Restoring the electricity required that the Serbs remove the many mines scattered around the electricity pylons leading into Sarajevo. He would buy more time for a revived military offensive. Getting gas to Sarajevo was a different matter: Sarajevo's gas was controlled by the giant Russian state-controlled firm Gazprom, which did not wish to turn on the pipeline to Bosnia until it had received a large cash payment for long-overdue bills. In the next few weeks, this unexpected side issue would greatly complicate our efforts and, ironically, bring Sarajevo and Belgrade together in a united front against Moscow and the man behind Gazprom, Russian Prime Minister Victor Chernomyrdin.

October 4: Belgrade. We quickly drafted a cease-fire agreement incorporating Izetbegovic's conditions and flew to Belgrade, leaving Hill and Pardew in Sarajevo to facilitate communications with the Bosnian government. We felt we had crossed a psychological divide in both Sarajevo and Washington, and wanted to see how far we could get in Belgrade. Milosevic was in an upbeat, almost celebratory mood. As he read the draft cease-fire agreement with his usual speed, he joked and continually offered us drinks, which I turned down. "Not until we have an agreement," I told him.

We soon began to argue over details. Milosevic gave us a large room in the front of the building, in which we set up word processors. We opened a direct telephone line to our Embassy in Sarajevo through the State Department Operations Center in Washington, and kept it open for several hours. Members of our support team typed and retyped the proposed cease-fire agreement as changes flew back and forth. When Washington heard that we were in the final stages of negotiating a nationwide cease-fire, Christopher, Lake, Tarnoff, Donilon, and Kornblum all joined the telephone marathon. At one point while I was talking to Christopher, Milosevic wandered into the room, drink in hand, and asked whom I was talking to. Hearing that the Secretary of State was on the line, he indicated a desire to speak to him. This was clearly not the right time for the two men to have their first conversation, and I mumbled an excuse.

For hours Milosevic and the Bosnians haggled long-distance, through us, over small changes of wording in the agreement, with Chris Hill relaying each of Milosevic's suggestion to Sacirbey. As the night progressed, we all became increasingly exhausted—except for Milosevic, who seemed to be enjoying himself thoroughly. In Sarajevo, Hill could not locate Sacirbey. Finally, after one of Sacirbey's unexplained disappearances, the normally dignified Roberts Owen slammed his fist against the wood paneling in our room in Belgrade and uttered a string of unlawyerlike oaths. From then on, he was affectionately known as "Mad Dog" Owen, or simply "Mad Dog."

At about one in the morning, we finally had a document acceptable to both Sarajevo and Belgrade. Izetbegovic had his conditions, almost exactly as he had demanded. Milosevic signed the document with a flourish. We still needed the signatures of Karadzic and his Bosnian Serb colleagues, who were waiting in a villa outside Belgrade. This task we left to Milosevic, who promised to return the document, "signed, sealed, and delivered," before we left in the morning. We stumbled back to our hotel, entering through the basement to avoid the press, and called Washington with the news. We would still have to get Izetbegovic and Tudjman to sign the next day.

October 5: Belgrade, Sarajevo, Zagreb, and Rome. In the morning Milosevic delivered the document signed by the Bosnian Serbs. After briefing the British chargé, Ivor Roberts, we raced (laboriously, via Italy, as usual) to Sarajevo to get Izetbegovic's signature.

Izetbegovic's withdrawn and unhappy face told the story. Flanking him were several members of his Cabinet and military. I assumed from the mood in the room that a number of his colleagues objected to the cease-fire. Izetbegovic took the document and read it carefully. We pointed out that Milosevic had agreed to most of Sacirbey's changes, including the immediate exchange of all prisoners of war and a tightening of the language regarding the restoration of full gas and electrical service to Sarajevo.

We were running far behind a difficult schedule: we had to fly to Zagreb to see Tudjman, then get to Rome in time for the first "expanded Contact Group" session we had promised the Italians. As Izetbegovic argued, Rosemarie handed me a note warning that we had five minutes left to make our "window" for the last flight of the day, after which we would be unable to get out of Sarajevo until the next day.

Izetbegovic's visceral fear of the cease-fire had to be resolved quickly. He studied it in silence, his eyes narrowed. Finally, pointing at the Serb signatures, he said emphatically that he could not affix his signature to the same piece of paper as his enemies. I asked Ambassador Menzies to make a photocopy of the document with the Serb names covered up, and again presented it to Izetbegovic for signature.

Still he hesitated. I pushed a pen toward him. "Mr. President, you can end four years of fighting in your country with a single signature," I said, "and on your terms."

His colleagues watched him in silence as he stared at the paper. Suddenly, he looked at me suspiciously. "Where is the American signature?" he said. "I don't see your signature on this document."

I grabbed his pen and took the paper from his hands. "Here it is, Mr. President," I said, and scrawled my name on the document in the lower left-hand corner. "We must leave immediately. If you don't sign now, the war will continue." I started to rise.

Izetbegovic took the paper. His hands shook as he held it. Finally, slowly and reluctantly, he signed the document. We shook hands and raced for the airport, taking the document with us and leaving Ambassador Menzies to call Washington with the news.

CHAPTER 14

Choosing Dayton,
Getting Ready

(October 5–25)

How did a snake get in the tower?
Delayed in the democracies
By departmental vanities,
The rival sergeants run about
But more to squabble than find out.

—W. H. AUDEN, *New Year Letter*

WE KEPT THE CEASE-FIRE SECRET long enough for President Clinton to break the news. At 11:00 A.M. on October 5, he announced "an important moment in the painful history" of the former Yugoslavia. A general cease-fire would take effect in five days, he said, if the gas and electricity were turned on in Sarajevo. This would be followed by talks among the three Balkan Presidents, which would take place in the United States.

At the very moment the President spoke, our team was in Zagreb, urging Tudjman to capture more territory before the cease-fire took effect. The Croatians had virtually stopped their advance, and Sanski Most and Prijedor still lay inside Serb lines. "You have five days left, that's all," I said. "What you don't win on the battlefield will be hard to gain at the peace talks. Don't waste these last days."

Tudjman requested that we delay the start of the peace conference until the beginning of November, so that it would not interfere with the Croatian parliamentary elections. We agreed. As it turned out, we needed every minute of that extra week to get ready.

Before leaving the region, we laid down three conditions for the negotiations:

- first, that each President come to the United States with full power to sign agreements, without further recourse to parliaments back home;

- second, that they stay as long as necessary to reach agreement, without threatening to walk out; and

- third, that they not talk to the press or other outsiders.

All three Presidents agreed to these conditions, although Izetbegovic and Sacirbey objected to the third provision, claiming that they had important friends in Congress and the press with whom they had to keep in touch. We said that serious negotiations were incompatible with the sort of outside contacts they had in mind. Milosevic, reading the document, protested mockingly that we were trying to make him a prisoner. Although this document had no official standing, the three parties generally stuck to its terms—until the final dramatic hours in Dayton.

Akashi. Our last call in Zagreb before returning to Washington was on U.N. Secretary-General Boutros-Ghali's senior representative in the former Yugoslavia, Yasushi Akashi, whom I had known since my two visits to Cambodia in 1992. Akashi had been harshly treated by the press and castigated by critics of the U.N. for his weakness. But it was not entirely his fault: he was operating under tight constraints imposed by Boutros-Ghali. Furthermore, Akashi was virtually ignored by General Janvier and the U.N. military.

We asked Akashi to make his first priority the quick reopening of the electrical lines, which had been cut and mined. Then we bade each other goodbye, almost emotionally. I felt sorry for Akashi. He was leaving Zagreb with his previously distinguished record blemished, but his mission had been doomed from the start because of limits imposed from New York. The United States was delighted with his replacement: Kofi Annan, who was already flying to Zagreb to take up temporary residence. Since the August bombing crisis, Annan was the U.N. official in whom we had the greatest confidence, and his arrival was good news.

Rome. As our team flew to Rome, Warren Christopher called each Contact Group Foreign Minister to propose that the talks be co-chaired by the United States, the European Union, and Russia at the "Holbrooke-Bildt-Ivanov level." He would participate only when required. Christopher was concerned that if he attended the entire conference, the other Foreign Ministers would also insist on attending, which would make the negotiations unmanageable.

The Europeans accepted the American decision to host the talks without complaint, with the exception of the French. To mollify them, Christopher kept open the possibility of a signing ceremony in Paris. Rifkind expressed concern, verging on anger, at the French position, stressing that the British government had never agreed to Paris. But not wishing to turn this into a public problem, he said that the British would be content to host an "implementation conference" shortly after a signing ceremony.

The expanded Contact Group meeting was designed to satisfy the Italians. Foreign Minister Agnelli began it on October 5 with a dinner in the Renaissance splendor of the Villa Madama, the official guest house of the Italian Foreign Ministry. For someone who had eaten breakfast in Belgrade and lunch in Sarajevo, the scene was disorienting, so enormous was the distance between Rome's classical grandeur and the ugly realities we had just left.

The Europeans who were not part of the Contact Group praised American diplomacy and leadership. But there was a clear undercurrent of resentment among some Contact Group members over American "unilateralism." When I noted that the U.N. seemed reluctant to try to open the roads around Sarajevo, Pauline Neville-Jones exploded, charging that I was trying to "set the U.N. and the Europeans up" to be blamed for a failure. I was unprepared for this outburst. I was not interested in discussing the possibility of failure, I said. We needed to lay the groundwork for a success in which we would all share. For that, the most rigorous enforcement of every detail of every agreement was essential. I expressed myself acidly, criticizing those mired in bureaucratic maneuvers at such a critical juncture in European history. It was probably unwise of me to rise to the bait, but I was trying to lay down a strong marker against unproductive procedural proposals. With her usual grace, Sunni Agnelli moved the discussion to less turbulent issues.

Despite this tense beginning, the Rome meetings were useful. The next morning, October 6, the Italians formally convened an expanded Contact Group meeting, followed by a special, even larger meeting designed to promote economic recovery of the region—the first time we had focused on the long-term economic needs of the region.

With Italy having finally hosted a Bosnia conference, Moscow wanted its moment in the limelight. Each major European nation wished to host an international meeting, designed in large part to demonstrate to its domestic audience that it was involved in the peace process. John Kornblum termed this phenomenon "conference proliferation," and we complained constantly about it as time-consuming and redundant. However, we recognized that these meetings were important for European-American unity.

Albright and the U.N. The United Nations intended to request a place as a fourth co-chair of the negotiations. Madeleine Albright and I were strong longtime supporters of the United Nations, but we both felt that the U.N.'s participation in the talks would further complicate them. In the end, we agreed that the U.N. representative, Thorvald Stoltenberg, would participate in the negotiations only when they involved eastern Slavonia, and over the next three weeks Madeleine held the U.N. at bay in its quest for a larger role. Telling the U.N. that its involvement would weaken the search for peace was painful, especially for those of us who had grown up believing in the importance of the world body. But Albright stepped up to the task without complaint, and performed with a toughness that was productive if not always popular. In this period, our working relationship became progressively closer and more effective. As she often put it, we had been "joined at the hip" on every key European issue. She also felt a special kinship with my wife, Kati, like herself a product of a Central European refugee family.

The struggle over the U.N.'s role foreshadowed the American determination a year later to oppose Boutros-Ghali's quest for a second term as Secretary-General. More than any other issue, it was his performance on Bosnia that made us feel he did not deserve a second term—just as Kofi Annan's strength on the bombing in August had already made him the private favorite of many American officials. Although the American campaign against Boutros-Ghali, in which all our key allies opposed us, was long and difficult—especially for Albright, who bore heavy and unjust criticism for her role—the decision was correct, and may well have saved America's role in the United Nations.

Albright and Talbott were also deeply involved in another complicated aspect of the cease-fire agreement—the effort to open the gas lines to Sarajevo. The Russians controlled the pipeline through Gazprom, which did not want to start the gas flowing until it received $100 million in unpaid bills. The Bosnians were furious; most of the debt, they said, was for gas that had been siphoned off by the Serbs. More important, they did not have the money.

To solve the impasse, Milosevic sent his Prime Minister to Moscow with a personal plea to Prime Minister Victor Chernomyrdin to open the gas lines immediately and work out the back payments later. Silajdzic also flew to Moscow, hoping to gain credit in Sarajevo for getting the gas turned on. Meanwhile, our Ambassador in Moscow, Thomas Pickering, struggled with the Russian Foreign Ministry and Gazprom through several long nights. Talbott and Leon Fuerth activated the Gore-Chernomyrdin channel, the key working-level mechanism for American-Russian cooperation. Participating in this frustrating subplot through constant telephone calls—the remarkable final conference call included Pickering, Albright, Menzies, Tarnoff, Donilon, Chris Hoh, Nick Burns, and me, all in different locations—I had the impression that for the Russians the issue was financial, not political; the famously powerful and greedy leaders of Gazprom were simply trying to squeeze the Bosnians for back payments, and only Chernomyrdin himself could break the logjam. Still, the gas was not turned on, and the fighting continued. While slamming Moscow for what it regarded as blackmail, Sarajevo took advantage of the cease-fire delay to accelerate the military offensive, which had picked up last-minute momentum.

The Birth of IFOR. On the same day that the President announced the cease-fire and we met in Rome, Secretary of Defense Perry concluded a special two-day session of the sixteen NATO Defense Ministers in Williamsburg, Virginia. The announcement of the cease-fire gave added urgency to his effort to forge a consensus on the first peacekeeping force in NATO's storied history. With surprisingly little difficulty, the ministers gave Perry support for a structure without precedent—one that would enforce a peace agreement and include both NATO and non-NATO troops. NATO's Supreme Commander, General Joulwan, told the ministers he wanted a force of fifty to sixty thousand troops, with separate American, French, and British operational zones. The United States would contribute about one third of the troops, at an estimated annual cost of close to $2 billion. The peacekeeping force would be called the Implementation Force—or IFOR.

Perry also planned to meet with his Russian counterpart, Marshal Pavel S. Grachev, in Geneva two days later to pursue a visionary goal: bringing Russian troops into a Bosnian peacekeeping force. Moscow bitterly opposed the enlargement of NATO, and we were often at cross-purposes over Bosnia, where the Kremlin resented and feared the reassertion of American leadership. Not since World War II had Russian, American, and other Western European forces served together under a common command. But President Clinton, Perry, and Strobe Talbott, the President's most influential advisor on Russian policy, believed that if Russia participated in Bosnia, it would be a historic step in the development of cooperation between countries that had been Cold War adversaries only four years earlier.

Site X. Tom Donilon took over responsibility for finding an acceptable place—which we code-named Site X—for the talks. He assigned the job to the Assistant Secretary of State for Administrative Affairs, Patrick F. Kennedy, an intense, no-nonsense official with over twenty years of government experience as an administrative specialist. Kennedy, with whom I had worked during the Carter Administration, came to my office on October 10 with his aide, Ken Messner, to find out what kind of site we wanted. I repeated our mantra: physical arrangements could make a difference; every detail mattered. Site X would have to hold nine delegations—each Balkan country, the five Contact Group nations, and E.U. representative Bildt. Ideally we wanted an area we could seal off from the press and all other outsiders, close enough to Wash-

ington so that senior Administration officials could visit, yet sufficiently remote, as Michael Dobbs later put it in *The Washington Post,* "to discourage
Balkan warlords from running off to television studios in New York and Washington every time the negotiations hit a snag."

The President's retreat at Camp David was too close to Washington, too
small, too "presidential," and too closely identified with the 1978 negotiations
between Egypt and Israel. Hearing our requirements, Kennedy observed that
a military base would best meet our needs. After Wes Clark and I called Jan
Lodal, the Principal Deputy Undersecretary of Defense for Policy, Bill Perry
ordered the Pentagon to help Kennedy find Site X immediately.

Kennedy quickly narrowed the search to three sites: the Navy base at Newport, Rhode Island; Langley Air Force Base in Norfolk, Virginia; and Wright-
Patterson Air Force Base in Dayton, Ohio. When the possibility of Newport
arose, Senator Claiborne Pell called to offer us access to some of the great
houses along the water in his home state. Though the idea of Milosevic,
Izetbegovic, and Tudjman wandering around The Breakers was amusing to
contemplate, the facilities at Newport were too spread out. Unable to make the
site inspections myself, I asked Rosemarie Pauli to help Kennedy. As they
drove around Wright-Patterson, a sprawling base that contained twenty-three
thousand government personnel, Kennedy noticed five visiting officers' quarters (VOQs) grouped around a central parking lot, only a few feet apart. He
and Rosemarie decided that while some of the rooms would need substantial
improvement, in all other ways Wright-Patterson filled our needs.

And so Dayton was chosen for the talks, to everyone's surprise. At the time,
it did not sound like an impressive place for a major international conference.
As Dobbs wrote in *The Washington Post,* "Camp David it isn't." When we told
Milosevic the news on October 17, he protested, half-jokingly, that he did not
want "to be locked up like a priest"—a remark that later leaked to Roger
Cohen of *The New York Times,* much to Milosevic's annoyance. The Europeans, used to negotiations in more opulent settings, literally had no idea
where Dayton was, and expressed open unhappiness with a site "somewhere
in the middle of America." Carl Bildt worried about the hawkish imagery of a
military base. But I thought that reminders of American airpower would not
hurt.

Studying Camp David. We could find no exact precedents for the negotiations on which we were about to embark. The closest model, of course, was
the Camp David talks in September 1978, when President Carter forged the
historic agreement between Egyptian President Anwar Sadat and Israeli Prime
Minister Menachem Begin that ended thirty years of armed hostility and wars
between Egypt and Israel. As we flew around the Balkans in October, I distributed to every member of our team Carter's own account of those thirteen

days, as well as the section on Camp David in Cyrus Vance's memoirs, *Hard Choices,* and William Quandt's *Camp David: Peacemaking and Politics.* Dan Hamilton of the European Bureau also interviewed Quandt and Harold Saunders, who had been Assistant Secretary of State for Near Eastern Affairs at the time of Camp David, about every detail, no matter how small, concerning the talks, including eating arrangements, telephone connections to the outside world, and the handling of the press. Of greatest interest to us was the question of personal relations between the leaders at Camp David. Had the Americans been able to create any sort of personal rapport between Sadat and Begin? Could we do so at Dayton? Do people become more malleable after being cooped up for days? Will sheer fatigue make tempers flare?

I phoned President Carter and listened in fascination as he described how he had tried without success to get Sadat and Begin to talk directly to each other. He had then reverted to "proximity talks," a diplomatic technique originating in Mideast negotiations held in the 1940s at the U.N., in which the mediator moves between the two parties, who rarely meet one another face-to-face—a sort of "shuttle diplomacy by foot." We already assumed that this would be our pattern, and always referred to Dayton as "proximity peace talks." Carter recounted his constant efforts to reduce the personal distaste between the two men. His most memorable effort was a field trip to the Gettysburg battlefield, where, he hoped, being at a site of wasted sacrifice would produce a breakthrough. No such thing happened, of course, and Carter sat in the car between Sadat and Begin for hours, their knees touching, while they ignored each other.

Preparations. By the second week of October, preparations had become frantic. Several task forces framed positions on every issue from elections to the creation of a joint railroad commission. Robert Gallucci, the former Assistant Secretary of State for Political-Military Affairs, was given responsibility for coordinating implementation of civilian activities if an agreement was reached.

Our strategy for Dayton was both ambitious and simple: we would never have a better chance to end the war in Bosnia—and therefore we sought to address as many issues as possible in the final agreements. What was not negotiated at Dayton would not be negotiated later. We recognized that implementation would be at least as difficult as the negotiations themselves, but we rejected the minimalist theory that we should negotiate only those matters on which implementation would be relatively easy. Later we would be criticized for being overly ambitious, but the alternative would have been a "small" agreement, not much more than a cease-fire—and an opportunity lost, perhaps forever.

While the preparations continued at home, teams spread out across Europe to conduct three simultaneous negotiations. First, Slocombe, Kornblum, and

Clark flew to Brussels to gain more support for a multinational NATO-led force. Observing the response to their trip, Perry said that NATO had finally "emerged from a long dark tunnel of indecision and irresolution."

Second, Perry and Talbott continued their negotiations with Moscow on Russia's role in a peacekeeping force. President Clinton discussed this with Yeltsin by phone on September 27 and in person with Kozyrev one week later; Perry, Slocombe, and Talbott saw Marshal Grachev in Geneva on October 8. The Russians wanted to participate in any military force in Bosnia, but they wanted it led not by NATO but by either the United Nations or some special coalition in which they played a role equal to that of the United States. Although the President, Perry, and Talbott had explained repeatedly to the Russians that this was impossible—"a deal breaker," as Strobe put it, because it would destroy the key principle of NATO, unity of command—the Russians did not budge.

The third negotiating track remained in the Balkans. I was already committed to a Contact Group meeting in Moscow, and the French had insisted that we stop first in Paris. We timed our travel so we could hold the Contact Group meeting in Moscow, join Talbott and Slocombe for the discussions on the Russian role in peacekeeping, and then return to the Balkans for a final "pre-Dayton systems check."

The fighting in western Bosnia intensified as the cease-fire approached. NATO planes swung back into action, attacking a Bosnian Serb command bunker after the Serbs shelled a U.N. base southeast of Tuzla and killed a twenty-nine-year-old Norwegian peacekeeper. Both sides tried to make last-minute gains, with the Federation forces having much the better of it. Facing the end of the fighting, the Croats and the Bosnians finally buried their differences, if only momentarily, and took Sanski Most and several other smaller towns. But Prijedor still eluded them. For reasons we never fully understood, they did not capture this important town, a famous symbol of ethnic cleansing.*

---

* In March 1997, I attended a showing at the Council on Foreign Relations in New York of a powerful documentary film, *Calling the Ghosts,* that recounted the brutal treatment two Bosnian women from Prijedor had suffered during their incarceration at the notorious Omarska prison camp. Following the film, the two women angrily asked me why they were still unable to return to their hometown. I told them we'd repeatedly encouraged an assault on Prijedor. They were astonished; they said General Dudakovic, the Bosnian commander, had told them personally that "Holbrooke would not let us capture Prijedor and Bosanski Novi." I subsequently learned that this story was widely believed in the region.

This revisionism was not surprising; it absolved Dudakovic and his associates of responsibility for their failure to take Prijedor. I suspect the truth is that after the September 18 disaster at the Una River the Croatians did not want to fight for a town they would have had to turn over to the Muslims—and the Bosnians could not capture it unaided.

Other parts of the cease-fire agreement were slowly falling into place. The power lines into the capital were steadily being restored as the Serbs and the Croats showed U.N. engineers the location of the mines. However, despite Russian promises, Gazprom continued to delay the reopening of the gas lines into Sarajevo. Finally, after several days of drama, Pickering obtained a serious offer from the Russians: they would agree to await later payment of the unpaid bills, and open the valves, provided the Bosnians agreed not to hold them responsible for any explosions or other damage caused when the gas went back on. When Sarajevo agreed, the gas began to flow (without any serious explosions). On October 11, in a dramatic moment, the lights began to flicker on all over the city, and the first tentative bursts of gas started through the pipes in Sarajevo. A few hours later, wild shooting broke out all over Sarajevo—not fighting, but celebrations. The cease-fire had officially started, although fighting continued for a few more days in the west.

Before leaving for Paris and Moscow, I planned a weekend on Long Island. The President wanted a final discussion, which could not be scheduled until I was already on my way in a car. This led to a surreal scene on the Long Island Expressway. Asked to call the White House on Friday afternoon, October 13, I found myself at the appointed hour trapped in heavy traffic with my family on the Long Island Expressway. The White House switchboard told me not to use a cellular phone for a conversation with the President. I called back from a service-station pay phone, and was connected immediately to Christopher, Lake, and Berger. With the deafening sound of truck traffic in the background, we chatted as we waited for the President to join the call. Two men in a pickup truck drove over, and after a short wait made it clear that in their view my time at the pay phone was up. Their cigarette packs were lodged inside the sleeves of their T-shirts, James Dean–style, and they looked increasingly annoyed. I imagined the headlines in the tabloids if I told them the truth: "Man Attacked in LIE Phone Booth; Claimed He Was Talking to Prez."

Finally, as we waited impatiently, the President came on the line, asking me where I was. "You won't believe it, Mr. President," I said, in a low voice. "Is this the envoy to *The Washington Post*?" he asked with amusement, referring to a favorable editorial a week earlier. "How do you get such an article?" he continued. "I can't get them to say anything nice about me." I replied that the editorial had not been all *that* laudatory, and that it came after "eighteen straight hits on me." "Don't complain," the President laughed. "You won't get many of those.

"Can we get a united Sarajevo?" he asked. "Could we protect it?" "The Serbs want a Berlin with guns," I said. "The two sides have incompatible positions on four or five key issues. Everyone knows that only a peace settlement will bring U.S. involvement. They can't have one without the other."

Areas of Control After Cease-fire, October 12, 1995

SLOV.

HUNGARY

SERBIA

Zagreb

CROATIA

Karlovac

EASTERN SLAVONIA

Bosanski Novi

Prijedor

Bosanski Samac

Bihac

Omarska

Sanski Most

Banja
Luka

Doboj

Brcko

Bosanski
Petrovac

Udbina

Tuzla

Mali
Zvornik

Jajce

BOSNIA-HERZEGOVINA

Srebrenica

Knin

Kiseljak

Zepa

Sarajevo

Pale

Rogatica

Mt. Igman ▲

Gorazde

Split

Foca

Mostar

MONTE-
NEGRO

Dubrovnik

Podgorica

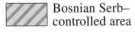

0   20 miles

0   20 kilometers

Bosnian Serb–
controlled area

Croat-Muslim Federation–
controlled area

"That's good," the President said. "It's the only dog we've got. Let's use it."

The President was particularly concerned about Yeltsin's support for the peace effort, and spoke with passion about the need to involve Russia in the peacekeeping force.

"We want the Russians in," I said. "But they cannot have their own sector. It would look like a Russian zone of occupation after World War II. Secondly, they cannot have any say in NATO decisions to use force, which they are seeking through some kind of council."

"We should try to involve Russia," the President replied. "It's important. And good luck on your trip."

Moscow. After a short stop in Paris to see Chirac, we landed in Moscow. The Russians were pleased at their first opportunity to act as host for the Contact Group. But the meetings, held at the Foreign Ministry, were confused and shapeless; the Russians, not used to running international meetings, had no set agenda. Foreign Minister Andrei Kozyrev, an affable and decent man, but under pressure from the nationalists in Russia, chaired the opening session.

The French representative, Jacques Blot, announced that it had been "unanimously decided" that Carl Bildt would be the senior civilian representative in Bosnia. Since we had already agreed that the civilian chief would be a European, I agreed to this suggestion despite the odd manner in which it had been sprung on us. To do otherwise would have opened a wide breach within the Contact Group. Besides, we could work with Bildt, whom we had strongly supported in early 1995 as E.U. negotiator.

Kozyrev suggested that the three Balkan Presidents visit Moscow prior to Dayton. His main purpose was to enhance the prestige of the Yeltsin government on the eve of the election for the Russian parliament, or Duma. The Russians promised that if we agreed to this meeting, they would restrict it to a "photo op" with Yeltsin.

I had doubts about this proposal. It risked derailing or delaying the negotiating process, notwithstanding the Russian pledge to stay away from substance. Scheduling would be difficult. It seemed unlikely that the meeting would have much impact on Duma elections. However, I knew Strobe would favor such a trip, and given our recent conversation I assumed President Clinton would also support it—so I told the Russians that Strobe would address it when he arrived in Moscow the next day.

That afternoon I went to the airport to meet him and his team, which included Slocombe and James Collins, the head of State's office for relations with the former Soviet republics.* We headed straight to the Russian Defense Ministry, where we met with a group of grim and skeptical-looking Russian

* Collins succeeded Pickering as Ambassador to Russia in 1997.

generals. They listened coldly to Strobe and Walt but seemed more receptive when American military officers spoke, especially Wes Clark; with his crisp military bearing and handsome uniform, he seemed to communicate to the Russians soldier-to-soldier, in a manner that we civilians could not match. When our team left for Belgrade the next day, Strobe asked us to leave Wes behind to participate in their discussions.

In order to join the Bosnia force, the Russians said, they needed joint authority over all decisions. Briefing the NATO Council in Brussels on October 18, Strobe predicted that Yeltsin would "reserve for himself the final say on what has been an extremely contentious issue." This meant the decision would not be made until the Clinton-Yeltsin summit, scheduled for Hyde Park, New York, on October 23.

Congress—and the Twelve–Month Limit. On October 17, Christopher, Perry, and Shalikashvili ran into difficulty during an unusual joint appearance before the Senate Armed Services Committee. Democrats joined Republicans in warning that the Administration had not yet made a convincing argument for deploying American troops in Bosnia.

Like most Americans, affected by endless images on television of U.N. forces killed and wounded in appalling conditions in Bosnia, Congress assumed that American troops would also suffer casualties. This expectation shaped the debate over the next few weeks. Had the public understood that Americans would be sent to Bosnia only in a radically different environment from the one they had seen on television, one that sharply reduced the risk of casualties, there would have been more support for the effort. It was virtually impossible to make the case in the absence of a peace agreement, but Congress demanded that the debate begin *before* the negotiations at Dayton.

Trying to bolster support, Perry told the Armed Services Committee that the NATO force in Bosnia would be "the biggest and the toughest and the meanest dog in town," adding that if it were attacked, "it would bring a large hammer down on them immediately." Still, the Senators were skeptical. "We haven't made the case yet," Christopher said, "but there's a case to be made and we'll make it."

Two issues dominated the hearing. First, would the Administration submit any decision to deploy troops to Bosnia to a formal vote of the Congress and would it respect the outcome of that vote? Senator Robert Byrd of West Virginia spoke for most of his colleagues in a letter to President Clinton that called for "the Congressional majority [to] share full responsibility, from the outset, for any decision to accept the costs and risks of this proposed operation." Other Senators, including John Glenn, Dan Coats, Kay Bailey Hutchison, and William S. Cohen all pursued this same line.

Christopher and Perry had prepared carefully for this. Though they said they would "welcome an authorization from the Congress," they refused to answer repeated questions as to whether or not they would recommend that the President seek such authority and be bound by a vote.

The second issue was fundamental: how long would American and NATO troops be deployed in Bosnia? Although the NATO plan had not yet been formally approved by the President, Perry and Shalikashvili told the Senators NATO would "complete its mission in twelve months and [then] withdraw."

The plausibility of this statement, even when slightly softened by the President a few days later, was widely questioned at the time—and would cause serious difficulty for the Administration later. It resulted from the deeply held conviction of the Pentagon and the NSC that the American people would not support involvement in Bosnia without an "exit strategy." There was merit to this theory, as all students of Vietnam and Somalia knew. Nevertheless, announcing *before the peace talks began* that we would withdraw in twelve months, no matter what happened on the ground, was not an "exit strategy," but an exit deadline—something quite different, and quite misleading.

The negotiating team knew that one year was not sufficient to succeed, no matter what happened in Dayton. But we were traveling between Moscow and Belgrade on the day this issue was decided, and after stating once in an earlier discussion that an arbitrary deadline—especially one so unrealistic—was a terrible idea, we were not consulted again. When we heard the news, we feared it would weaken our negotiating hand as well as threaten successful implementation. But the decision had been made, and we had no choice but to defend it publicly.

A Final Systems Check in the Balkans. As Washington announced its decision on the troop commitment, we began our "final systems check," visiting all three Balkan capitals. As a display of Contact Group unity, I asked Bildt and Ivanov to travel with us. It was the only joint trip of the three Dayton co-chairmen, and gave us a chance to develop closer working relationships.

It had been almost two weeks since we had seen Milosevic. He began the October 17 meeting with a strong effort to get the sanctions lifted or suspended prior to Dayton. We rejected his request. John Shattuck had called from the Bosnian town of Zenica that same day to report that several thousand Muslim refugees had been driven toward central Bosnia by paramilitary Serb units, perhaps led by Arkan. At the same time, we had received intelligence reports of continued Yugoslav resupply to the Bosnian Serb Army, despite many assurances from Milosevic to the contrary.

Milosevic waved off Shattuck's information. Was the Serbian President lying about what was going on, or was he so isolated that he did not know what his own forces were doing? We did not know, but since he consistently claimed to be uninformed about what was happening in the Banja Luka area, I asked the CIA to prepare a "sanitized" (or unclassified) document that laid out evidence of the ties between Arkan and the Yugoslav Army. We planned to give the document to Milosevic on a second trip to Belgrade on October 19, after Bildt and Ivanov had left. Although the document did not link Arkan directly to the recent events, it was powerful and incriminating.

When I raised the subject again at lunch on October 19, Milosevic tried to brush it off. "No, no, no," he said. "Your information is wrong." At this point, by prearrangement, Pardew pushed our document in front of Milosevic. "Our evidence is all in there, Mr. President," I said.

Milosevic looked away. He would not touch the paper lying directly in front of him. I urged him to read it, but he went on eating. Hill observed later that Milosevic acted as if by touching the document he would be physically connected to the charges it contained. When the meal ended, a Serb official came up to Pardew and said that he had left *his* paper on the table. "No, I didn't forget it," Jim said. "It belongs to President Milosevic."

Hyde Park. On October 23, a gorgeous fall day, a frail Boris Yeltsin met President Clinton at Franklin Roosevelt's home at Hyde Park high above the Hudson. Jim Collins had suggested the beautiful setting in the hope that its reminders of FDR's great wartime alliance with the Soviet Union would encourage a new security relationship, beginning in Bosnia. In a speech to the United Nations General Assembly the previous day, Yeltsin had delivered a blistering attack against NATO expansion and indicated that Russia would not participate in any force under NATO command in Bosnia.

The President's goal was to get Yeltsin to agree to participate in a Bosnia peacekeeping force even if the Russians continued to object to NATO enlargement, on the theory that what we did together in the Balkans would become a partial antidote to Russia's neuralgia about NATO and would, in Talbott's words, "lubricate the NATO-Russia track." Talbott and Perry had spent a great deal of time discussing this nuanced approach to Bosnia and NATO during their frequent trips to Geneva to see Grachev; now, with Dayton only days away, it was up to the President to pull at least the first track—Bosnia—across the finish line while holding firm on NATO.

The President succeeded brilliantly. After hours of intense and often highly personal discussion, the two men agreed that two battalions of Russian troops, totaling about two thousand soldiers, would participate in the force in Bosnia. President Clinton defended the integrity of the Bosnia command structure—a sacred "red line" for NATO, which would rather have a command without the Russians than the kind of messy structure, with separate chains of command, that the Russians sought. The two Presidents did not attempt to settle this complicated problem, instead handing it back to Perry and Grachev, who were scheduled to meet at the end of the week in Fort Leavenworth, Kansas. But they did agree on the size and functions of the Russian contingent, and the meeting set a positive tone for Perry's closing efforts with Grachev.

One other issue concerning Bosnia came up at Hyde Park: Yeltsin's desire for a pre-Dayton summit in Moscow of the three Balkan Presidents. All three Balkan Presidents had told us they would rather not go to Moscow. From their point of view, it would be exhausting, unproductive, and politically undesirable. But Yeltsin was adamant: he did not care that none of the presidents wanted to make the trip to Moscow. Knowing that President Clinton would meet with Izetbegovic and Tudjman the next day in New York, Yeltsin asked him to use "all his influence" to make the meeting happen. Reluctantly, President Clinton agreed.

Izetbegovic and Tudjman at the Waldorf. The day after Hyde Park, October 24, President Clinton met Izetbegovic and Tudjman together at the Waldorf-Astoria Hotel in New York. Seeking to put the Dayton talks in a larger framework, the President began on a high note. "We have seen things in the last few years that we never expected to see," he said. "Israel and the PLO sitting down after thirty years of fighting; the IRA laying down their arms. But what the world wants most is the end of the war in Bosnia." The President praised the Muslim-Croat Federation as essential. "Without the Federation," he said, "I am not sure that the NATO bombing or Dick Holbrooke's diplomacy would have worked."

Seated on both sides of President Clinton, the two Presidents barely acknowledged his point. Rather, Izetbegovic immediately complained about the Croatians. "All parties here support the Federation in words," he said, "but the process of implementation has not taken place as it should." He then listed areas in which the Croatians had failed to live up to their commitments. Tudjman ignored Izetbegovic, and made another strong pitch that eastern Slavonia had to be part of any deal at Dayton. The President agreed. Then the two men took a few more shots at each other, and the meeting ended. Its main value was that it had given the President and his senior advisors a rare firsthand sense of how much these two men disliked each other, and how difficult Dayton would be.

With the formal meeting over, President Clinton asked me and Sandy Vershbow to join him and the two Presidents in a corner. "I want to ask you to do something for the peace process that I know will be hard on both of you," he said to Izetbegovic and Tudjman. "I want to ask you both to go to Moscow before Dayton. It would be better to get the Moscow visit over with before the

Duma elections, and that means before Dayton." The main purpose of the meeting, President Clinton concluded, would be to allow Yeltsin "to send a signal to the Serbs, and to allow the Russian people to see that he is part of the process." Despite their previous misgivings, Izetbegovic and Tudjman agreed immediately. To ease the physical strain on Izetbegovic, President Clinton offered an American plane for the trip; Tudjman had his own plane.

The pre-Dayton Moscow summit, which would delay the start of Dayton by one day, was announced by the Russians and confirmed by the White House on October 25. Two days later, on October 27, Perry and Grachev agreed to put two thousand Russian troops directly under General Joulwan.

This arrangement told a great deal about the complicated mind-set of the Russians in the fourth year of the post-Soviet era. The great World War II alliance of Americans and Russians still echoed in the minds of the Russian military. Having regarded themselves as our only "fellow superpower" for fifty years, they seemed to be ready to accept the U.S. military as a worthy superior or commander in Bosnia. The negotiations over Russia's role in Bosnia thus helped us understand how to approach the next big strategic goal of America's post–Cold War European policy—enlarging NATO.

This was a historic achievement. From the patient negotiating style of Perry and Talbott, strongly supported by General Joulwan, had come an unprecedented command arrangement: for the first time since World War II, U.S. and Russian troops would operate in a unified command. Even Strobe was surprised at the speed with which everything fell into place on the eve of Dayton. "The Russians were unbelievably sanguine about being under American command in Bosnia," he observed later—"but NATO was still a four-letter word in Moscow."

But the same day brought stunning news that temporarily overshadowed the agreement between Perry and Grachev. For the second time in three months, Yeltsin entered the hospital with severe heart disease. Ambassador Pickering predicted that the country was entering a period of crisis and uncertainty. There was, however, a small plus from this frightening development: the pre-Dayton Moscow summit was canceled. As Chris Hill said, "If Yeltsin *had* to get sick, at least he picked a good time from our standpoint." Still, we all knew that a great deal depended on his speedy recovery.

CHAPTER 15

Decisions with Consequences

(October 25–31)

> . . . our theories, like the weather,
> Veer round completely every day,
> And all that we can always say
> Is: true democracy begins
> With free confessions of our sins.
>
> —W. H. AUDEN, *New Year Letter*

> Now the man who has risen to the top [of the military] finds him-
> self with new concerns, political and diplomatic. He is not simply
> directing the Army or Navy or Air Force. He is consulting with his
> colleagues and advising his civilian superiors. . . . He is advising
> them on matters having to do with the goals and ends of peace and
> war. For this he has certainly not been trained.
>
> —BERNARD BRODIE, *War and Politics*

AS DAYTON APPROACHED, THE PRESSURE INCREASED. It was the most brutal bureaucratic effort I had ever been involved in. Some bureaucratic bruises were
made in the process that did not heal quickly. But in retrospect, the amazing
thing was not how tough it was to get ready for Dayton, but how hard everyone worked to make it happen. The State Department was swarming with activity. Conference rooms had been turned into messy drafting rooms, where
people drawn from various parts of the government were working together,
minus most of the normal bureaucratic wrangling. There seemed to be a certain air of destiny, as if everyone working on the preparations for Dayton felt
they might be part of a decisive moment in American foreign policy.

The Role of IFOR. However, the Administration remained divided over the
most important question it faced: if we got an agreement in Dayton, what
would the NATO-led Implementation Force, IFOR, do? Of course, if Dayton
failed to produce a peace agreement, such deliberations would be inconse-

quential. Assuming success in Dayton, however, they would define the most important action in the history of NATO—its first deployment outside its own area, its first joint operation with non-NATO troops, and its first post–Cold War challenge.

There was no disagreement over the first two tasks of IFOR personnel: first, to use whatever force or other means was necessary to protect themselves; and, second, to separate the warring parties and enforce the cease-fire.

But aside from separating the forces and protecting themselves, what else should the peacekeepers do? The disagreement on this critical issue between the "maximalists," like myself, and the "minimalists," mainly at the Pentagon, was profound. With Dayton days away, and our NATO allies sending military representatives to Washington to work out a common position, two high-level White House meetings were scheduled for October 25 and 27 to resolve these questions.

The military did not like civilian interference "inside" their own affairs. They preferred to be given a limited and clearly defined mission from their civilian colleagues and then decide on their own how to carry it out. In recent years, the military had adopted a politically potent term for assignments they felt were too broad: "mission creep." This was a powerful pejorative, conjuring up images of quagmires. But it was never clearly defined, only invoked, and always in a negative sense, used only to kill someone else's proposal.

The debate over mission creep raised an extremely important issue: the role of the American military in the post–Cold War world. The Pentagon did not want to fragment its forces in the pursuit of secondary objectives, especially in the twilight zone between war and peace. Given budgetary constraints, the Chiefs did not think they could pursue these objectives and fulfill their primary missions as well.

America's modern fighting force, primarily the creation and pride of the Reagan era, had handled challenges in Iraq, Panama, Grenada, and elsewhere with courage, skill, and low casualties. But two less pleasant memories still hung like dark clouds over the Pentagon. Phrases like "slippery slope" and "mission creep" were code for specific events that had traumatized the military and the nation: Mogadishu, which hung over our deliberations like a dark cloud; and Vietnam, which lay further back, in the inner recesses of our minds.

Vietnam had affected almost every American who had lived through the 1960s and early 1970s, including myself. But the "lessons of Vietnam" divided people almost as much as the war itself had. The leaders of the military establishment in the 1990s, all of whom had been company or field-grade officers in Vietnam, had derived a lesson substantially different from that of opponents of the war, including Bill Clinton. Colin Powell spoke eloquently for the military in his memoir. "Many of my generation," he wrote, "the career captains, majors, and lieutenant colonels seasoned in that war, vowed that when our turn came to call the shots, we would not quietly acquiesce in half-hearted warfare for half-baked reasons that the American people could not understand or support."[1]

The power of that distant yet living memory was visible on the right shoulder of General John Shalikashvili. As Chairman of the Joint Chiefs of Staff, he was entitled to wear the patch of any military unit on his uniform. He chose the insignia of MACV—the long-decommissioned Military Assistance Command Vietnam. When I first commented on the powerful emotions the once-ubiquitous MACV shield evoked in me, Shalikashvili said he was "surprised a civilian recognized" the symbol. "I spent three years in Vietnam," I explained, "part of it living in a MACV compound in the Mekong Delta." He wore the patch, he said, as a silent tribute to the Americans who served and died in that faraway war.

Despite some major successes, at least three times in the twenty years since Vietnam the military had stumbled. In April 1980, the attempt to rescue the American hostages in Tehran had failed in the Iranian desert, leaving eight Americans dead and contributing heavily to Carter's defeat by Reagan. In Lebanon three years later, 241 marines had been killed when their barracks was bombed, Reagan's worst moment as President. Then, on October 3, 1993, came a new disaster, which rocked the Clinton Administration and traumatized the military. Eighteen Americans, serving as part of the U.N. force in Somalia, were killed in the streets of Mogadishu while trying to capture a Somalian clan leader, Mohammed Farah Aideed. The scars from that disaster would deeply affect our Bosnia policy. Combined with Vietnam, they had left what might be called a "Vietmalia syndrome" in Washington.

To be sure, there were fundamental differences between Bosnia and "Vietmalia." Our goals and stakes were different. The Bosnian Serbs were neither the disciplined, ruthless revolutionaries of North Vietnam nor the drunken rag-tag "technicals" who raced around Mogadishu shooting people. But discussion of such distinctions was not welcome: most officials felt they already knew the meaning of Somalia and Vietnam without giving them more than cursory analysis.

In their hearts, American military leaders would have preferred not to send American forces to Bosnia. They feared that the mission would be "fuzzy" and imprecise, like Somalia. Tony Lake, who shared their concerns, argued against a "nation-building" role for the military, and worried aloud about the "slippery slope" in Bosnia. Of course, if they were ordered to go, they would do so quickly and successfully. But the leadership of the military would resist "tasking" for anything beyond self-protection and the implementation of the military provisions of any peace agreement. The JCS and NATO believed that these two tasks would probably absorb all their resources.

American Casualties. Basing their predictions on another misreading of the Bosnian Serbs, as had been the case throughout the war, the military viewed the Serbs as a potent military force that would threaten IFOR as it had the U.N. Our negotiating team, including its two generals, Clark and Kerrick, believed these fears were greatly exaggerated. The Bosnian Serbs were a spent force, and we were confident that Milosevic would no longer come to their aid militarily. We believed that if sent to Bosnia, the U.S. military and NATO would be able to control the situation on the ground with little difficulty or challenge from the Serbs. In any case, we would not deploy American or other NATO troops absent ironclad guarantees from all three parties concerning their safety, access, and authority.

I reflected my belief that American and NATO casualties would be low— far lower, in fact, than any official predictions—in meetings and in several interviews just before Dayton. On Friday, October 27, I told Rowland Evans and Christiane Amanpour of CNN that

> While we have to anticipate that it's not a risk-free situation, we're not going to send people into combat. This is not Somalia, and it's not Vietnam. . . . We're not anticipating the kind of casualties and body bags that your question presupposes. *There is no peace without American involvement, but to repeat, there's no American involvement without peace.*
>
> EVANS: Well, I hate to belabor the issue, but this is what Americans are asking themselves. [General] Michael Rose, who ran the U.N. operation for at least a year—and you may disagree with him, but he certainly knows the situation on the ground—estimates that the casualties from this operation that you're planning will exceed the casualties from the Gulf War, which were three hundred and ninety dead. Is he crazy?
>
> HOLBROOKE: He's not crazy. He's wrong. His predecessor in Bosnia, General Morillon, said, "Hit them the first time they challenge you and they won't respond again."*

The Great Debate. Our team argued that after IFOR carried out its primary missions in Bosnia it should undertake additional tasks in support of peace—

---

* At the end of the program, Evans accurately summarized my views:
> Ambassador Holbrooke was very hardheaded on casualties, Christiane. To me at least, he indicated that, if they get what they want from the three parties, there may not be many casualties. He wouldn't say there wouldn't be any, but, Christiane, he really emphasized an aspect of this that may be getting overlooked a little bit here, that the casualties and the body bags, despite Sir Michael Rose's prediction, may not be as bad as everybody here is afraid they will be.

including keeping roads open, assisting in the election process, and arresting war criminals. Without the backing of IFOR, the civilian parts of an agreement—the test of true peace—could not be carried out. And if the civilian provisions of a peace agreement were not carried out, then withdrawal of NATO forces would be more difficult.

In my view, this could create a self-defeating cycle: the narrower the military mission, the longer they would have to stay. But the military saw things quite differently: anticipating a huge security problem that would tie down their forces, they believed that any additional responsibilities would require additional forces, well beyond the sixty thousand troops in the plan.

The disagreement with the military was not personal. My respect for the senior military officers with whom we worked was enormous, especially General Shalikashvili, a friend whose support of the negotiating team had been exemplary. His unusual background added to his charm. He was born in Warsaw of Georgian parents three years before Hitler invaded Poland. English was his fourth language. Once, when several Americans were describing their first memories of Berlin, Shalikashvili quieted the others by recalling his first visit there—in 1943! He and his family came to the United States in 1954 when he was sixteen years old, and he learned English from American movies (especially, according to legend, John Wayne's). His military career had begun in the enlisted ranks, not at West Point.* Low-key but forceful, he was less imposing than Powell, and far less of a public figure. But, like Powell, he conveyed confidence and trust. With a quick smile and a disarming manner— "Call me Shali," he would say to anyone stumbling over his five-syllable surname—he was open and friendly, and universally liked by his civilian colleagues. He never tried to strong-arm or overwhelm civilians in a discussion, but simply stated his position and held his ground as long as possible. That we had good personal relations was important, since we had to work together closely, whatever happened.

With only a year to go until the presidential election, public opinion was heavily opposed to deployments—at that time some 70 percent of the American public did not want troops in Bosnia under any circumstances. The White House was understandably averse to a direct confrontation with the military. If the military openly opposed the deployment, our political difficulties would be vastly increased. We had to have their backing to get congressional and public support for the mission, which meant that they had the upper hand in the debate over what their mission would be.

---

* It was unusual for the nation's top military officer not to have gone to one of the service academies, but it was also true of two of Shalikashvili's three immediate predecessors, General Powell, an ROTC student at City College of New York, and General John Vessey, who won a battlefield commission on the Anzio beach during World War II.

So the lines were drawn, although not precisely, between two points of view concerning the mission of the peacekeepers: on one side, a narrow approach, backed by the JCS and NATO; on the other side, a broader, more ambitious maximalist approach in which IFOR would support the civilian aspects of a peace agreement if and when it had completed its primary missions.

Less than a week before Dayton, the battle lines were clear. Even after Sandy Berger's Deputies' Committee had resolved many secondary issues, there were still eleven major disagreements between State and the JCS. Some of them were fundamental, as identified in a study by Sandy Vershbow:

1. The JCS wanted to locate IFOR headquarters in Zagreb or Naples, rather than Sarajevo. Quarters suitable for a four-star admiral did not exist in Sarajevo, they said, and they worried about the security of their headquarters. We argued that if the senior American were not in Sarajevo the entire operation would be fatally weakened.

2. They wanted to deploy IFOR only in the Federation, and not in Republika Srpska. State argued that this would turn the Inter-Entity Boundary Line between the two parts of Bosnia into the equivalent of the DMZ in Korea—and effectively partition the country.

3. The Pentagon did not want to place IFOR troops on Bosnia's international borders, despite a strong request from Izetbegovic. We argued that troops had to be placed on the international border to support our position that Bosnia was a single country.

4. The JCS opposed "requiring" that the parties withdraw all heavy weapons from a "heavy weapons exclusion zone." Instead, it proposed that the peace agreement simply "encourage" the parties to withdraw their heavy weapons "on a voluntary basis." We found this position incomprehensible from the military's own point of view. The word "voluntary" did not exist in the Balkan lexicon, and leaving heavy weapons near the IFOR troops would only increase their vulnerability.

5. The Pentagon opposed the cantonment of weapons—that is, the stockpiling in isolated areas open to NATO inspection—by the two sides on the grounds that it was unenforceable. We argued that cantonments would protect IFOR and reduce the chances of incidents.

6. They opposed giving IFOR the authority to investigate "past incidents of attacks, atrocities or human rights violations." We said this was essential.

7. The Pentagon resisted any obligation to respond to "over the horizon" reports of attacks on international civilian personnel or gross

violations of human rights, on the grounds that this would "lead to mission creep and increase force requirements." In plain English, this meant that the Pentagon did not want to go to the aid of international civilian aid workers if a problem arose outside their immediate line of sight. We argued that it was inconceivable that the military could stand by if civilians, some of whom might be Americans, were endangered.

8. The military wanted little or no role in any aspect of civilian implementation, including elections and securing freedom of movement; we argued that its visible presence would be essential for the first series of elections after the war.

9. The Pentagon not only rejected any police functions for themselves, but also opposed giving the International Police Task Force (IPTF) a strong mandate and authority to arrest people. This, they said, would constitute the most dangerous form of "mission creep." If the IPTF got into trouble, the military argued, this could "lead to the assumption by IFOR of police functions throughout the country." I argued that this would weaken the chain of enforcement. Either the military should have arrest authority or else the IPTF should be given such powers.

10. The Pentagon wanted to exclude eastern Slavonia from the IFOR area of responsibility on the grounds that it would require more troops and raise more problems with Congress. We argued that eastern Slavonia, small, adjacent to Bosnia, and directly on the route that U.S. troops would travel to resupply their forces in Bosnia, was an integral part of the region, and would be easy to place under IFOR.

11. Finally, the Pentagon opposed any mandate or obligation to arrest indicted war criminals. Needless to say, I disagreed.

Over the last few days before Dayton we contested every one of these issues, winning some, losing many others. The implementation of Dayton, as it turned out, was determined in these meetings, with decidedly mixed results.

I appealed privately to Perry and Shalikashvili for a more robust IFOR mission. After personal review, Perry and Shalikashvili reversed two of the Pentagon's positions. The first was the location of IFOR headquarters; they realized that it had to be in Sarajevo rather than in Zagreb—a bizarre suggestion that had come up through the chain of command.

They also agreed that IFOR had to deploy some forces in the Serb portion of Bosnia; otherwise we would divide the country instead of unifying it. Perry also agreed to deploy IFOR forces on the international borders, although the number was smaller than we wanted or Izetbegovic had requested.

The first of the two White House meetings on the State-Pentagon disagreement took place on October 25. The JCS agreed to a *required* twenty-kilometer heavy-weapons-free zone adjusted to fit the demarcation of territory, and a four-kilometer zone of separation free of all weapons. This was a significant step forward from the original JCS-NATO plan. (I argued unsuccessfully for a ten-kilometer weapons-free zone.)

Two days later, with the European military representatives already arriving in Washington, we returned to the Situation Room to resolve the rest of our differences. Despite its significance, the debate on October 27 was never personal or tense. In our private meetings, Shalikashvili had promised to look for ways to reduce the gap between State and the JCS. Nonetheless, there were still serious disagreements.

"The issues before us are the ones that will determine the success or failure of the mission," I said. "Elections and the right of refugees to return may not be in IFOR's mandate, but they may be the key. We are deciding here whether or not we will end up with partition or a single country. If we succeed at Dayton, we will then face very tough real-life cases, such as people who want to return to their homes, say Muslims who once lived in Banja Luka—"

Shalikashvili broke in. "That's not IFOR's mission. We can't get every bus through. We should not sign a document we can't implement. I hope police will do their utmost to provide security for returning refugees. If there is an incident and the police are overwhelmed, then the IFOR commander has the authority to assist. But there could be days when he can't do this because his resources are stretched too thin."

Finally, Shalikashvili offered a compromise. "Supposing we accept the 'authority' to do additional tasks," he said, "but not the 'obligation.' " There was some confusion until Shali explained the distinction, which had a clear meaning to the military: if IFOR completed its required missions, it would have the *authority, but not the obligation,* to undertake the additional tasks. "For example, we do not wish to be obligated to arrest war criminals," he explained, "but we will accept the authority to arrest them if we get the chance." This was a big step forward from the military's opening position, which had opposed any widening of IFOR's role. But the meaning of this finely crafted compromise would not be determined until the commanders on the ground decided how to use their "authority."

This compromise was swiftly accepted by Christopher, Perry, and Lake. I did not object. It gave us a unified American position, which was essential for the weekend meetings with our European allies and the NATO Council, and in Dayton.

But had I known then how reluctant IFOR would be to use its "authority," I would have fought harder for a stronger mission statement, although I would probably have lost. But, like all the civilians in the meetings, I believed that IFOR would do more than it did, especially in the critical first year.

The "Silver Bullet." I still did not feel that IFOR's mandate was sufficient. Clark agreed, and he and his staff added a "silver bullet" clause to the military annex. Although phrased in bureaucratese, it gave the IFOR commanders freedom to use force whenever they felt it was necessary, without recourse to civilian authorities. In its final form, it read:

> The Parties understand and agree that the IFOR Commander shall have the authority, without interference or permission of any Party, to do all the Commander judges necessary and proper.... The violating Party shall be subject to military action by the IFOR, including the use of necessary force to ensure compliance with the Annex.

On the day between the two White House meetings, October 26, Christopher took the Dayton team and a number of senior officials, including Madeleine Albright, to a government training center in the Virginia hills near Warrenton for a strategy session. By now our team had expanded substantially. Warrenton was a dress rehearsal for Dayton, and we walked through every detail of the talks, presenting to Christopher and his team a ninety-two-page draft peace agreement and volumes of backup material. We agreed on a basic concept: Christopher would open the talks, then return to Washington, where he would remain available for visits whenever his presence might make a difference. After five hours of discussion, Christopher pronounced himself "satisfied and impressed" and we drove back to Washington.

The Consultations Intensify. The Europeans waited impatiently. The civilian implementation structure would be headed by Carl Bildt, and the military force would be at least two-thirds European—yet we had spent almost no time talking to the Europeans while our internal debate proceeded. When the consultations with the Europeans finally began, time was short, and the agenda massive. A visitor to the sixth floor of the State Department that weekend would have seen an unusual sight—dozens of people from at least seven countries wandering up and down a long corridor arguing in small groups over hundreds of pages of draft agreements and backup papers. Kornblum and I moved from room to room, encouraging and guiding the process.

I wish that cynics about government service had observed these meetings. It was one of those lovely Washington fall weekends that make the capital seem invigorating, but inside, oblivious to the weather, dozens of bureaucrats and military officers from many countries sweated through intense, seemingly endless meetings. By late Sunday afternoon, they had resolved many issues, especially those involving the deployment and role of IFOR. But we could not finish work on several key matters, including the authority of the senior civilian in Bosnia, and the role of the International Police Task Force. We agreed to complete our discussions in Dayton.

As the meetings continued, Owen, O'Brien, Menzies, and Jack Zetkulic of the Balkan desk flew to New York with me to talk to the Bosnians. Despite our pleas, they had done nothing to prepare for Dayton. Six weeks earlier, on September 18, I had raised my concern over this issue with Muhamed Sacirbey over a late-night conversation at the Inter-Continental Hotel in Zagreb. "Mo, I'm concerned that your government isn't ready for a peace conference," I had said. "Every time we try to discuss the key issues, you guys disagree with each other. You can't go into a big conference like that."

"We need help," he had replied. One of Sacirbey's charming qualities was his ability to admit, when he was alone, the mess in his government. "You're the Foreign Minister," I had said. "You are going to have to keep your team focused." I remembered his reply: "I know, I know. But it won't be easy." A few days later, Owen gave Sacirbey a list of fifteen international legal experts, but the Bosnians ignored the list and the idea until the last moment. On the eve of the talks, the Bosnians still had serious internal divisions within their government, few clear positions, and no qualified international legal experts, except one overworked and underconsulted international lawyer, Paul Williams.

The meeting in New York was intended to help the Bosnians prepare for Dayton. "Think strategically about what you want to achieve in Dayton," I said. Sacirbey, however, told us his government would not negotiate with the Serbs until we had forced the Croats into a new and better Federation agreement. This threatened our original scenario for Dayton, but Sacirbey had a point.

Negotiating requires flexibility on tactics but a constant vision of the ultimate goal. Sacirbey's demand would slow Dayton down and could even sink the conference, but there was no alternative. Putting the Federation first would give the Sarajevo delegation a chance to settle down, while pressuring us to produce a better Federation agreement.

On Monday, October 30, I flew to Dayton for my first look at Wright-Patterson Air Force Base. Dozens of workmen swarmed over the site in preparation. The Air Force, working closely with Pat Kennedy and Rosemarie Pauli, had repainted and rebuilt parts of the five facing visiting officers' quarters so that the three Balkan delegations, the United States, and the Europeans each had its own building. The Air Force had knocked walls out and created "presidential suites" for some of the participants. They turned over to us the

Hope Conference Center, a two-hundred-room hotel (which we filled completely with administrative and security personnel) with conference rooms. The Air Force had built a high barbed-wire fence around the entire area and had secured the entrances with heavy concrete barricades, which were heavily guarded by military police and security personnel.

With large areas for private walks, many private rooms, and even tennis courts, the final result was close to our dreams for Site X. The Air Force had even built, in the words of Tom Shoup, the deputy director of the 88th Civil Engineer Group that readied the site, a "very lovely meandering walkway, complete with lighting, so that delegates could walk this peaceful path from their quarters to the meeting rooms."* When Donilon saw the facilities, he was impressed. "This is as close as it gets to a perfect setup," he said. "Now all we have to do is get a deal."

Our tour was made more poignant by the vice commander of the Air Force Materiel Command who showed us around. He was Lieutenant General Lawrence P. Farrell, Jr., Joe Kruzel's brother-in-law, whom I had last seen more than two months earlier when he spoke over Joe's grave at Arlington. He was businesslike throughout, but at the end of my visit he told me that he and his family had a special reason to pray for success at Dayton.

That same evening, October 30, the House of Representatives delivered a serious public blow to the Administration, voting three to one for a nonbinding resolution that the Administration not deploy troops to Bosnia without prior congressional approval. Gingrich called the vote "a referendum on this Administration's incapability of convincing anyone to trust them."

Mike McCurry answered immediately. "The President will live up to his responsibilities as Commander in Chief and be true to his oath of office," he said. "If he needs to act to protect America's interests in the world, he will act." While Leon Panetta predicted ultimate congressional support for a deployment, telling *The Washington Post* that "the American people are not going to walk away from a peace settlement," Senator Patrick Leahy of Vermont, one of our supporters, warned that "the President would lose" if it came to a vote right away. The President told the press that the resolution would have no effect on the talks, but there was no denying that if we succeeded in Dayton, the vote's damage would have to be undone.

The Last Briefing. Our last meeting before Dayton was on October 31, with President Clinton and Vice President Gore in the Cabinet Room. Trying to

---

* Two years after the conference, the walkway was formally dedicated and named the Wright-Patterson Peace Walk.

start on a light note, I denied rumors that we had picked Dayton because it was Strobe Talbott's birthplace. Thin laughter. I gave the President a T-shirt from Wright-Patterson showing a dove superimposed over the map of Ohio, and he predicted it would become a collector's item. I noted that Ohio's population included people from every ethnic community of central Europe and the Balkans. "There are more Serbs and Hungarians in Cleveland than any other American city," I said. "The area is filled with Croats, Albanians, Hungarians, Slovaks, and other groups who understand the tragedy of their original homelands. We hope the fact that they confine their rivalries to the football fields will send a signal to the participants."

This interested and pleased the President. He knew the area well, and spoke with feeling about the way people from different backgrounds lived in harmony in Ohio.

Regarding the talks themselves, I said we were on our own thirty-yard line. "That's not bad, considering we started on our own goal line," I said. "Dayton's a gamble, but the shuttle phase has run its course. Even if we fail, our nation can be proud that we made an all-out effort for peace. But there are practical limits to how long we can keep people cooped up at Wright-Patterson. We'll hit a wall by day ten or fifteen."

The President said that he hoped Dayton would be successful, but if it was he would face the most difficult decision any President has to make: sending thousands of young Americans into a dangerous, possibly lethal situation. "Given Somalia, we must have a clearly defined goal so that there's no mission creep," he said.

"I have especially strong feelings about Sarajevo," he went on. "It would be a mistake to divide the city. We don't want another Berlin. If you can't unify it, internationalize it." Turning to me, he said we should not be "constrained by artificial deadlines."

I said that there was one critical issue I had to raise, even though it was difficult. "If we are going to create a real peace rather than an uneasy cease-fire," I said, "Karadzic and Mladic will have to be captured. This is not simply a question of justice but also of peace. If they are not captured, no peace agreement we create in Dayton can ultimately succeed." There was silence at the Cabinet table.

"We can only go to the Hill with a full agreement," I went on. In the continuing silence, it seemed like a good time to raise some other important issues, even though they would not be resolved that day. "I know that this still concerns the military, but we cannot give up Gorazde and create sixty-five thousand more refugees. Also, there is real tension over what we are doing on the Zones of Separation. If we patrol only on the internal demarcation line, we will be partitioning the country. We must prevent Bosnia from becoming a Cyprus or a Korea.

"Finally, there is a political dilemma. The Hill sees us as replacing the U.N. in the middle of the war, although of course this is not the case. We need to explain better that we won't send troops without an agreement, and we won't participate in an operation like the U.N."

We broke up with many expressions of support. The President led us into the Roosevelt Room, where he told the press, "This is the best chance for peace we've had since the war began. It may be the last chance we have for a very long time." Then he and Vice President Gore posed for pictures with the negotiating team, wished us success, and left.

Our preparations were complete. We drove directly to Andrews and boarded an Air Force plane for Wright-Patterson Air Force Base in Dayton, Ohio.

BOOK THREE

DAYTON

(November 1–21, 1995)

Now sits expectation in the air.
—SHAKESPEARE, *Henry V*

CHAPTER 16

Going in Circles

(November 1–9)

The most gifted man can observe, still more can record, only the *series* of his own impressions; his observations, therefore, . . . must be *successive,* while the things done were often *simultaneous.* . . . Actual events are nowise so simply related to each other as parent and offspring are; every single event is the offspring not of one, but of all other events, prior or contemporaneous, and will in its turn combine with all others to give birth to new; it is an ever-living, ever-working Chaos of Being, wherein shape after shape bodies itself forth from innumerable elements. And this Chaos . . . is what the historian will depict, and scientifically gauge, we may say, by threading it with single lines of a few [inches] in length!

—THOMAS CARLYLE

DAYTON. THE WORD CONJURES UP INTENSE memories: the peace agreement that lasted thirty-seven minutes; our main gathering place, Packy's All-Sports Bar; midnight shrimp and steak dinners with Milosevic; the barren parking lot that separated the buildings where we lived; our cramped quarters, the lack of privacy; the effort of our European colleagues to adjust to diplomacy far removed, geographically and stylistically, from what they were used to; tennis matches with a surprisingly agile Tudjman; the emotional visit of the families of our lost colleagues; "napkin diplomacy" in the Officers' Club; dinner with Izetbegovic and Milosevic under the wing of a B-2 bomber; long walks with Silajdzic in the bitter cold; Krajisnik slamming his fist against a map of Sarajevo; Milosevic singing "Tenderly" with the pianist at the Officers' Club; the family of an imprisoned American journalist pleading his case; Izetbegovic refusing to touch his food during a meal with Milosevic; the stunning breakthrough on Sarajevo; the unforgettable final hours and our ultimatum; Silajdzic bursting into my room, shouting "You've ruined everything!"; Kati finding Milosevic waiting in a snowy parking lot outside my room; Tudjman emotionally telling Warren Christopher to "get peace now"; and Washington—waiting and worrying . . .

We thought we were ready. But nothing had prepared us for the pressure we encountered within the compound at Wright-Patterson. We estimated the conference would last fifteen to seventeen days; surely it would be impossible to keep three Presidents and hundreds of other people cooped up much longer. But twenty-one days later, on the last morning inside the high wire fence, we were facing defeat, with only twenty minutes left before we closed down the negotiations.

"Dayton." Since November 21, 1995, "Dayton" has entered the language as shorthand for a certain type of diplomacy—the Big Bang approach to negotiations: lock everyone up until they reach agreement. A "Dayton" has been seriously suggested for Northern Ireland, Cyprus, Kashmir, the Mideast, and other festering problems.

Those considering other Daytons should proceed with caution. It is a high-wire act without a safety net. Much work must precede the plunge into such an all-or-nothing environment. The site must be just right. The goals must be clearly defined. A single host nation must be in firm control, but it is high risk for the host, whose prestige is on the line. The consequences of failure are great. But when the conditions are right, a Dayton can produce dramatic results.

The translators' booths in the two large conference rooms came to symbolize for me the stupidity of the war. Our system had six language channels on the headsets. The first three were for English, French, and Russian.* Channel 4 was for translation into Bosnian, 5 into Croatian, and 6 into Serbian. This puzzled outsiders, since the same language, with minor differences, was spoken throughout the region. The answer came when one looked at the translation booths a few feet from our table. Each participant from the Balkans could choose his or her channel of preference—but one interpreter translated for channels 4, 5, and 6. When I noted this absurdity to Sacirbey, he said that "Serbo-Croatian" no longer existed—or, perhaps, had never existed. Nationalistic leaders were aggressively developing distinctive vocabularies for each ethnic group. Language, which had once helped unify Yugoslavia, was now another vehicle through which people were being driven apart.

Our goals were ambitious: first, to turn the sixty-day cease-fire into a permanent peace and, second, to gain agreement for a multiethnic state. Many observers believed these were impossible goals. Whatever we did, critics said,

* The Germans did not need, or ask for, a German translator. The French insisted on a French one, even though they all spoke excellent English.

Bosnia would eventually divide into three parts, after which the Croat and Serb portions of Bosnia would join their neighboring "motherlands." We could not ignore the possibility that this might eventually happen. But not at Dayton— and not under American leadership. We would not legitimize Serb aggression or encourage Croat annexation. Furthermore, such an outcome might unleash a new round of ethnic and border conflicts in Central and Eastern Europe.

To reach our goal required agreements on many issues: eastern Slavonia, the Federation, a constitutional framework, elections, a three-person presidency, a national assembly, freedom of movement and the right of refugees to return to their homes, compliance with the International War Crimes Tribunal, and an international police force. Finally, we would face our most contentious task: determining the internal boundaries of Bosnia, those between the Serb portion of Bosnia and the Croat-Muslim Federation.

Our governing principle for this daunting agenda was simple: what we didn't get at Dayton we would never get later, so we would try to put everything on paper rather than settling for the sort of short and vague (and ultimately ignored) agreements that had been the products of all previous peace efforts. Better a high benchmark than a weak compromise. Despite the difficulties that implementation was to encounter, this approach proved to be correct. Any lesser goal at Dayton would have resulted in larger problems later. While some people criticized us for trying to do too much at Dayton, my main regret is that we did not attempt more.

The Compound. The size and diversity of Wright-Patterson impressed the participants. We wanted them to see this physical symbol of American power. But the small inner compound where we lived and negotiated was a different story. We placed the American, Bosnian, Croat, and combined Serbian– Bosnian Serb delegations in the four nondescript visiting officers' quarters that faced each other around a drab rectangular parking lot. The Europeans occupied a fifth building off the quad, but only thirty feet away. To emphasize Europe's co-chairmanship of the conference, we gave Carl Bildt a VIP suite directly above mine in the American building. The Bosnians were to our left, the Croatians to the right, and the Serbians and the Bosnian Serbs directly opposite us. The ground-floor windows of my rooms looked straight into those of Milosevic across the parking lot, about sixty yards away, thus allowing us to see if he was in his suite. The buildings were adequate, but hardly elegant. Our rooms were small, sound carried through the thin walls, and the corridor was only about six feet wide. During a preview tour of the facilities for journalists before the talks began, someone compared them to college dormitories. Sacirbey thought they looked like a Motel 6.

These were true "proximity" talks; we could walk from President to President in about a minute. On some days we would visit each President in his

quarters a half-dozen times. Our days (and nights) became a blur of unsched-
uled meetings.

Dayton. There was also a real Dayton out there, a charming small Ohio city, famous as the birthplace of the Wright Brothers. Its citizens energized us from the
outset. Unlike the population of, say, New York, Geneva, or Washington, which
would scarcely notice another conference, Daytonians were proud to be part of
history. Large signs at the commercial airport hailed Dayton as the "temporary
center of international peace." The local newspapers and television stations covered the story from every angle, drawing the people deeper into the proceedings.
When we ventured into a restaurant or a shopping center downtown, people
crowded around, saying that they were praying for us. Warren Christopher was
given at least one standing ovation in a restaurant. Families on the air base placed
"candles of peace" in their front windows, and people gathered in peace vigils
outside the base. One day they formed a "peace chain," although it was not large
enough to surround the sprawling eight-thousand-acre base.

Ohio's famous ethnic diversity was also on display. We did everything possible to emphasize the fact that in the American heartland people from every
part of southeastern Europe lived together in peace, their competition restricted
to softball games, church rivalries, and the occasional barroom fight. Once, as
Milosevic and I were taking a walk, about one hundred Albanian Americans
came to the outer fence of Wright-Patterson with megaphones to plead the case
for Kosovo. I suggested we walk over to chat with them, but he refused, saying
testily that they were obviously being paid by a foreign power, and that Kosovo
was an "internal" problem, a position with which I strongly disagreed.

Our team arrived in Dayton on October 31, in time to greet the Balkan delegations. The wind whipped across the airstrip at Wright-Patterson and there
was a cold, light drizzle—weather we would soon become used to. Shortly
after 6:00 P.M. on October 31, Milosevic arrived, proclaiming his confidence
that a peace agreement would emerge from Dayton. Then, on an American
military plane, came Izetbegovic, withdrawn and apprehensive, calling for
"peace with justice." Finally Tudjman landed, proud and haughty. From the
outset, he wanted to show he had finally become more important than his
longtime rivals, and that he was in Dayton only to regain eastern Slavonia. We
agreed he would stay for two days, go back to Zagreb for the opening of the
new parliament, and then return.

I accompanied each President to his quarters, then returned to the airstrip to
wait for the next arrival. Tudjman and Izetbegovic went directly to bed, but
Milosevic, ever the night owl, was restless as usual, and asked to tour the
grounds. I took him, naturally, to Packy's All-Sports Bar.

Packy's was Wright-Patterson's answer to the United Nations Delegates Lounge, and a lot more fun. Pictures of Bob Hope—for whom the Hope Conference Center was named—entertaining American troops in four wars covered the walls. Four giant television screens, tuned to CNN and various all-sports channels, dominated the main room. Each table had its own small speaker, which could tune to any of the four channels, so the room usually resounded with overlapping broadcast sounds. On nights when the Chicago Bulls played, the Croats gathered to cheer their hero, Toni Kukoc; the Serbs waited to cheer Vlade Divac, then with the Los Angeles Lakers.

When Milosevic and I arrived on that first evening, Haris Silajdzic was sitting with Chris Hill. I went over to their table, but Milosevic pointedly held back, shaking Silajdzic's hand brusquely and then turning away to chat with people at other tables. Watching Milosevic turn on the charm, Warren Christopher later observed that had fate dealt him a different birthplace and education, he would have been a successful politician in a democratic system.

The waitress serving Milosevic was a pleasant woman who had no idea that she was serving one of the most reviled people in the world. "What's your name?" he asked her. "Where are you from?" Charmed by the attention, she told us she was Vicky. In Milosevic's excellent but accented English, she became "Waitress Wicky." Whenever he came to Packy's, he would ask her to serve him. A local legend was born, and a year later, during the first-anniversary celebrations at Wright-Patterson, I was served by Waitress Wicky herself, now a proud part of the Dayton story.

Milosevic was seething about the press, especially a profile of him by Roger Cohen in *The New York Times* that morning. "It is unbelievable," the Serb leader said, "that such shit can be printed." He singled out the references to his parents—his father, "an Orthodox priest who had committed suicide when his son was 4," and his mother, "a schoolteacher who committed suicide several years later."

"Why do they print such stupid things," he asked, neither confirming nor denying their accuracy. "How can you permit it?" Milosevic complained that some of the information in Cohen's article came from within our delegation. This was true, although unintentional, and I made no effort to deny it.

DAY ONE: WEDNESDAY, NOVEMBER 1

"The eyes of the world are on Dayton, Ohio," Warren Christopher said on his arrival at 9:00 A.M. As we drove to the "quad," I warned Christopher that all three sides had hardened their positions in anticipation of the opening bell. This was to be expected at the beginning of such an event. More discouraging was the disarray within the Bosnian delegation and the dissension between the Croatians and the Bosnians over the Federation.

Christopher and I met with each President privately, reviewing once more the ground rules that we had presented to the parties almost a month earlier. The most important rule, of course, was that no one should talk to the press. Carl Bildt had agreed to our proposal that State Department Spokesman Nick Burns would be the only authorized spokesman on Dayton, and he would brief the world from Washington. We did not even have a press briefing officer in Dayton.

Each President made his priority clear in these initial meetings. For Tudjman, of course, it was eastern Slavonia; he did not even mention Bosnia. We told him eastern Slavonia could be settled only within the framework of a larger agreement. For Milosevic, it was sanctions. Christopher offered a slight change in the American position: we would agree to suspension of the sanctions upon *initialing* an agreement, instead of waiting for its formal *signing*. This was significant because we anticipated that about a month would elapse between initialing in Dayton and signing at a formal ceremony. This small change in our position would give Milosevic more incentive to reach agreement in Dayton, and simultaneously relieve some of the strain within the Contact Group over the sanctions issue.

Izetbegovic and Silajdzic told Christopher again that we had to renegotiate the Federation agreement before the start of serious territorial discussions with the Serbs. We had already agreed to this, even though it would delay us. The Federation was indeed weak, and no peace with the Serbs would work unless Croat-Muslim tensions, especially in Mostar, were contained. I asked the number-two man in the German delegation, Michael Steiner—the most knowledgeable and tenacious of the Europeans working on Bosnia—to lead the Federation negotiations, along with Dan Serwer, our tenacious Federation special envoy.

With our calls completed, Christopher and I walked the hundred yards to the Hope Center for lunch with the Contact Group. Handling them at Dayton would be a problem. They could, of course, meet whenever they wished with the Balkan leaders. But the real negotiations, with the exception of Steiner's Federation efforts, would be conducted by the United States. "Some of you," Christopher said at lunch in an effort to prepare them for some frustration, "may not be happy with every aspect of the negotiations, but we are all pursuing the same result together. Let us not lose sight of that."

Finally it was time to begin. The opening event was planned for maximum symbolic value: a public face-to-face meeting among the three Presidents, the first in more than two years, and the first ever under American auspices. In the B-29 Superfortress Room (each room at the Hope Convention Center carried the name of a military plane)* hundreds of journalists waited behind ropes.

Every detail had been choreographed carefully by Donilon, Burns, and my-self. Christopher and I entered first. Tudjman, Izetbegovic, and Milosevic came next, escorted by Galbraith, Menzies, and Perina to their seats at a small round table—a duplicate of the one we had used in Geneva and New York. Then came the most hotly debated and closely watched moment of the day— the handshake among the three men. Christopher and some of his staff feared that they might refuse, embarrassing us in full view of the world's press. I felt a handshake was essential as a symbolic act before we disappeared from pub-lic view. After some discussion, we decided to stage a handshake, but when the critical instant arrived, there was, in the words of *The New York Times,* an "awkward" pause. After a moment Christopher rose and asked the three Pres-idents to shake hands. The photographs—almost the last that would come out of Dayton for three weeks—sent the right signal around the world: the three Presidents were finally in one room and talking, however hesitantly, to one an-other.

"We are here to give Bosnia and Herzegovina a chance to be a country at peace, not a killing field," Christopher said. He laid out four conditions for a settlement: Bosnia had to remain a state with "a single international personal-ity"; a settlement must take into account "the special history and significance" of Sarajevo; human rights must be respected and those responsible for atroci-ties be brought to account; and, finally, eastern Slavonia must be resolved. When Christopher had finished his remarks, we adjourned immediately, with-out letting the warring Presidents make public statements. Nick Burns took a heavy assault from several reporters who understandably wanted more than a short and well-staged public event. But that would have started us off on a contentious note, and we had enough problems already.

Tudjman and Eastern Slavonia. Christopher originally planned to return to Washington soon after the ceremony, but in the first example of a pattern that would emerge at Dayton, we changed the schedule at the last moment so that he could attend a hastily arranged meeting between Milosevic and Tudjman on eastern Slavonia. We met in a small VIP cottage about a mile from the Hope Center. The two Presidents sat opposite each other, while Christopher and I sat side by side on a couch between them; Hill and Galbraith also participated. Their greeting was far warmer than their performance for the press; Milosevic jovially hailed Tudjman as "Franjo." Tudjman called Milosevic "Slobo."

Ambassador Galbraith started by saying that he believed the solution to eastern Slavonia, on which he had worked tirelessly, lay in the resolution of

---

* Carl Bildt suggested that we redesignate the rooms with more peaceful names for the duration of the conference, a proposal that was impractical.

several relatively small matters. Tudjman replied testily that these so-called technical problems begged the fundamental question, on which he demanded an answer from Milosevic: would the Serbs accept the full reintegration of eastern Slavonia into Croatia? Milosevic replied that the technical issues were really about another core question: would the Serbs have rights as a minority in eastern Slavonia? Milosevic seemed oblivious to the irony that he was arguing a human-rights case on behalf of Serbs from a region that his army had reduced to rubble. Still, he had a point. The Serbs who had lived in eastern Slavonia and the Krajina for generations should have had the same rights as other dispossessed people in the region.

The conversation began with consecutive translation, but as it heated up, we invited the two men to proceed in their native language (or languages), while we tried to follow with the assistance of an interpreter and Chris Hill. Once they were liberated from the civilizing restrictions of English, the decorum of the meeting rapidly deteriorated. "Franjo!" "Slobo!" They shouted with increasing intensity, half in Serb, half in English. Finally I interrupted. "Let's do something about eastern Slavonia right away," I said. "Mr. Holbrooke, you are too unrealistic," Milosevic replied. "This issue must be settled in the field. I cannot control those people in eastern Slavonia."

Nonetheless, Milosevic agreed to "use his influence," which he continued to claim was nonexistent, with the eastern Slavonian Serbs. Given this small opening, I suggested that Galbraith and the U.N. negotiator, Thorvald Stoltenberg, return with Tudjman to Croatia the next day, in order to seek an agreement among the local leaders. I thought of the stoic Stoltenberg, who was at that moment on a plane en route to Dayton; he would have time only to grab fresh clothes and take a short nap before returning to Croatia.

Although there had been no change in the positions of the two parties, Milosevic had made two important implicit concessions. For the first time, he had agreed that eastern Slavonia would be discussed at Dayton. And he had previously claimed he had no influence over the Serbs of Slavonia; now he seemed ready to "recommend" a solution to the local Serbs.

Tudjman had gained a point. Events had given him a central role in the peace process. Some critics charged that we had made a deliberate decision to overlook Croatia's often brutal policies toward Muslims and Serbs in exchange for Zagreb's support of a peace agreement in Bosnia. The truth, however, was different: we did not empower Tudjman, the situation did. Tudjman could prevent a settlement in Bosnia until he got control of eastern Slavonia, the last piece of Serb-controlled land in Croatia. Given his previous behavior, his threats to go to war again soon after Dayton if he did not get the region back peacefully had to be taken seriously. Tudjman's ability both to prevent a

Bosnia agreement and to threaten another war was his primary leverage over Milosevic. His influence over Izetbegovic came from his ability to break up the Croat-Muslim Federation, whose continued survival was essential for Dayton to work. For years Tudjman had been regarded with contempt by Milosevic and hatred by Izetbegovic; now he had the upper hand over his two rivals, and he knew exactly how to exploit it for his own goals.

Warren Christopher. Christopher was appalled by the behavior he had just witnessed. But it was useful that it had happened in his presence; he could warn Washington, as he said, that "it is going to be tough the whole way." Otherwise, he was pleased with the day—more so than I was. It had gone smoothly, and the press coverage appeared to be excellent. Christopher said he would return whenever it was useful, but would leave the timing to the team at Dayton. As we drove to the airstrip, I asked if he was comfortable with the chaotic nature of the process—so alien to his methodical style. "I'm not always sure what you are doing, or why," he replied, "but you always seem to have a reason, and it seems to work, so I'm quite content to go along with your instincts."

I thanked him for his confidence. As he left for Washington, I reflected on the long road we had traveled together. I had known Warren Christopher since 1977, when Cy Vance had made him Deputy Secretary of State and me Assistant Secretary for East Asian and Pacific Affairs. My relationship with him in the Carter Administration had been close, and it became even closer in December 1978, when he undertook a difficult and dangerous mission to Taiwan immediately after President Carter had announced the full normalization of relations with the People's Republic of China. When a screaming crowd of thousands of angry Taiwanese surrounded and attacked his car as he tried to leave the airport, he handled himself with courage and calm.

In the 1980s, Christopher and I kept in regular contact. He invited me to address his partners at O'Melveny & Myers in Los Angeles. We dined together in Los Angeles and New York, and worked on several business deals together. Despite our close association over eighteen years, we were obviously different in style, age, and background. Where he was cautious and methodical, I tended to be intuitive and impatient. While he looked at issues as a sort of lawyer-judge, adjudicating the differences between the two sides, I was more likely to focus on the historical causes of the problem and its internal dynamic. He came to Washington from California, a Norwegian American raised in North Dakota; I was a New Yorker with a mixed Central European Jewish background and had lived overseas for many years, on three continents. Almost twenty years separated us in age.

I never felt we were competitors. But starting in 1992, some mutual friends, perhaps trying to stir things up, began saying that Chris viewed me with concern. When Christopher was appointed head of the transition task force for the President-elect, the press printed rumors of friction and rivalry between us. When I raised these stories with him, he dismissed them. Whatever the truth about the past, it was extremely unusual for a Secretary of State to give a subordinate the kind of support and backing Christopher had given us during the shuttle. Now, with identical interests, fate had made us an inseparable team.

That evening, after Christopher left, we handed each Balkan delegation the draft annexes on the constitution, elections, and IFOR. Amazed at the detail and length of the documents, the three Presidents began to realize that when we said we wanted a comprehensive agreement, we meant it.

DAY TWO: THURSDAY, NOVEMBER 2

Trying to create a little order out of chaos, we divided our efforts into six areas:

- First, Michael Steiner and Dan Serwer, assisted by their diligent German colleague Christian Clages and Chris Hill, would negotiate a new and tougher Federation agreement between the Croats and the Muslims;

- Second, Bildt, Owen, and I would negotiate constitutional and electoral issues with Milosevic and the Bosnians;

- Third, Clark and Pardew would begin discussions on the military annex with the parties, which I would join later;

- Fourth, we would conduct a two-track negotiation on eastern Slavonia, led by Hill and me in Dayton and Galbraith and Stoltenberg in the region;

- Fifth, we would try to complete unfinished business internal to the Contact Group, with Robert Gallucci taking the lead on two issues that we had not resolved on that last pre-Dayton weekend, the role of the international police task force and the mandate of the senior civilian implementation official, who would be Carl Bildt;

- Finally, we would continue to defer most discussion on the territorial issues ("the map") until we had made progress on other matters.

What Is the Federation? The distinction between the two levels of government—the central government and the entities—was still confusing, even to many people at Dayton. This was understandable: the designations had changed several times during the war, and were poorly defined. The Republic of Bosnia and Herzegovina had been at war since the moment it declared independence in 1992. Its predominantly Muslim government, headed by Izetbegovic, contained some Croats and Serbs, but it had control only over the Muslim part of Sarajevo and the area around Tuzla. Other Muslim areas, such as Bihac and Goradze, were, for all practical purposes, autonomous. The Croat part of Bosnia was run separately out of Mostar by a group of Bosnian Croats whom we considered crooks; they were the people who had waged the terrible war-within-a-war that had torn Mostar and several other mixed Croat-Muslim towns apart in 1993–94. To stop this war and create a common front against the Serbs, the United States, under the leadership of Charles Redman, had created the Federation in early 1994. But we had not followed up. Until the fall of 1994, when I appointed Dan Serwer, no American official was assigned to work on the Federation. His thankless task was to hold the fragile, virtually nonexistent coalition together.

Out of makeshift wartime structures, we sought to create two functioning levels of government: a central government, with its capital in Sarajevo; and two regional entities, one a functioning Croat-Muslim Federation, the other a Bosnian Serb entity with no claims to sovereignty. Steiner and Serwer wanted the Federation to turn responsibility for certain functions, such as foreign affairs and finance, over to the new central government, which would include Muslims, Serbs, and Croats. In turn, local matters such as police, education, and internal security would be assigned to each of the entities—the Federation and the Republika Srpska. The para-state that the Croats called the "Republic of Herzog-Bosnia" was supposed to disappear, turning over its functions to the Federation.

For the first week, Steiner, Serwer, and Hill would struggle with Tudjman, Izetbegovic, and Kresimir Zubak, the President of the Federation, while I worked on other issues.

DAY THREE: FRIDAY, NOVEMBER 3

The Contact Group was already restive. We had agreed to meet each morning at 9:00 A.M. The first two meetings were a mess, and we wasted almost two hours on trivial matters. This was not why we had come to Dayton. The Europeans had a great deal to contribute, and would be essential for success. But they seemed addicted to interminable meetings focused mainly on procedure, while the three Balkan Presidents waited a few hundred feet away.

We could not afford to waste so much time, yet we had to keep the Europeans involved. After three days, we dissolved the large daily Contact Group meeting and replaced it with a smaller meeting restricted to the six senior representatives at Dayton: Carl Bildt, Pauline Neville-Jones, Wolfgang Ischinger, Jacques Blot, Igor Ivanov, and myself. For symbolic reasons, I suggested we meet in Bildt's room each morning.

"What Is Europe's Phone Number?" This arrangement reflected a deeper difficulty within the European Union: who spoke for Europe?

This problem had been famously described by Henry Kissinger when someone in the State Department had said that they had better consult Europe on some issue. "And what," Kissinger had rumbled to his staff, "is Europe's phone number?" Now, two decades later, and despite the E.U.'s frequent lip service to a common defense and foreign policy, Kissinger's question was still relevant.

At Dayton, it was a problem from the outset. Although Carl Bildt was one of the three co-chairmen, Pauline Neville-Jones and Jacques Blot told us privately that Bildt could not speak for their governments on certain issues. This made a mockery of both the theory and the practice of having a E.U. representative as co-chairman, and raised other questions. Whom did Bildt speak for? And when? What, in fact, was his authority? Did he represent only the E.U. countries that were *not* there? Where did the Germans, who had not made a similar statement, stand?

No clear answers were forthcoming from Neville-Jones or Blot. In fact, they seemed annoyed when we raised the problem, saying, "We'll sort it out as we go along." It was a sad admission, on the one hand, that the E.U. did not exist as a single negotiating entity. On the other hand, it was not surprising that nations which still aspired to greatness and global influence wanted to retain an independent voice on foreign policy. What troubled us most was the hypocrisy of the European Union in giving a distinguished former Prime Minister such a grandiose title, then undermining and hamstringing him from the outset, and later blaming us for friction in the negotiations. Reflecting on this situation a year later, Carl Bildt observed philosophically, "Europe lacks the capacity to act because of too many competing interests, while the U.S.— when it sorts out its own mess in Washington—has the capacity to act. The Europeans are good at coordinating with each other, while the U.S. is not, but our internal coordination takes up all our time, and you are more decisive when you get your act together."

David Rohde. In the midst of our negotiations, a new problem arose. An intrepid young *Christian Science Monitor* journalist, David Rohde, had rented a car in Vienna and, without telling anyone, set out for Srebrenica, hoping to write a follow-up account of its fall, a story that he had been one of the first to cover. On October 29, showing more courage than wisdom, he began digging in the red dirt of the mud dam near Zvornik, the presumed site of a mass grave. Not surprisingly, he was picked up by Bosnian Serb police. As Dayton opened, he was missing somewhere in Republika Srpska.

Rohde's absence complicated our work considerably. Although he was a private citizen and had knowingly taken great risks—traveling without papers or permission, apparently without the full knowledge of his own editors—we could not ignore the situation. I told Milosevic that while we would continue to discuss the issues, no agreement would be possible at Dayton unless Rohde was found unharmed.

Milosevic was astonished. "You would do all this for a journalist?" he said incredulously. "Yes," I replied. "We would have no choice." It was the beginning of a dramatic subplot at Dayton.

The Bosnian Serbs. The joint Yugoslav–Bosnian Serb delegation at Dayton included Momcilo Krajisnik and Nikola Koljevic, and one of General Mladic's top deputies, General Zdravko Tolimir. Milosevic relegated them to the second floor of the two-story Serb quarters, and treated them with open contempt. This was in sharp contrast to his treatment of Momir Bulatovic, the genial, low-key president of Montenegro, whom he often brought to meetings to demonstrate that the Federal Republic of Yugoslavia consisted of more than just Serbia.

On November 2 and 3, Jim Pardew met with Krajisnik and his colleagues to test their attitudes. The meetings were unproductive but revealing. Krajisnik, an unreconstructed opponent of a single state, proposed that Sarajevo be divided, and that the airport be moved so that the land it occupied could be converted into a new Serb downtown area. After five hours, Jim told them their positions were completely unrealistic, and left.

From then on, the Bosnian Serbs were essentially isolated at Dayton. Dark and brooding, they hovered on the edge of the conference, eating alone at Packy's, avoiding contact with the other national delegations, and trying to communicate with Carl Bildt and Wes Clark, whom they thought would be more accessible. Within a few days, Krajisnik began sending us angry letters demanding to know what was going on. I showed them to Milosevic, observing how odd it was for us to receive missives from members of his delegation asking *us* what was going on. Milosevic took each letter, crumpled it up without reading it, and threw it ostentatiously into his wastebasket. "Pay no attention to those guys," he said. "I'll make sure they accept the final agreement."

The Museum Dinner. We constantly looked for ways to break down the barriers of hatred and distrust. The most ambitious effort took place on the evening of the third day: a large dinner for all the delegations at the Wright-Patterson Air Force Museum.

We picked the site with great care. The Wright-Patterson Air Force Base included the greatest military air museum in the world, with a collection that covered the entire history of aircraft, from before the Wright brothers to the cruise missile. Hangar after hangar held priceless airplanes, beautifully displayed. For an hour before dinner, the delegations walked through the exhibition with museum guides. Izetbegovic showed little interest, but the others were fascinated by this brief diversion. With controlled emotion, Wolfgang Ischinger pulled me aside in front of a Messerschmitt. "This was the plane my father flew during the war," he said quietly. "I have never seen it before." Ischinger was a true son of modern Germany—sensitive, urbane, and determined to see his country play a positive role in the world.

Jacques Blot, however, was nowhere to be seen. When Rosemarie called to find him, she discovered that he was boycotting the dinner because the security guards at the gates of Wright-Patterson had stopped his car, forced him to walk around the inspection post, and then searched him using dogs trained to smell explosives.

We put an end to this excessive zeal the next day by ensuring that all senior personnel would be treated with respect and allowed to pass unimpeded through the gates. But it was too late to soothe Jacques Blot's wounded pride. I called him to apologize and promised it would never happen again, but, enraged, he said my apology was insufficient. The insult was not simply to him, but "to all of France." He would not leave the compound for our dinner—but he would make a formal protest to Washington and consider returning to Paris. "I will not," he said, "be sniffed." He pronounced it "sneefed."

Apologizing again, I asked Jacques to come to the dinner. Again he refused. When I offered to send my vehicle, he reluctantly agreed, and arrived at the dinner in a foul mood. When Igor Ivanov heard the story, he laughed, "Blot should not complain until he has been searched at the Kremlin. They used to do it to us every day." But Blot remained angry, and, irritated by other real or imagined insults in the following days, he was dyspeptic throughout the rest of the conference.

We arrived in the last hangar—the largest one in the museum—to find a great array of modern warplanes and missiles. The tables were laid out beneath the wing of an enormous B-2 suspended from the ceiling. Along the wall, in a fortuitous coincidence, was an exhibit that intrigued Milosevic—a Tomahawk cruise missile. Hill and Kerrick took him and some of the Bosnian Serbs over to the missile that had so impressed the Serbs in western Bosnia. It was only about twenty feet long. "So much damage from such a little thing," Milosevic said, almost wistfully, looking up at it.

Kati had come to Dayton for the weekend, along with several other wives. We seated her between Milosevic and Izetbegovic. Bildt and I took our places on the other sides of the two Presidents, and Croatian Foreign Minister Mate Granic, representing Tudjman, joined us, along with the still-seething Jacques Blot and Haris Silajdzic.

As entertainment, Wright-Patterson had provided the local Air Force band, which played World War II songs in the style of Glenn Miller. Three black women sergeants performed as the Andrews Sisters, and as they sang "Boogie Woogie Bugle Boy" Milosevic sang along, while Izetbegovic sat sullenly. The scene was surreal: the warplanes and cruise missiles, Glenn Miller and the Andrews Sisters act, my wife seated between Izetbegovic and Milosevic.

This bizarre feeling increased when we tried to engage Izetbegovic and Milosevic in a single conversation. To break the ice, Kati told Milosevic that in 1980 she had covered Tito's funeral in Belgrade for ABC. When she was growing up in Hungary during the Cold War, she went on, Yugoslavia had represented the best face of multiethnic socialism. "We always admired Yugoslavia so much," she said. "What happened to you?" Milosevic shrugged, as if he had been no more than a passive victim of events.

Kati asked Izetbegovic how he and Milosevic had first met. The two men had been avoiding direct conversation, but this question triggered an exchange. "Alija, I remember calling on you," Milosevic said, "in your office in Sarajevo. You were seated on a green sofa—Muslim green." Izetbegovic nodded, and said that he remembered the meeting well. "You were very brave, Alija," Milosevic said, trying to charm the man he had been trying to destroy. Izetbegovic tried to avoid all eye contact with Milosevic, but the Serbian President was undaunted.

"How did the war start?" Kati asked. "Did you know that your initial disagreements would lead to this terrible conflict?"

"I did not think the fighting would be so serious," said Izetbegovic. Milosevic nodded in agreement, and added, "I never thought it would go on so long."

It was a striking conversation. They both professed surprise at the dimensions of what they had unleashed. Yet neither man had made a serious effort to stop the war until forced to do so by the United States.

DAY FOUR: SATURDAY, NOVEMBER 4

Several participants wanted to unwind on the first Saturday. Sacirbey took Izetbegovic to Louisville for a football game between the University of Louisville and his alma mater, Tulane. I asked Sacirbey several times not to do this, concerned that a football game was not in keeping with the seriousness of the peace conference. In addition, I worried about the added strain on the frail Izetbegovic of a three-hour car ride and the bitter cold and rain of an outdoor stadium. But Sacirbey insisted. With his usual dour expression, Izetbegovic merely shrugged when I suggested it was a bad idea. When he returned, I asked him who had won. "I don't know," he said. "I think it was the people in the red clothes." (In fact, Louisville—the people in red—had clobbered Tulane.)

David Rohde. With Izetbegovic and Tudjman away, the pace slowed down that afternoon. We organized soccer, football, and bowling for the delegations, hoping this would diminish their hostility. But for me the afternoon focused on David Rohde. We received word that he was definitely alive, and being held in the northwest Bosnian Serb town of Bijeljina on charges of illegally entering Bosnian Serb territory and falsifying his ID papers. The Bosnian Serbs had threatened to indict him for espionage. At some personal danger, Walter Andrusyzyn, an officer from the Embassy in Sarajevo, had driven one hundred miles through a brutal snowstorm and forced his way into the Bijeljina jail to see Rohde. It was the first trip by any Embassy officer deep into the Serb portion of Bosnia since the war began. When he saw Andrusyzyn, Rohde became quite emotional. He was in reasonable physical shape but was worried that he would be convicted of espionage.

Violating our rule on no contacts with journalists, I took a call from Ted Koppel, who told me Rohde had worked for him and urged me to make his case a high priority. Then Menzies and I met with ten members of Rohde's family and two of his editors from *The Christian Science Monitor,* who had come to Dayton en masse to plead his case. Menzies had already spent a great deal of time with them, as had Nikola Koljevic, who saw this as an opportunity to ingratiate himself with the Americans. When we arrived at the meeting, the little Shakespearean was in full rhetorical plumage, talking, as he had in Geneva, about his profound love of America and his hopes for peace. Rohde's family did not realize that Koljevic, widely regarded as a drunk and a Milosevic stooge, had no influence over the men holding their relative.

Asking Koljevic to leave, we had an emotional meeting with Rohde's family, whom I liked at once. Mostly from Maine, they had gathered in Dayton at their own expense to impress upon everyone that David was not alone. I told them that we were, in effect, ready to hold up the negotiations on David's behalf—that we would not announce any final agreements while their son was incarcerated.

Rohde's family and his editors, including Clayton Jones, the foreign editor of the *Monitor,* were unsure whether to believe us. Jones wanted us to negotiate with Koljevic over the terms of David's release. This was not a good idea; it would have made Rohde a pawn in the larger negotiations and prolonged his captivity. The best chance for an early release was simply to hold to the line that there would be no Dayton agreements while David was being held. We would not bargain for David's release, we would demand it. I said I was certain he would be freed if we stayed firm. Two of his relatives assailed us for not doing enough, but others in the room seemed more sympathetic. We parted on a hopeful note.

That evening, while Izetbegovic was on his way back from Louisville, we dined at the Officers' Club as the guests of Chris Spiro, an American who was part of Milosevic's delegation. Spiro, chairman of the New Hampshire Democratic Party and an early supporter of Jimmy Carter in 1976, had been an intermediary between Carter and the Serbs, and had become Milosevic's closest American advisor. (He had also run unsuccessfully for Governor of New Hampshire against John Sununu.) I was uneasy about an American in the Yugoslav delegation, but there was nothing illegal about it, and Spiro—a colorful Greek-American who liked to tell us that we "didn't know shit about the Balkans"—did no apparent harm.

Before we sat down to a splendid dinner of lobsters that Spiro had flown in from Maine, Kati cornered Milosevic. Speaking in her capacity as the chair of a humanitarian organization, the Committee to Protect Journalists, she said that if Milosevic did not free Rohde he would face overwhelming pressure from the world's press. Milosevic claimed he did not know where Rohde was, or anything about the case. By prearrangement, I joined the conversation and told Milosevic again that we would not make a final agreement until Rohde was freed. When Milosevic knew the game was up on an issue, he often grumbled and murmured, as if to himself. Now he did just that. "I guess I'll have to see what I can do," he said. I stressed the need for speed; after his visit to the prison, Andrusyzyn had reported that Rohde was "pretty strung out," and urged us to get him released as quickly as possible.

The day ended with tragic news: the assassination of Yitzhak Rabin, Prime Minister of Israel, at the hands of a fanatic Israeli in Tel Aviv. He had been murdered because he had been willing to consider a compromise for peace. The reaction of the Balkan Presidents was cold-blooded and self-centered; this showed, each said separately, what personal risks *they* were taking for peace. None expressed sorrow for Rabin or the Israeli people or concern for the peace process. The only Bosnian who seemed stricken was the Ambassador to the United States, Sven Alkalaj, who was from an ancient and distinguished Sephardic Jewish family from Sarajevo. Izetbegovic let him leave immediately for Israel to represent Bosnia at the funeral. The contrast between Rabin and the Balkan leaders could not have been more evident than it was in the following days, as we watched the funeral on television and simultaneously struggled to find a way forward in the Balkans.

DAY FIVE: SUNDAY, NOVEMBER 5

We were determined not to let Sunday become a day of rest. It was time to intensify the effort. To test this proposition, we asked Izetbegovic to meet alone with Milosevic. With a notable lack of enthusiasm, he agreed. From the reports we received from both sides after the meeting, it was clear Milosevic had made an effort to persuade Izetbegovic that they had mutual interests and could make a deal, perhaps at the expense of the Bosnian Serbs. The meeting was inconclusive, but Izetbegovic later told Chris Hill that he felt that Milosevic was "sincere" in wanting to make peace at Dayton—a small but significant step forward in Izetbegovic's thinking.

That same day, we turned to the issue of Sarajevo—the Jerusalem of Bosnia, the divided city where the war had started. The Bosnian Muslims had never wavered in their quest for a unified capital city under their control. Although President Clinton had publicly supported this goal, it seemed unlikely we could achieve it at Dayton. As an alternative, we devised something we called the "District of Columbia" or "federal" model, in which Sarajevo would be part of neither the Federation nor Republika Srpska. Instead, it would become an independent enclave governed by representatives of all three ethnic groups. The post of chief mayor of the "Federal District of Sarajevo" would rotate among the three ethnic groups.

Silajdzic and Sacirbey were intrigued by this idea, although it provoked some jokes about who would be the Marion Barry of Bosnia. While they still hoped for a unified Sarajevo, they said they could live with the federal model if the Muslims had a majority in all joint commissions. I asked Owen and his associates to draft a detailed proposal for Sarajevo as an autonomous city.

At the same time, we pursued the unresolved issue, left over from New York, on the powers of the presidency and the parliament. Izetbegovic still wanted broad powers for a directly elected presidency and national parliament, while Milosevic continued to favor a narrower mandate without direct elections. But Milosevic left us with the impression that this was a secondary issue to him, and he would bargain it away later.

DAY SIX: MONDAY, NOVEMBER 6

"We've already been here six days. You may be enjoying Dayton, but we Americans want to go home. We can't stay here beyond November fifteenth." It was the first morning of a new week, and I was alone with Milosevic in his suite.

We had made no significant progress on the key issues. In a sense, our efforts to break the personal ice had been too successful. People were too comfortable at places like Packy's All-Sports Bar. Milosevic had a reserved table at the Officers' Club and knew many of the waiters by name, one of whom he jokingly invited to work for him in Belgrade.

Milosevic complained about the confusion on eastern Slavonia, and said that he thought the Galbraith-Stoltenberg talks were not going well. With this, he in effect invited us to negotiate eastern Slavonia in Dayton. We seized the opening. With Chris Hill taking the lead, we wrote a draft agreement based on

Galbraith's original text, reworded and simplified. The Croatians wanted the agreement to make every detail concerning the return of the region explicit—flags, postage stamps, and so on. Milosevic, on the other hand, was trying to soften the fact that he was ready to give up the region. Among other things, he hoped to reduce the risk that Serbia would be flooded with a hundred thousand Serb refugees. Hill had an idea designed to bridge the gap: to place the eastern Slavonia negotiation within the larger context of Croatian-Yugoslav relations. He proposed that the eastern Slavonia agreement be negotiated side by side with a larger agreement on mutual recognition and respect for the international borders that the Serbs had challenged with the original 1991 invasion. Both Foreign Ministers in Dayton—Milutinovic of Yugoslavia and Granic of Croatia—agreed to this approach.

As for Sarajevo, the Bosnians showed increasing interest in the "D.C. model" during long morning meetings. Owen, Pardew, and Miriam Sapiro had reduced the idea to a simple ten-point plan. It contained all the main components of a workable solution: a City Council, a rotating mayor, a unified police force, and local control of educational, cultural, and religious activities—and the demilitarization of the entire city.

I asked Milosevic to join Hill, Owen, and me at the Officers' Club for lunch. We expected the "D.C. model" to appeal to Milosevic, but he resisted it strongly. A joint city, Milosevic said, would involve a degree of cooperation that the parties had not shown. "These people," he said, "would kill each other over who would run the day-care centers." The only way he would consider it was if there was absolute political equality between the ethnic groups in Sarajevo. Milosevic's position was tantamount to killing the idea, since it would neutralize the huge population advantage of the Muslims. Tired of the charade, I grabbed Owen's draft from Milosevic's hands and tore it up. "If you don't like this proposal," I said, dropping the torn paper in the ashtray, "this is what we'll do with it. But that's the end of it. We'll go back to our original position—an undivided Sarajevo under the Bosnians." Owen, who had worked all night on the proposal, looked crestfallen and stared in disbelief at the torn pages of his masterpiece. Milosevic laughed at the theater and said he would reconsider the entire problem.

A Visit by Strobe—and Sanctions. As we had proposed in October, we wanted regular visits from senior Washington officials. Our first visitors were Strobe Talbott and his wife, Brooke Shearer, accompanied by Jan Lodal, the Principal Deputy Undersecretary of Defense. We gave a dinner for the three delegations at Dayton's Racquet Club, the first time we had taken the participants off the base as a group. Through the panoramic windows Strobe proudly showed us landmarks of his birthplace. He brought a fine, conciliatory tone to

Dayton, and added to this graceful stories about Belgrade, where he and Brooke had spent two years while he was with *Time* magazine and she was writing for *The Christian Science Monitor* and *The Sunday Times* of London. At the head table, the mood was spirited and relaxed. The two Presidents, still enjoying the absence of Tudjman, told each other jokes—jokes from Izetbegovic!—and tested Brooke's language abilities. The mood, almost giddy at times, even produced a rare moment of consensus.

The issue that created the good feeling, ironically, was sanctions—but this time with a twist. In the harsh Balkan winter, Belgrade was facing an energy crisis. Milosevic requested permission to import oil to his capital immediately. The humanitarian agencies supported part of Milosevic's request—twenty-three thousand tons of heavy heating oil into Belgrade. In addition, Milosevic asked for help on natural gas, and permission from the U.N. sanctions committee to export a limited amount of grain to pay for the fuel. According to the agreement that accompanied the cease-fire in October, when the gas went on in Sarajevo it was also supposed to have gone on in Belgrade. However, the Russians had not allowed the gas to reach Belgrade, claiming that the United States had blocked them in the U.N. sanctions committee.

These requests kicked off another round of intense discussions between Dayton and Washington. Leon Fuerth, still the main engine in Washington on sanctions, believed that Milosevic's requests far exceeded Belgrade's needs. He estimated that Milosevic's "grain-for-fuel" proposal would give him a profit of between $20 million and $80 million. Still, Fuerth concluded that the problem was real. After a protracted discussion, we reached a common position: we should not let people freeze in Belgrade—but at the same time we should not let the Serbs turn a humanitarian gesture into a profit-making arrangement.

Izetbegovic and Silajdzic told Strobe that the October 5 cease-fire agreement had been intended to permit "unrestricted natural gas flow" to both Bosnia and Serbia. "Millions of people are freezing in both countries," Silajdzic said emotionally, "and with the fighting over, this should be stopped." Milosevic was clearly relieved. It may have been sunny in Dayton that day, he said, but it was already below zero in Belgrade.

It was the first time Izetbegovic and Milosevic had found common ground on any issue. Little surprise then, that we ended dinner hopeful that Dayton's spirit was permeating the drab rooms at Wright-Patterson. Strobe and Brooke left for Washington impressed.

We could not realize it then, but the dinner Strobe and Brooke co-hosted was Dayton's high-water mark in terms of good feelings. Never again would there be such a friendly atmosphere among the warring leaders, and never again would Dayton feel as promising.

DAY SEVEN: TUESDAY, NOVEMBER 7

"All going well," Don Kerrick reported that morning to Washington. "Just unclear where all is going. No evidence anyone—parties or Euros—want to close deal. [Holbrooke] intends to rachet up pressure today."

At our 8:00 A.M. staff meeting, we agreed that while the spirit of the previous evening was encouraging, the parties still seemed to be enjoying themselves too much. We still hoped to end the conference at the end of the following week, but we had no idea how to get there.

The Weak Police. Even some of the annexes remained a problem with the Europeans. The most important was Annex 11, regarding the international police. Bob Gallucci commuted from Washington to negotiate a deal. NATO continued to refuse to accept any responsibility for arresting people. We could not leave this responsibility solely to the local police, who represented, in all three communities, the worst and most extreme elements. In my view, therefore, it was essential to have a strong international police task force with the authority to arrest people who violated the agreements. The three Balkan Presidents were not opposed to this: since they distrusted one another, they would have accepted an external force to impose compliance with the agreement.

Regrettably, the problem with the police annex came from within our own ranks, from both NATO and the Europeans. Pauline Neville-Jones, supported by her E.U. colleagues, took the strongest position, saying that British tradition and the legacy of Northern Ireland precluded her government from allowing police officers to make arrests on foreign soil. The connection between Ireland and Bosnia was not clear to us. Supporting the position the JCS had taken in the White House meetings in late October, NATO also opposed giving the international police enforcement power, on the grounds that if they got into trouble the military would have to come to their aid.

Distressed over the deadlock on the police annex, I called Tom Donilon and told him that to get the annex right, we would have to "foot more of the bill." Such a commitment, I said, would allow us to insist on a robust police. A day later, Tom called back with bad news. He had discussed the issue with the White House, he said, and, in light of the crisis over the entire federal budget—the Gingrich assault had reached its height and a shutdown of most of the government was imminent—they felt we could put up no more than $50 million. This meant we could not write the rules. Gallucci had to yield, agreeing to an International Police Task Force (IPTF) consisting of advisers and "monitors"—a favorite Euro-word that could mean almost anything. In addition, the IPTF was put under the United Nations, a change from our previous decision not to let the U.N. play any role in implementation. In the final draft of Annex 11, the IPTF was given responsibility for an "assistance program" *restricted* to:

(a) monitoring, observing, and inspecting law enforcement activities and facilities; (b) advising law enforcement personnel and forces; (c) training law enforcement personnel.

Article V of the same annex further limited the IPTF's effectiveness by imposing on it a convoluted appeal system that did not involve IFOR:

[In the event of a] failure [by the Parties] to cooperate with the IPTF, the IPTF Commissioner may request that the High Representative take appropriate steps, including calling such failures to the attention of the Parties, convening the Joint Civilian Commission, and consulting with the United Nations, relevant states, and international organizations on further responses.

I worried about the police annex from the beginning. Even without Washington's support, I should have fought harder against it, and rejected the compromise with the Europeans. As Clark, who openly disagreed with his own military colleagues on this point, observed, "We are leaving a huge gap in the Bosnia food chain." Events were to prove him right.

That afternoon, Clark, Kerrick, Pardew, and I drove across the base to the national intelligence headquarters of the U.S. Air Force to participate, by closed-circuit television, in a two-hour White House meeting. Milosevic was fuming over the continued delays in getting heating oil and gas into Serbia; he thought the dinner with Strobe Talbott had resolved the problem, and he did not understand why we were still blocking fuel for the freezing people of Belgrade. Izetbegovic and Silajdzic had raised the issue again, in effect on Belgrade's behalf, and urged us to withdraw our "hold" in the U.N. Sanctions Committee on heating fuel for Serbia. Kerrick told the White House the situation was "explosive."

As we watched from Dayton the discussion seemed distant and strange. Twenty of the top people in the U.S. government were debating the amount of heating oil and natural gas Belgrade needed during the winter. None of them knew enough to form an opinion, let alone a policy, yet the argument in the Situation Room became intense. Tony Lake, trying futilely to control the meeting, actually banged his head on the oak table in frustration. To break the impasse, Fuerth finally recommended that we offer Serbia significantly less oil and gas than Milosevic had asked for, and, desperate to move on to some other issue, everyone agreed. But after the meeting Lake put another personal hold on the decision so that he could consider its ramifications again.

The Prince of Darkness. After a week of confusion, the Bosnians finally took a close look at Annex 1-A, the military annex that would govern the role of IFOR. They did not like what they saw. From their point of view, the annex seemed to imply that IFOR would enforce partition rather than create a single state.

The Bosnians had a point. As Don Kerrick put it in a terse message late that night, "[They] will not accept [Annex 1-A] without change. Surprise is length of time it took Bosnians to recognize [the problem]."

To deal with Annex 1-A the Bosnians turned for advice to an unusual source—former Assistant Secretary of Defense Richard Perle, the Prince of Darkness, as he had been called by critics and friends alike during the Reagan Administration. When Washington heard that Perle was advising the Bosnians, reactions ranged from controlled concern (Strobe Talbott) to outright horror (Tony Lake and many of Perle's former associates at the Pentagon).

Richard Perle, originally a conservative Democrat, first came to prominence in the 1970s while a foreign policy advisor to Senator Henry "Scoop" Jackson, the conservative Democrat from Washington State. Joining the government as Assistant Secretary of Defense in the 1980s under Caspar Weinberger, Perle became the leader of the arms-control hard-liners within the Administration.

When the Bosnians approached Perle for advice, he called to ask if I had any objection if he came to Dayton. It was an odd situation, rich in irony: Perle had been a vociferous and influential critic of the Clinton Administration's policies in Bosnia, which he regarded as weak. Only a month earlier he had told a House committee that the American mission in Bosnia was "hopelessly ill-defined." He had been a supporter of proposals to give the Bosnians enough military equipment and training so they could defend themselves—an idea to which both the Pentagon and the Europeans strongly objected. His rise to public attention had been greatly aided by Strobe Talbott, whose 1984 book, *Deadly Gambits,* celebrated Perle as one of the leading figures in the shaping of Reagan's arms-control policy. Our relationship—we had known each other for twenty years—had been strained because we were usually on different sides of the political and ideological fence. Yet, to the surprise of most of my colleagues and the press, I urged Perle to come to Dayton immediately. "Richard, the Bosnians need you desperately," I said. "They do not know how to read or interpret a military document, and they are completely disorganized." Perle took the first available plane to Dayton and, with the help of Douglas Feith, a lawyer who had worked for him in the Pentagon, started analyzing the military annex, whose bureaucratic language the Bosnians had been unable to decode. Within a few minutes of his arrival in Dayton, he closeted himself with the Bosnians, showing them the real, often hidden meaning of the jargon in Annex 1-A.

Well after midnight, Pardew, Clark, Kerrick, and I sat down with Richard Perle in the bleak surroundings of the small conference room next door to my suite. Stale pizza and empty Diet Coke cans littered the room after a day of continuous meetings by others. After listening impatiently to our comments, Perle said he would encourage the Bosnians to put the maximum possible pressure on us to make the role of IFOR stronger. In its current form, Perle said, he considered Annex 1-A a "pathetic evasion of responsibility by the Pentagon." He had already begun to identify scores of changes that would strengthen the role of IFOR; I agreed with most of them, but it was not clear how many could be sold to a Washington and NATO bureaucracy that had already gone through a difficult negotiating process and that deeply distrusted Perle. The White House feared he might denounce the Pentagon publicly, which gave him a certain leverage, as long as he did not push it too far. My goal was to use Perle's presence to improve the military annex while keeping him from criticizing the Administration publicly—another subplot of the increasingly complex proceedings at Dayton.

Late that evening, Milosevic asked me to come to his room. When I arrived, he said, "This time you must join me in a drink—because your American journalist, Mr. Rohde, will be released in the morning and sent across the border. This was very difficult."

DAY EIGHT: WEDNESDAY, NOVEMBER 8

We awoke to learn that David Rohde was safe in Belgrade. His relatives, many of whom had stayed in Dayton, were euphoric, and asked to convey their appreciation to Milosevic. Christopher also sent his thanks to Milosevic. It was interesting to watch Milosevic turn the Rohde affair into a public plus for himself by presenting himself as the problem solver, the indispensable peacemaker.

President Clinton, Christopher, and I all spoke to Rohde by phone. He said he hoped he had not "screwed up" the negotiations. A few months later, he sent me a gracious handwritten letter of appreciation from Tuzla which concluded,

> I apologize if my detention complicated your efforts in Dayton. The last thing I wanted was to be an obstacle to peace. You made me a priority when you didn't have to, and I thank you. I saw two survivors here recently. One told me I was a hero. The other told me I was a fool. I think the latter got it right. My family and I cannot thank you enough. I am a very, very lucky person.*

---

* Rohde won a Pulitzer Prize in 1996 for his articles on Srebrenica, and later joined the staff of *The New York Times*. His book *Endgame* describes the fall of Srebrenica in impressive detail.

The Map—at Last. "Intensive U.S.-led face-to-face negotiations begin in earnest Wednesday," General Kerrick reported to Washington. With progress on the Federation, with political and constitutional discussions moving forward, and with Rohde released, we thought it was time to plunge into the most difficult issue: territory. We called a large meeting of all three sides in the B-29 Room and assembled large maps for discussion.

The meeting was a disaster. Putting the principal actors together in front of maps brought out the worst in all of them. Milosevic participated only after predicting that it would be either a waste of time or a mess. He sat relatively silent most of the time, enjoying the spectacle, which he knew would strengthen his hand. After a six-hour meeting, we had accomplished nothing, and perhaps even set ourselves back. As Kerrick described the ordeal:

> In scene reminiscent of *The Godfather,* two families (don Slobo and outcast Serbs; don Izzy and Federation) held truly remarkable six-hour map marathon. Despite hours of heated, yet civil exchanges, absolutely nothing was agreed. Astonishingly, at one moment parties would be glaring across table, screaming, while minutes later they could be seen smiling and joking together over refreshments. Bosnians presented country-wide 60% map proposal—rejected by Serbs. Serbs will present map Thursday. Saga continues.

Instead of offering an "American map," we invited each side to make an opening proposal. This approach only widened the differences between the sides. The Federation team was composed of Muslims, Croats, and Serbs, who argued continually with one another. As he had many times before—but never directly to the Bosnian Serb delegation—Izetbegovic demanded a unified Sarajevo. This led to one of the most remarkable scenes of the entire Dayton negotiations: the explosive response of the senior Bosnian Serb at Dayton, Speaker of the Bosnian Serb Assembly Momcilo Krajisnik.

As everyone who met him noted, Krajisnik had only one long and extraordinarily bushy eyebrow, which spanned his forehead, creating what looked like a permanent dark cloud over his deep-set eyes. Although Krajisnik had not been indicted by the War Crimes Tribunal—and could therefore participate in Dayton—it was hard to distinguish his views from those of his close friend Radovan Karadzic. Milosevic had often said that Krajisnik was "more difficult" than Karadzic, but we had little basis on which to make an independent judgment. Krajisnik had participated in our epic twelve-hour meeting outside Belgrade on September 13–14, but had said little.

He and Izetbegovic knew each other well, from lengthy meetings in the Bosnian Assembly before the war. Krajisnik owned a five-hectare farm on the edge of Sarajevo, in an area that would probably revert to the Muslims in any settlement, and we often made bitter jokes that the war was really over "Krajisnik's five hectares."

Enraged at the idea of a united Sarajevo, Krajisnik rose from the table, and strode to the huge map of Sarajevo on the easel in front of us. "I've lived here all my life," he shouted, hitting the map with his fist, "and I will never give it up. This land is ours. We cannot lose it." We thought he had hit the map at the point where his own farm was, although we were not sure.

It was evident we could not make progress in such a forum, and we never again assembled so many people in a single meeting. And from that point on, Krajisnik and his Bosnian Serb colleagues were truly nonpersons at Dayton.

Milosevic enjoyed reminding us that he had predicted the failure of the map session. "I told you not to bring those idiots to any meeting," he said. He had frequently told us that the Bosnian Serbs were a breed apart from the more "civilized" Serbs of the big cities in Serbia itself. "They have more in common with the Bosnian Muslims than with us," he said.

Meanwhile, Steiner reported gains in his efforts to build a new Federation structure that could run the Croat-Muslim half of Bosnia. His agreement defined which powers would be assigned to the central government and which to the two entities, the Federation and Republika Srpska. It split customs revenues between the Federation and the Serbs, and created a new structure for Mostar, which we hoped would eventually become the capital of the Federation in order to make the distinction between the central government in Sarajevo and the Federation government. To this end, we invited to Dayton the two mayors of Mostar—one Croat, one Muslim—and the courageous European Union chief representative in Mostar, Hans Koschnik, who had survived several attempts on his life. Tudjman would return to Dayton the next day, and his approval of these arrangements was essential. Then, we hoped, Christopher would return to Dayton one day later to announce the Federation agreement.

David Lipton and the Central Bank. One of our main goals at Dayton was to create the framework for a single currency and a central bank. When the Europeans first heard that we wanted to create a single currency, most thought we were wholly unrealistic. In the fall of 1995, the Croat portions of the Federation used Croatian currency, the Serb parts used their own currency or Yugoslav dinars, and the Bosnians also had their own money. Everywhere the German mark was the real benchmark currency. But a single country needed a single currency and a central bank—otherwise it would be a fraud from the outset.

No one on our core team—in fact, no one in the State Department—knew enough to negotiate these goals. We turned to David Lipton, then a Deputy Assistant Secretary of the Treasury. Lipton was one of the most talented young government officials I had ever met. A former Harvard faculty member, he was an expert in the brave new field of converting communist economies to free-market economies. In one of the most satisfying moments of my government career, I had taken him and Dan Fried of the NSC staff to Budapest in the spring of 1995 to present Hungary with a strong, single American voice to urge them to carry out a controversial new austerity plan. Senior Hungarian officials told us later that our meetings had been critical in Prime Minister Gyula Horn's decision to back the unpopular program, which was ultimately successful. Remembering how persuasive Lipton's presentations during that trip had been, I asked Secretary of the Treasury Robert Rubin and his deputy, Larry Summers, if Lipton could come to Dayton, and they agreed. In the final two weeks of Dayton, he would visit us four times, and spend a total of ten days with us.

Lipton flew directly to Dayton from Mexico City, where he had been working on the problems of another shaky currency far more important to the American economy, the Mexican peso. It was the day before his birthday, but he said he would delay his celebration in order to help us. "It will be good to deal with a currency that does not end in a vowel," he joked. As soon as he landed, we went to dinner with Milosevic.

Milosevic, who prided himself on his experience as a banker, enjoyed the discussion with Lipton but said that he did not see how there could be a single central bank. There would be a constant struggle over the ethnicity of its head, and over who got loans. We suggested that the head of the bank be from a Western European country, probably France. Lipton also proposed that the central bank not make loans directly, but restrict its activities to buying and selling foreign currencies. This arrangement, which Lipton called a "currency board," would prevent the Federation from taking loans and imposing the inflation on the Bosnian Serbs. Milosevic, who was familiar with the concept of a currency board from the dying days of Yugoslavia, was delighted with Lipton's proposal. Slapping me on the back, he said, "I like this guy. You diplomats talk bullshit, but this guy talks sense. He is a real banker. I can talk to him." Nonetheless Milosevic expressed doubt that the Bosnians would agree. (He was wrong; Lipton persuaded them over the next few days.)*

Lipton remained in Dayton for another day. He met with Tudjman and Silajdzic, whose understanding of economic issues was better than that of any other Bosnian. Silajdzic was obsessed with the question of his country's debt to the international financial institutions. Although it amounted to only $400 million, he feared that after Dayton the financial institutions would, in effect, foreclose on Sarajevo and bring it to its knees economically. Lipton said this

---

* Lipton's subsequent rise through Treasury was rapid and well deserved: after two quick promotions, he became the Undersecretary for International Affairs. He continued to play an important role in Bosnia, where his proposals, originally regarded as completely unrealistic, gradually were implemented.

would never happen. If there was a viable peace at Dayton and the central banking institutions put into place, he said, then Bosnia would have no trouble recycling the old debt into new lending facilities.

Lipton returned to Dayton after his birthday. He became an important part of the core team. In the close quarters of Wright-Patterson, we included him in small meetings that normally did not involve Treasury officials, and the payoff was enormous.

Nothing was more important to peace in the former Yugoslavia than rebuilding economic ties that transcended ethnic divisions. Shortly before Dayton, the World Bank had drawn up a $5 billion economic reconstruction plan designed to bring the per capita income in the country up to two thirds of its prewar levels by the year 2000. It had, of course, suspended negotiations on the program pending the outcome of the Dayton talks. Lipton and I both called James Wolfensohn, the President of the World Bank, who promised to support our efforts; his representative, Christine Wallich, was already inside the compound at Dayton.

Meanwhile, Perle spent the day with the Bosnians producing a long list of requested changes in the military annex. It ultimately ran to over one hundred suggestions, ranging from tiny word corrections to major changes. In several places Perle simply caught errors in the draft that the rest of us had missed. Elsewhere he and the Bosnians, now following his advice closely, sought significant revisions in the mission of IFOR. Ironically, Perle's proposed changes moved the military annex back toward State's original goals.

Most senior officials in Washington were still unhappy that Perle was in Dayton. Donilon warned me that the Washington consensus was to tell the Bosnians they had to accept Annex 1-A as originally written, and reject all of their proposed changes. "Tell Perle to shove his goddamn changes up his ass," one angry Pentagon official said when I warned him what to expect. "Let's see what they propose," I replied. "We can't reject them all, and some of them make sense."

Perle would depart after three days in Dayton, on November 11, leaving behind the official Bosnian response to the military annex. Although he kept in touch with us by phone, he did not return. When he finished the work on November 11, Clark, Kerrick, Pardew, and I began a careful review of each suggestion, trying to decide how to deal with both the substance and the politics of his proposals.

In Brussels that day, Defense Secretary Bill Perry and Russian Defense Minister Pavel Grachev watched as General Joulwan and General Shevstov signed an agreement that would place Russian troops under the commanding general in the American Sector of Bosnia. As previously agreed, Joulwan signed the agreement with the Russians wearing his hat as the commanding general of U.S. forces in Europe, and not as NATO Supreme Commander. It was, Perry said, "a truly historic moment." This agreement not only made possible the Russian role in Bosnia but also went a long way to ameliorating Russian antagonism toward NATO enlargement.

Every meeting with Milosevic that day turned into an argument about sanctions. "Talbott promised action on the heating oil and gas for Belgrade," he said angrily. "Why hasn't it happened yet?" On this issue, everyone at Dayton was in accord, and Kerrick spent much of the day on the phone with Washington trying to get it done. Finally, late that evening, Lake agreed that the United States would accept the flow of a limited amount of natural gas and heating oil to Belgrade for home use.

Late that night, President Tudjman returned to Dayton. We hoped that his reappearance would lead to breakthroughs on the two matters whose immediate resolution was essential—the Federation and eastern Slavonia. Driving from the airstrip to Tudjman's quarters, I told him that when Warren Christopher returned to Dayton in two days, we had to present him with completed agreements on both issues.

DAY NINE: THURSDAY, NOVEMBER 9

It was one of those days when, despite intense activity on all fronts, nothing significant happened. We used Christopher's impending trip as pressure for concessions from all parties, but with little success. Over lunch at the Officers' Club, Milosevic accepted the new American position on heating fuel with undisguised annoyance, pointing out that it fell short of what even the Bosnian Muslims had supported. On the "D.C. model" for Sarajevo, he remained elusive, neither accepting nor rejecting it. He still sought political equality among the ethnic groups in Sarajevo, a proposal we rejected because it would disadvantage the Muslims, who would be vulnerable to a Serb-Croat coalition or Serb obstructionism. "We will not even submit this to Izetbegovic," I told Milosevic. "It would raise questions about your sincerity." So the question of Sarajevo remained at ground zero.

During the lunch, Milosevic sought to appeal to Kerrick as a professional soldier. With Rabin's funeral fresh in everyone's mind, Milosevic switched from his normal role as the boss of the Serbs to that of a man taking risks for peace. "General Kerrick," he said, "you are a military man, and while America's prestige is on the line, my head and life are at stake, literally." The exchange was fascinating, but it was more theater than substance. Although they often disagreed vehemently, Milosevic controlled the political situation in Belgrade and dominated the Pale Serbs.

Overnight, the Croatians increased the pressure by moving their military forces closer to eastern Slavonia. Tudjman hinted again that he might prefer to conquer the region outright in a military action—as he had in the other three parts of the Krajina earlier in the year—rather than make a deal with Milosevic. On the other hand, because eastern Slavonia was on the Serbian border, Tudjman could not be as confident of the outcome. Tudjman requested that some American troops and an American commanding general be part of a "transition force" that would enforce its peaceful turnover.

Putting a few American troops there as part of an international force under IFOR made sense; it would ensure the successful implementation of whatever was agreed to. And it would be easy: the route from the NATO staging area in Hungary to the bases planned for the American troops in central Bosnia actually ran through eastern Slavonia.

The Pentagon, however, had a different view. Supported by the NSC, they argued that adding a Croatian mandate to the one in Bosnia would create an insurmountable problem with Congress. The White House quickly decided not to send any American troops to eastern Slavonia, a decision I regretted; the additional forces could have been limited to only a few hundred, as in Macedonia, but they would have ensured success in a dangerous sliver of the region.

The Tennis Match. Late that afternoon, Tudjman invited Chris Hill and me to play doubles at the indoor courts at Wright-Patterson. Tudjman, in remarkable condition for a man of seventy-three, took no chances; his official delegation included an outstanding tennis player, a gynecologist from Zagreb. On the first point of the match, with the gynecologist serving, Hill fired a hard volley past Tudjman at net. I walked over to Chris, "Go easy on Tudjman; we need eastern Slavonia," I whispered. Hill, a fine player, nodded. I served again. On my second serve Tudjman rifled a passing shot down the line past Chris. I walked over to him. "The hell with eastern Slavonia," I said, "our national honor is at stake. Let's beat these guys." We lost anyway, 6–2, 6–1, 6–4.

After tennis, we went to the Officers' Club with Tudjman for a dinner with leading Croatian Americans from all over the country. On the margins of this event, which had been planned to show us that the Croatians had significant domestic American support,* we continued to discuss eastern Slavonia. In

---

* There were about 540,000 Croatian Americans, according to the 1990 U.S. Census, with nearly half of them in the Midwest and concentrations in southern California and New York.

many ways the negotiations on eastern Slavonia reminded me of those two months earlier between Athens and Skopje; most of the details were settled, but the political will to solve the problem was still lacking, and a big final push would be essential. The main sticking point seemed to be the length of time a U.N. "transitional administration" would remain in place in eastern Slavonia. Tudjman still insisted on one year, while Milosevic was equally set on three. The obvious answer—a compromise of two years—had been rejected with equal vigor by both men.

Chris Hill stayed up until after 3:00 A.M., working with Foreign Minister Milutinovic. Using the Galbraith-U.N. paper as a starting point, he made progress, although, as usual, Milutinovic said they had to "consult" the local authorities. Meanwhile, Galbraith and Stoltenberg were pressing forward with their negotiations in the region.

We remained deeply concerned with human rights and war criminals; Dayton had to be about more than a political settlement. To this end, I asked Milosevic to extend his earlier support of Shattuck's trips into Srpska. A few days later, this request produced a strange sight: Milosevic's special military security forces escorting Shattuck into Banja Luka, which no American official had visited in several years, as he sought access to mass grave sites of massacres allegedly committed by Serbs. The trip was also designed to answer the charge that we were not sharing enough information with the International War Crimes Tribunal.

We had achieved very little in the first nine days at Dayton. Late that night I expressed my frustration to Kati, telling her I thought our chances of getting an agreement were poor. "There is simply too much work and too little time left," I said. "Milosevic is playing statesman without giving up anything important." My greatest concern that night, however, was with the Bosnians. Their internal splits, which were becoming increasingly acrimonious, were paralyzing us. "They are refusing to give us serious responses on most major issues," I said. "The Croat, Muslim, and even Serb members of the Bosnian delegation are all screaming at one another. Without clear positions from them, it will be impossible to end this negotiation."

CHAPTER 17

"Peace in a Week"

(November 10–17, 1995)

> [British Prime Minister] Lloyd George is trying his hand at reaching a settlement with the Italians on the Adriatic Treaty. . . . They all sit round the map. The appearance of a pie about to be distributed is thus enhanced. Lloyd George shows them what he suggests. They ask for Scala Nova as well. "Oh, no!" says Ll. G., "you can't have that—it's full of Greeks!" . . . "Oh, no," I whisper to him, "there are not many Greeks there." "But yes," he answers, "don't you see it's coloured green?" I then realise that he mistakes my map for an ethnological map, and thinks the green means Greeks instead of valleys, and the brown means Turks instead of mountains. Lloyd George takes this correction with great good humor. He is as quick as a kingfisher.
>
> —HAROLD NICOLSON, *Peacemaking 1919*

DAY TEN: FRIDAY, NOVEMBER 10

CHRISTOPHER AND HIS TEAM RETURNED TO Wright-Patterson at 9:30 A.M. on November 10, planning to announce the new Federation agreement that morning. But shortly before he landed, the Bosnian Croats told us they would not sign Steiner's agreement as scheduled because it did not give them enough power. "Blood pressure up"—Kerrick's laconic phrase—was an accurate description of our reaction. Once again, our game plan was scrapped, as we scrambled to prevent an embarrassing setback.

Christopher and I went immediately to see Tudjman, and asked him to get the Croats under control. Without apologizing for the delay, Tudjman said his problem was not with the Federation agreement itself, but with Izetbegovic's refusal to reserve one of the top three posts in the *central* government—president, prime minister, or foreign minister—for a Croat. Tudjman could be brutal at times, but he had a valid point.

We told Tudjman that we would insist that one of the three top posts in the central government be assigned to a Croat if he would support our Federation agreement. Tudjman assented, and the ceremony was rescheduled for the afternoon. Walking across the parking lot immediately to see the Bosnians, we urged them to accept a Croat as Prime Minister or Foreign Minister of the central government in order to save the Federation agreement. This was the essence of statesmanship, I said, a reasonable concession for a major gain. But this one would add to the tension within the Bosnian camp, already seething with intrigue, since either Prime Minister Silajdzic or Foreign Minister Sacirbey would have to step aside in favor of a Croat. Sacirbey was clearly upset. If anyone had to leave, he knew it would be him, and not Haris, who had a political base in Bosnia.

Less than an hour before the public signing of the agreement, Federation President Kresimir Zubak sent me a letter stating that he would neither attend the ceremony nor sign the agreement. Hill and I immediately went to see Tudjman, who read the letter and laughed. "If Zubak doesn't sign it," he said, "we'll get someone else to."

"That's not good enough," I replied. "Zubak must be part of the event, or else he should be replaced as Federation President. He cannot have it both ways, and we cannot allow him to wreck Dayton." We sent Hill and Menzies to see Zubak. A Croat distrusted by many of the Muslims, he worried that the new agreement would weaken him. We had not paid enough attention to the dapper and normally polite Zubak, partly because he did not speak English well, partly because he was overshadowed by extroverted people like Sacirbey and Silajdzic. He had become difficult, withdrawn, and sullen. Hill and Menzies said that if Christopher and I sat down for a few minutes with Zubak, the problem would be solved. And indeed it was. Flattered by the personal attention of the Secretary of State, who met with him for fifteen minutes, Zubak said he would attend the signing.

Still, the ceremony unveiling the new Federation agreement, while important to the future of Bosnia, was a sour affair. We met again in the B-29 Room, with the press allowed back into the base for the first time since the opening ceremonies. Izetbegovic and Tudjman barely acknowledged each other. (Since the agreement did not involve the Serbs, Milosevic, who mocked the whole process, was not present.) In his prepared remarks, Christopher gave the sort of upbeat speech that the event required. "Today's agreement will bring the Federation to life," he said. "It will create common political and economic institutions that will unite the two communities." He went on:

> The agreement finally gives the Federation the authority to govern effectively. The central government of Bosnia and Herzegovina will keep the powers it needs to preserve the country's sovereignty, including foreign affairs, trade, and

monetary policy. It will transfer most of its other responsibilities, including police, courts, tax collection, health, and education to the Federation. . . . The agreement provides for the sharing of revenues and a joint customs administration. Internal customs checkpoints, which had marred the Federation before, will be removed. Finally, the parties have agreed to the reunification of the city of Mostar under a single administration.

Of course, this impressive agreement was on paper only. After watching the terrible body language between the two delegations, I was as worried about the Federation as about the negotiations with the Serbs. Events would bear this concern out. Two years after Dayton, much of what had been announced that day to make the Federation viable was still not implemented, and Mostar was only beginning to settle down.

A Semibreakthrough on Eastern Slavonia. Milosevic and Tudjman were still divided over the time for a transitional period prior to the reversion of eastern Slavonia to Croatia—a seemingly small issue, but one on which both men were dug in. After three meetings with each President, neither had moved an inch. We returned to our quarters to examine our choices. Christopher had to leave in two hours, and while we wanted his day to end with a breakthrough, none was in sight. "Chris, what about a two-phase approach—with certain specified events happening in each phase?" I said, adding, half-teasing, "You're a great lawyer, can't you think of something creative?"

Standing up, Christopher started writing rapidly on a legal-sized yellow pad. One rarely saw this side of Warren Christopher anymore, yet it was him at his best—the skilled lawyer drafting an agreement. "The transition period shall last twelve months," he read, "and, on the determination of the Transitional Administration, may be extended for a second period not to exceed the duration of the first."

It was simple. Christopher's wording used only Tudjman's number—twelve months—but in fact allowed up to two years, which Milosevic probably could accept, for eastern Slavonia's transition back to Croatian rule. Tudjman and Milosevic could each present the agreement differently at home, and the length of the transition would be determined a year hence.

We almost ran to Milosevic's room to present Christopher's idea. Without hesitation, Milosevic said he would accept the proposal if Tudjman did. "Mr. President, let's close this now," I responded. "Let's go to Tudjman's room together and work this out before the Secretary has to leave for Washington."

"No," said Milosevic. "Let me see Tudjman alone. I'll come back to you with a solution." He was suddenly cocky, convinced he could deliver a deal, and get credit for it.

We returned to my room, where we waited anxiously with our colleagues. Through Milosevic's windows across the parking lot, we could see the two Presidents walking back and forth, gesturing and apparently yelling at each other. An hour passed. Finally, someone glanced out the window and said, in an almost awed voice, "Look at that!"

It was, indeed, an amazing sight. Milosevic and Tudjman were walking side by side, almost shoulder to shoulder, across the parking lot toward our building. The rest of our team quickly slipped out the door, while Christopher, Hill, and I awaited our guests. After a moment the two Presidents entered and sat down facing us on a small sofa. Seated so close that their knees were touching, the two men seemed like schoolboys proudly reporting to the teacher that they had finished their homework. "We have solved the problem, Mr. Secretary," Milosevic said. "We can agree to your formulation. However, we need a few days to work this out so that it looks like the issue was determined by the local leaders in eastern Slavonia." Tudjman nodded, but said nothing.

This did not seem specific enough; experience had shown that if there was an escape hatch, someone would use it. "Excuse me," I interrupted, "but the Secretary of State will return here Monday on his way to Japan. When he gets back, eastern Slavonia must be completed so that we can move on to our main work."

Looking straight at Christopher, Milosevic said, "The two of us pledge that it will be finished, completely finished, in seventy-two hours." Again, Tudjman nodded in agreement. As soon as the meeting ended, he sent one of his closest aides, Hrvoje Sarinic, back to Croatia to make sure everything went according to plan.

With the negotiations moving to a new level of intensity, I could no longer reserve an hour or more each morning for the daily Contact Group meeting. The less time I spent with the Europeans the more upset they became, but the more time I spent with them the less we accomplished. But we could not ignore the Europeans, so I asked John Kornblum, who had arrived with Christopher, to remain in Dayton. Although this left the European Bureau almost leaderless in Washington, it freed up a great deal of time for me to work directly with the Presidents, while John handled the Contact Group and other duties. We kept Carl Bildt closely informed of our activities, and left it to him to inform the other Europeans. We knew this would leave bruised feelings among a few Europeans, but there was little we could do about it.

The lesson from Christopher's trip was clear: he should visit Dayton only when a problem was nearly solved, so that he could push it across the finish line. Summarizing the mood in Dayton that day, General Kerrick discerned a cyclical pattern in our moods that he jokingly speculated was "directly linked to tidal Potomac." "Every twelve hours [we are] sure we will fail," he wrote, "only to find real chances for success at next high tide."

When I called Kati late that night, I said that the next week would probably be decisive—but could go either way. "If these guys want peace, they can get it in a week," I said. "If they do not, we could be here for a year. We do not want to return to the shuttle, and I don't want to spend the rest of my life in Dayton."

DAY ELEVEN: SATURDAY, NOVEMBER 11

The weather was miserable. A sleeting rain came down intermittently during the day, and the wind made it feel colder. The short walk from our quarters to Packy's left us shivering and wet.

In the late morning, Tudjman placed a wreath at the Wright-Patterson memorial to the American war dead. Alone of the leaders present, he had remembered that November 11 was an American national holiday—Veterans Day, or Armistice Day to an older generation, which, like Tudjman, would forever know the eleventh day of the eleventh month as the day World War I came to an end. General Clark and I drove with him to the memorial, which was next to a replica of a briefing hut used by pilots during World War II. As we sat on wooden benches in front of an easel showing targets for a 1945 bombing run over Germany, Tudjman made an impassioned speech stressing his own role as a member of the anti-Nazi resistance in World War II. This was part of Tudjman's effort to emphasize that he had been an opponent of fascism, so as to counter widespread international criticism of him for rehabilitating the pro-Nazi Ustasha regime of 1941–45—an action he presented as nationalist but others saw as racist and anti-Semitic. His own television crews filmed the entire scene for home consumption, as the rain pounded on the roof of the small shrine.

Tudjman was feeling good—as Galbraith might have said, he was on "one of his highs." He sat in his room savoring his impending triumph on eastern Slavonia, which would complete his liberation of the territories lost during the 1991 war with Serbia. But reports from Galbraith were confusing; the local authorities in eastern Slavonia had apparently not received the order from Milosevic to sign the agreement, and Peter, shuttling between Zagreb and eastern Slavonia in bad weather, feared that the agreement being discussed in Dayton was not going to be accepted by the local authorities. When Hill and I complained strongly to Milosevic, he laughed at our concern. The deal, he said flatly, was done. Galbraith confirmed this by phone later that day.

For Milosevic, the key to the agreement was that it would be signed far from Dayton by a local Serb leader. While Milosevic wanted credit in Dayton for the breakthrough, he did not want his fingerprints visible in the region. For Tudjman, the results were spectacular: he would get eastern Slavonia back without a war. For the United States, it meant that we had successfully brought a part of Croatia back to its rightful owner without another war, one that had seemed inevitable only weeks earlier. In so doing, we had also settled an issue that was an absolute prerequisite to the broader peace.

The main beneficiaries of the agreement would be the Croatians and a significant number of ethnic Hungarians who had lived in the area before 1991 and would now be able to return to their homes. But the agreement would not have been possible unless the Croatians had also guaranteed the rights of the Serbs in the area, who feared, with reason, that they would be driven out once Zagreb took over. Given the brutal manner in which the Croatians had treated the Serbs in the other areas they had "liberated," this was not an unreasonable concern. The problem was still alive in May 1997, when, during a trip to the region, the new Secretary of State, Madeleine Albright, publicly criticized the Tudjman government for violating the rights of the Serbs of eastern Slavonia and other parts of Croatia.

The November 11 eastern Slavonia agreement gave Dayton instant credibility after eleven days of stalemate. We hoped it would stimulate a productive map discussion. But when the maps came out, we hit the wall again, just as we had during the six-hour map session three days earlier. There was no momentum—no carryover from eastern Slavonia, no value from the progress we had made on political issues.

Milosevic began what Kerrick called "the day of the maps" by presenting us with one that was ludicrous. When I showed Milosevic's map to Izetbegovic, he reacted badly, adding to the tension inside the Bosnian delegation, which seemed to be getting worse. Silajdzic sat in his own room, six feet across the hall, watching us come and go with maps, but he did not join us, so after the meeting with Izetbegovic I went to see him.

"What's going on here?" I asked. "Why aren't you in these meetings? We've started the map discussions and you are not even in the room."

Silajdzic was visibly depressed. His mood seemed to combine despair and barely suppressed fury. "You see what I'm up against! I don't know what's going on in there! You see what a terrible mess they are making of this?"

"You have to get back into this thing, Haris," I said. "Your country needs you, and so do we. In forty-eight hours Secretary Christopher returns here. If there is no progress, I am going to recommend to him that we close this down—"

"Suspend it or end it?" Haris asked, calming down a bit. It was the same question that our team had been debating.

"I think suspend. Maybe resume the shuttle. I'm not sure."

"That's wrong," Haris said emphatically. "Threaten to end the conference once and for all. That will get his attention."

Silajdzic's point made sense. I went directly to Milosevic's room and told him that unless he took the territorial issues seriously, we would consider closing down the conference.

"It's the fault of the Muslims," Milosevic replied. "They are pigheaded and stupid. They—"

"That's not the issue. We need to make progress, or else shut down. The time has come for private, face-to-face talks between you and the Bosnians. I suggest you start with Silajdzic. He's in his room. Will you see him right now?"

I went back to the Bosnians, dropping in on Izetbegovic to get his approval for the meeting. Izetbegovic, seeing the advantage to himself if Silajdzic took the lead—and therefore the risks—on the territorial issues, readily agreed.

As Silajdzic and I walked through the rain and sleet to the Serbian building, with the precious maps covered in plastic, I put my arm on his shoulder and said, "Haris, this may be the most important meeting of your life, and if it works, there will be more like it." He nodded silently. "I'm going to leave the two of you alone," I said as we reached the door of the building. "Just one thing, Haris. Please do not lose your temper. Hang in there. If it is anything like some of our sessions with Milosevic, the meeting may begin to get interesting just when you think it is over."

I went out for a rare treat—a relaxed dinner in town with some colleagues. When we returned late at night, we heard that the two men had spent over two hours alone together. It was too late to learn more until morning, but that, at least, seemed encouraging.

DAY TWELVE: SUNDAY, NOVEMBER 12

The day began with long-awaited news from Croatia: the fourteen-point agreement on eastern Slavonia had finally been signed. There was elation over the agreement in Washington, Zagreb, and Western Europe, and resignation among the Serbs. "I think we have experienced the start of the end of the war in the ex-Yugoslavia," said the tireless Thorvald Stoltenberg, who witnessed the agreement on behalf of the United Nations in the region. President Clinton called it "a major step toward peace."

A Visit from the Families. This particular Sunday would always remain special in our memory because of the visit to Wright-Patterson by the widows and children of Bob Frasure, Joe Kruzel, and Nelson Drew.

December 31, 1992. With Lionel Rosenblatt, president of Refugees International, in Kiseljak on the road to Sarajevo, just before entering Serb-controlled territory. In the background, a U.N. soldier heads for his compound.

September 1994. In Mostar, standing on the makeshift bridge that replaces the ancient one that was the city's symbol, with General Charles Boyd, Deputy Commander-in-Chief U.S. Forces Europe, during a trip just prior to becoming Assistant Secretary of State.

August 21, 1995. Andrews Air Force Base: Kati, the author, and Strobe Talbott. WASHINGTON *TIMES* PHOTO.

August 21, 1995. A decisive moment: President Clinton pulls the government and the negotiating team back together in a dramatic meeting in a small room behind the chapel at Fort Myer immediately after the memorial service. *Clockwise from the President:* Tony Lake, General Wes Clark, Leon Fuerth (standing), Leon Panetta (partially hidden behind Clark), Warren Christopher, Chris Hill (standing), General Don Kerrick (standing), CIA Director John Deutch, the author, William Perry, Jim Pardew (standing), Madeleine Albright, General John Shalikashvili. Just out of camera range to the left were Sandy Berger and Strobe Talbott. WHITE HOUSE PHOTO.

August 28, 1995. With Bosnian Foreign Minister Muhamed Sacirbey in front of the Crillon Hotel in Paris hours after the marketplace bombing in Sarajevo. We are awaiting word as to whether or not there will be NATO bombing. In the background, Ambassador Pamela Harriman and, far right, Robert Owen. AP/WIDE WORLD PHOTO.

The team on the plane. *Left to right:* General Kerrick, General Clark, Jim Pardew, Chris Hill. STATE DEPARTMENT PHOTO.

October 5, 1995. Outside the Bosnian Presidency in Sarajevo. Carl Bildt (behind author); General Clark and Jim Pardew (right background) conferring with Bosnian officials. REUTERS/DANILO KRSTANOVIC/ARCHIVE PHOTOS.

October 16, 1995. A typical scene during the shuttle, taken leaving the Quai d'Orsay after a meeting with French Foreign Minister de Charette. *Left to right:* Chris Hill, Lt. Col. Dan Gerstein (recovered from his injuries on Mt. Igman), the author, General Clark (on the phone), General Kerrick, Jim Pardew. AP/WIDE WORLD PHOTO.

November 28, 1995. Discussion of U.S. force levels in Bosnia in the Oval Office. Chart shows a possible drawdown schedule for IFOR based on a twelve-month withdrawal plan. WHITE HOUSE PHOTO.

February 20, 1996. Reporting to the Principals Committee in the White House Situation Room, one day after the Rome compliance summit and one day before I left the government. *Left to right, at the table:* the author, Deputy Director of Central Intelligence Admiral Dennis Blair, General Shalikashvili, Secretary of Defense Perry, Vice President Gore, President Clinton. *Left to right, behind the table:* General Clark, Undersecretary of Defense Walt Slocombe, White House deputy press spokesman David Johnson (standing). *Back to the camera:* OMB Director Alice Rivlin. WHITE HOUSE PHOTO.

April 4, 1997. Two guys on crutches, taken during a White House ceremony. (Paul Nitze is in center background.) WHITE HOUSE PHOTO.

August 7, 1997. A meeting of the joint presidency in Sarajevo during a return trip as special envoy. *Left to right:* the author; Robert Gelbard, the implementation "czar" for the United States; and the three "co-Presidents": Izetbegovic, Zubak, and Krajisnik. This photograph was taken at the start of a ten-hour negotiating session that ended at 4:00 A.M. AP/WIDE WORLD PHOTO.

A Dayton Portfolio

October 31, 1995: The core team arrives at Wright-Patterson Air Force Base. *Left to right:* Hill, Kerrick, Clark, Owen (partially hidden), the author, and Pardew. At Pardew's left is Lt. Gen. Lawrence P. Farrell, Jr., base commander and Joe Kruzel's brother-in-law. STATE DEPARTMENT PHOTO/S. SGT. BRIAN W. SCHLUMBOHM.

November 4: Before a private dinner, Milosevic and the author argue over the release of *Christian Science Monitor* journalist David Rohde, who is being held in a Bosnian Serb jail. STATE DEPARTMENT PHOTO/S. SGT. BRIAN W. SCHLUMBOHM.

November 8: Milosevic and Izetbegovic lead a group from the barracks to the Hope Center to begin discussions of the map. The remarkable rapport the two men show—Milosevic laughing, apparently at a comment of Izetbegovic—will disappear within hours, and they will almost never meet face-to-face again. The author is far back, talking to Silajdzic. STATE DEPARTMENT PHOTO/ARIC R. SCHWAN.

Warren Christopher meets with the Contact Group in Carl Bildt's suite. *Left to right:* Christopher, Jacques Blot, Wolfgang Ischinger, Igor Ivanov, Pauline Neville-Jones, Bildt. STATE DEPARTMENT PHOTO/ARIC R. SCHWAN.

An American staff meeting over sandwiches and soft drinks at the Hope Center. *Left to right:* the author, Hill, Kerrick, Ambassador John Menzies, Rudy Perina, David Lipton (U.S. Treasury), Nick Burns, policy planning chief Jim Steinberg, Christopher, Chief of Staff Tom Donilon, Assistant Secretary of State John Shattuck. Also present were Robert Owen, John Kornblum, and Wes Clark. STATE DEPARTMENT PHOTO/S. SGT. BRIAN W. SCHLUMBOHM.

November 12: The core team meets in the author's suite as the map discussions begin. *Clockwise from lower left:* Pardew, Perina, Kerrick (leaning forward), Clark, Rosemarie Pauli, Owen, Hill, the author, Menzies. The issue is the width of the corridor linking Bihac and Sarajevo. STATE DEPART-MENT PHOTO/ARIC R. SCHWAN.

November 14: On a typically windy Dayton day, Christopher and the author, carrying a map, walk from the Bosnia delegation building to see Milosevic. STATE DEPARTMENT PHOTO/ARIC R. SCHWAN.

November 17, 1:00 A.M.: Drawing the map. As Milosevic stares at the high-tech computer screen, the search for a secure path to Gorazde continues. *Left to right:* Kerrick (back to camera), Menzies, Clark, Perina, the author. DEPARTMENT OF DEFENSE.

November 20, 2:00 A.M.: Milosevic and Silajdzic, negotiating in an American conference room, close in on an agreement that would last thirty-seven minutes. *Left to right:* Silajdzic, Milosevic, Clark, Christopher, the author. In the left background, Bosnia's main map expert watches to make sure that Silajdzic does not give anything away. STATE DEPARTMENT PHOTO/ARIC R. SCHWAN.

November 20, 4:05 A.M.: The negotiators toast the Milosevic-Silajdzic agreement, sipping wine from Christopher's personal supply. (Christopher is at author's right, just out of the photograph.) The author watches without drinking, concerned that the "agreement" is somehow flawed. *Left to right:* the author, Clark, Hill, Silajdzic, Milosevic. STATE DEPARTMENT PHOTO/ARIC R. SCHWAN.

November 20, 4:15 A.M.: Ten minutes later, the negotiators relax during the lull before the storm. Silajdzic is asking Izetbegovic's interpreter to wake up the Bosnian President so he can review the agreement. Moments later, Izetbegovic and Croatian Foreign Minister Granic arrive, and the agreement blows up. *Left to right:* Christopher, the author, Clark, Hill, Silajdzic, and Milosevic. STATE DEPARTMENT PHOTO/ARIC R. SCHWAN.

November 20, midafternoon: Reconvening in the author's suite after the disaster of the previous night, Izetbegovic and Milosevic go at it again. Milosevic is pushing hard for an agreement, but as the photo shows, Izetbegovic has withdrawn. STATE DEPARTMENT PHOTO/ARIC R. SCHWAN.

November 21, 11:45 A.M.: Donilon, the author, and Christopher watch President Clinton announce the agreement from the Rose Garden as Christopher works on his own remarks for the afternoon ceremony. STATE DEPARTMENT PHOTO/ARIC R. SCHWAN.

November 21, 1:00 P.M.: The three Presidents meet in Christopher's suite at the Hope Center prior to the initialing ceremony. STATE DEPARTMENT PHOTO/ARIC R. SCHWAN.

November 21: Bildt tries to encourage Izetbegovic before the initialing ceremony. STATE DEPARTMENT PHOTO/S. SGT. BRIAN W. SCHLUMBOHM.

November 21, 3:15 P.M.: The initialing ceremony begins. *Left to right:* Germany's Wolfgang Ischinger (partially hidden), Britain's Pauline Neville-Jones, Milosevic, Izetbegovic (showing his ambivalence), Tudjman, Christopher, Bildt. STATE DEPARTMENT PHOTO/S. SGT. BRIAN W. SCHLUMBOHM.

November 21: After the ceremony, talking to Silajdzic. In the right background, Christopher's executive assistant, Robert Bradkte. STATE DEPARTMENT PHOTO/S. SGT. BRIAN W. SCHLUMBOHM.

Not everyone approved of the visit. Several of my colleagues feared it would divert us from our primary mission or unduly distress the families. The first point seemed wrong; we could handle the extra burden. As for the second, I insisted that we let them decide. All three wives said they wanted to visit, with their children. They wanted to understand better what their husbands had lived and died for, and they wanted to meet the three Presidents. In order to ensure that the trip in no way exploited the tragedy, we told almost no one about it, and the press never reported it. This was a private event.

Jan Lodal, the Principal Deputy Undersecretary of Defense, who had done so much to support our team, brought them to Dayton on a military plane. General Farrell and I met the plane, which landed in a gusty crosswind and freezing temperatures. We took the families—Katharina Frasure, Gail Kruzel, Sandy Drew, and six children, two from each family—directly to the B-29 Room and showed them how the conference was set up. The children reacted in various ways. Some were excited about the visit, but others hung back, still depressed, unable to connect this sterile conference room with the loss of their fathers. After everyone had settled down, I said, "We would not be here today if it were not for Bob, Joe, and Nelson. They are with us here in Dayton at all times." In the midst of our tense confrontations with the parties, it was a suddenly emotional moment, and I had difficulty finishing my remarks.

Rosemarie arranged for each family to have a separate private meeting with each President. At the end of the afternoon, we gave a reception that included all three Presidents. I repeated my earlier remarks, and we ended by asking for a moment of silence. Then the families were gone.

"Shouts, anger highlight map talks," Kerrick told Lake. That was, in fact, an understatement. Even while the three families held emotional meetings with the three Presidents, we were enduring an endless series of setbacks with the same men.

Silajdzic began the day in an upbeat mood. He thought his session with Milosevic the night before had produced real movement. But Milosevic produced another ridiculous map that put five important cities in central and western Bosnia under Serb control. Milosevic also made a strange suggestion—that we present *his* map as an American proposal.

After lunch with the families, we showed Silajdzic Milosevic's map. I first warned him that he was not going to like what he was about to see, but my admonition had little effect. When Silajdzic saw the map he became furious. Waving his arms violently, his eyes darting around the room as if looking for escape, he paced up and back in an extremely agitated manner. He finally calmed down, but his reaction disturbed me. He should not have been so shaken; this was all part of the theater Milosevic was putting on. Was this the "cabin fever" Jimmy Carter and Hal Saunders had warned us about?

We now realized that each map drawn by the parties would be worse than its predecessor. We would have to present our own map—the long-awaited "American map"—the next day. If we did not, we would never move forward.

The "Perle Markup." Although it was now well past midnight, the long day was far from over. I returned to the American building to find almost everyone still awake and working feverishly to prepare for Tuesday, when Christopher would return. While Clark and Pardew prepared our first "made in the USA" map, Chris Hill worked on the final details of the eastern Slavonia agreement. Owen and his team of lawyers continued to draft election laws, constitutional amendments, and various versions of the "D.C. model" for Sarajevo. Meanwhile, Kornblum and I went through the Bosnian response to Annex 1-A, which, for shorthand purposes, we called the "Perle markup."

While many of Perle's suggestions were unacceptable or irrelevant, there was no question that their general thrust was to strengthen the role of IFOR— something we also wanted. In the end, we boiled Perle's 150 suggestions down to about 50 clusters. We recommended acceptance of 35 of these and rejection of only 15. Some of the changes were significant, but to get them through Washington, we needed to downplay that fact. I called both Sandy and Strobe to stress the importance of approving as many of the changes as possible. Sandy Berger scheduled a Deputies' Committee meeting for the next day to give us a final American position.

At the same time, we sent back to Washington the only document the Russians ever produced at Dayton: their review of the military annex. While the Perle markup sought to strengthen IFOR, the Russian draft emasculated it, gave the U.N. a larger role, curtailed the authority of the IFOR commander, and limited the use of force to self-defense only. Since the Russians had chosen to serve under the American commander but not be part of IFOR, it was relatively easy to ignore their suggestions. We handed the problem over to Strobe and Walt Slocombe, and asked them to handle the discussions with the Russians directly.

DAY THIRTEEN: MONDAY, NOVEMBER 13

We pumped ourselves up by telling one another that this would be the decisive week. We noted that we had now equaled Camp David's thirteen days.

It was not a good day. Izetbegovic and Tudjman both withdrew to their rooms, and refused to see each other or Milosevic. Izetbegovic also had ceased talking to Silajdzic. Thus we were back to true "proximity" talks, and every member of our team was in motion, working on annexes, arguing map details, negotiating the Perle markup with the Deputies' Committee in Washington.

. . .

Clark and Pardew represented the delegation in the teleconference with Sandy Berger and his Deputies' Committee on the military annex. Sandy steered them through the document, and the deputies accepted almost all of the thirty-five proposals we had supported. One suggestion they rejected, unfortunately, was to delete the reference to a one-year limit for IFOR. I thought such a self-imposed limit did not belong in the Dayton documents. But the White House and the Pentagon, which had overruled us before on this point, did so again, fearing that its omission would trigger a congressional backlash. The one-year time limit remained in the draft agreement.

The deputies also rejected another major Perle proposal: to create a "mechanism" to investigate suspected war criminals, "in particular all current or former soldiers . . . [and] oversee [their] discharge from such forces." I thought that, while sloppily drafted, this was a creative idea that deserved to be refined and incorporated into the final Dayton agreement. Washington did not agree; it viewed it as a step toward mission creep. In retrospect, it is still odd, and sad, that the Pentagon and NATO so vigorously rejected such proposals, which would have given IFOR greater authority in Bosnia—and greatly aided the implementation of the agreements.

Berger pushed most of the rest of the changes through the Deputies' Committee without much problem. We could now put this important part of the Dayton agreements, which would give the NATO-led forces their authority and the ability to defend themselves, into final form. There was no question about it: the military annex had been improved by Richard Perle's involvement. So valuable was his contribution that I called him a few days later to suggest that he come back to assist the Bosnians on other issues, but his schedule did not permit it.

Engaging the Bosnians. Of the many difficulties we faced that day, the one that disturbed us most was, as I wrote Christopher late that evening, the "immense difficulty of engaging the Bosnian government in a serious negotiation." Desperate to find the key to the increasingly fractious Sarajevo delegation, I took Silajdzic on a long walk at noon. Although it was still cold, the sun was finally out, and as we walked across the quiet streets of the military base, I tried to reach out to this intelligent, remote, often tortured man by appealing to his sense of history. This approach went nowhere; Haris was furious with the Serbs and Croats and gloomy about his own situation within the Bosnian delegation.

Changing my tone, I warned him that Christopher would consider closing down the talks if we could not make progress. We had said this before, but I added that "if the breakdown were attributable to Sarajevo, there would be serious consequences" to their government, including the possible suspension of our plan to equip and train the Federation forces.

This infuriated Haris. "You must never, ever threaten us in such a manner," he said, as we walked past the orderly houses of majors and colonels, trailed by security personnel. "We will never yield to blackmail." There was an almost uncontrolled fury in his voice. "We're not threatening you, Haris," I said, "only trying to convey to you the situation as we see it. We cannot stay in Dayton forever, and we are getting nowhere on the map." I felt sorry for Haris: he was alternately a belligerent defender of his nation and a beleaguered victim of a conspiracy within his own delegation led by Sacirbey.

The Key Map Issues—Defined at Last. We began to move rapidly back and forth across the quad, with Clark carrying the precious maps himself. Each President took hard positions on the key issues, although Milosevic conceded a few areas that were already in Federation hands, such as the Livno Valley linking Sarajevo and Bihac. By the end of the day we had our first clear picture of the most important territorial issues:

1. *Sarajevo.* The "D.C. model" was still on the table; the issue was still unresolved.

2. *Brcko and the Posavina Corridor.* In the original 1994 Contact Group plan, Brcko, the disputed city on the Croatian border on the Sava River, had been "solved" by a complicated proposal that returned the city to the Muslims and narrowed the Serb-controlled Posavina Corridor—the all-important link between Serbia proper and the Serb portion of western Bosnia—to a *thirty-meter* underpass below a railroad bridge. This idea had been "accepted" by Milosevic, who knew it would never be implemented. But that same agreement obsessed Izetbegovic, who insisted it be honored. Milosevic, on the other hand, demanded its widening.

3. *Gorazde.* We had to create a defensible land connection between this last Muslim enclave in eastern Bosnia and Sarajevo.

4. *The Posavina "Pocket."* Not to be confused with the neighboring Posavina Corridor, the Posavina was a fertile area just south of the Croatian border, comprising about 3 percent of the entire landmass of Bosnia. Early in the war, the Serbs had seized it and driven over 135,000 Croats from their land. Importantly, Posavina was near the home of Federation president Zubak.

5. *Srebrenica and Zepa.* Izetbegovic wanted it clearly understood that these two towns in eastern Bosnia, the ultimate symbols of ethnic cleansing, were still on his list of objectives at Dayton. He knew that he would not get them back, but since they were assigned to the Fed-

eration in the 1994 Contact Group map, he did not want to give up his claim to them without something in return.

6. *Bosanski Novi.* This was the town, on the international border with Croatia, where the Serbs had stopped the Croatian Army in mid-September. It was another important railroad junction, as well as a vital link on the river route for goods going down the Sava River to the Adriatic.

There were many other disputed areas, but these seemed to be the most important. Of the six, the most critical were certain to be Gorazde, Sarajevo, and Brcko. And tough as the first two were, we suspected that Brcko would be the most difficult of all.

"Closure or Closedown." Through the day and well into the night the map team and the political-constitutional teams negotiated on parallel tracks with the three presidents and their entourages. Near midnight Silajdzic and I took a second, shorter walk. Haris was in a much better mood than I was. "Today has been the best day so far," he said, to my surprise. "Peace is within sight." He was excited that we were finally engaged on the last and most critical set of issues; I was depressed because of the difficulties that we still encountered at every turn, especially within his delegation.

When we had finished our walk, I sent Warren Christopher a fairly downbeat "scene setter" in preparation for his visit the next day. It was the first time we confronted Washington with our view that if we did not succeed, we wanted to close down rather than suspend. "We have to recast your trip," I wrote:

> Initially conceived of as a possible closer trip, it now becomes a last warning to get serious stopover on your way to Japan, with the clear message that when you return we must have either closure or closedown. . . .
>
> On Day 14, we are about where should have been on Day 8 or 9. Much has been accomplished here . . . but the issues that remain include most of the core issues except elections, where we have made remarkable progress. Most disturbingly, we have had a series of emotional map discussions in which the Bosnians constantly changed their minds. While the Bosnians are the sort of friends that try one's patience, Milosevic has often lied outright about factual data or changed his position after we thought we had locked something in. As for Tudjman, he is fast becoming the King of Dayton. . . .
>
> You can jump-start this conference by a combination of pressure, rhetoric, and direct involvement on some issues where you can break a logjam. . . . All the parties want peace, but they still don't know how to get it. They look forward to your helping them stop killing each other—and so do we.

DAY FOURTEEN: NOVEMBER 14

The struggle in Washington over the federal budget was casting dark shadows over Dayton, hard to define but increasingly noticeable. With the day-to-day operations of the federal government shut down except for "essential operations," the fact that an agreement in Dayton would result in the commitment of twenty thousand American troops to Bosnia at a cost estimated at $2 billion for the first year created conflicting emotions in the White House. On one hand, everyone understood the consequences of failure at Dayton. On the other, the domestic advisors to the President were deeply worried that the Congress and the American people would be doubly resistant to a Bosnia troop commitment in the face of such budgetary problems.

The domestic crisis took its toll in other foreign-policy areas as well. At the last moment, President Clinton decided it would not be appropriate to attend the Osaka summit of Asian-Pacific leaders when many government services were shut down, and sent Vice President Gore and Secretary Christopher to represent the United States. Christopher planned to spend the day with us, then fly to Osaka for the meeting of the leaders of the Asian-Pacific region, drop out of the rest of the Asian trip, and return to Dayton.

He began the day, as usual, with a detailed briefing at the Hope Center, where a suite of rooms was always reserved for him. From then until midnight, he and I crisscrossed the quad, arguing, pleading, threatening, and cajoling the three Presidents. In every meeting, we stressed the new theme outlined in the previous night's memo to Christopher, although he held back from stating that a shutdown of Dayton would be permanent; he wanted to keep open the possibility of a return to the shuttle or a resumption of the talks to Europe. I felt, however, that after Dayton another American shuttle effort would not be effective. Some people in Washington thought moving the talks to Europe would shift the burden of failure from the American hosts to the Europeans, but the core team had gradually concluded that it was all or nothing at Dayton.

Christopher hoped that his visit to Dayton might result in a breakthrough on Sarajevo. But there was no such luck. Milosevic toyed throughout the day with the "D.C. model," trying out on us various unacceptable versions of it. At the end of the day, we had gone nowhere on Sarajevo.

The most difficult meetings were with Izetbegovic. In the last of our three meetings that day, we tried to talk in personal terms to the Bosnian leader. We reminded him of all the benefits peace would bring, and listed the substantial achievements the process had already brought Bosnia: a cessation of hostilities, the lifting of the siege of Sarajevo, the partial opening of roads, the damage NATO bombing had done to the Bosnian Serbs, the $5 billion World Bank package that awaited the country after a peace agreement, the equip-and-train program for the Bosnian Army. Christopher concluded with a drama unusual for him. "President Clinton has put an enormous amount on the line to save Bosnia," he said. "But he will no longer assist your government if you turn out to be the obstacle to an agreement in Dayton." Izetbegovic said nothing in response, and outwardly seemed unmoved by Christopher's statement.

Christopher left for Asia late that night, frustrated that he had spent a day at Dayton and accomplished nothing. To the President, Christopher gave a mixed report. "Dayton," he said, "offered tantalizing hints that a peace agreement might indeed be possible. It is possible, in the good moments, to see the final shape of the map. . . . But it is a very fragile system." He expressed the hope that, in his absence, the negotiators would be able to "fill in the success" of his visit under what he called "Holbrooke's aggressive tutelage." While the "optimistic scenario may well not happen," he added, the "prospect [is] good enough to justify missing the State Visit to Japan." Christopher still resisted the idea of a choice solely between closure and closedown, and told the President that if we had not finished the agreement by early the following week, "it will probably be necessary to suspend the negotiations on the best possible basis."

DAY FIFTEEN: WEDNESDAY, NOVEMBER 15

There was no movement on the core territorial problems, but the negotiators made progress on other issues, including elections. One election issue, however, remained unsolved: how and where refugees should vote. Should they be allowed to vote in their countries of sanctuary, or should they be required to return home? And what was home, for example, to a Bosnian Muslim who had been driven from his house in Banja Luka and now lived in Frankfurt with little prospect of returning? Did he vote in Banja Luka, or for candidates in some Federation area in which he had never lived? On such complicated, but real-life, questions the success of Dayton would depend. During the United Nations–sponsored negotiations on Cambodia in 1992, the problem of refugee voting had been the last issue resolved; we expected a similar last-minute drama on this question in Dayton.

The Germans felt especially strongly about this. With over three hundred thousand Bosnian refugees in their country, Germany wanted to reduce the burden that the refugees had put on its social services and budget. Other countries had similar problems, although not as severe. Bonn had given Wolfgang Ischinger one firm instruction: any agreement must encourage the refugees to return home. Ischinger proposed that the refugees be allowed to vote only if they stated at the time of the voting their intention to return to Bosnia. We incorporated this proposal into the draft agreements, although it was clearly not sufficient for Germany.

Late in the afternoon, Tudjman left for Zagreb to preside over the opening of the new Croatian Parliament. He promised to return in a few days. In our last meeting before his departure, he again asked that an American general officer be put in charge of the United Nations Transitional Authority in eastern Slavonia—a request I promised to support strongly.

We reached agreement that day on another important issue: the relationship between the IFOR commander and the High Representative—although it was not, to my mind, a good agreement. From his headquarters in Belgium, General Joulwan had called Clark and me repeatedly since the beginning of the negotiations to warn that he "would never accept" any arrangement, no matter how weak, that institutionalized a relationship between the IFOR commander and Bildt, who was slated to be the first High Representative. Because, as the Supreme Allied Commander Europe, General Joulwan was not part of the American military chain of command, he had the authority to reject "guidance" from Washington on any issue involving his own command arrangements. His veto of any formal ties between the two senior people in Bosnia was to leave an unfortunate legacy, as Pauline Neville-Jones wrote later:

> Either the High Representative should have been given more authority, or civilian implementation should have been made considerably less ambitious. . . . Much acrimony had surrounded the role played by the senior UN official in theatre, who had come in some quarters to signify civilian interference in the military chain of command. This situation led US negotiators in Dayton to resist including in the implementation structures any sort of body which would provide a forum for the civilian administrator and military commander to discuss and find solutions to problems and issues which spanned their separate responsibilities. . . . Preventing interference should not be confused with promoting cooperation.[1]

Buildup and Build–down. On this, the fifteenth day of negotiations, there was a White House principals' meeting to settle the last outstanding internal issues. Clark, Kornblum, and Gallucci attended by secure video. A decision was also reached on the most controversial and criticized aspect of our policy: whether we should train and arm the Federation, or try to reduce the overall level of armaments in Bosnia.

This was one of our greatest dilemmas. In an ideal world, the several armies of Bosnia-Herzegovina should have been sharply reduced in size and merged into a single force controlled by the central government. However, NATO refused to accept implementation of such a policy as part of its mission. This eliminated any hope, as Pauline Neville-Jones wrote later, "of getting the parties to agree at Dayton to share military power."[2] Sadly, we would have to allow each entity within a single country to maintain its own military force—a fundamental flaw in our postwar structure, but nonetheless inevitable, given the self-imposed constraints on what the outside powers were willing to do.

Thus the most controversial of all programs for Bosnia—to arm and train the Bosnian Muslims—resurfaced. The version under discussion was a postwar variant of the original proposal to arm the Muslims, which had been championed by a powerful group of Senators led by Republican Majority Leader Bob Dole and two senior Democrats, Joe Lieberman of Connecticut and Joe Biden of Delaware. Some bitter Washington debates had been fought over their proposal, which the Administration had opposed on the grounds that it would have violated the United Nations arms embargo.* Facing a defeat in Congress on this issue, President Clinton had pledged that in the event of a peace agreement, the United States would lead an effort to equip and train the Federation in order to "level the playing field" so that it could defend itself. The military hated this idea, which they believed would increase the chances of another war and undermine their desire to be "evenhanded" in enforcing a peace agreement. They also feared that if the United States took part in "Equip and Train," as the program was renamed, its peacekeepers would become targets for Serb reprisals. Our European allies took an even stronger position against Equip and Train.

Despite the commitment of the President, the Pentagon continued in every internal policy debate to oppose military assistance to the Federation. Led by Shalikashvili and Slocombe, they gained agreement during the November 15 White House meeting for a series of measures that did not kill the program but limited American visibility and involvement in it. Specifically, the principals agreed that there would be no active American involvement by American military personnel in Equip and Train, and that the weapons should come from other nations.

To bridge the gap with the Pentagon we added another annex, one that would reduce the level of armaments on all sides—a sort of modified arms-control policy for Bosnia that we called "build-down." Like Equip and Train, build-down was in part a result of congressional pressure. It originated in discussions in late 1994 between Perry and Senators Sam Nunn, Democrat of Georgia, and Dick Lugar, Republican of Indiana, two influential moderates who had supported the Administration's effort to defeat Dole and Lieberman. (It was an interesting feature of Bosnia policy that the congressional debate did not follow party lines.) Whether one supported Equip and Train or not, build-down was an inherently good idea, an indirect step toward disarming the

---

*As recounted earlier, I had advocated a variant of this idea in 1992–93.

swollen armies of Bosnia—provided it did not become a vehicle for weakening the Muslims.

In the end, after much debate in the principals' meeting on November 15, the Administration reached a compromise that confused people at first, but made sense: it decided to support *both* buildup and build-down—that is, an Equip and Train program, accompanied by an arms-control annex. These two programs would be carried out at roughly the same time, according to carefully calibrated schedules and ratios.

We thus added a new annex to the draft agreements for Dayton—Annex 1-B, "The Agreement of Regional Stabilization," commonly referred to as the "arms-control," or "build-down," annex. This annex required the parties to reduce their armaments to ratios that had been carefully calibrated by the Pentagon. Under this concept, a 5:2:2 ratio would be established among Yugoslavia, Croatia, and Bosnia, respectively. The Bosnian allotment would be further divided between the Federation and Republika Srpska, with the Federation getting twice as many armaments as the Bosnian Serbs. These ratios were designed to protect the Federation from ever again being overwhelmed by Serb military power. Unfortunately, the Pentagon once again refused to include an enforcement provision in Annex 1-B. Thus some of the most difficult of all goals—general arms reduction, "restrictions on military deployments and exercises," and the "immediate establishment of military liaison missions"—were left to the goodwill of parties who had no goodwill.

There was one provision I insisted on, over the initial objections of the Pentagon: the "withdrawal of Forces and heavy weapons to cantonment/barracks areas." The Pentagon had objected to every attempt to include cantonment in Annex 1-A, which would have made it an IFOR obligation, but they reluctantly agreed to include it in Annex 1-B, which meant that while it would be a goal it would not be an IFOR task. Months later, when IFOR was on the ground, its commanders finally saw the value of the cantonment provision, and informed the Bosnian Serbs that they would insist on it as part of their core mission. Once IFOR took this line, the Bosnian Serbs began to respond, and, although compliance was never perfect, the cantonment provision proved to be extremely useful.

To many people, these two programs—one to *build up* the strength of the Federation, the other to *build down* the overall military forces in the country—seemed contradictory. But it was the best course available to us. Under Annex 1-B, there was room to build up the Federation forces and stay within the 5:2:2 ratio. But if the Serbs did not respect the annex on build-down, the Equip and Train program was already in place to strengthen the Federation. And when it came time, in early 1996, to set up the Equip and Train program, Christopher and I chose the best possible person to head it—one of its authors, Jim Pardew.

Dinner with Haris. We were still worried about Haris Silajdzic. Menzies, who knew him well, described him as a "caged panther." Frozen out of important discussions by Izetbegovic or Sacirbey, the Bosnian Prime Minister became depressed and increasingly fatalistic. Still looking for ways to reach out to him, I invited him to dinner, and Kati returned to Dayton specifically for the event, since on her first visit Haris had talked to her several times about his dreams for his country and himself.

To emphasize the special nature of the occasion, we took him to L'Auberge, an excellent French restaurant in Dayton. As we ordered caviar and a fine meal, I tried to talk about something other than the details of the negotiation. What were his hopes—personal and political? What did he want for his country? Could he re-engage himself in the talks? Could he negotiate directly with Milosevic?

Relaxing after days of isolation within his own delegation, Silajdzic talked movingly about his family in Istanbul, his young son, and his early days as a student in Sarajevo. But when we said that the future of Bosnia depended on rebuilding multiethnic co-existence, he retreated into an unreachable pessimism. I cited Nelson Mandela as a true leader, a man who could forgive his jailers and embrace power sharing with the very people against whom he had struggled for thirty years. The connection did not seem relevant to Haris. "You don't understand," he said bleakly. "You don't understand what we have been through."

"Perhaps we *don't* understand what you have been through," I replied, "but it was your request that we create a single country, and we are well on the way to accomplishing this. You were one of its chief proponents. Why are we trying to do this if you don't think it can work? Unless you and Izetbegovic reach out to your adversaries, both Serb and Croat, you will isolate yourselves and fail."

Haris did not dispute that he and Izetbegovic had both asked us to negotiate a single country. Instead, he returned to the horrors of 1992. "What you want would have been easier in 1992 or even 1993," he said, "but now it may be too late. Where was the world then? Where was the United States?"

More deaths would not honor the dead—only create more dead, I said passionately. We wanted the war criminals brought to justice, and would not compromise on this issue, but if the Muslims wanted a central government for Bosnia—again, I stressed, *their* own choice—they had to find a way to work with some of the Croats and Serbs, hard though that would be.

These were bleak thoughts, in sharp contrast to the surroundings. Haris was somewhere else, far away. But he had calmed down, and our arguments turned out to have a positive effect on him. Moreover, the evening helped make him feel that he still had an important role to play.

DAY SIXTEEN: THURSDAY, NOVEMBER 16

How much longer could we continue without significant progress on the key territorial issues? The question hung over us during a particularly gloomy 8:00 A.M. staff meeting. Having worked on Silajdzic the previous evening, I decided the next target should be Milosevic, and shortly after 10:00 A.M. Chris Hill and I invited him to take a walk.

It was a clear, dry day—and extremely cold. Dressed in bulky ski jackets and overcoats, we paced the perimeter of the base, trailed discreetly by security guards, for almost two hours. Chris and I put it to Milosevic bluntly: Secretary Christopher was returning to Dayton the next day, and we had no progress to report. Rather than ask for specific concessions, we called for a major gesture of "goodwill" from Milosevic to show he was serious about an agreement. I offered Milosevic two models for Dayton. In one, he could "play Sadat," and show the Bosnians he was ready to make major concessions to get peace. In the other, we could shut down without an agreement, in which case the sanctions on his country would remain in place and the war might resume. Milosevic, in a thoughtful mood, said he would consider "what kind of gesture" he could make.

By a long and roundabout route we arrived at the Wright-Patterson Officers' Club around noon and went to the table that was always reserved for Milosevic. I called Rosemarie, who had taken Silajdzic on a similar walk. She decided to bring him to the club for lunch. Arriving fifteen minutes later, she led Silajdzic and John Menzies to a table at the opposite end of the large central dining room, as far from Milosevic as possible.

Thus the stage was set for an unusual diplomatic effort that was later termed the "napkin shuttle." Leaving Milosevic, I walked across the long dining room to greet Silajdzic. "Are you ready to negotiate right now?" I asked him. "Milosevic is willing to talk about Gorazde." Haris was interested, but when I invited him to join our table, he refused.

I returned to Milosevic, who was eating his steak with Chris Hill. "Silajdzic is ready to discuss Gorazde," I reported. Taking out a napkin, Milosevic started drawing a rough map of the area between Sarajevo and the beleaguered enclave. "We can offer safe conduct along these two roads," he said, indicating the two existing routes between the cities, both now under Serb control. Hill and I objected, saying that the Bosnians would not feel that "safe conduct" would be very safe in light of the last four years. "They will need a genuine, defensible corridor," I said. "Okay, then I will give them a kilometer on each side of the road," Milosevic replied.

Carrying Milosevic's napkin sketch across the room, I sat down with Silajdzic, who, after a moment's thought, replied with a countersketch showing a much wider corridor and substantially more land for the Muslims. As the other diners looked on in astonishment, I walked rapidly across the room carrying the two precious napkin sketches, and sat down again with Milosevic.

This scene was repeated half a dozen times over the next hour. Neither man would move to the other's table, but they eyed each other carefully across the room. Bit by bit, Milosevic yielded land and territory, until the gap between the two men was fairly narrow. Haris went to a phone and called Izetbegovic, who told him to keep negotiating. Finally, I said to Silajdzic, "Don't you realize that you are gaining something important here? You have to sit down with him. If you come over to Milosevic's table now you might get what you need." Reluctantly, Haris followed me to Milosevic's table. The two men greeted each other in characteristic fashion—Milosevic clapping Silajdzic on the back with false camaraderie, Silajdzic unwilling to look Milosevic in the eye.

The other diners gradually left, and by three in the afternoon we were alone in the large room, Milosevic, Silajdzic, Hill, and myself. Rosemarie and Menzies, having delivered their man, had silently slipped away. The two men argued, in English and in their common tongue, over every detail of the area between Sarajevo and Gorazde. The road, the hydroelectric plants, the destroyed mosques, the small village along the road where General Mladic came from—all were discussed with passion and anger.

They did not resolve their differences, and the meeting ended without agreement. *But for the first time the two sides had actually negotiated on a territorial issue.* Our long talks with each man had had an effect; there was a noticeable change in tone. For the first time, Milosevic accepted the need to create a secure land corridor to Gorazde. Once we had crossed this mini-Rubicon—"actually, the Drina," Hill joked—we were, in essence, arguing over the location and width of the corridor. These were negotiable. Although we did not resolve the Gorazde issue in the "napkin shuttle," the meeting marked the first time anyone on either side had shown a readiness to look for territorial compromises.

During the day, Federation President Zubak again threatened to resign. This time his anger was aimed at Tudjman and his fellow Croats, who, he felt, were selling out the Posavina, his home area. He did not feel he could go home again if the territorial agreements at Dayton did not include a Serb "giveback" of some of this land. He felt that the land negotiations were, so far, effectively conceding the Posavina to the Serbs. If this happened, he said, he would have to resign and leave Dayton immediately.

My first instinct was to let him depart. Zubak had been nothing but trouble at Dayton. Susak had always told us to ignore him. But Izetbegovic and Sacirbey both said we should help retain Zubak. After several emotional meetings and a pledge from both Tudjman and Izetbegovic not to ignore the Posavina, Zubak again backed off, and agreed to stay.

It was time for our next high-level visitor from Washington, Tony Lake. Accompanied by Sandy Vershbow, he arrived in the midafternoon at the base. After a briefing at the Hope Center, Tony and I called on the two Presidents. Tony had decided not to try to negotiate during his short visit, but rather to send a strong message, in President Clinton's name, to reinforce our effort.

The meeting with Izetbegovic was fairly routine, but the Lake-Milosevic meeting set off some sparks. Milosevic began with a typical ploy. "I hear you're the most anti-Serb official in Washington," he said. Tony was pleased by what he considered an implicit compliment. At my request, Tony stayed for an early dinner at the Officers' Club so that we could discuss sanctions. Milosevic came right at Tony, making an all-out effort to change American policy, but Tony held his ground, telling Milosevic that while initialing at Dayton would result in suspension, lift could come only with full implementation. This set off a heated debate over what constituted implementation. But Milosevic knew that in real terms suspension of the sanctions would give him what he needed most, immediate relief for his people.

After two brief calls, one on Izetbegovic and the other on Silajdzic, Tony left for Washington. His trip had conveyed the urgency we attached to the negotiations. I summarized his core message late that evening in a memorandum to Warren Christopher: "Tony said there was no second chance for the U.S.; that this was our last, best shot and that Congress was going south on us; that if they didn't reach agreement when you get here we will turn them over to Carl, Pauline, Jacques, and Wolfgang, and our role will greatly diminish."

It had also given Tony and Sandy Vershbow a sense of Dayton. At one point, as we walked alone through the parking lot, Tony leaned toward me and said, "This is the craziest zoo I've ever seen." This was, in fact, exactly what we hoped our colleagues in Washington would remember; it helped if they understood the special weirdness of Dayton.

After Tony left, Hill and I went to see Izetbegovic, hoping he would be encouraged by the progress Silajdzic had made on Gorazde. Instead, I encountered more tension and disarray within the Bosnian camp. The immediate cause was an article by Roger Cohen in that day's *New York Times* in which unnamed "western diplomats" said that Silajdzic, whom Cohen described as "a brilliant, whimsical man with a Hamlet-like tendency to speak in riddles," had emerged as "the key figure—or 'swing vote' in the Bosnian delegation." Seated next to Izetbegovic, Sacirbey began reading excerpts from Cohen's article in a voice dripping with anger and sarcasm. After he finished, Sacirbey paused. "There is only one 'swing vote' in this delegation," he almost shouted, "and that is Mr. President, sitting right here." Throughout this charade Izetbegovic sat motionless, with a slight smile playing across his face. What had happened seemed all too clear: Izetbegovic had been unnerved by Tony Lake's private call on Silajdzic and the direct Milosevic-Silajdzic talks. Encouraged by Sacirbey, he had slapped Haris down—hard.

The Clark Corridor. During the meal with Tony Lake, I had suggested to Milosevic that we resume the negotiation over Gorazde after dinner. After his humiliation, Silajdzic could not continue the negotiation, so we invited Milosevic to our building. We hoped to find a route between Sarajevo and Gorazde that would satisfy the Bosnians. To do this, we decided to introduce Milosevic to PowerScene.

General Clark had brought to Dayton a special unit of the Defense Mapping Agency, personally headed by Major General Philip Nuber. Among other tasks, the map experts were supposed to compute the exact percentage of land that each map proposal gave the sides. They brought with them a highly classified $400,000 imaging system, called PowerScene, first used during Desert Storm. The entire country of Bosnia had been filmed and stored in this extraordinary "virtual reality" machine, visible in three dimensions, accurate down to two yards. Simply by manipulating an ordinary joystick, the viewer could "fly" fast or slow, look straight down, straight ahead, or sideways at any angle. PowerScene was impressive. To foreigners especially, it was a vivid reminder of America's technological prowess.

The Mapping Agency installed its large computers in a room directly across from my bedroom, with a huge sign warning all unauthorized personnel to stay out. Only a handful of people had access to the American building to begin with, so this sign—the only one of its sort inside the compound—naturally attracted endless visitors, who found "flying" the roads and mountains of Bosnia even more enjoyable than Packy's All-Sports Bar. As visitors dropped in, noise from this accidental video arcade often went on late into the night. But the video game would play an important role in the resolution of the Gorazde problem.

Clark and his colleagues had prepared well for the meeting. Flying the land between Sarajevo and Gorazde endlessly on PowerScene, they had found a route that could link the two cities. It was a small dirt track located halfway between the two roads, both now controlled by the Serbs, that had once connected the two cities.

Milosevic arrived alone at the room containing the PowerScene computers around 11:00 P.M. He was fascinated by the technology and spent some time playing with the joystick, "visiting" portions of Bosnia. Then we began an in-

Key Territorial Issues at Dayton

SLOV.

HUNGARY

SERBIA

Sava R.

Karlovac

CROATIA

Drava R.

EASTERN SLAVONIA

Danube R.

Sava R.

Posavina Pocket

Posavina Corridor

Bosanski Novi

Prijedor

Bosanski Samac

Sava R.

Sanski Most

Banja Luka

Doboj

Orasje

Brcko

Drina R.

Kljuc

Mrkonjic Grad

Jajce

BOSNIA-
HERZEGOVINA

Srebrenica

LIVNO VALLEY

"The Egg"

Zepa

Sarajevo

Pale

Rogatica

Mt. Igman

Gorazde

Split

Mostar

"The Clark Corridor"

Drina R.

MONTE-
NEGRO

0   20 miles

0   20 kilometers

- - - - - Dayton Agreement inter-entity boundary line, November 21, 1995

Bosnian Serb–controlled area, November 1, 1995

Croat-Muslim Federation–controlled area, November 1, 1995

tense examination of the dirt track that Clark thought we might upgrade. Milosevic began by offering a three-kilometer corridor through the mountainous terrain. This was far too narrow, we told him, and demonstrated the point by showing him, on PowerScene, that the ridgelines had a clear line of sight on the road and his proposed corridor was therefore too narrow to defend.

For almost two hours we examined the maps and "traveled" across the hills and valleys of the Gorazde area, courtesy of PowerScene. The session was made far livelier, even raucous, by the substantial amount of scotch consumed by some of the participants. This later led people to say that Milosevic had made some key concessions under the influence. But, as usual, I saw no evidence that the alcohol affected him. Milosevic knew what he was doing, and he remembered every detail of the discussion the next morning.

Using maps and an old-fashioned technology—crayons—Clark sketched a corridor that cut a wider swath through the hills east of Sarajevo. As he drew the connector, it was no longer simply a narrow, indefensible road. Instead, its width now averaged 8.3 kilometers, and stretched from ridgelines to hilltops so as to minimize the areas in which the road was vulnerable to direct fire from the high ground. After hours of argument, Milosevic offered us a substantially revised, widened version of this route between Gorazde and Sarajevo. It was after 2:00 A.M. We shook hands, and Milosevic drained his glass again, saying, "We have found our road."

We called it the "Clark Corridor," or, sometimes, the "Scotch Road." In his report the next day, General Kerrick said he was "still recovering from scotch exchange with Milosevic [which I drank] for my country—and I don't even drink scotch."

When the lengthy session on the Clark Corridor finally ended, I sent a long message, entitled "Closure or Closedown: The Situation as of 2:00 A.M.," to Warren Christopher, who was about to leave Osaka for the long return flight to Dayton:

> The Bosnians still wish us to believe that they are getting a lousy deal. Yet they know it is not only a good deal but the best they will ever get. Logically, therefore, they should accept. But the dynamics of their delegation make this a very close call. Izetbegovic spent nine years of his life in jail, and is not a governmental leader so much as a movement leader. He has little understanding of, or interest in, economic development or modernization—the things that peace can bring. He has suffered greatly for his ideals. To him, Bosnia is more an abstraction, not several million people who overwhelmingly want peace. Haris, on the other hand, is more modern and focused heavily on economic reconstruction, something Izetbegovic never mentions. . . .
>
> Milosevic seems to be enjoying himself at Dayton Place, although he likes to intimidate people. Standing up to him when he attacks is the key; he respects

people who act as tough as him. He is always testing us. In order to move him, we must lay down very firm markers and not move them unless we know exactly what we are getting in return. I'll see you at the airport. Have a good trip back.

DAY SEVENTEEN: FRIDAY, NOVEMBER 17

When the Bosnians saw the Gorazde map early the next morning, they were impressed, but did not accept it. This did not worry us: it was standard Balkan negotiating procedure not to accept anything that came from the other side without trying to change it. (This tendency was so pronounced it had become a joke: the best way to confuse someone in the Balkans, we often said, was to accept his initial proposal without change, at which point he would change his own position.) The Bosnians wanted two things: more land south of Gorazde, and firm assurances from the United States that the dirt track would be upgraded into a paved, all-weather road. After discussions with Joulwan and the Army Corps of Engineers, Clark informed us that IFOR engineers would upgrade the road during the summer months and added a key sentence to the military annex: "a two-lane all-weather road will be constructed in the Gorazde Corridor." This satisfied the Bosnians. But they still wanted more territory around Gorazde, especially some land on the south bank of the Drina River, the river that carried so much historical and emotional importance to all former Yugoslavs.*

We planned a day of high-level visitors who would increase the pressure on the reluctant parties. Perry and Slocombe were due at 10:00 A.M., General Joulwan would arrive from Europe at noon, and Christopher would return in the late afternoon. These visits were carefully sequenced: Perry and Joulwan would symbolize American military power and determination, and set the stage for the final push when Christopher returned.

The meetings left a powerful impression on the delegations. Izetbegovic, who knew from Sacirbey and Perle that the Pentagon was opposed to the Equip and Train program, asked for Perry's personal commitment to it. After an edgy exchange, Perry gave Izetbegovic what he wanted, using words that would be cited often by the Bosnians later: "If we get a peace agreement, I will make the Equip and Train program happen." This was no more than a repetition of commitments made by Christopher, Lake, and myself, but it was important that Izetbegovic hear it directly from the Secretary of Defense.

Joulwan joined the meetings two hours later, bringing with him Major General William Nash, the blunt, cigar-smoking First Armored Division comman-

---

* The Yugoslav writer Ivo Andric won the Nobel Prize in Literature in 1961 for his epic novel *The Bridge over the River Drina.*

der, who was scheduled to lead most of the American troops in Bosnia. It was symbolism at its best. With their straightforward warnings and uniforms bristling with medals, the generals made a powerful impression. It was Joulwan's inspired idea to bring Nash, whose no-nonsense style impressed the Balkan leaders; this was, after all, the man who would actually command the American troops on the ground in Bosnia.

With the exception of Perry, the visitors did not get into the details of the negotiations. But they sent a potent message: the physical presence of Joulwan and Nash in Dayton gave NATO a tangible reality in the eyes of the parties, and set the right tone for the final phase of the negotiations, which we planned around Christopher's return. Thirty minutes after they left, at 4:30 in the afternoon, the Secretary of State's big plane touched down from Osaka.

CHAPTER 18

Showdown

(November 18–21, 1995)

Human error is a permanent and not a periodic factor in history, and future negotiators will be exposed, however noble their intentions, to futilities of intention and omission as grave as any which characterised the Council of Five. They were convinced that they would never commit the blunders and iniquities of the Congress of Vienna. Future generations will be equally convinced that they will be immune from the defects which assailed the negotiators of Paris. Yet they in their turn will be exposed to similar microbes of infection, to the eternal inadequacy of human intelligence.

—HAROLD NICOLSON, *Peacemaking 1919*

DAY EIGHTEEN: SATURDAY, NOVEMBER 18

Deadlines. Negotiations have a certain pathology, a kind of life cycle almost like living organisms. At a certain point—which one might not recognize until later—the focus and momentum needed to get an agreement could disappear. *Something* could happen to break our single-minded commitment. Either endless squabbles over small details would replace the larger search for peace, or the Europeans would leave, publicly signaling an impending failure. We worried that if we were still at Wright-Patterson over the Thanksgiving holiday, only a few days away, it would create the impression that we had stayed too long and accomplished too little.

That morning I wrote a short note to myself:

There is a sense here that peace is probably inevitable because of the dangers if we fail. That may be true, as far as it goes. But the critical question—will the Bosnians grasp an imperfect peace or let the war resume—remains unresolved. Their delegation is divided and confused. Silajdzic told me that he had not talked to Izetbegovic in over twenty-four hours. They have let other opportunities for peace slip away before. It could happen again.

Kerrick was even bleaker in his daily report:

> Endgame personal dynamics taking downward spiral. Milosevic and Pale
> Serbs never seen together—rarely speak. Izetbegovic, Mo, Haris continue to
> amaze us all with their desire to torpedo one another—and possibly even peace.

Christopher did not want to leave Dayton again without a deal. Tired from
his quick round-trip to Asia, he had met briefly with Izetbegovic and Milosevic on arrival Friday night, and then went to sleep. The rest of us went to the
Officers' Club for another lobster dinner with Chris Spiro and Milosevic.
Milosevic seated Tom Donilon next to him to discuss American politics. Tom
said that if Dayton failed, the congressional backlash would leave Serbia even
more isolated, and the embargo would never be lifted. Donilon's straight-
talking style appealed to Milosevic, and he engaged Tom in a sophisticated
discussion of American politics, even offering his thoughts on how to handle
the budget confrontation with Gingrich.

We thought Saturday would be "the big day, a hell of a day." We told the
parties that we wanted to finish the negotiations by midnight Saturday, spend
Sunday morning cleaning up final details, and make the announcement later
that day. This was obviously unrealistic, but it gave us a twenty-four-hour
cushion for our real deadline, which was completion of the negotiations Sunday night and an announcement on Monday.

In the morning staff meeting, we reviewed the status of the negotiations
with Christopher. Most of the General Framework Agreement—the umbrella
document—had been accepted by the parties, except for the issue of mutual
recognition among the three states. Of the eleven draft annexes, agreement
was in hand or within sight on nine: the military annexes (Annexes 1-A and
1-B), the constitution—with the exception of the central bank, which was still
in dispute (Annex 4); arbitration (5); human rights (6); refugees/displaced
persons (7); national monuments (8); public services (9); civilian implementation (10); and the International Police Task Force (11). This was more than
we had originally thought possible. But the two toughest problems were still
unresolved—the map (Annex 2) and elections (Annex 3):

- *The map.* Of the big issues, only Gorazde seemed close to resolution.
  Sarajevo, Brcko, the Posavina Corridor, and the Posavina pocket were
  unresolved. Contrary to our initial hopes, there had been no trade-offs
  between Dayton's political provisions and the map. We would have to
  negotiate the remaining map issues literally kilometer by kilometer.

- *Elections.* The problem of refugee voting still stymied us. Milosevic
  held to his view that voters must register in person in Bosnia. The
  Bosnians wanted to allow absentee registration and let people vote

where they had lived in 1991, the year of the last prewar census of Yugoslavia. In practice, this would mean that Muslims from, say, Banja Luka who were now refugees in Germany would be allowed to vote in the Banja Luka district for a Serb presidential candidate, opening the possibility that Muslims could become a swing bloc in an election between Serb candidates. To the Serbs, of course, this was unacceptable.

Elections and the OSCE. Just before Christopher arrived, we settled a serious disagreement over how to conduct elections. Everyone agreed that an international body should oversee the elections, but there had been an early disagreement over which organization should have the job, and a more serious problem over what the international community's role should be. Organizationally, the choice came down to the U.N. or the Organization of Security and Cooperation in Europe (OSCE). At the urging of John Kornblum, who had served as Ambassador to the organization, the United States opted for the OSCE, which had been created to monitor the 1975 Helsinki Accords.

Known until 1994 as the Conference on Security and Cooperation in Europe (CSCE), the fifty-two-nation OSCE was the only regional "security" organization that included both the NATO nations and all the countries of the former Soviet bloc.* During the Cold War, it had been little more than an occasional forum for meetings, but it was part of our vision for European security to transform the OSCE into a significant component of what President Clinton called "an undivided Europe."

The European members of the Contact Group readily agreed to assign the OSCE responsibility for the elections. But they simultaneously proposed to limit its role simply to *monitoring* the elections. This view ran directly counter to that of President Clinton, who told me, just before Dayton, that "a credible election would be the most important single event" of the first year after Dayton. This would be possible only if the international community ran it; "monitoring," a vague and elusive concept, would result in a stalemate, and either no elections or disputed elections. While an international organization was no guarantee of a "free and fair" election, the larger its role, the better. With the President's words as our marching orders, we insisted that the OSCE *run* the elections. Otherwise, they would either never take place, or be worthless. Finally, after days of argument, we gained agreement at Dayton that the OSCE would "*supervise,* in a manner to be determined by the OSCE, . . . the preparation and *conduct* of elections [emphasis added]."

Although this was still not perfect, I felt this language was strong enough so that the OSCE could interpret it any way it wanted to. Thus the selection of an

---

* Even neutral countries like Switzerland and Malta, and tiny states like Andorra and Liechtenstein, were members. The chairmanship rotated annually, and in 1996 fell to the Swiss, who did an excellent job.

aggressive head for the OSCE mission in Bosnia would become important later.*

That morning, we learned that Muhamed Sacirbey had held a rather casual press conference the night before at the Holiday Inn outside the air base to announce his resignation as Foreign Minister, thus complying with the terms of the November 10 Federation agreement. He would be replaced by an ethnic Croat—Jadranko Prlic—as part of the agreement. This was a necessary step, but it had no effect on the proceedings at Dayton, or on Sacirbey's role.

Sarajevo Breakthrough. Milosevic continued to play with variations of the District of Columbia model, making a series of proposals that would have given the Serbs a voice equal to that of the Muslims in the city. Finally, early Saturday afternoon, I asked Milosevic to take a short walk around the inner compound. I complained bitterly that his behavior was going to cause a breakdown of the talks, and concentrated on Sarajevo. "Some issues can be set aside or fudged," I said, "but Sarajevo must be settled in Dayton." "Okay," he said with a laugh, "I won't eat today until we solve Sarajevo."

A short while later, while I was chatting with Hill and Clark, the door to my suite opened without warning, and Milosevic walked in. "I was in your neighborhood and did not want to pass your door without knocking," he said, smiling broadly. Clearly, he had something important to tell us.

"Okay, okay," he said as he sat down. "The hell with your D.C. model; it's too complicated, it won't work. I'll solve Sarajevo. But you must not discuss my proposal with anyone in the Serb delegation yet. I must work the 'technology' later, after everything else is settled.

"I tell you," he continued, "Izetbegovic has earned Sarajevo by not abandoning it. He's one tough guy. It's his."

These words were probably the most astonishing and unexpected of the conference. As he talked, Milosevic traced on a map with a pen the part of Sarajevo he was ready to give to the Muslims. Immediately Chris Hill objected: it was a huge concession, but it was not all of the city. Milosevic had retained for the Serbs Grbavica, a key area across the river from the center of town. Although a dramatic step forward, Milosevic's proposal did not quite unify Sarajevo.

When Hill pointed this out, Milosevic exploded. "I'm *giving* you Sarajevo," he almost shouted at Chris, "and you talk such bullshit!" We told Milosevic that while his proposal was "a big step in the right direction," it was likely Izetbegovic would reject it.

Hill and I went immediately to see the Bosnian President. Izetbegovic did not acknowledge the importance of the offer, but focused solely on its defects.

---

* This led to an argument with the French a month later. See chapter 19.

"Sarajevo without Grbavica cannot exist," he said with passion. The area that Milosevic wanted to retain for the Serbs jutted directly into the center of the city and was known to Western journalists as "Sniper Alley." Still, we all recognized that the negotiations over Sarajevo had entered a new phase.

Taking a detailed street map of Sarajevo, Hill, Clark, and I went back to Milosevic's suite. We began examining every road and every terrain feature. Milosevic seemed flexible; Hill predicted after the meeting that if we stuck to our position we would get all of Sarajevo the next day. Feeling suddenly encouraged, we adjourned with our hopes soaring.

Joined by Christopher, we reassembled in my suite to assess what had happened. We had not expected this. We agreed to support Izetbegovic's claim to Grbavica and the hills above the city. Then we sat around debating the possible reasons for Milosevic's astonishing decision.

"Why did Milosevic do this?" I asked. "And can he actually make it happen? Has he decided to abandon the Bosnian Serbs? Can he really force the Bosnian Serbs to give up their parts of the city?"

Reunifying Sarajevo Under Dayton

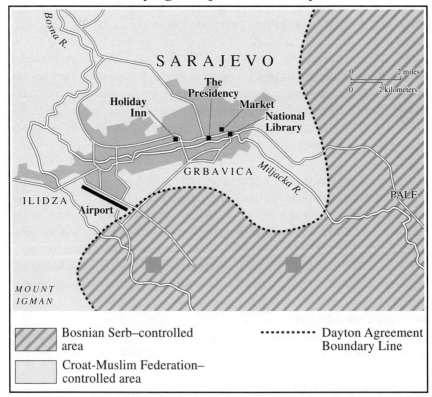

We never fully understood why Milosevic decided to give Sarajevo to the Muslims. But in retrospect, the best explanation may be that he was fed up with the Bosnian Serbs and had decided to weaken their Pale base by giving away the Serb-controlled parts of Sarajevo. By giving the Federation all of Bosnia's capital, perhaps Milosevic wanted to weaken Karadzic and strengthen the Serbs in other parts of Bosnia, especially Banja Luka.

This explanation was consistent with one of Milosevic's main themes at Dayton: that the Bosnian Serb leadership had become an impediment, even though he had earlier made common cause with them. Milosevic had often talked of strengthening the "intellectuals" and businessmen of Banja Luka in order to weaken Pale; now he seemed to be putting this theory into action.

To further weaken Pale, I proposed that the Dayton agreement include a provision moving the Bosnian Serb capital to Banja Luka. Milosevic seemed interested in this proposal, but, to my surprise, Izetbegovic demurred. Even though he hated the leadership in Pale, he seemed to think he could work with them, especially his old associate from the Bosnian Assembly, Momcilo Krajisnik. Izetbegovic also saw value in keeping the capitals of the two entities close to each other so that Sarajevo remained the only important political center in Bosnia. He may also have feared that if the Bosnian Serb capital moved to Banja Luka, which is closer to Zagreb than Sarajevo, it would accelerate the permanent division of the country and strengthen Tudjman.

Whatever Izetbegovic's reasons for not wanting to close Pale, it was a mistake. The mountain town was solely a wartime capital, established by an indicted war criminal and his henchmen. It was the living symbol—and headquarters—of his organization. We should have pushed Izetbegovic harder to agree to establish the Serb capital at Banja Luka. It would have made a big difference in the effort to implement the Dayton agreements.

DAY NINETEEN: SUNDAY, NOVEMBER 19

This would be our longest day. Twenty-two hours after it had begun, we would still be at it—without success.

A Bluff Fools No One. Christopher and I agreed to make an all-out effort to complete the talks Sunday. In an attempt to convince the parties we were serious about this deadline, I asked every member of the American delegation to pack his or her bags and place them in the parking lot where the other delegations could see them. After the bags lay outside for several hours, I asked the Air Force to put them on a truck and take them to the airstrip. Rosemarie began to try to collect the payment of bills from the parties—an effort in which she was entirely unsuccessful.

Of all the gambits we tried at Dayton, this proved to be the most pathetic. Everyone saw through our bluff; nobody else made the slightest effort to prepare for departure. Early in the evening, we gave up and brought the bags back to our rooms.

To bring the conference to an end, in fact, would require much more than a theatrical ruse. We needed to tie up the loose ends on a dozen secondary issues, resolve the question of refugee voting, and settle Sarajevo. But each time Christopher met with Izetbegovic, the Bosnian President pointedly brought up Brcko, referring to the unrealistic 1994 Contact Group map with its railroad bridge and tiny underpass.

The Chart Fiasco. How could we convince Izetbegovic that he was now at the decisive moment? Knowing he was under conflicting pressures from his own delegation, we looked for ways to convince him to take the leap for peace. Through Neville-Jones and Blot, we asked Prime Minister Major and President Chirac to call Izetbegovic. Both men did so immediately, telling the Bosnian President that "if this moment is lost, the opportunity might not easily come again." Izetbegovic conceded to Major that they had made progress, but added that he needed more land to make up for the lost towns of Srebrenica and Zepa. In Ankara, Ambassador Grossman also arranged a call between Izetbegovic and Turkish president Suleyman Demirel, the foreign leader whom Izetbegovic probably respected most.

We asked Menzies to compile a list of everything the Bosnians had already achieved in the negotiations—and would lose if the talks did not succeed. Working with the graphics division of Wright-Patterson, Menzies produced two large posters, listing the "gains of Dayton." On Saturday afternoon—at the same time we were arguing over the Serb portions of Sarajevo—Christopher, Menzies, and I took these to Izetbegovic's suite. In large block letters, they listed everything that had been achieved in the negotiations. Reviewing the charts before we showed them to the Bosnians, Christopher laughed and said, "Well, *I'm* impressed, even if Izetbegovic is not," and added that he did not see how anyone could "responsibly walk away from these gains and allow his country to go back to war."

The posters contained one particularly sensitive item. Measuring the territorial concessions that Milosevic had already made, the Defense Mapping Agency team had determined that 55 percent of Bosnia was now conceded to the Federation. This was a negotiated increase of about 5 percent during the first eighteen days at Dayton over the battlefield situation—and left us with something halfway between an opportunity and a dilemma. The opportunity was obvious: a chance to gain more territory for the Federation. But so was the dilemma: under the 1994 Contact Group plan, all five Contact Group Foreign Ministers and the leaders of all three countries had formally agreed to a 51–49 split of Bosnian territory between the Federation and the Bosnian Serbs.

Were we still bound by 51–49? Given that the Serbs had conquered so much territory through infamous methods, it would have been just for the Federation to control more than 51 percent of the land. Unexpectedly, we had gained 55 percent for Sarajevo. We decided to see if we could retain this higher percentage, since it would significantly strengthen the chance to create a viable country. But we knew that if Milosevic objected we would have little choice but to fall back to the 51–49 formula, given the prior commitments of the United States and the four other nations of the Contact Group. Tony Lake had reaffirmed this as a core American position during his August trip to the European capitals before the start of our shuttle, and it had been included in the September 9 Geneva agreement.

Menzies had placed the dramatic percentage figures in a prominent position on the first poster. We hoped the Bosnians would recognize what a significant achievement it was, and move rapidly to lock it in by finishing the rest of the negotiations. With Sarajevo close to solution, we felt this was possible within hours if we worked fast. But while the Bosnians were fascinated with our charts, they continued to argue over minor issues. Their delay, and what happened next, doomed any chance we might have had to get more than 51 percent for the Federation.

When the meeting was finished, Izetbegovic and Silajdzic asked to keep the charts. Menzies placed them beside the couch, partially concealed. A short time later, Milosevic unexpectedly called on Izetbegovic—in itself an unusual event—to discuss Sarajevo and the need to finish the conference quickly. As the two men talked, Milosevic noticed the top of one of our charts peeking out from behind the couch. On it was written, in bold capital letters: "FEDERATION TERRITORY INCREASED FROM 50% TO 55% DURING DAYTON TALKS."

For the first time, Milosevic realized how far his territorial concessions had gone. Ending the meeting quickly, he walked directly to my room, and entered without warning. I was sitting with Warren Christopher and several of our team. When Milosevic entered, everyone left except Christopher.

"You tricked me," he said angrily. "You didn't tell me that the percentage was no longer 51–49. I asked you but you didn't reply. I saw your charts. How can I trust you?"

At first we could not understand what had happened. Had the Bosnians boasted to Milosevic about the percentage in order to goad him? We had no idea. The truth—that the Bosnians had left the charts partially in view when Milosevic visited them—did not occur to us, and we did not know if it was a deliberate provocation or simply a stupid oversight. (Later, Silajdzic told me that it was just bad luck that Milosevic showed up without warning and saw the charts.)*

"I can do many things," Milosevic said, "but I cannot give you more than fifty-one percent. This is my bottom line with Republika Srpska. We agreed to this before Dayton."

We pointed out that Milosevic had already accepted territorial changes that exceeded 51 percent. "I didn't know what the percentage was," he replied, "and I can't force Pale to accept a deal for less than forty-nine percent. Please believe me. This is the end of the matter."

Christopher and I glanced at each other. The Secretary of State could not re-nege on a public commitment if any of the parties insisted on sticking to it. Other parts of the original Contact Group map had been changed "by mutual consent," as called for in the plan, but 51–49 had taken on an almost theolog-ical force.

Milosevic had a suggestion as to how to return to 51–49—and it was unac-ceptable. He asked for a widening of the Posavina Corridor from three miles to ten miles. This was, of course, the same corridor that Izetbegovic continu-ally insisted be reduced to a thirty-meter-wide underpass beneath the railroad bridge to the adjoining city of Brcko. The existing corridor, connecting the Serbs of western Bosnia with Serbia itself, hung like a noose around the Serb neck.

Having repeatedly told Izetbegovic that we could not reduce the width of the corridor, we now rejected Milosevic's demand to widen it. But the issue of the Posavina Corridor and Brcko were still not settled, and would, as we had expected, prove to be the toughest of all issues at Dayton.

The day continued with endless meetings over maps. Clark and the military map experts looked for ways to change the percentage from 55–45 to 51–49 without asking the Federation to give up any "important" land. Since a sig-nificant portion of the terrain in Bosnia consisted of sparsely inhabited mountain areas ("worthless land," in Silajdzic's dismissive phrase), there was room for some compromise, but not much. Using their computers, the mapping team could measure the land to one one-hundredth of 1 percent (.01 percent!), an absurdly false precision; the thickness of the map lines themselves amounted to at least 1 percent of the land. But, with both sides now obsessed with this issue, the precise percentage of land each controlled was central.

---

* In *The Death of Yugoslavia,* Brian Lapping and Laura Silber's superb six-part documentary for the BBC, Silajdzic recounts this incident in detail. He describes it as an accident, and laughs as he recalls how upset both Milosevic and the Americans were. To those involved in it at the time, however, it was no laughing matter.

The most disturbing aspect of this obsession with 51–49 was that it revealed how little each side trusted the political aspects of the Dayton agreements to which they had both agreed. As Izetbegovic once said, a "mountain of corpses" between the two sides prevented trust. The argument over the land was, in effect, a continuation of the war in Dayton, while the political discussions were a tentative effort to build a political framework for a joint future. We were all too aware of the internal contradiction, but there was nothing that could be done about it.

Milosevic and Silajdzic. The long day dragged on. Milosevic, still fuming over our "clever trick" with the percentages, refused to make any further concessions on Sarajevo or settle the final details on Gorazde. After several hours, he gradually regained his composure, and the talks inched forward again. But Milosevic still held out on the land south of the Drina near Gorazde, on the hills to the southwest of Sarajevo, and, most important, on the Grbavica portion of Sarajevo. Shortly before 8:00 P.M., while Milosevic argued with Hill and me, we looked out the window and noticed Silajdzic walking toward Packy's. The two sides had not met face-to-face since Milosevic had walked out of Izetbegovic's suite after seeing the offending poster hours earlier. Running into the parking lot, I grabbed Haris. "You might get what you want on Sarajevo if you meet Milosevic right now," I said, and pulled him into my rooms. Asking the two men to negotiate face-to-face, I left them alone with Chris Hill, our "language officer."

For hours the three men argued, while Christopher, Donilon, Jim Steinberg, and I waited in another room down the hall. Periodically Hill would appear to give us a progress report or get new maps. A careful man not given to overoptimism about the Balkans, which he knew so well, Hill was now relatively upbeat. As we ate sandwiches in Christopher's room, we thought the end might be in sight. Donilon and Burns began discussing with Washington how to arrange the initialing ceremony.

At 10:00 P.M., Tudjman returned from Zagreb to join the final push. Christopher and I met him at the airport and told him that he had to exert direct pressure on both Izetbegovic and Milosevic. He said he would do whatever he could the next morning, but preferred to stay away from the Milosevic-Silajdzic marathon, already in its third hour.

Under Hill's insistent pressure, Milosevic finally gave more ground near Gorazde. At one point, Silajdzic asked for Ustkolina, a small town near Gorazde, primarily because it held the oldest mosque built in Bosnia. Milosevic laughed sardonically. "Oh, Haris," he said, "don't you know that those idiots"—he meant the Bosnian Serbs—"blew it up?"

"But the location is sacred," Silajdzic replied.

"Haris," Milosevic joked, "now you sound like Karadzic." But he yielded, and Ustkolina was Muslim again.

Shortly thereafter, Milosevic agreed to give the Federation a symbolically important strip of land on the southern bank of the Drina. Four days after the napkin diplomacy at the Officers' Club shuttle, Gorazde was settled. We had come a long way from the original U.S. position in July that Gorazde was indefensible and might have to be sacrificed in a negotiation. Gorazde was saved.

The three men shifted back to Sarajevo, drawing lines on the map. Milosevic's lines did not include Grbavica. Silajdzic said that without it, there was no deal; it was an integral part of the capital. Hill drew a line that included Grbavica and said, "This is *our* line, the American line." Suddenly, Milosevic did not object.

Silajdzic demanded land that overlooked the city so that it could never again be used for artillery and mortar attacks on Sarajevo. Part of it contained a Serb cemetery. "Now you want our dead too!" Milosevic exclaimed. But again he relented. Almost without realizing it, the two men had won an undivided Sarajevo.

But, Milosevic said, all his other agreements were contingent on returning to 51–49. Pulling Silajdzic out of his session with Milosevic, Christopher and I told him that we could not hold to the percentages of the posters any longer. This did not surprise Silajdzic, who had always maintained that the quality of the land was more important than its quantity. He agreed to negotiate land readjustments that would get the map back to 51–49.

Shortly after midnight, the three men broke off their talks. Silajdzic, feeling extremely good, went back to his building to consult Izetbegovic and his own map expert.

In the American building, members of our team crowded in the hallway and the small conference room. Stale air and the smell of pizza filled the corridor. In the workrooms, Tom Malinowski, one of Warren Christopher's best speechwriters, worked on two public statements—one for success, the other for failure. I looked at the failure statement, which tried to put a positive face on events, and tossed it into the air. I wrote a new draft that presented failure, if it came, honestly, bluntly, and unapologetically. "To put it simply," the draft ended,

we gave it our best shot. By their failure to agree, the parties have made it very clear that further U.S. efforts to negotiate a settlement would be fruitless. Accordingly, today marks the end of this initiative. . . . The special role we have played in recent months is over. The leaders here today must live with the consequences of their failure.

"The Thirty-seven-Minute Peace." The evening was far from over. Milosevic did not leave our building, but instead moved from my suite to the conference room, where he waited, with Christopher, Hill, Clark, Menzies, and myself, for Silajdzic to return. Shortly after 2:00 A.M., Silajdzic returned with his map expert. Huge maps had been set up by Clark.

For two more hours Milosevic and Silajdzic argued, yelled, and drew wide, sweeping lines on the maps. Translation was almost unnecessary—the body language, the hand gestures, the emotions told the story. Silajdzic—on the attack, demanding one concession after another from Milosevic, a railroad station here, a hilltop there—was picking up more territory. At one point the Bosnian map expert pointed out that the water reservoir at Faletici northeast of Sarajevo had been left outside the line of Federation control. When Silajdzic raised this, Milosevic said, "I am not a louse," and yielded immediately. It was clear: Milosevic wanted an agreement then and there. But he insisted, at all times, to 51–49.

This was not easy, given the concessions Milosevic had already made. More than minor "shaving" of lesser Federation-controlled areas would be necessary. Well after 3:30 A.M., Silajdzic hit upon a solution that retained for the Federation all the key gains of Dayton but returned to the sacred percentage. He outlined a large egg-shaped area on the map south of Highway 5 in western Bosnia, and offered the land to Republika Srpska. This was a mountainous, lightly populated Serb region south of the town of Kljuc that had been taken during the recent Croat offensive—precisely what Silajdzic had meant when he talked of "worthless land." Because of its shape, Hill dubbed it "the egg," while Milosevic, thinking it resembled Spain, called it "the Iberian peninsula." Both men agreed to calibrate its exact size so as to reach 51–49 for the whole country.

Suddenly Milosevic stuck out his hand. Slightly surprised, Silajdzic took it. Except for some details, the deal was done. It was 4:00 A.M. For a moment, we sat silent, too stunned to react. They talked with sudden ease, and, for the first time, joked. Silajdzic seemed euphoric at his negotiating triumph, Milosevic relieved that it was over. Christopher went outside and asked Bob Bradtke, his faithful executive assistant, to fetch a bottle of his favorite California Chardonnay from the supply with which he always traveled. Out of plastic cups, we drank to peace. (Silajdzic, a practicing Muslim, drank a Coke.) An Air Force photographer came in to record the triumphant scene.

After a drink or two Silajdzic went off to get Izetbegovic, who appeared wearing an overcoat over pajamas and looking sleepy and annoyed. He refused a drink, even a soft drink, while he stared at the map without comment.

As we drank, I had been studying the map, puzzled. Something was wrong, but at first, I was too tired to see what was it was. Then it struck me: all of

Silajdzic's "givebacks" were from Croat-controlled territory—and no Croatians were present. I whispered to Hill to get Tudjman.

Ten minutes later, Hill appeared with Mate Granic. Although it was now after 4:00 A.M., the Croatian Foreign Minister was dressed impeccably and looked as if he had just stepped out of his office on a relaxed day. Sitting down, he politely shared a drink with us and listened to the explanation of the deal. Then, quite calmly, Granic asked to see the map, which was leaning against the wall. As he studied it, an extraordinary transformation came over him. When I thought about it later, it reminded me of the way Zero Mostel had turned himself into a rhinoceros in Ionesco's play. Turning red and barely able to speak at first, Granic slammed his fist into the map. "Impossible! Impossible!" he finally said, walking rapidly around the small room. "Impossible. Zero point zero zero chance that my President will accept this!" He stormed out, almost tripping over Jim O'Brien, who was sitting on the floor in the corridor drinking a beer and chatting with Jim Steinberg.

Within minutes, Granic returned with Defense Minister Susak, who took one look at the map and turned on Silajdzic. "You have given away the territory we conquered with Croatian blood!" he yelled, in English, at Silajdzic, who sat motionless at the table. Milosevic said nothing. Izetbegovic was leaning forward now, listening carefully. This, his body language seemed to say, was getting interesting.

There was still a chance to salvage the evening's gains. If the problem was simply that Haris had given away too much Croat land, perhaps we could redistribute the "givebacks" more equitably between the Croats and the Muslims. I suggested that we try to do just this, "shaving a bit here and bit there."

Izetbegovic still had not said a word. I turned to him, fearing his response, "What do you think, Mr. President? Can we finish the negotiation right now?"

His answer sealed the long day. "I cannot accept this agreement," he said in a low voice, in English.

"What did you say?" Christopher asked, in astonishment.

More loudly: "I cannot accept this agreement."

We sat absolutely silent for a moment. Suddenly Silajdzic took the papers in front of him, slammed them down on the table with great force, and shouted, "I can't take this anymore." Then he stormed out into the cold Dayton night, leaving the rest of us behind.

"Let's deal with this in the morning," I said, and Izetbegovic, suddenly quite animated, walked out, followed by Granic and Susak. We were left alone with Milosevic, who had said nothing during the entire scene.

The "peace" had lasted thirty-seven minutes. We sat with Milosevic for another half hour, utterly spent. The twenty-two-hour day had ended in disaster. Nothing since the Mount Igman tragedy had hit us as hard. Finally, shortly after 5:00 A.M., we parted to get short naps before resuming. We were too exhausted to imagine a way out.

DAY TWENTY: MONDAY, NOVEMBER 20

We rose again after one hour of sleep. (Christopher told me later that he had not slept at all.) The conference was now stalled within sight of its goal, and after the drama of the previous night, emotions were raw in all three delegations. Christopher, Donilon, Steinberg, and I met early in the morning, and agreed that it was time to bring in the heaviest weapon we had: President Clinton.

Intervention (but not a visit) by the President had always been part of our operating assumptions for Dayton, but the questions were when and how. It was important not to weaken the President. The presidential coin is precious, and should not be devalued. The rest of us could rise or fall, succeed or fail, be replaced or repudiated if necessary. But the President represents the nation. There is no higher authority, and his failure or error can hurt the national interest. Thus any involvement of the nation's chief executive is something that White House staffers debate strenuously.

We called Tony Lake, and asked him to arrange two calls—one to Tudjman, the other to Izetbegovic. (No call to Milosevic was needed or desirable.) We recommended a simple presidential message: You are very close to success, and I am asking you, in the name of peace, to work out your differences.

Lake said he wanted to delay any presidential calls until the afternoon, while we made another try to reach agreement. More important, Lake opposed any call to Izetbegovic, on the grounds that the President should not appear to be pressuring the Muslims. Christopher and I felt differently. Both calls, we said, were essential.

Lake was adamant. He would oppose a call to Izetbegovic, he said, even though Christopher and I said that without it the risks of failure increased substantially. When we argued that the call could be couched in a manner that would not be construed as pressure, he still objected.

The core team at Dayton was not happy. Kerrick, using his direct channels to the NSC, tried again, but with no success. Then he wrote the first draft of the "talking points" that the President would use with Tudjman. I suggested that Christopher call the President directly to get him involved immediately and more deeply. But the Secretary was reluctant to get in an argument with Tony over whether the President should call Izetbegovic.

We called on Tudjman, who told us that his ministers had acted with his full support in killing the Milosevic-Silajdzic agreement the previous evening.

"We cannot be the only ones who give up land," Tudjman said. "The Muslims must give up something too."

We saw Bildt at 9:15 A.M. and asked him to meet separately with each of the three Presidents, starting with Tudjman. After calling Spanish Foreign Minister Javier Solana in Brussels, Carl went to each delegation with a simple, but important, message: "Don't hold out for a better deal in Europe. Make it here."

Tudjman walked across the parking lot to see Izetbegovic to see if together they could force Milosevic to accept less than 49 percent of the land. They concluded, as we had, that it would be impossible.

At 11:00 A.M., Bildt came to my room to ask how we were doing. "We are deeply concerned," I said, "that even if Milosevic makes more concessions, the Bosnians will simply raise the ante."

"Do you think Izetbegovic even wants a deal?" Carl asked. It was a question that Warren Christopher had also been asking. "I'm never quite sure," I replied. "Sometimes he seems to want revenge more than peace—but he can't have both." Chris Hill, normally highly supportive of the Bosnians, exploded in momentary anger and frustration. "These people are impossible to help," he said. It was a telling statement from a man who had devoted years of his life to the search for ways to help create a Bosnian state.

It was a beautiful sunny day, clear and crisp, not too cold. People walked around outside to relieve the tension. A sort of "parking-lot diplomacy" took place as people ran into each other and discussed the situation. At one point Bildt ran into Milosevic in the barren asphalt between our buildings, and found him "desperate." "Give me anything," he said, "rocks, swamps, hills—anything, as long as it gets us to 49–51."

At about three in the afternoon, President Clinton made the call to Tudjman. "I am impressed with how much has been achieved in the overall agreement, and with the benefits that will come to all the parties," he said. "A very difficult trade-off will have to be made to resolve the map. I'm calling to ask you to give back a small percentage of nontraditional Croatian territory in western Bosnia in order to bring the map back in line with the basic 51–49 territorial concept of the Contact Group plan."

Tudjman's reply baffled the President and his advisors in Washington, listening in and taking notes. "We have already made such a proposal," Tudjman said, adding that we were only two or three hours from a final agreement. This brought the short conversation to an end.

As soon as Sandy Vershbow, who had listened to the conversation, briefed us on it, Christopher and I went to see Tudjman. Contrary to what he had told the President, Tudjman had made no proposal prior to the call—but he knew that he would have to do so now. "In response to President Clinton's request," he said, "I will instruct my negotiators to give up seventy-five percent of the land needed to reach 49–51." This was good news. But then came two important conditions: "The Muslims must give some of their land up—and I must get back at least part of the Posavina pocket."

President Clinton's call had given us a new lease on life. We returned to Izetbegovic's suite immediately, hopeful that reason would prevail once again. We told him and Silajdzic that, with the President's personal intervention, we had gained agreement from Tudjman that he would "contribute" 75 percent of the land required to reach 51–49. The remainder—just 1 percent of the land—would have to come from them. This would not be difficult to accomplish, we said, especially since the Bosnians would not have to give back any land they currently controlled, only land that they had been given in the last few days by Milosevic—"theoretical land," as we called it.

To our consternation, Izetbegovic refused to budge. While Silajdzic sat silent, Sacirbey argued that the Croat position was still unfair. And, to Christopher's amazement, Izetbegovic began talking again about Brcko, Srebrenica, and Zepa. We returned to my rooms, where Christopher expressed himself in unusually vivid terms on the performance we had just witnessed.

Our next call was on Milosevic. We told him that we could achieve 51–49—but only if he gave back part of the Posavina pocket. Although this request momentarily stunned Milosevic, he understood its importance to Tudjman. Working with detailed maps, Milosevic, Hill, and I started a protracted subnegotiation that went on intermittently for the next six hours. Milosevic finally agreed to return to the Federation a sliver of the Posavina pocket that contained the town of Orasje, which had been the scene of ethnic cleansing of Croats early in the war, and the town of Samac, which lay on the Sava River. A deadlock developed over the exact boundary of Samac. Thinking of Harold Nicolson's negotiators at Versailles, who drew lines on maps with almost no understanding of what they were doing,* I drew a line on the map that ran down the middle of the Sava River, directly on the international border, and then curved around the town's boundaries.

Tudjman accepted this last-minute return of Bosnian Croat land with pleasure. In addition to eastern Slavonia, Tudjman could now show the Croatian people that he had regained some Croat land in Bosnia. And since it was near the home area of Federation President Zubak, it had special value.

By 9:00 P.M., Tudjman had given us enough land in return so that the map stood at 52–48. A shift of only 1 percent, and the deal was done. Yet the

* See opening quotation, chapter 17.

Bosnians still refused to share this tiny amount of land. We met in Christopher's room to discuss the situation—Christopher, Donilon, Steinberg, Kornblum, Hill, Burns, and myself. We were depressed and tired. "The land the Bosnians have to give up is only theoretical," I said again. "We are not asking them to give up one inch of land they actually control."

"It's truly unbelievable," Christopher said. "The Bosnian position is irrational. A great agreement is within their grasp, and they don't seem able to accept it."

"What more can we do?" Christopher continued, almost rhetorically. "We have gotten them everything they asked for."

"Chris," I said, "this game has gone on long enough. We must give everyone a drop-dead time limit." I then recommended that we tell Izetbegovic that he had one hour to decide, after which we would close down the conference. "And I really mean close Dayton down," I added. "This should not be a bluff."

It was a huge decision, foreshadowed days earlier in my "Closure or Closedown" memorandum. A heated debate broke out in the room between those who wanted to keep trying and those who thought that our best chance for success was to force everyone to confront failure. The argument went on for close to an hour. Would we resume the shuttle if we closed Dayton down? Would we let the conference continue in Europe under Bildt's chairmanship? It was a gamble. Some people shifted sides, but Kornblum and I held firm for absolute closedown, without resuming the shuttle. Finally, after protracted debate, Christopher agreed that we had to give the Bosnians an ultimatum. We suggested a flat midnight time limit.

"I'd better get the President on board," Christopher said. Over a secure phone line, Christopher told the President what we proposed to do, listened for a moment, and said, "Thank you for your confidence, Mr. President." Then, turning to us, he said, "The President is comfortable with this approach. He will give us complete support."

Kornblum alerted the Bosnians that we wanted to see them immediately, and told Bildt that we were going to deliver an ultimatum. At 10:30 in the evening, Christopher and I walked slowly to the Bosnian President's suite.

Izetbegovic, Silajdzic, and Sacirbey sat in the room waiting for us. Christopher and I took up our usual places next to each other on the couch, and Christopher began.

"Mr. President, we have come a long way in Dayton, and we are very close to a successful conclusion. If you will reduce by one percent the amount of land you claim, we can make a final deal. You do not have to give up any land that you currently control. It's a very good deal, Mr. President. We have obtained almost everything you asked for."

Izetbegovic was visibly uncomfortable. He began to review his griev-ances—a familiar litany. We tried to reason with him, but he became increasingly obdurate. He mentioned the city of Brcko several times. He felt that he had become the object of all the pressure at Dayton, and he hated pressure. He was tired and beleaguered, and his delegation was about to explode. His eyes narrowing almost to the vanishing point, he looked away from us and mumbled something to his colleagues.

Christopher's famous politeness and patience finally ran out, and he delivered the ultimatum in a tone that conveyed genuine anger. "Mr. President, I am truly disappointed," he said, "at the fuzzy, unrealistic, and sloppy manner in which you and your delegation have approached this negotiation. You can have a successful outcome or not, as you wish. But we must have your answer in one hour. If you say no, we will announce in the morning that the Dayton peace talks have been closed down." We rose to leave, and I added, "Not suspended—closed down. In one hour."

Exhausted, Christopher went directly back to the Hope Center to sleep—his first in three days. I promised we would call as soon as we heard from the Bosnians. Less than a minute after Christopher had left, the door to my room burst open and Haris Silajdzic entered, in a towering rage. "You and Christopher have ruined everything!" he screamed. "How could you let this happen? Don't you know that we can never give in to an American ultimatum—never!"

"You are the ones who have ruined it," I said. "You have at least ninety-five percent of what you wanted, and now you are about to piss it all away, because you can't get your own act together." Silajdzic continued to argue, and I asked him to leave. "Use the next hour to get your President to accept this offer and the war will be over. You will not regret it."

At precisely 11:30 P.M., John Kornblum went to the Bosnians' building to receive their reply. Sacirbey stopped Kornblum in the hall. The Bosnians, he announced, would agree to shave the necessary 1 percent of the land in order to get to 51–49, but they wanted something in return—Brcko.

"You have added a new condition," John said. "You know that we cannot agree." John gave Sacirbey the draft failure statement, and told him it would be issued at 10:00 A.M. the next day.

I called Christopher with the news. "It's over—but maybe it's not over," I told him. "Perhaps confronting the abyss will clear some heads overnight. Please get some sleep, because we are going to have a tough day tomorrow."

Hill delivered the failure statement to Tudjman, who was playing cards with his aides. As befitted a man who already had most of what he wanted, Tudjman laughed, and asked Hill if the United States was really ready to blame the Bosnians publicly for failure. He urged us not to quit.

I sent Kerrick and Hill to deliver the failure statement to Milosevic. Clark, Pardew, Kornblum, and Perina joined the meeting as it went on. Before they left, I told them to make clear that we really were going to close down in the morning—unless Milosevic could save the negotiation. I deliberately stayed away in order to avoid another negotiating session.

It had been, without question, the most depressing day of my professional life. It was hard to believe that the Bosnians would let the agreement slip away over so little, but they seemed ready to do so. I fell asleep quickly, without awaiting the news of the meeting still going on with Milosevic.

Kornblum described the meeting to me later: Milosevic began in a jovial mood, and offered everyone scotch. But when he realized that we would really close the conference the next morning, he reacted strongly. "You can't do that," he said, his voice showing the strain. He became emotional. "We've got this agreement almost done, you can't let this happen. You're the United States. You can't let the Bosnians push you around this way. Just tell them what to do." When the Americans replied that the United States had done a great deal already, but we could not dictate the terms of peace to any party, Milosevic pleaded: "Try some more, don't give up."

Distraught, Milosevic said he would see "Franjo" right away, and propose that the two men sign the Dayton agreements with or without Izetbegovic. Milosevic sent faithful Goran to set up a meeting, but the Croatian President was asleep. Milosevic said he would see Tudjman in the morning. At about 2:00 A.M., the Americans departed, leaving behind a deeply concerned, perhaps even confused Milosevic, who could not believe that we would not be able to force the Bosnians to sign. "Mr. President," Kornblum said as he left, "it's up to you. We've done everything we can."

At 6:30 A.M., the phone rang in our room. It was David Martin, the CBS Pentagon correspondent. It was the first time a journalist had managed to get past the Air Force switchboard since the talks began. "I'm going on the air in a few minutes," Martin said, "and I need you to confirm something. Sacirbey has been at the Holiday Inn all night long, telling everyone that you gave them an ultimatum, they refused, and you are calling off the talks."

Suddenly I was wide awake. "David," I said, "I don't know what Sacirbey said to you, but you can say that we are at a moment of absolute crisis."

"Thanks, that's all I need." A few minutes later, I watched Martin say on television that we had reached "a moment of absolute crisis." It was indeed. As I showered and dressed, I mentally composed a personal statement to accompany the formal announcement that Dayton was closing down. I would thank everyone for their support, and state that I was withdrawing from the effort, since it was clear that I could accomplish nothing further.

The television was now filled with reports similar to David Martin's. Donilon and Kerrick had briefed the White House, and even as we held our final staff meeting in Dayton the President gathered with his senior advisors. One of the people in the Oval Office that morning, George Stephanopoulos, later described the scene to me:

> We all woke that morning to hear television reports from Dayton that you had failed. When we gathered in the Oval Office to discuss the situation, there were mixed emotions. Some people, primarily on the domestic side, were relieved, because they knew that if you got an agreement the President would have to make the single most difficult decision of his presidency—to send troops to Bosnia—and then defend it during the 1996 elections. Our polls showed the public overwhelmingly opposed to sending American troops to Bosnia. Yet everyone knew what an enormous amount of prestige we had invested in the effort. The President did not express his own views, but followed the discussion carefully.
>
> I would summarize the general attitude as follows: if Dayton failed, there would be a combination of relief and disappointment. If you succeeded, there would be a combination of pride and apprehension.

Through Tom Donilon, we were already aware of Washington's ambivalence about our efforts. Lake had also told us the previous day that "not everyone in Washington wants you to succeed." This neither surprised nor alarmed me; every Administration contains different points of view. The responsibility for failure or success rested with us, and this was no time to worry about Washington's ambivalence.

As I dressed for the 8:00 A.M. staff meeting there was an insistent knock on the door, and Chris Hill came in. "Something's up," he said, excitedly. "Milosevic has just gone to see Tudjman. I think Slobo is going to suggest that the two of them sign the agreement even if Izetbegovic does not."

This did not constitute a breakthrough, but at least they were still talking. After the terrible feeling of failure and exhaustion, I was suddenly, perhaps irrationally, optimistic. As Christopher arrived from the Hope Center for the staff meeting, I pulled him aside and whispered, "We're going to get an agreement!" He looked at me as if I had lost my mind.

The staff meeting was a gloomy affair. Twenty tired people crowded into every corner of the small, messy room. With no more business to conduct, I said this was our last staff meeting, our "shutdown meeting," and started a final statement of appreciation. "The Secretary and I would like to thank everyone for their magnificent efforts. We gave it everything we had, and, no matter what happens today, we should not feel that we have failed, but—"

Suddenly Kati burst into the room. "Milosevic is standing out in the snow in the parking lot waiting to talk to you," she said. For the first time I noticed that it was snowing. She ran back out and pulled him into my room, where Christopher and I met him. He looked as if he had not slept all night.

"Something has to be done to prevent failure," he said wearily. "I suggest that Tudjman and I sign the agreement, and we leave it open for Izetbegovic to sign later."

"That's quite impossible," Christopher said firmly. "We cannot have an agreement that is not signed by everyone. It is not a viable contract."

"Okay, okay," Milosevic said. "Then I will walk the final mile for peace. I will agree to arbitration for Brcko one year from now, and you can make the decision yourself, Mr. Christopher."

Christopher said that he could not personally be the arbitrator. I said we would choose Roberts Owen for the task if we completed the rest of the agreement. I said we had to see Tudjman and Izetbegovic immediately to see if we had an agreement. We ended the brief meeting, and raced to Tudjman's suite.

Tudjman listened intently as I outlined Milosevic's offer. When I finished, he slammed his hands on his knees twice, and, leaning as close to Christopher's face as he could get, said, in English, "Get peace. Get peace now! Make Izetbegovic agree. You must do it now!" Shaking with emotion, he got up, almost pushing us out of his room.

Christopher and I walked back to my suite. I locked the doors so that we could be alone. As we talked, other staff members stood outside, banging on the door, but we ignored them. It was essential to have a single focus for the next meeting, and not a cacophony of voices. This was not a time to consult anyone.

"Chris," I said, "the next meeting may be the most important of your entire tenure as Secretary. We can get this agreement—or we can lose it. Forget Washington. It's entirely in our hands. We must go into the meeting with an absolute determination to succeed."

Christopher listened silently, then nodded. Without stopping to talk to anyone else, we walked directly to Izetbegovic's rooms, where the three Bosnians waited for us. We outlined the offer from Milosevic. Silence. I repeated it, slowly and carefully. There were seven hundred journalists waiting outside the base, I said. They had been told by Sacirbey that the talks were over, and, in fact, we would make such an announcement at 10:00 A.M. unless the offer to put Brcko under arbitration was accepted. Time had run out, and we needed an answer immediately.

There was a long, agonizing pause. We watched Izetbegovic carefully. No one spoke. Finally, speaking slowly, Izetbegovic said, "It is not a just peace." He paused for what seemed like a minute, but was probably only three seconds. My heart almost stopped. Then: "But my people need peace."

Remembering how often things had unraveled with the Bosnians in the past, I did not want to discuss anything else. Leaning over to Christopher, I whispered, "Let's get out of here fast," and rose. Christopher shook Izetbegovic's hand and turned rapidly away. As we reached the door, I said to Sacirbey, "Why don't you come with us and work out with General Clark the final details of 51–49 right now." He said he would be over in a minute, and we left.

Christopher and I called President Clinton from my room, as our team crowded around, excited and relieved. The President offered to fly to Dayton for the announcement. "Mr. President," I said, "you don't want to be anywhere near these people today. They are wild, and they don't deserve a presidential visit." Instead, we suggested that the President make the initial announcement as quickly as possible from the White House, and we rescheduled the ceremony for 3:00 P.M. We also suggested that Secretary Perry and General Shalikashvili fly out to symbolize the Pentagon's support of the agreement.

When he heard that Izetbegovic had accepted his offer, Milosevic came to our rooms. He was in a highly emotional state. As he entered the room, he hugged Don Kerrick, and we saw tears in his eyes. He shook everyone's hand.

There was plenty of unfinished business in Dayton. Focused on the problems that still remained, we could not relax or celebrate yet. A re-energized negotiating team went into action across many fronts at once. Clark and Sacirbey began the tricky process of shaving the map by 1 percent. Kornblum, Owen, and Miriam Sapiro convened the three Foreign Ministers to work out several details of the political annexes. The refugee voting issue was settled by a compromise that permitted people to vote in the area where they had lived in 1991, as the Bosnians wanted, but allowed them to apply to an electoral commission for the right to vote elsewhere, as the Serbs wanted. Two years later this provision would be important, enabling Muslims to elect eighteen members of the eighty-four seat Republika Srpska Assembly.

President Clinton made the announcement from the Rose Garden at 11:40 that morning. "After nearly four years, two hundred and fifty thousand people killed, two million refugees, and atrocities that have appalled people all over the world, the people of Bosnia finally have a chance to turn from the horror of war to the promise of peace," he said. He called on the American people—

and especially Congress—to support the agreement with American troops. "Now that a detailed settlement has been reached, NATO will rapidly complete its planning for IFOR. American leadership, together with our allies, is needed to make this peace real and enduring. Our values, our interests, and our leadership all over the world are at stake."

We briefed the Contact Group, and then brought the three Presidents to Christopher's suite at the Hope Center for lunch and discussion of the remaining details. In order to strengthen our case with Congress, I drafted a letter to President Clinton, which I insisted that all three Presidents sign, in which each man personally guaranteed the safety of the NATO/IFOR troops.

By prearrangement, President Clinton called Christopher's suite during the lunch. The three men huddled around the speakerphone, leaning closer and closer to one another as they strained to listen to President Clinton as he congratulated them. Christopher and I glanced at each other, half amused, half astonished at the sight of Izetbegovic, Tudjman, and Milosevic with their heads almost touching.

Meanwhile, Hill and Kerrick had made an alarming discovery. In conversation with Foreign Minister Milutinovic, they learned that no Bosnian Serb would initial the agreement. In fact, Milutinovic told them, the Bosnian Serb delegation had seen the map for the first time just before lunch. "They went completely crazy," Milutinovic said with a laugh. Milosevic had decided that Milutinovic would initial for the Republika Srpska.

This was unacceptable. What good would the agreement be if the Bosnian Serbs refused to initial? And why would the signature of the Foreign Minister of the Federal Republic of Yugoslavia be valid for Pale? I asked Hill and Kerrick to find Milosevic and tell him that we would delay the initialing ceremony until he got the Bosnian Serb signatures.

Milosevic professed amazement at our attitude. "Why are you making such a big thing of such bullshit?" he asked. "I'll get the Republika Srpska signatures as soon as I return."

"Why can't Krajisnik initial now?" they demanded. Milosevic laughed. "Because he is in a coma after seeing the map."

After further discussion, we decided to accept Milosevic's initials—though not those of his Foreign Minister—in place of Republika Srpska, but on one condition: that Milosevic sign a separate letter, addressed to Christopher, promising that he would deliver the Pale signatures within ten days. He mocked this letter as completely unnecessary. "I guarantee you that I will have the signatures within twenty-four hours of my return to Belgrade," he said. (And he was right; the Bosnian Serbs, including Karadzic, signed the agreement the day after Milosevic returned to Belgrade.)

. . .

The ceremony that we had not even dared dream about—"a day that many believed would never come," as Warren Christopher put it—began at 3:00 P.M. in
the same room at the Hope Center where it had all begun twenty-one days earlier. Facing the press and our colleagues, I could see in the front row Katharina Frasure, Gail Kruzel, and Sandy Drew—proud, silent witnesses to the
price we had paid for the agreement. Around them were the members of the
Contact Group, our negotiating team, and General Shalikashvili and Deputy
Secretary of Defense John White, filling in for Perry.

Christopher began the ceremonies by outlining the positive features of the
agreement, but cautioned that the road to full implementation would not be
easy. Carl Bildt followed with a short and generous statement of praise for the
Americans, with special thanks to the staff of Packy's All-Sports Bar. Knowing that he would now be the senior civilian responsible for implementation,
Bildt talked of the "massive effort by the international community" that would
be required.

As the third co-chairman of the conference, Igor Ivanov had not played a
major role, but he spoke next. To our surprise, he announced that his government would "reserve its position in regard to the military and arms-control annexes." It was a minor hiccup on a day of great achievement, and was soon
ironed out. More importantly, President Yeltsin had spoken to the Russian
people about his country's support for the basic agreement at Dayton immediately after President Clinton's first announcement, and pledged his country's
participation in the effort.

Milosevic was next, his first public words since arriving. He spoke opti-
mistically about the future, calling November 21, 1995, the day that "will
enter history as the date of the end of the war." All sides, Milosevic said, had
made "painful concessions," but now "the war in Bosnia should be left to the
past."

Washington was most concerned about what Izetbegovic would say. Jim
Steinberg worried that Izetbegovic would repeat publicly his private comment
that the agreement was an "unjust peace," and asked Menzies to try to talk the
Bosnians into a positive statement. But Izetbegovic's real audience was in
Bosnia, and he was not ready to give unequivocal praise to an agreement that
troubled him and that he was not sure the Serbs would respect. After calling
this "a historic day for Bosnia and for the rest of the world because the war,
we hope, will be replaced by peace," Izetbegovic began the delicate process of
gaining support for the agreement at home:

> And to my people, I say, this may not be a just peace, but it is more just than a
> continuation of war. In the situation as it is and in the world as it is, a better peace
> could not have been achieved. God is our witness that we have done everything

in our power so that the extent of injustice for our people and our country would be decreased.

In the crush of last-minute problems and details, I had not thought about my own remarks until after the ceremony was already under way. I therefore had to write my statement while half-listening to the previous speakers. My mood was more one of relief than exhilaration, more weariness rather than euphoria. I could not find a way to share in the joy that some of the participants showed, even though I wanted to. After the behavior we had seen from some of the participants at Dayton, I was more worried than ever about implementing the agreement. As several reporters pointed out the next day, my remarks were notable for their cautionary tone, far more so than that of any of the other speakers that day. They began with a tribute to Bob Frasure, Joe Kruzel, and Nelson Drew, and continued:

> The agreements and territorial arrangements initialed here today are a huge step forward, the biggest by far since the war began. But ahead lies an equally daunting task: implementation. On every page of the many complicated documents and annexes initialed here today lie challenges to both sides to set aside their enmities, their differences, which are still raw with open wounds. On paper, we have peace. To make it work is our next and greatest challenge. . . .
>
> It's been a long and winding road for all of us, and it's not over yet—far from it. The immense difficulties and the roller-coaster ride we have lived through in Dayton over the last twenty-one days, and especially in the last few days, only serve to remind us how much work lies ahead. Let us pledge, therefore, that this day in Dayton be long remembered as the day on which Bosnia and its neighbors turned from war to peace.

BOOK FOUR

IMPLEMENTATION

Between the idea
And the reality
Between the motion
And the act
Falls the Shadow.

—T. S. ELIOT

CHAPTER 19

Slow Start

(November 21, 1995–February 21, 1996)

In 1884, at the International Meridian Conference in Washington, D.C., representatives from twenty-six countries voted to make . . . the Greenwich meridian the prime meridian of the world. This decision did not sit well with the French, however, who continued to recognize their own Paris Observatory meridian, a little more than two degrees east of Greenwich, as the starting line for another twenty-seven years, until 1911. Even then, they hesitated to refer directly to Greenwich mean time, preferring the locution "Paris Mean Time, retarded by nine minutes twenty-one seconds."

—DAVA SOBEL, *Longitude: The True Story of a Lone Genius Who Solved the Greatest Scientific Problem of His Time*

AN HOUR AFTER THE DAYTON INITIALING CEREMONY, Kati and I flew with General Shalikashvili to New York. Leaving Wright-Patterson Air Force Base was like release from a comfortable prison; we slowly rediscovered the outside world. Still, after twenty-one days of isolation, normal life seemed far away. The extraordinary public reaction to the Dayton agreement was immensely gratifying, but in the rush of tasks that needed to be done, there was no time to savor it.

Meeting with the President. The next day, November 22, we met at the White House in an atmosphere that combined relief, pride, and apprehension. Lake's opening quip reflected the tone: "We're in a heap of trouble now—but it's the right kind of trouble." The President, arriving with Gore a few moments later, thanked everyone, and joked, "I was all set for a disappointment."

Asked to begin, I said that the arrest of Karadzic and Mladic was the most critical issue that was not resolved at Dayton. I repeated my view that if the two men, particularly Karadzic, the founder and leader of a still-unrepentant separatist movement, remained at large, full implementation of the agreement would be impossible. The President concurred, saying, "It is best to remove both men." Without giving a direct instruction, he asked the military to reconsider the issue.

He then shifted to a more immediate issue: gaining public and congressional support for the policy. "I must be brutally honest with the American people," he said. "When I address the people I must be sure our military and intelligence people have signed off. I must be honest about what we are getting into."

Vice President Gore said Dayton was a gamble worth taking. He paused for a moment, and his face took on a sharp focus. "I want to make an important practical point regarding the JCS and the Pentagon," he said, looking directly at the Defense representatives in the room. "I've had lots of conversations with the Congress. They have told me that our military representatives on the Hill usually leave their audience more uncomfortable than when they arrived. I'm not saying they are trying to undercut our policy, but they are losing us votes up there."

After a brief, stunned silence, Deputy Defense Secretary John White took up the challenge: "We need answers that Shali and his colleagues can all feel comfortable with."

The President stepped in to support Gore. "My sense," he said, "is that the diplomatic breakthrough in Dayton has given us a chance to prevail in Congress and in the nation. People see the stakes and the big picture. But we can't get congressional support without Defense and the military fully behind this. We must show Congress the stakes and the consequences. We can't promise them zero casualties, but we have to convey a high level of confidence in our capacity to carry out the mission and to manage the gaps in the agreement. Your people have body language. It's not a question of being dishonest, but we can't close the deal without the Pentagon's support." He looked directly at Shalikashvili. "I know there has been ambivalence among some of your people—not you, Shali, but some of your people—about Bosnia," he said, "but that is all in the past. I want everyone here to get behind the agreement."

The two men rose to leave, and we all rose with them. Their message would have a substantial effect. When the President and Vice President tell their senior aides to get with the program, and when they say it with vigor and even an unmistakable sternness, it does wonders for a divided or reluctant bureaucracy. I wondered if the two men had coordinated their comments; a year later the President told me that they had.

Congress and the Public. While the public applauded our diplomatic efforts, opinion polls put public opposition to the deployment of American forces to Bosnia at around 70 percent. This was understandable. For almost four years, Americans had watched television pictures of United Nations troops being killed and wounded while unable to defend themselves adequately. Most Americans assumed we were sending our own troops into a similar situation, where they would suffer heavy casualties.

Sending American troops to Bosnia would be the single most unpopular action of President Clinton's entire first term. Although the public was proud of the American diplomatic role in ending the war, we had to convince them that the American deployments would be different from those of the U.N., that NATO would shoot first and ask questions later—and that the deployment was in our national interest. *Newsweek* wryly captured the paradoxical situation in its first post-Dayton issue in an article by Evan Thomas and John Barry:

> Hail Pax Americana! Salute the return of the superpower! Or, then again, maybe not. The foreign-policy establishment may cheer, and Balkan brigands may head for the hills, but ordinary Americans are decidedly wary of sacrifices ahead. . . . Most voters regard Bosnia as someone else's civil war. It will be up to President Clinton to convince them otherwise. . . . Baffled by Bosnia or distracted by domestic concerns, most Americans have not begun to realize the reach and depth of the U.S. commitment made last week in Dayton.

Some important members of Congress immediately came to our support: Senators Lieberman, Biden, and Lugar once again were in the forefront. Some qualified their support by tying it to a tight "exit strategy." Since the Administration had written a one-year timetable into the Dayton agreement, we could not object. Many others opposed the policy outright. Such a position was essentially cost-free, since the Congress knew that the President would send troops regardless of what it did (barring an absolute cutoff of funds, which was very unlikely). Thus members of Congress could take a politically popular position without having to worry about its consequences. Speaker Gingrich predicted that the Administration would win "guarded approval, even acquiescence through inaction" and produced an artfully evasive resolution that allowed his colleagues in the House to vote both sides of the issue; they could give, as he put it, "very strong support for the troops [while objecting to] the president's policy."

In this atmosphere Donilon, and at the White House McCurry and Donald Baer, coordinated an intense public relations campaign. The President invited many members of Congress to the White House for briefings. In December we organized two large congressional delegations to the Balkans. Almost seventy members, an astonishing 15 percent of the entire House, went on these trips. Without exception, the members who went came back swayed in favor of the policy, although participation did not automatically mean full support. Cynthia McKinney, a first-term Democrat from an overwhelmingly black district in Georgia, who had previously focused on domestic issues and expressed great skepticism about foreign "giveaways," was typical. She told me later, "The trip changed my life. It made me realize that we have to undertake some of the same responsibilities overseas that we need to do at home, and that we must find a way to do both."

Europe: Applause and Shock. Dayton shook the leadership elite of post–Cold War Europe. The Europeans were grateful to the United States for leading the effort that finally ended the war in Bosnia, but some European officials were embarrassed that American involvement had been necessary. Jacques Poos's 1991 assertion that Europe's "hour had dawned" lay in history's dustbin, alongside James Baker's view that we had no dog in that fight.

"One cannot call it an American peace," French Foreign Minister de Charette told the press, "even if President Clinton and the Americans have tried to pull the blanket over to their side. The fact is that the Americans looked at this affair in ex-Yugoslavia from a great distance for nearly four years and basically blocked the progression of things." But de Charette also acknowledged that "Europe as such was not present, and this, it is true, was a failure of the European Union." Prime Minister Alain Juppé, after praising the Dayton agreement, could not resist adding, "Of course, it resembles like a twin the European plan we presented eighteen months ago"—when he was Foreign Minister. Agence France-Presse reported that many European diplomats were "left smarting" at Dayton. In an article clearly inspired by someone at the French Foreign Ministry, *Le Figaro* said that "Richard Holbrooke, the American mediator, did not leave his European colleagues with good memories from the air base at Dayton." They quoted an unnamed French diplomat as saying, "He flatters, he lies, he humiliates: he is a sort of brutal and schizophrenic Mazarin."* President Chirac's national security assistant, Jean-David Levitte, called to apologize for this comment, saying it did not represent the views of his boss. I replied that such minidramas were inevitable given the pressures and frustrations we faced at Dayton and were inconsequential considering that the war was over.

With two weeks remaining before the formal signing of the agreement in Paris, Karadzic raised temperatures again in the region. Although he had signed the agreement under Milosevic's pressure, he announced that Sarajevo would "bleed for decades" unless we changed the Dayton terms. In response, we said that we would not change the agreement. Defending the most prob-

* Cardinal Jules Mazarin, a famously cunning and powerful seventeenth-century prelate, succeeded Cardinal Richelieu as chief minister to Louis XIII.

lematic part of American policy, Perry predicted that "one year will be sufficient to break the cycle of violence in Bosnia." Perry broke the year down into two phases, four to six months to enforce a truce and disarmament, and another six months to create a secure environment. As it turned out, he was overly pessimistic on the first task, and overly optimistic on the second.

There was much work left before the signing ceremony. NATO had to send sixty thousand troops to Bosnia—the largest troop movement in Western Europe since World War II—and deploy thousands more off the Adriatic coast and at a forward logistics base in Hungary. On the civilian side, a series of high-level conferences were jammed into the two weeks immediately preceding the Paris ceremony. First came the annual NATO Foreign Ministers meeting in Brussels on December 5 and 6, which focused heavily on Bosnia. One day later, the scene shifted to Budapest for the annual meeting of the Foreign Ministers of the OSCE, who had to set up the machinery to oversee the elections in Bosnia as called for in the Dayton Peace Agreement. On December 8, the British convened a high-level "Implementation Conference" in London to discuss how to handle the nonmilitary parts of Dayton. Warren Christopher and John Kornblum attended the first two conferences, while Strobe Talbott and Bob Gallucci led the American team to London and Budapest. Meanwhile, I reassembled the negotiating team and returned to the Balkans to pin down the final details for the Paris ceremonies.

This blizzard of diffused activity demonstrated the key difference between the negotiations and the phase that was beginning. The previous fourteen weeks had been highly focused. Now a wide-ranging effort, involving thousands of civilian and military personnel from the United States and other countries, was about to begin. Unfortunately, we had created a structure for implementing Dayton in which responsibility and authority would rest with no single individual or institution. Although Bosnia would play host to fewer agencies than it had during the U.N. days, too many still remained in the process, including NATO, the U.N. and the UNHCR, the OSCE, the E.U., the World Bank, the IMF—and an organization with no precedent, the Office of the High Representative, headed by Carl Bildt.

"Foreign Forces and Elements." When our team met Izetbegovic in Sarajevo on December 8, he was animated and jovial. But his mood darkened when we pressed him on the presence of "foreign forces and elements" in the Muslim portion of Bosnia. These were the Iranians and mujahideen who had been helping the Bosnian Muslims for the previous three years. American intelligence had long known of their existence—they were prominently mentioned, in fact, in my January 1993 memorandum to the incoming Administration—but during the war Washington had not made an issue of their presence since they were helping the otherwise isolated Bosnians to survive. The Dayton agreement required their complete withdrawal within thirty days after the arrival of IFOR, scheduled for December 20. I told Izetbegovic we would withhold our support for the Equip and Train program unless the Iranians and the mujahideen left. The press, aware of their presence, was running stories with headlines that particularly alarmed Congress (*The Washington Post,* November 30: "Foreign Muslims Fighting in Bosnia Considered 'Threat' to U.S. Troops"; *The New York Times,* December 10: "What's Iran Doing in Bosnia Anyway?"). With NATO forces about to arrive in Bosnia, we could not tolerate the continued presence of these people in Bosnia, especially since some had ties to groups in the Middle East that had committed terrorist acts against American troops.

Extremely uncomfortable with this subject, Izetbegovic pledged that the foreign elements would leave within the Dayton timetable "if there is peace." This was only the first of many conversations we would have on this troublesome issue.

In Pale, Karadzic was still giving inflammatory interviews, to our intense annoyance. On December 2, I wrote Milosevic an angry letter demanding that he get the Bosnian Serbs under control. After reading the letter, Milosevic told Rudy Perina that he had been meeting with Bosnian Serb leaders all week, pressing them to "support" Dayton. Six days later, when we met with Milosevic, he told us confidently that he was succeeding. But on the future of Karadzic and Mladic, Milosevic remained adamant; he could not, and would not, deliver the two men to an international tribunal.

I was concerned that we would not get off to a fast enough start. "Everything depends on a vigorous implementation by IFOR *from the first day,*" I cabled Christopher at the end of the trip. "A slow start would be a mistake."

One day before the Paris ceremony, under pressure from the White House, Congress voted on the deployments. In the Senate, with crucial support from Senator Dole, the Administration won a surprisingly easy 69-to-30 victory. In the House, Gingrich's odd approach produced a 287-to-141 vote to oppose the Administration's policy while "supporting" the troops. Coupled with defeats in each house for proposals to cut off funds for the mission, it was enough for Mike McCurry to claim victory. "This is probably the strongest statement of support they could possibly make," he said. "Having voted overwhelmingly not to shut off funding is, in a sense, supporting the President's judgment."

Paris. By the time of the vote, the negotiating team was already in Paris. The day before the ceremonies, in the midst of a gigantic strike of transit workers that paralyzed Paris, I met Foreign Minister de Charette alone to discuss the unresolved issue of whether an American or a European would run the OSCE election unit in Bosnia.

The meeting quickly turned into a general discussion of the relationship between our two countries. I observed that no nation had done more in Bosnia than France. President Chirac's personal intervention with President Clinton during his June trip to Washington had been vital in focusing the Administration. Success in the future depended critically on close French-American cooperation, especially since the French military would be responsible for the Sarajevo Sector, as it had been during the war. Finally, I reminded de Charette that we had kept our promise to have the formal signing ceremony in Paris.

We had agreed to let Europeans head every civilian implementation institution in Bosnia, I said. But there was one exception: we would not yield on the OSCE election unit. The reason was simple: the final wording at Dayton—that the OSCE would "oversee and conduct" the elections—was sufficiently ambiguous that we wanted to ensure a maximalist approach. This required someone of our own choosing.

He and President Chirac, de Charette said, were equally adamant that this position go to a Frenchman. These elections would take place in Europe, and they required a European to head the OSCE team. We went back and forth for a while. I ended the discussion by noting that when President Clinton arrived in the morning, he would take the matter up directly with President Chirac—and he would not yield.

On the morning of December 14, President Clinton and his team arrived in Paris for the signing of the peace agreement. He met in the dining room of the Ambassador's residence with the three Balkan Presidents prior to the formal ceremonies at the Élysée Palace. Two weeks earlier he had made a spectacularly successful trip to both Ireland and Northern Ireland; now he made an eloquent comparison between Bosnia and Ireland. After fifteen months of cease-fire in Ireland, he said, "it is unthinkable for the people to go backward. The whole situation has changed. You need to do the same."

After the meeting, we eased the three Presidents into separate parts of the room, and President Clinton moved among them, spending a few minutes with each. The President told Tudjman that we would send Jacques Klein, a career Foreign Service officer who was also a retired Air Force Reserve general, to eastern Slavonia to oversee the transition of the area to Croatia. With Izetbegovic, the President focused on the dangers posed to the NATO troops by the Iranians and the mujahideen. "If any action is taken against our troops," he said, "it could shatter the whole venture and jeopardize our ability to equip and train your forces. I want to do what I promised, but this could undermine my commitment." Izetbegovic told the President that the bulk of such personnel "had already left," a statement we knew not to be true.

Finally came the President's first discussion with Milosevic. The White House had taken care to ensure that there would be no photographs of the encounter. Still, this was a meeting Milosevic had long wanted; it put him on a plane with other world leaders after years of isolation. "I know this agreement would not have been possible without you," President Clinton said, cool and slightly distant. "You made Dayton possible. Now you must help make it work."

Milosevic said that the key to peace lay in strict implementation of the Dayton agreements. Then he requested full normalization of U.S.-Yugoslav (i.e., Serbian) relations. We swiftly ended the discussion.

Ceremony. Minutes later we were at the Élysée Palace, the home of the President of France, for the formal signing ceremony. First, however, President Chirac wanted to see President Clinton alone. As we waited outside their private meeting room, de Charette approached Warren Christopher and me. "Our President has decided to give you Americans the OSCE election position," he said dryly. "We have our doubts it will work. I hope this is satisfactory to you."

We walked to the ballroom of the Élysée Palace, where we were led to assigned seats facing a long table at which sat the three Balkan Presidents. Behind them stood President Chirac, President Clinton, Chancellor Kohl, Prime Minister Major, and Prime Minister Chernomyrdin, filling in for the ailing Boris Yeltsin. One by one the leaders signed, as either principals or witnesses. The Presidents and Prime Ministers spoke, as did Carl Bildt and, oddly, a man whose actions had contributed so little to the ending of the war, Boutros Boutros-Ghali.

In a strange, almost touching footnote to its sense of injured pride, the French Foreign Ministry called the Dayton Peace Agreement the "Treaty of the Élysée," and asked the speakers to omit any references to Dayton in their remarks. In addition, it seated Tony Lake, Sandy Berger, General Clark, and me near the back of the room, behind many officials and guests who had played no role in the negotiations. This was inconsequential (and Levitte apologized for it later), and if several newspapers had not noted it the next day, it would not be worthy of recording. I did not judge these sad actions by one or two *functionnaires* as representative of the country in which I had lived as a teenager, which had influenced me so much, and for which I had such affection. By wielding the ephemeral power of protocol with such a heavy hand, a few Foreign Office bureaucrats only trivialized their country's important contributions to achieving peace in Bosnia.

After the ceremony, we all moved on to the Quai d'Orsay, where Chirac hosted a large banquet. At the end of the meal, the French president pulled me aside for a moment. "*Mon cher* Holbrooke," he said, in great good humor, "you have won your point on the elections, but you will see that it is inappropriate for any American, even any European, to conduct these elections in such a place as Bosnia." I said I hoped events would prove him wrong. At that moment, Milosevic came up to us and, picking up on the subject, told Chirac that he would make the elections work.

Once again the scene became somewhat surreal. Smoking a cigar, Milosevic sought out President Clinton, with whom he engaged in small talk. Milosevic clearly relished the moment; as Pardew told Bill Perry later, "the Serbian President was last seen in the magnificent hall of the Quai d'Orsay puffing on a cigar half the size of a fence post while making one last—but futile—effort to charm the U.S. President."

We flew home on Air Force One, exhausted but awed by what we had witnessed. Despite the minor irritations, the event had been successful in giving the Dayton Agreement the aura that came with a formal ceremony, witnessed by five of the world's most powerful leaders. It was entirely appropriate that it was formally signed in Europe, the continent on which the war had been fought.

The President was in a good mood as we flew home. He came back to the second cabin to ask Clark, Kerrick, and me how we thought implementation would proceed. "We will have far fewer casualties than the public and the Congress expect," I said. The President seemed skeptical; after all, he had heard ominous scenarios from the Pentagon. Clark and Kerrick pointed out that official estimates had to be cautious. But none of us could have imagined just how low the casualty rate actually would be—*zero* American forces killed or wounded from hostile action in the first three years after Dayton.

There was a more difficult discussion I had to have with the President, and about an hour out of Paris I sat down alone with him in his office near the front of the plane.

"Mr. President, the time has come for me to make a tough decision," I began, somewhat stiffly. "I want to ask your support and understanding for my request to leave the government early next year." Before leaving Germany, I told him, I had promised Kati—and told Christopher and Talbott—that, since she could not move to Washington because of her children, I would return to New York within a limited period of time. This had already been extended because of the negotiations, but the time had come.

The President was gracious and compassionate. "Family is terribly important," he said, and we talked about the strains that public service puts on families. This was one of the most difficult decisions of my life—a choice between a job to which I was fully dedicated and a personal commitment that was precious to me, and I was touched by the President's support. He asked me to stay on as long as possible to get implementation headed in the right direction, and requested that I remain available for special assignments in the future.

For Deploys. On December 16, General Joulwan issued the order to begin moving NATO and other forces to Bosnia. It was the first such troop-deployment order since NATO had been formed in 1949.* Most of the U.N. troops already in Bosnia repainted their vehicles from white to a more military-looking olive green, traded in light weapons for heavier ones, and were reassigned to IFOR, the Implementation Force.

American journalists flooded Bosnia to cover the arrival of U.S. troops, led by two of the three network anchors, Tom Brokaw and Dan Rather. Modern journalism requires that if such stars go out on a story, the story has to be good—that is, dramatic. But the only story was the bad weather, which delayed the crossing of the Sava River for several days. Unable to show any tension or conflict between the arriving American forces and the local population, television exaggerated the dangers facing the troops, and covered the arrival in a sort of retro-Vietnam style that misled the American public as to the dangers the troops faced.

Attention would shift away from Bosnia fairly soon, when it became apparent that IFOR was having an easy, untroubled entry. Of course, *this* was the real story, and it was important; there was to be no repetition of the U.N.'s dreadful experience.

A Slow Start for the Civilians. The same was not true on the civilian side. At first, Carl Bildt, now the High Representative, had so little money and support that he was forced to operate without an office or telephones, and used his personal cellular telephone as his primary means of communication. After appeals to the European Union, he received enough funding to open his offices in Sarajevo, where he presided like an elegant squatter over a building filled with wrecked rooms, broken toilets, shattered windows, and almost no staff.

This lag in civilian implementation troubled us enormously, although we shared in the blame for it. While the military, sixty thousand strong, met every early deadline, the civilian side, functioning out of Carl Bildt's cellular telephone, met almost none, and fell steadily behind schedule. For this Bildt was personally criticized, but the fault was more in the structures we had imposed on him, particularly the failure to give him sufficient funding or stronger backing from IFOR.

Furthermore, with a weak police advisory effort, Bildt had no enforcement capability for his task. Now the full consequences of the absurd position taken

---

* Forces normally assigned to NATO were reassigned for use in the 1991 war against Iraq, but Desert Storm was not a NATO operation.

by NATO—opposing a police force with enforcement capability while itself refusing the task—began to come home to roost.

To say that I was concerned would be an understatement. Having announced my early departure, I agreed to a one-month delay at the request of Christopher to help address the mounting problems. I realized later that I should have stayed longer, but by then we were locked into a firm departure schedule.

The President Visits Bosnia. The President wanted to visit the troops as soon as possible, and scheduled a trip for mid-January. The trip was unusually difficult, posing, as one White House official said publicly, "more logistical, security, and weather variables" than they had ever encountered before. I had hoped that the President would be able to visit Sarajevo, but the risks were deemed too great by those responsible for presidential security, so it was decided that the only stop in Bosnia would be the American military base at Tuzla.

On Friday afternoon, January 12, we flew to the American air base at Aviano, Italy, landing before dawn. As the President spoke to American soldiers and their families, bad weather reports poured in from the Balkans, delaying our departure. After two hours on the ground in Italy, we piled into a C-17, a modern, high-performance military cargo plane, for the flight to Tuzla. Four parallel rows of plastic seats facing each other down the middle of the plane created an unusually egalitarian arrangement: the President, his top advisors, and a bipartisan congressional delegation sat almost at random next to journalists, camera crews, enlisted men and women, and a cargo of food for the troops.

With the weather playing to stereotype, we circled over the landing strip at Tuzla for almost an hour. Finally we landed at the American staging area in Taszar, Hungary, where six thousand American troops had established a forward logistics base for Bosnia. We had planned a brief stop at Taszar later in the day, but we arrived almost seven hours ahead of schedule. Moving fast, the American military took the President to a large tent, where he spoke to American troops while we waited for the weather in Bosnia to clear. I wandered around the base, marveling at how quickly the U.S. military could re-create a special universe and culture almost overnight in any corner of the world. The ankle-deep mud, the wooden pathways, the signs stressing communications security and safety, the individual unit insignias, the small PX, the troops, slightly uncertain of what they were doing in Hungary but ready to carry out their mission—all reminded me vaguely of a war thirty years earlier on the other side of the world. But there were also noticeable differences from Vietnam: most markedly the presence of so many women in uniform, and the cleaner, tighter look of the troops.

Early in the Administration, the President had had well-publicized difficulties dealing with the military because of questions over why he had not served in Vietnam, but by 1996 these were a fading memory. A generation of soldiers who were born after the war in Vietnam ended looked at Bill Clinton as *their* President. They seemed pleased he had come to see them, and he was at ease as he chatted with them. The military's greeting of the President, it seemed to me, was genuinely enthusiastic, and the troops filled the tented area with a war whoop—it sounded like they were grunting "Hoo-aa!"—that shook the ground.

Eventually Hungarian President Arpad Goncz, Prime Minister Gyula Horn, Foreign Minister Lazlo Kovacs, and Ambassador Donald Blinken arrived in two small planes. In the chaos and the excitement of President Clinton's presence, no one met the Hungarian officials, arriving on their own soil, except me and, by chance, Dan Rather, covering the trip for CBS. We squeezed the Hungarians and Ambassador Blinken into some mud-caked military vehicles and sped off to meet President Clinton, driving past a row of broken-down MiG fighter planes, a relic of the Cold War. The presence of six thousand American troops on Hungarian soil only four years after the end of the Cold War—and forty years after the 1956 Soviet invasion—was in itself a remarkable symbol of the transformation of Europe. The Hungarians had one message for President Clinton: that they were ready for NATO membership and that the staging area at Taszar was part of that goal. "Stay as long as you like," they said. "Turn this into a permanent NATO installation—and let us join the West."

The weather at Tuzla was clearing, but by the time we landed, just before 3:00 P.M., daylight was fast disappearing, and the Secret Service put an absolute time limit on our stay. A trip originally scheduled for eight hours was now down to less than three; the schedule collapsed into a makeshift set of quick meetings. The President, dressed in a brown leather bomber jacket and khakis, addressed the troops, who had waited for over two hours outside. Under slate-gray skies, as Apache attack helicopters flew overhead and Secret Service sharpshooters followed his every move, he called the troops "warriors for peace" who had the support and prayers of the American people, and gave promotions to five enlisted men.

After the speech and a meeting with senior military officers, we had originally scheduled three important meetings: first, with President Izetbegovic and members of his government; then, with representatives of the leading nongovernmental organizations in Bosnia; and finally, with civic and religious leaders of Bosnia. The last meeting, planned at my request, was designed to stimulate the leaders of the Muslim, Orthodox, Catholic, and Jewish communities to work for reconciliation. The religious leaders of the region had done great damage since 1991, stirring up ancient but long-submerged desires for revenge among their followers. This meeting appealed to President Clinton's sense of the importance of religious leaders for good and bad, derived from his own Southern Baptist background. But with the schedule in disarray, we had to reduce the meeting with Izetbegovic to ten minutes, and combine the last two sessions, turning the plan into a shambles. The President entered a small, overheated room crowded with a diverse group: Catholic priests (including Vinko Cardinal Puljic), Orthodox prelates (led by the Metropolitan Nikolaj), Muslim mullahs, the Muslim and Serb mayors of Sarajevo, Jewish community leaders, Americans and Europeans representing a dozen humanitarian organizations, journalists, and security personnel—and three widows who had lost their husbands during the war. As everyone else yelled and pushed, the President calmly walked through the room, greeting almost everyone individually. Then, as he spoke movingly about the need for religious reconciliation, Harold Ickes, the White House Deputy Chief of Staff, pulled me aside and said that the Secret Service insisted that we leave within five minutes. As the astonished and disappointed Bosnians watched, I almost yanked the President out of the room. Our ambitious game plan to use the trip to begin a multiethnic dialogue had gone down the drain with the weather.

As we were leaving, an American colonel handed me a small plastic bag with something inside it. "A Bosnian soldier found this near the wreckage on Mount Igman and turned it in to the American Embassy," he said. "It's Nelson Drew's Air Force Academy class ring. Would you deliver it to Mrs. Drew?" Sandy Drew has carried it with her ever since.

Another Shuttle—and Problems. A week later, on January 18, our team was back in Sarajevo. While most people were saying that implementation had just begun, I was acutely conscious of a different equation: the IFOR year was already one twelfth over, and nothing had been accomplished on the political front.

Still, the trip from the airport into Sarajevo was exhilarating. For the first time we drove through Serb-controlled areas of the city, cutting fifteen minutes off the trip and using roads that had been closed for years. The city was showing more signs of recovery; in a particularly bold move, one merchant had opened a store with a large plate-glass window.

Our meeting with Admiral Leighton Smith, on the other hand, did not go well. He had been in charge of the NATO air strikes in August and September, and this gave him enormous credibility, especially with the Bosnian Serbs. Smith was also the beneficiary of a skillful public relations effort that cast him as the savior of Bosnia. In a long profile, *Newsweek* had called him "a complex warrior and civilizer, a latter-day George C. Marshall." This was quite a journalistic stretch, given the fact that Smith considered the civilian aspects of the task beneath him and not his job—quite the opposite of what General Marshall stood for.

After a distinguished thirty-three-year Navy career, including almost three hundred combat missions in Vietnam, Smith was well qualified for his original posts as commander of NATO's southern forces and Commander in Chief of all U.S. naval forces in Europe. But he was the wrong man for his additional assignment as IFOR commander, which was the result of two bureaucratic compromises, one with the French, the other within the American military. General Joulwan rightly wanted the sixty thousand IFOR soldiers to have as their commanding officer an Army general trained in the use of ground forces. But Paris insisted that if Joulwan named a separate Bosnia commander, it would have to be a Frenchman. This was politically impossible for the United States; thus, the French objections left only one way to preserve an American chain of command—to give the job to Admiral Smith, who joked that he was now known as "General" Smith.*

Smith treated us like VIP tourists visiting Sarajevo for the first time, offering us a canned briefing full of military charts and vague "mission statements." Close to thirty of his multinational staff sat behind us, saying nothing. On the military goals of Dayton, he was fine; his plans for separating the forces along the line we had drawn in Dayton and protecting his forces were first-rate. But he was hostile to any suggestion that IFOR help implement any nonmilitary portion of the agreement. This, he said repeatedly, was not his job.

Based on Shalikashvili's statements at White House meetings, Christopher and I had assumed that the IFOR commander would use his *authority* to do substantially more than he was *obligated* to do. The meeting with Smith shattered that hope. Smith and his British deputy, General Michael Walker, made clear that they intended to take a minimalist approach to all aspects of implementation other than force protection. Smith signaled this in his first extensive public statement to the Bosnian people, during a live call-in program on Pale Television—an odd choice for his first local media appearance. During the program, he answered a question in a manner that dangerously narrowed his own authority. He later told *Newsweek* about it with a curious pride:

> One of the questions I was asked was, "Admiral, is it true that IFOR is going to arrest Serbs in the Serb suburbs of Sarajevo?" I said, "Absolutely not, *I don't have the authority to arrest anybody.*" [Emphasis added.]

This was an inaccurate way to describe IFOR's mandate. It was true IFOR was not supposed to make routine arrests of ordinary citizens. But IFOR had

---

* Joulwan finally got the command structure that he wanted—the right one—in 1997, when a four-star Army general took over the Bosnia command.

the authority to arrest indicted war criminals, and could also detain anyone who posed a threat to its forces. Knowing what the question meant, Smith had sent an unfortunate signal of reassurance to Karadzic—over his own network.

An hour after our meeting with Smith, we met Izetbegovic and asked him to urge the Serbs who still lived in Sarajevo to stay after the city was unified under Muslim control on March 19. Izetbegovic said he would make the statement, but stressed that it could apply only to those Serbs who had lived in Sarajevo before the war, and not those who had seized Muslim apartments after April 1992, often with a sniper or soldier as a live-in member of the family. Within two months, this issue—the unification of Sarajevo—would emerge as the first true post-Dayton crisis, and the international community would fail it.*

I returned to Washington to warn Christopher and his colleagues again that the civilian effort was already dangerously behind schedule. Christopher talked to Lake and Perry. But bureaucratic inertia and the resistance of the military prevented any serious effort to change the behavior of IFOR. Lake was especially wary of pressuring IFOR, arguing in public and private against anything that suggested that the military should engage in "nation building," a phrase that had been transformed since the sixties from a noble goal to a phrase meaning "mission creep."

Ron Brown. On January 31, I made a farewell call on Ron Brown, the Secretary of Commerce, who had given me exceptional support in Germany and Washington. In addition to thanking him, I asked him to undertake an important mission to Bosnia. Brown had been exceptionally effective in strengthening American exports and supporting business, and I thought his imagination and drive could give a huge boost to the economic reconstruction effort, one of the key long-term tests of our policy. Brown enthusiastically said he could lead a high-level trade delegation to Bosnia in March or April. He asked only that I get Warren Christopher to support the trip with the White House, which I assured him I would do.

Our friendship, like many in Washington, was political and professional, not personal, but I truly liked Ron Brown. He was then involved in several well-publicized investigations into his personal financial affairs, but of these I knew nothing. What I saw was a superb Cabinet member who had made a significant contribution to the resurgence of the American economy. Now he had agreed to launch an essential part of our Bosnia policy. I thanked him for his willingness to make the trip, added that perhaps I might travel with him as a private citizen, and said farewell. I would never see him again. Nine weeks

* See chapter 20.

later, on April 3, his plane, which also carried several other friends and associates, including Assistant Secretary of Commerce Charles Meissner, crashed into a mountain trying to land at Dubrovnik, on the Croatian coast, in a driving rainstorm. Thirty-five people died.

Jacques Chirac. On February 1, President Chirac visited Washington. The mood was strikingly different from his first trip in June 1995, when his blunt warnings had contributed to the re-evaluation of American policy. Now the agenda could focus on other issues, especially bringing new nations into NATO, the Administration's next big policy move in Europe.

In a moving and thoughtful gesture, Chirac held a ceremony at Blair House on February 1 to present the widows of Bob Frasure, Joe Kruzel, and Nelson Drew with the French Medal of Honor. What moved us most was the openness of Chirac's emotions. Standing next to Katharina Frasure as he gave her Bob's medal, I could see a large tear running down the cheek of the President of France.

The Last—and Longest—Trip. This was Warren Christopher's first trip to the region, and my last as a government official. At first, unlike for previous trips, there was no specific objective—only to say good-bye and bring Christopher and John Kornblum, who had been selected as my successor, up to speed. But by the time it ended, seventeen days later, it had become my longest trip, and it ended with a hastily planned Balkan summit in Rome.

We left Andrews Air Force Base on the Secretary's big jet on the morning of February 2, and met with Tudjman late that night in Zagreb. The next morning, after a briefing by Admiral Smith in Tuzla, we flew to Sarajevo. Christopher and his staff were fascinated to see the city they had read about for three years but never visited. Though rebuilding was under way and most of the barricades and wrecked vehicles had been removed, the sight of so much damage stunned them. To his pleasure, Christopher was greeted with cheers and applause when he ventured on a short walk. The next day, after lunch with Milosevic, Christopher headed toward the Mideast, and I took a commercial flight to Switzerland to attend the annual World Economic Forum meeting in Davos. After this, I hoped to launch our diplomatic initiative on Cyprus, accompanied by our Presidential Special Envoy for Cyprus, Richard Beattie, who would carry on the negotiation.*

The Davos conference was a strange affair. Several thousand people, most of them wealthy businessmen, milled around in groups, attending meetings, setting up meetings, skiing, or socializing. The press was everywhere. So were

---

* Beattie, a senior partner at a New York law firm, was appointed under government regulations that allow private citizens to serve on a part-time basis. In June 1997, he became a senior advisor to Secretary Albright for the reorganization of the State Department, and I became the envoy for Cyprus.

Russians and other leaders from the former Soviet Union, who set up shop in one of the many hotels and filled the lobby with the stench of cigarettes and spilled alcohol. The State Department set up a series of high-level meetings for me with leaders from Europe and Asia.

When I returned to my room there was an urgent message from Tom Donilon, who was in Syria with Christopher. "The Secretary has become increasingly concerned about Bosnia since his trip," Tom began. "He would like to take advantage of your last few days in government to ask you to return to the region, assemble the three Presidents, and hold a short follow-up summit, perhaps in Rome. He will join you."

"While Europe Slept . . ." There was one other event of note at Davos. During a meeting I thought was off the record—but nothing is off the record at Davos—I was asked why it took the Americans to solve "another European problem"—a reference to a recent American diplomatic effort that had averted a small war between Greece and Turkey over Imia/Kardak, a tiny islet off the Turkish coast inhabited only by sheep. My answer was honest but undiplomatic. "While President Clinton and our team were on the phone with Athens and Ankara, the Europeans were literally sleeping through the night," I said. "You have to wonder why Europe does not seem capable of taking decisive action in its own theater."

These remarks were picked up by *The Washington Post*'s chief European correspondent, William Drozdiak, who used them as a metaphor for the confusion and drift that seemed to have settled over the European Union since the end of the Cold War. Although several European commentators had written similar assessments of Europe's political paralysis, Drozdiak's article kicked up an unexpected furor and provoked a surprising number of articles in the European press. Several European officials complained to Tarnoff, Talbott, and Kornblum. It was clear the mini-uproar was really about Dayton, not Imia. The commentary fell into two categories: first, those who said my remarks were right but rude; and second, those who said that they were right and needed to be said. No one took issue with the basic thesis. As Philip Gordon of the International Institute for Strategic Studies wrote in the *International Herald Tribune* on February 17, the comments "hurt so much because Europeans know that such comments are right."

I never expected these remarks would be so widely discussed and remembered. Two years later, people were still asking me about the "While Europe slept thesis."* Of course, my goal had been not to insult the Europeans, but to

---

* British Foreign Secretary Malcolm Rifkind gently objected to the phrase for a personal reason: he told the press later that he had stayed up until 4:00 A.M. working on the same problem. Introducing him at a speech in New York a year later, I offered a customized amendment to the quote: "While Europe, with the exception of Malcolm Rifkind, slept . . ."

encourage them to deal with the unresolved problems of their own history and the convoluted E.U. system. "My comments were not a criticism of any individual nation or any individual," I told Agence France-Presse, "but of an institutional structure which makes it hard for Europe to use its full moral, political, and diplomatic authority in a coherent and consistent way. Every European in Western Europe knows this. It is no secret."

Drama in Sarajevo. We chose Rome for the first post-Dayton summit as a way of emphasizing the importance of Italy. Christopher proceeded with his Middle East diplomacy, and I visited Poland and Hungary before returning to Sarajevo on the morning of February 11 to set up the Rome meeting.

We arrived just in time to be confronted by an unexpected problem: the local police had arrested two senior Bosnian Serb officers, General Djordje Djukic and Colonel Aleksa Krsmanovic, as they entered Sarajevo in a civilian car. The Bosnians claimed the two men were war criminals.

Since the two men had been apprehended in a manner that violated the free-movement provisions of Dayton, we would normally have insisted that the Muslims release them immediately. But Justice Goldstone complicated matters considerably; from the International War Crimes Tribunal in The Hague, he issued a warrant for the two men—even though they had not been indicted. When Shattuck called Goldstone to find out what was going on, he told us he wanted the two men for questioning and possible indictment.

Milosevic, on the other hand, demanded their immediate release. The Bosnian Serbs said they would not cooperate any further with IFOR until they were freed. The Muslims, meanwhile, threatened to try them in a Bosnian court.

In this tense atmosphere, Clark and I met with Admiral Smith on the afternoon of February 11, and asked if he could get the two men out of Sarajevo swiftly and safely. Smith said he could not guarantee that it would be low-risk, but he would develop a plan right away. For once there was no question about IFOR's authority; Smith saw the danger if they remained in the Sarajevo jail.

Our team flew to Belgrade, where Milosevic again demanded the immediate release of the two men, saying that they were simple soldiers. The general, he added, was dying of cancer and needed medication urgently. We told Milosevic that the two men could not be released. As for the health of General Djukic, we would ensure that if he was as sick as Milosevic said, he would get the proper medication. (It turned out that he did indeed have cancer.)

We returned to Sarajevo early the next morning, February 12, tense with concern. Unexpectedly, our visit had turned into a decision-making trip on a risky operation. At 2:00 P.M., I called Goldstone again. He said he had sent the formal request to IFOR two hours earlier for their removal to his jurisdiction. Smith was back in Naples, but he had authorized General Walker to carry out the operation. Walker described the plan: with the prior knowledge of the Bosnian prison authorities, a small group of specially selected French soldiers would move into the jail at night, grab the two prisoners, and move them quickly to American helicopters for transport to The Hague. The greatest danger, in Walker's view, was that the Serbs would get wind of the operation and try to block it on the roads or shoot the helicopter down, but he felt the risks were acceptable provided they moved fast.

We left Sarajevo just before the operation was to begin. Most of the negotiating team went to Zagreb, while I went to Bucharest for a long-planned visit. The operation went smoothly, but an alert television crew filmed the dramatic nighttime transfer at the prison. The two men were safely delivered to The Hague, where they were held for months by Goldstone before the charges against Colonel Krsmanovic were dropped and General Djukic, now close to death from cancer, was released.

Christopher and I were greatly disturbed by this incident. The seizure of the two men, neither of whom was ever indicted, had disrupted the implementation process and set a bad precedent for the future. We determined to try to prevent any repetition of such an incident before it became a pattern.

Anglo–American Ties. The next three days were a continuous whirl—Zagreb again, then Frankfurt, London, and Paris—before the main event in Rome. My farewell calls with Foreign Secretary Rifkind and Defense Minister Michael Portillo were personally warm, but Ambassador Crowe and I had the sense of meeting government officials who, more than a year before the next election, felt they were already lame ducks.* We had worked together under the most difficult circumstances. When I returned to Washington in September 1994, the strains in the Anglo-American alliance had been at a level that was nearly intolerable, and rebuilding the relationship, which I still believed was "special"—a once-standard phrase that had been banned by the Major government—had been a high priority. At a small farewell dinner at Ambassador Crowe's residence, both Foreign Secretary Rifkind and his predecessor, Douglas Hurd, offered their appreciation for the closing of the gap during the last seventeen months. I repeated my mantra: that when the two nations stood side by side, they could change history, but when they split on an important issue the consequences were invariably disastrous.

Rome. After more farewell calls in Paris, we flew to Rome on February 16 for the first meeting of the three Balkan Presidents since the signing ceremony

---

* Although neither man could have imagined that he would lose his own House of Commons seat in the landslide victory of Tony Blair and the Labor Party in May 1997.

in December. Admiral Smith, who came to Rome for a few hours, took a dramatic step on the eve of the conference to show that he intended to enforce the military provisions of Dayton. Sending a commando team deep into a mountain area of the Federation on February 17, IFOR raided a "terrorist training camp" and captured eleven "freedom fighters" whom they identified as Iranians, as well as sixty heavy weapons, booby-trapped plastic toys, and a model of an American military headquarters building. Stunned, Izetbegovic claimed that he was unaware of the presence of this group until the raid. Joulwan and I told him that it was immaterial whether or not he knew; the presence of such people on Bosnian soil violated Dayton and constituted a threat to the IFOR troops.

With this dramatic event as background, the first Compliance Summit began on the afternoon of Saturday, February 17, with a welcoming speech by Foreign Minister Susanna Agnelli. Christopher and General Joulwan, as well as our team and the Contact Group, sat around a large conference table for the opening session; then we broke down into smaller groups, placing each delegation in separate rooms. For the next two days the corridors of the normally sedate Italian Foreign Ministry reverberated with the arguments of the Balkans—a veritable mini-Dayton. Specific agreements were reached that were designed to get the implementation process back on track: an agreement on what Christopher called the "rules of the road" so that we would never again have to struggle with the consequences of a surprise arrest; a compromise on Mostar that pulled that city, the most explosive in Bosnia, back from the brink of renewed fighting between the Croats and the Muslims; an understanding on improving the performance of the International Police Task Force; and an agreement to hold similar summits regularly.

We returned to Washington on February 19. Two days later, after some more farewell calls and a generous ceremony on the eighth floor of the State Department for the entire negotiating team attended by Secretaries Christopher and Perry, I resigned as Assistant Secretary of State, and immediately signed papers as an unpaid advisor to the Secretary of State. This meant little, except that I would retain my security clearances and be available on short notice to the Administration. That evening, February 21, I left Washington for a new life in New York.

CHAPTER 20

Disasters and Progress

(February 1996–April 1998)

This even-handed justice
Commends the ingredients of our poison'd chalice
To our own lips.

— SHAKESPEARE, *Macbeth*

ON PAPER, DAYTON WAS A GOOD AGREEMENT; it ended the war and established a single, multiethnic country. But countless peace agreements have survived only in history books as case studies in failed expectations. The results of the international effort to implement Dayton would determine its true place in history. And the start was rocky.

The First Setback. The unification of Sarajevo under Federation control ninety days after the establishment of IFOR was the first major political deadline of the Dayton agreement, and in many ways the most important. Before Dayton, no outside observer had thought it could happen, and many still doubted that it would. It was, without question, the first key civilian test of Dayton.

Sarajevo was unified precisely on schedule. On March 18, 1996, a group of ragged Bosnian Serb policemen, their voices barely audible over a scratchy recording of the anthem of precommunist Yugoslavia, lowered their flag from the police station in Grbavica and left for Pale. "We saved this area militarily," said Milenko Karisik, a Bosnian Serb Deputy Interior Minister, "but we lost it at Dayton." The next day, the Bosnian Serbs handed over to the Federation the Serb-controlled portions of Sarajevo. There was no fighting, no attempt to prevent the event.

But at the moment that was one of Dayton's greatest achievements, the Bosnian Serbs exploited the passivity of IFOR and the weakness of the enforcing powers to salvage something for their separatist cause. In the two weeks before Sarajevo's unification, Pale ordered all Serbs in Sarajevo to burn down their own apartments and leave the city. They even broadcast detailed instructions on how to set the fires. (Pile all the furniture in the middle of the room, douse it with kerosene, turn the gas on, and throw a match into the room as you leave.) Young arsonists, mostly thugs from Pale, roamed the streets warning Sarajevo Serbs that if they did not destroy their homes and leave, they would be punished severely, perhaps even killed.

For those Bosnian Serbs who had moved into Sarajevo from the country-side during the war, destroying apartments they would have to leave anyway was easy. But tens of thousands of Sarajevo Serb families had lived in peace for generations in the once-cosmopolitan city. Most were ready to stay had they not been forced to leave. Kris Janowski, the spokesman for the United Nations High Commissioner for Refugees, estimated that before the exodus there were seventy thousand Serbs in Sarajevo, of whom at least thirty thousand wanted to stay. After the intimidation tactics of Pale, fewer than ten thousand remained, many of whom would leave soon thereafter. In the week before March 19, a steady stream of Serbs clogged the roads out of Sarajevo, most carrying furniture, plumbing fixtures, and even doors. Behind them rose the smoking remains of Grbavica and Ilidza. "We must not allow a single Serb to remain in the territories which fall under Muslim-Croat control," said Gojko Klickovic, head of the Bosnian Serb Resettlement Office (and later Prime Minister of Republika Srpska).

Journalists reported nearly incomprehensible scenes: a Serb woman beaten and raped by a young Serb thug before he set fire to her apartment; an elderly Serb couple who survived the entire war in Sarajevo appealing futilely to Italian troops as a Serb thug blew up their apartment. Robert Gelbard, Assistant Secretary of State for International Narcotics and Law Enforcement, was visiting Sarajevo at the time at my suggestion; he watched in disgust as IFOR and the International Police Task Force refused to apprehend the marauding arsonists and IFOR kept its own fire-fighting equipment inside the IFOR compound. Desperate, the Muslims sent their antiquated fire-fighting equipment into the Serb portion of the city, where they were attacked by rock-throwing Serb arsonists. But their requests for IFOR protection were refused. Gelbard watched buildings burn as IFOR troops stood by less than 150 meters away, and observed British General Michael Walker, IFOR's second-ranking officer, coolly reject the pleas of the Deputy High Representative, Michael Steiner, for IFOR intervention. "I was ashamed to be associated with it," Gelbard told me later, "to be unable to get IFOR to do anything." A year later, appointed by President Clinton and Secretary Albright to coordinate the faltering implementation effort, Gelbard would make a difference.

This tragedy could have been easily prevented if IFOR had taken action. But although unchallenged and feared, NATO/IFOR did almost nothing. An IFOR spokesman said that while the burnings were "unfortunate," the Serbs "have the right to burn their own houses." IFOR, said another spokesman, "is not a police force and will not undertake police duties." Shocked by IFOR's sudden passivity, U.N. officials, in an ironic role reversal, now criticized NATO for *its* inactivity. "If [NATO] had been tougher, things would be different," said Kris Janowski. "We're seeing a multiethnic Bosnia being flushed down the toilet."

It was my first month as a private citizen; I realized too late that I had left too early. Watching with growing anxiety from New York, I called Washington frequently, pleading for action, pointing out that Dayton's "silver bullet" clause gave IFOR full authority in such a situation. But Admiral Smith refused to act, repeating his mantra that IFOR was not a police force, that putting out the fires or arresting the arsonists would be mission creep. That IFOR's passivity was endangering fundamental policy goals of the United States and NATO seemed unimportant to him.

Warren Christopher and Bill Perry finally stepped in and insisted that NATO take action. Reluctantly, Smith and Walker ordered their troops to detain a few of the young arsonists and turn them over to the local authorities, while IFOR put out some of the fires. It was too little, too late. "If anyone thinks this is a success," said U.N. spokesman Janowski, "that would be rather silly. There has been millions of dollars' worth of property damaged in looting and fires, and an exodus when we were supposed to see people returning to their homes."

This was the worst moment of the first two years after Dayton. Not only was it a disaster on its own terms, but it ended the sense of hope and momentum that had begun in late November. Pale used the very exodus it had created as an excuse to prevent Muslims from returning to their homes in the Serb portion of Bosnia. Muslims and Croats read the events as evidence that multiethnic cooperation would not be encouraged by NATO. The message seemed clear: leaders and thugs who preached ethnic division would not be punished or constrained.

Stung by international criticism, the military struck back, publicly blaming the international civilian agencies, particularly Carl Bildt, for the "slippage" in implementing Dayton. But assigning blame was pointless. The events of mid-March provided an object lesson in the tenacity and ruthlessness of the Serbs—and the confusion of the implementing organizations in Bosnia. They also illustrated one of Washington's most important but least understood maxims: *good policy badly executed becomes bad policy.*

The Toughest Issue. Until the March disaster, all three ethnic groups in Bosnia, awed by the sight of sixty thousand heavily armed IFOR soldiers, were prepared to do almost anything that IFOR asked. The Bosnian Serbs, in particular, had been so badly battered, both militarily and politically, that they would have offered little resistance had IFOR enforced tough guidelines. Even Milosevic had encouraged IFOR at first to take a firm line, although he would soon cease to do so. Rallying from the despair they had felt since November, the Bosnian Serbs began to resist on almost every nonmilitary issue, while remaining careful to avoid provoking IFOR. It was almost as if they had an implicit understanding with the IFOR command: we will not attack your forces if you leave us alone to pursue an ethnically divided country.

Of all the things necessary to achieve our goals in Bosnia, the most important was still the arrest of Radovan Karadzic. But Karadzic surfaced after a few months of near seclusion and began issuing orders and giving interviews, signaling his followers that they could still safely pursue their separatist goals. With his military forces neutralized, Karadzic used the "special police," a vestige of the communist police state, to threaten any Bosnian Serb who showed support for Dayton. Even though these units were also covered in the Dayton agreement, IFOR pointedly ignored these "police" as they crossed the Serb portion of Bosnia intimidating anyone who cooperated with Muslims or spoke favorably of Dayton. Karadzic's first major target was the first politician to support Dayton publicly, the mayor of Banja Luka, Predrag Radic, whom he prevented from attending the meeting with President Clinton at Tuzla in January.

While the arrest of Karadzic would not have solved all the problems the international community faced in Bosnia, his removal from power was a necessary, although not sufficient, condition for success. As we had told the President and his senior advisors before Dayton, Karadzic at large was certain to mean Dayton deferred or defeated. Nothing had changed six months later, except that Karadzic was rebuilding his position. While the human-rights community and some members of the State Department, especially John Shattuck and Madeleine Albright, called for action, the military warned of casualties and Serb retaliation if an operation to arrest him took place. They said they would carry it out only if ordered to do so directly by the President; thus if anything went wrong the blame would fall on the civilians who had insisted on the operation, especially on the President himself. This was a heavy burden to lay on any president, particularly during an election year, and it was hardly surprising that no action was taken to mount, or even plan, an operation against Karadzic in 1996 or 1997.

Paradoxically, the same officials who opposed capturing Karadzic supported a tight deadline for American troop withdrawal. The two goals were obviously incompatible; if you wanted to reduce troop levels, capturing Karadzic was essential. Yet still NATO refused to consider arresting Karadzic, arguing that it was too risky and not an IFOR mission.

. . .

I raised the issue with Admiral Smith on my "farewell" trip to Sarajevo on February 11, during the same meeting in which we discussed the detention of the two Bosnian Serb officers by the Muslims. The previous day, *The Washington Post* had published John Pomfret's dramatic description of Karadzic driving unchallenged through four NATO checkpoints—two of them manned by Americans—on a trip from Pale to Banja Luka. When I showed Admiral Smith the article, he tossed it contemptuously to an aide while offering a few pithy comments about interfering, know-nothing journalists. He did not deny the story, however. He remained adamant: his forces would not go after indicted war criminals.

A Letter to the President. When I left the government, President Clinton had invited me to send him my views from time to time. By early June of 1996, I felt that the situation had reached a point where such a message was justified. I sent copies to Christopher, Lake, and Talbott.

Dear Mr. President:

We are at a decisive moment in the Bosnia peace process. I would like, therefore, to take up your request to send you my views:

The success of IFOR so far is now threatened by Karadzic's success in defying the political portions of Dayton. If he continues to thwart the Dayton powers, the peace process will fail.

This would result, at a minimum, in Bosnia's partition, with the real possibility of further division into three parts within a few years—all of which we have said we oppose. While our national interests are not directly affected by whether Bosnia is one country or two or even three, the outcome in Bosnia will profoundly affect our overall role in the emerging *post*–post–Cold War world. . . .

Of the many organizations in the former Yugoslavia in the last five years, only NATO—that is, the United States—has been respected. What NATO/IFOR demands, happens.

But the reluctance of NATO to go beyond a relatively narrow interpretation of its mission has left a gaping hole in the Bosnia food chain. Recognizing this, the Bosnian Serbs have increasingly defied the Dayton powers. In response, the Bosnian Muslims have moved further from a multiethnic state, as Izetbegovic starts building an undemocratic and fundamentally (although not fundamentalist) Muslim state in his half of the country. . . .

The implications of Karadzic's defiance go far beyond Bosnia itself. If he succeeds, basic issues of American leadership that seemed settled in the public's eye after Dayton will re-emerge. Having reasserted American leadership in Europe, it would be a tragedy if we let it slip away again. . . .

It may seem odd that so much can hang on such a matter as the fate of two odious war criminals. But history is replete with examples of small issues leading to the unraveling of larger ones. The question of Radovan Karadzic is such an issue. . . . Our goal should be Karadzic's removal not only from his presidential post, but from power. . . .

There are other things that should have been done earlier—but which, if done now, will still make a difference. Several examples:

—Every day Karadzic uses television and the controlled media to prevent local reconciliation efforts. IFOR has the ability and authority to cut these lines, but has refused to do so. These communication lines should be cut—now. This would be a devastating blow to Karadzic, and popular in the United States. . . .

—Sanctions reimposition. We wrote into Dayton the ability to reimpose sanctions if necessary. This is our strongest remaining leverage. . . . I would suggest Milosevic be given a clear message. . . .

Return to Bosnia. Calls to capture Karadzic and Mladic were mounting. They came from newspapers around the world, and from Carl Bildt and Senator Dole; from Mort Abramowitz, the respected president of the Carnegie Endowment for International Peace; and from the American philanthropist and financier George Soros—who, astonishingly, had spent more of his own money on aid projects in Bosnia than had the United States government.

On the evening of Friday, July 12, the Administration, facing growing international criticism, asked if I would return to the region immediately on a special mission. With the understanding and support of my new colleagues at Crédit Suisse First Boston, I left three days later, after a day in Washington.

The Administration's goal was to remove Karadzic from power or significantly weaken him through diplomatic pressure, thus defusing the pressure for a military operation. As I had written a few weeks earlier to the President, our most potent nonmilitary weapon was the reimposition of economic sanctions against Serbia and the Bosnian Serbs—a right we had carefully retained for ourselves in the Dayton agreement, but only until ten days after the national elections scheduled for September 14.

When I saw Christopher, Talbott, Tarnoff, and Berger separately on Monday, July 15, it was clear that Washington was uneasy about using sanctions. With only hours left before departure for Bosnia, I argued that the threat of sanctions was important if our team was to have a chance of success. When several officials expressed concern that reimposition would upset the Europeans, I reminded them that we would lose the power to reimpose sanctions in only seventy days. "Use it before we lose it," was my slogan for the day.

The key meeting took place with Sandy Berger in the late afternoon. Lake was away; we met in his empty office. He said no consensus could be forged in time for our trip. After close to an hour of intense discussion, Sandy said, "Look, you and I have been friends for twenty years. Don't ask for something we can't give you. Just go out there and do what you can. We know you will make it sound better than it is." He laughed, and clapped me on the shoulder. "That's why we asked you back," he said. On the way to the airport I called Strobe to describe the meeting. He confirmed my impression. "Just use that old creative ambiguity," he said.

"We are here," I told the press when we landed at the Sarajevo airport on Tuesday, July 16, "because we are not satisfied with the degree of compliance we are seeing, particularly on the part of the Bosnian Serbs." Our first meeting was with Robert Frowick, the urbane American diplomat whom we had chosen to head up the OSCE mission in Bosnia and run the elections. He was at a crossroads. So far he had allowed Karadzic's party, the SDS, to take a major role in the election preparations, but he was increasingly troubled by their behavior, which included stuffing the registration rolls and intimidating potential voters. Frowick had the authority to declare any party or individual ineligible. The deadline for a final decision was almost upon him—within three days he had to decide whether or not to allow Karadzic's party to participate in the elections, scheduled for September 14.

Disenfranchising the SDS was tempting but risky. It might provoke a boycott of the elections, but it would remove from the electoral process the party that was, more than any other force in Bosnia, trying to prevent Dayton from succeeding. But before we came to any conclusions, it was essential to find out what Izetbegovic wanted to do; his views would be critical.

Izetbegovic, whom I had not seen in five months, seemed a changed man, cracking small jokes and smiling. He thanked me profusely for what I "had done for Bosnia," and noted that we had kept our promises to his government. When we were alone I outlined the core issue. "Mr. President," I said, "we can disqualify the SDS from the election process if we wish, by declaring that the entire party is in violation of the Dayton agreement. On the other hand, if Milosevic helps us remove Karadzic from power, we can allow the SDS to participate in the elections. What we do next with the SDS is essentially in our hands, and we need to know your views."

This was a huge decision for Izetbegovic, and he said he would have an answer for us when we returned from Belgrade and Zagreb in somewhat more than twenty-four hours.

The next day, July 17, our team met with Milosevic over a long lunch in Belgrade. We were blunt: if we were unable to get a satisfactory agreement, we would "recommend" that sanctions be reimposed and that Frowick disqualify the SDS from the elections. Incredulous, Milosevic was asked to see me alone. Members of our team, including Goldberg and Owen, could hear his voice through the doors between the two rooms, as he angrily charged that we were wrecking the Dayton agreement. I replied that it was Karadzic who was trying to destroy Dayton. Our goal was to get him "out of power and out of country." After a prolonged argument, we agreed to meet again the next day.

We returned to Sarajevo on the morning of July 18. It was another of those meetings whose consequences would be felt for a long time.

"The SDS is the Nazi Party of our country," Izetbegovic began. "But if we throw them out of the elections, they could organize a boycott, like they did the last time. If you can get Karadzic out of power, I think it is much better to let them run. I can work with Krajisnik. I know how to deal with him."

Izetbegovic could work with Krajisnik? The comment was surprising. The speaker of the Pale assembly, the man who at Dayton had slammed his fist into the map of Sarajevo, widely known as "Mr. No," was as much of a rejectionist as Karadzic. But Izetbegovic was worried about the effect of an SDS boycott. While the decision remained ours, Izetbegovic's desire not to throw the SDS out of the elections, his fear that they could wreck the elections, was a powerful message that the international community could not ignore.

Milosevic moved our July 18 meeting to a new venue, a government villa in the residential section of Belgrade. At 4:00 P.M., seated in the garden of the villa, we began a ten-hour negotiating session that mirrored some of the early shuttle drama and produced an agreement that defused the crisis—but at a price.

Milosevic came to the point quickly. "Krajisnik and Buha are upstairs," he said, pointing to windows on the second-floor of the villa. "They are ready to negotiate right now over the future of Karadzic." This tactic, so stunning eleven months earlier when Milosevic had produced Karadzic and Mladic, was no longer shocking. Asking to meet first without the two Bosnian Serbs, we presented Milosevic with a tough document, announcing the resignation of Karadzic from the presidencies of both Republika Srpska and the SDS, effective the next day. Our draft also announced that Karadzic would leave Bosnia and comply with the International War Crimes Tribunal.

Milosevic objected strongly to almost every detail of our draft. Finally, we agreed to bring the two Bosnian Serbs into the discussion. They were in a sullen mood. Krajisnik made not the slightest attempt to be civil; Buha simply sat in silence. But as Krajisnik realized that the removal of his friend and mentor Karadzic would directly benefit him, he became increasingly interested in our proposals. Still, Krajisnik was immovable on the possibility that Karadzic leave Bosnia. "Maybe later, but never tonight, with the world watching," Krajisnik said emotionally as Buha, thin-faced and gaunt, glared at us. "And there is nothing we can do to force him."

"Why don't you send him to stay with his mother and his smuggler brother in his native village in Montenegro?" I asked, half-seriously, half-facetiously. Krajisnik seemed stunned at this reference to the private activities of Karadzic's brother; we believed that Krajisnik was part of the same smuggling operations. I thought of an earlier conversation with a senior Serb official who had told us that Karadzic and Krajisnik had become friends when they were both jailed, one for passing bad checks, the other for stealing cement from public projects. We did not know if this story was true, but, as Phil Goldberg said, "it felt right."

Shortly after ten in the evening, after a great deal of argument, the Bosnian Serbs signed an agreement that removed Radovan Karadzic "immediately and permanently [from] all public and private activities," including his two official positions—President of Republika Srpska and president of the SDS. Mrs. Biljana Plavsic, one of the Vice Presidents of the Bosnian Serbs, would be named President the next day, and Buha would become the acting head of the SDS. Stressing the importance of the pledge that Karadzic also cease "public activities," I cited a number of examples, especially his appearances on television and the use of posters bearing his likeness, that would constitute violations. Although clearly unhappy, Krajisnik and Buha agreed; Karadzic would not appear on television, and his image would not be displayed.

We were still lacking the most important signature, that of Karadzic himself. Milosevic proposed that we obtain it by fax. I rejected this; we did not want Karadzic to claim later that his signature was a faxed forgery. So at our insistence, Milosevic sent his intelligence chief, Jovica Stanisic, to Pale by helicopter to obtain Karadzic's signature personally. After dinner—the best he had ever offered us, lamb, yogurt, and spinach—we left to call Washington. I read the draft statement to Tarnoff, who walked it through "the system" with impressive speed, obtaining Washington's support in less than ninety minutes. We returned to Milosevic's villa at about 2:00 A.M. to meet Stanisic, who presented us with the original document, now signed by Karadzic. Stanisic told us Karadzic seemed "resigned to the end of his political career." But he was not ready to leave Pale, Stanisic said. I wondered aloud if Karadzic's political career had *really* reached the end of the road.

Karadzic stepped down from both posts the next day, and faded out of public sight—even television—for the rest of the year. The world's press hailed the agreement and praised our efforts; in the words of the *Financial Times,* it was "another success."

Our team, drained by two almost sleepless nights and the long flight back from Belgrade, the last hour of it bouncing through violent thunderstorms, drove directly to the White House to join a Principals' Committee meeting already in progress, where we were greeted with a standing ovation that left us moved but a bit stunned. Our colleagues were more impressed with the July 18 agreement than we were. We were ambivalent about what we had done. We had achieved *just enough* to allow elections with SDS participation, and *just enough* to relieve the pressure for the rest of the year for a military operation against Karadzic—an operation I still favored. We might be "whistling past the graveyard," as Strobe put it, but it was just what Washington wanted.

I repeated my earlier recommendation that we close down the SDS television network, but this was again rejected on the grounds that it was either too provocative or impossible to carry out.* I also told the Principals' Committee that we had to move immediately against Pale if there were the slightest violation of the July 18 agreement. But by the beginning of 1997, these admonitions and proposals would be forgotten or ignored, and Karadzic, sensing another opportunity, would emerge once more.

The September 14 Elections. Two months later, I was back in Bosnia, this time as the head of the Presidential Observer Mission to the elections. The team, which had been assembled by the White House, consisted of a group of private citizens and several Congressmen, including two powerful Democrats, John Murtha of Pennsylvania and Steny Hoyer of Maryland, and Peter King, a Republican from New York. Thousands of other international supervisors, observers, monitors, and journalists were crawling all over the country.

The elections chose the three-person presidency and the national assembly established by the Dayton agreement. They were relatively trouble-free, and unquestionably constituted progress—Warren Christopher called them a remarkable success. But none of the winners was in favor of a truly multiethnic government. The election strengthened the very separatists who had started the war.

Many observers later cited this as proof that the people of Bosnia wanted to separate along ethnic lines. I did not share this assessment; the elections took place in an atmosphere poisoned by a media controlled by the same people who had started the war. Advocates of reconciliation in all three communities were intimidated by thugs and overwhelmed by media that carried nothing but racist propaganda. The full costs of failing to close down the SDS television stations now came home. And on the Muslim side, all was not well either; in one particularly ominous incident, zealots from Izetbegovic's party beat up Haris Silajdzic, almost killing him, as he spoke in favor of a multiethnic

---

* Neither argument against action had merit. Fourteen months later, on October 1, 1997, the NATO forces finally closed down the Pale television transmitters, depriving Karadzic and his party of one of their most powerful instruments of power. Although controversial to the last moment, when it took place the action was accomplished without incident or injury—and had the desired effect.

Bosnia during an election rally. On the Serb side, Milosevic ran a handpicked candidate, but the victory that he had long promised never materialized; Krajisnik won the Serb seat in the three-person co-presidency of Bosnia by a vote of 508,026 to 240,000. Biljana Plavsic won the presidency of Republika Srpska with ease. She was, at the time, the most popular Bosnian Serb. Nothing could have prepared us for the open confrontation she would have with her Pale mentors in less than eight months.

Clinton II and the Together Movement. Bosnia faded as an issue in the 1996 presidential campaign. In addition to the relative success of the effort, Senator Dole also deserved credit as well; he ignored every opportunity to exploit the issue because, as he told me later, he did not want to hurt a policy he now "basically agreed with." Dole even said publicly that he would favor extending IFOR beyond its one-year limit, but the Administration failed to seize this generous opening to get out from under the twelve-month deadline, and, with Dole's defeat in November, it was gone.

Even a re-elected president goes through a transition period, although it is almost invisible to the public eye. Outgoing officials tend to lose interest in the details of policy, as they prepare to return to the private sector. The Clinton Administration effected a smooth transition in most areas, especially at State, where the new Secretary, Madeleine Albright, was familiar with most of the major issues from her U.N. tour, and at the NSC, where Sandy Berger simply moved up (without the need for Senate confirmation) to replace Tony Lake.

Still, the new team—much of it far below the Cabinet level—had to await Senate confirmation. Even the smoothest shifts take time, and in the Balkans events did not pause for our transition. A remarkable challenge to Milosevic unfolded in the streets of Belgrade in December, led by three politicians who banded together into a movement they called Zajedno, or the Together Movement. For weeks, hundreds of thousands of Belgrade citizens braved subfreezing weather to call for democracy. But Washington missed a chance to affect events; except for one ineffectual trip to Washington, Zajedno had no contact with senior American government officials, and the Administration sent no senior officials to Belgrade for fear that their visits would be used by Milosevic to show support. For the first time in eighteen months, Milosevic felt no significant American pressure, and turned back toward the extreme nationalists, including Karadzic, for support. His tactical skills saved him again, and within weeks, the Together Movement was together no more, as its leaders split among themselves.

On Sunday, December 8, three days after Madeleine Albright was named Secretary of State, we met at her house in Georgetown. I offered her my full support, and noted that her well-known tough line on Bosnia made her the ideal person to reinvigorate the policy. She said this was her firm intention. Nonetheless, by April there was a general impression that "Clinton II" was downgrading Bosnia. In Europe, the emphasis was almost entirely on a critical summit meeting with Boris Yeltsin, planned for Helsinki, that would determine the fate of the Administration's plan to enlarge NATO. China also took center stage in internal policy discussions. The comparative silence on Bosnia during the early months of 1997 was broken primarily by the incoming Secretary of Defense, Senator William Cohen, who made a series of statements that the United States would end its troop presence in Bosnia in eighteen months—that is, June 1998.

Sensing that high-level American interest had declined, Karadzic ventured once more into public view, testing how flagrantly he could violate the agreement I had negotiated the previous July without provoking a NATO response. Finding nothing in his way, he even gave on-the-record interviews to European journalists. His re-emergence went unchallenged by the military, and suggested, as many journalists reported, that personnel in IFOR—now renamed SFOR, or Stabilization Force—were simply counting the days until their departure.

Finally, in April, after a highly successful Clinton-Yeltsin summit in Helsinki—in which President Clinton obtained Yeltsin's acceptance of NATO enlargement—the Administration, led by Madeleine Albright and Sandy Berger, began to focus again on Bosnia. As part of this process, Robert Gelbard was appointed to coordinate all U.S. government efforts to implement Dayton. This made sense; Washington needed a tough, full-time "czar" and Gelbard, who had been working on Bosnia sporadically since I had asked him to strengthen the International Police Task Force in December 1995, was an excellent choice. Gelbard's background was unusually varied for a Foreign Service officer; in addition to both economic and political experience, he had extensive firsthand knowledge of law enforcement and counterterrorism, and was a skilled bureaucratic infighter.

An Unusual Birthday Party. Washington is well known as a city where social events can have policy consequences. Such was the case with a memorable party given by Liz Stevens on Friday, April 4, in honor of her husband, the gifted filmmaker George Stevens, and Kati, who shared the same birthday. Without telling us or most of the other guests, Liz had invited the Clintons. We arrived early to find Secret Service agents all over the house. A few minutes later, ahead of other guests, the Clintons walked in.

To be precise, Hillary walked; the President limped in on crutches. Only a month earlier he had famously, and seriously, injured himself in a fall outside the home of the golfer Greg Norman. Less famously, I had injured myself at about the same time, tearing ligaments in my ankle. When we met, I was also on crutches, to the President's amusement, and we spent a few minutes comparing our rehabilitation programs. As he left, the President pulled me aside for a moment and said, "Come by tomorrow and we can do some therapy and talk."

The next day, Saturday, April 5, I presented myself at the White House and was ushered upstairs to the family quarters, where the President was already working out on a bicycle machine. Gesturing me into an adjoining room, he asked his therapist, a Navy commander, to look at my injury. We worked out in silence for a while as if it were the most natural thing in the world, and then adjourned to another room to cool down.

Members of his family, including Hillary and her mother, Dorothy Rodham, stopped by to chat. It seemed simultaneously completely ordinary and completely extraordinary, casual conversation with this nice, average American family—except that one of them happened to be the President. As I was beginning to wonder if we would ever discuss Bosnia, he said, "Let's go downstairs." With that we hobbled down to his office in the family quarters.

It is in the nature of the hierarchical relationship of the Executive Branch that such a meeting would have been almost impossible while I was still in the government. There are simply too many layers between an Assistant Secretary and the Chief Executive, and everyone in the chain of command would have insisted on either being there, changing the nature of the meeting, or preventing such a discussion from even occurring.

"What's going on out there?" the President began. Before the meeting, I had decided, with Strobe's enthusiastic urging, to be completely candid if the opportunity arose. I listed the series of reverses and lost opportunities since December: the collapse of the Together Movement; increasingly public activity by Karadzic; brutal behavior by Tudjman toward the remaining Serbs in Croatia; heightened tensions between the Croats and the Muslims within the Federation, especially at Mostar; and American passivity or worse.

"While NATO policy and your achievement with Yeltsin have been historic," I said, "Bosnia has gone nowhere since Dayton. These issues are interrelated. We said that we'll leave Bosnia in June 1998, which is not possible. People out there are not even sure we still support Dayton, or if we still care what happens in Bosnia. And we are losing irretrievable time."

I urged him to give Albright and Gelbard his full backing. Sensing that he was receptive, I spoke even more bluntly than I had planned, urging him to speak out forcefully on the issue. Finally, the President walked me to the elevator, and then, crutches and all, accompanied me all the way to my car, which was waiting at the South Portico of the White House.

The "therapy session," as Strobe called it, was timely. Both Berger and Albright said later that it was important in getting policy focused and revitalized at a critical moment. Meanwhile, Berger's formal policy review proceeded, and Gelbard "went operational."

The Policy Toughens. With the press filled with stories about Albright-Cohen and State-Pentagon conflicts over Bosnia, the President flew to Europe twice: first, to sign the NATO-Russia Founding Act on May 27 in Paris, which formalized Russia's role in the security architecture of post–Cold War Europe; and second, to attend a historic NATO summit on July 9 in Madrid that invited Hungary, Poland, and the Czech Republic to join NATO. It was a remarkable achievement, defying the predictions of many critics who said that NATO enlargement would do irreparable damage to relations between Russia and the United States.

In May, Berger overrode the doubts of some Pentagon officials; his study reaffirmed a solidly pro-Dayton policy. At the suggestion of several Administration officials, I spoke to the President again on Sunday, May 24, three days before his meetings with Yeltsin in Paris, to argue that if we did not revitalize Bosnia policy immediately it might be too late to salvage Dayton.

Meanwhile, the new British Prime Minister, Tony Blair, and his Foreign Secretary, Robin Cook, made clear that they would follow a more aggressive policy, and urged the same from the United States. When the President, during a joint press conference with Blair in the garden at 10 Downing Street on May 29, was asked about reports of a conflict between Albright and Cohen over Bosnia, he sidestepped the controversy but made it clear that he wanted Dayton to succeed.

As the President returned to Washington, Albright and Gelbard went to Sintra, Portugal, for a meeting of the NATO Foreign Ministers. The NATO countries invited the leaders of Bosnia to Sintra, and, after intense meetings, issued a statement that recommitted them to Dayton. From Sintra, Albright made her first trip to the region as Secretary of State, traveling to Zagreb, Banja Luka, Sarajevo, and Belgrade on May 31. Given her high profile—"the most popular political figure in America," in the words of Joe Klein—her trip brought attention back to American policy in Bosnia. We talked several times before and during the trip, and she called one last time around midnight, from Zagreb, the evening before she went to Belgrade for her first meeting with Milosevic. She was the first Secretary of State to visit Belgrade since James Baker's unfortunate trip in June 1991.

Throughout her visit, Albright showed a deft sense of how to communicate with the people of the region. Perhaps this was a function of her background; after all, she had not only been born in Czechoslovakia but spent part of her childhood in Belgrade. This special understanding was most in evidence when she met Biljana Plavsic in Banja Luka. Albright had added the stop almost as an afterthought on the advice of her closest aide, Assistant Secretary for Public Affairs Jamie Rubin, but the brief visit would have important consequences, emboldening President Plavsic to break publicly with her former mentors in Pale.

Ever since Dayton we had anticipated, even hoped for, a split between Pale and Banja Luka. (It will be recalled that at Dayton we had considered designating Banja Luka as the capital of Srpska, but held back because Izetbegovic objected.) Now it arrived in a most unexpected form. Plavsic publicly attacked her closest colleagues where they were most vulnerable: corruption. Presenting herself as a still-patriotic Serb nationalist, she lashed out publicly at Karadzic and Krajisnik, calling them "criminals" who were living well while stealing from their own people. To almost everyone's surprise, she struck a responsive chord among many Serbs in western Bosnia, and weakened Pale.

The Team Changes. Major personnel changes were under way within the international effort. Carl Bildt stepped down as High Representative to return to political life in Sweden, replaced by Carlos Westendorp of Spain. I urged Albright and Gelbard to send Jacques Klein to Sarajevo as Westendorp's deputy. In his tour overseeing the transition of eastern Slavonia to Croatian control, Klein had shown a flair for the sort of forceful, even melodramatic performance that impressed the people of the region.

Another appointment changed the equation significantly: President Clinton and Secretary Cohen chose as NATO's new Supreme Commander none other than Wes Clark. In naming Clark, they had, in effect, sent Dayton to NATO— an important signal of determination. At the same time a new SFOR commander, General Eric Shinseki, and a new Ambassador, Richard Kauzlarich, took over in Sarajevo.

Bosnia Once More. On July 18, Bob Gelbard, relatively new in his job as the "implementation czar," asked to have breakfast with me in New York. His drive and focus were impressive, but the situation on the ground was still unsatisfactory—to him as well as to me. Near the end of the breakfast, he asked if I would be willing to make another trip to the region as soon as possible. Its purposes would be to talk to an increasingly obstructionist Milosevic, and help revitalize the implementation effort. Agreeing at once, I proposed that we travel together to show a united front and maximize American pressure. I met Gelbard and his team, including Treasury's David Lipton, in Paris on August 6. President Clinton himself had talked publicly in recent weeks about "saving Dayton," a phrase that disturbed some of his senior advisors but that vividly conveyed his own sense of concern. I had told him that we were about one year behind where we should be.

We flew first to Split to join a meeting between Izetbegovic and Tudjman. They met against the backdrop of highly publicized actions by both the Croat and Muslim communities against refugee return; each had recently mobilized mobs to prevent other ethnic groups from returning to their homes. In the Vogosca suburb of Sarajevo, a mob of Muslim women—many Srbrenica widows—had blocked Serbs from returning to their homes. In Jajce, a Croat mob had done the same thing to five hundred Muslims.

When we were ushered into the meeting room, we were confronted with an unexpected sight. Instead of facing each other with the previous air of hostility, the two leaders were seated side by side at the end of the table, their shoulders almost touching. I remembered the meeting in Zagreb on September 19, 1995, when Tudjman had yelled at Izetbegovic in front of forty people. Now, as one of Tudjman's senior aides explained, they wanted to show us—and a large press corps waiting outside—that they could collaborate without American direction. With great pride, Tudjman and Izetbegovic gave us a joint announcement intended to strengthen the Federation. But it was vague and filled with generalities that meant little.

Gelbard and I had never worked closely together before, but we operated easily. I began, "We congratulate you on producing a joint statement. However, if you want us to praise it publicly, you must agree to a second statement with specific deadlines. You must condemn the mob actions against refugee return in both Jajce and Vogosca, and pledge that you will not permit it again."

We presented a draft that we had drafted during the flight to Split, and settled down to a five-hour negotiation that ended with an announcement containing ten new commitments and specific deadlines. As always in Bosnia, one could not be sure that these deadlines and goals would be honored. But based on the pattern of the previous eighteen months, we knew that the best way to make progress was to forge public agreement on specific dates and goals, and then hold the parties to them.*

In a private meeting, Tudjman complained bitterly to Gelbard, Galbraith, and me about his treatment by Washington. He had been hospitalized with a bout with cancer since I had last seen him, but it was in remission, and he showed only a few effects of his illness. But he believed that the United States had leaked information about his health after an examination at Walter Reed Army Hospital in Washington. The United States had also hardened its policy in the face of Croatia's continued expulsion of Serb families from land they had lived on for generations, slowing down or withholding aid to Croatia.

---

* To almost everyone's amazement, the refugees who had been forcibly prevented from returning to Jajce in early August returned peacefully a few weeks later, and more followed after that.

We said that he had to give Dayton more than lip service if he wanted Washington to ease up. I said that we were outraged by the Croat mob in Jajce only three days earlier. "By the way," Gelbard added dramatically, "I know for a fact that Dario Kordic [the most prominent indicted Croat war criminal] was personally directing that mob. You must send him to The Hague if you want things to change between us." Tudjman protested that he had no idea where Kordic was or what he was doing. But he did not really expect us to believe this; he was only testing the importance of the issue. We were immovable; Kordic had to be brought to justice.

Eight weeks later, on October 6, 1997, Kordic and nine other indicted Bosnian Croats "voluntarily" surrendered under pressure from Zagreb. It was an important step forward in the quest for war criminals.* Watching Kordic make his farewell statement on television before flying to The Hague, I noticed a small but revealing detail: Kordic's remarks at the Split airport were translated by Tudjman's personal interpreter, a clear signal that Tudjman and Kordic had reached some sort of private understanding regarding the future.

After our day with Tudjman and Izetbegovic, we spent the night at a resort hotel in Trogir, a beautiful walled city near Split. It was a soft August evening, and my thoughts went back to the last night I had spent in Split, almost exactly two years earlier, before setting out for Mount Igman.

Tuzla and the Generals. The next morning, August 7, we flew to Tuzla at dawn for a meeting with the three senior commanders in the American and NATO chain of command: General Shalikashvili, who had changed his schedule to join us for what was also his final visit to the region; General Clark, now the NATO commander; and General Eric Shinseki, the new SFOR commander. For over a year the Bosnian Serbs had been "cheating" on Dayton by putting military police uniforms on regular soldiers and claiming that they were no longer in the Bosnian Serb Army, even though the military annex of the agreement, anticipating such games, had specifically included "military uniformed police" in the definition of armed forces. These paramilitary police were, I said publicly, "racist, fascist, anti–peace agreement, anti-democratic, and a potential threat to the international community." Yet until Clark took command of NATO, SFOR had ignored them. Clark instructed Shinseki to issue a warning, followed by enforcement, that henceforth the military uniformed police would be treated the same way as regular forces.

When the weather cleared, we headed for Sarajevo, after bidding an especially warm farewell to Shalikashvili, whom I would not see again until his emotional retirement ceremony on the parade grounds at Fort Myer at the end of September. I had never known a military officer of whom I was fonder. It

* More voluntary surrenders—including a number of Serbs—followed in 1998.

was impossible to dislike him, and I was grateful for his personal support even when we occasionally disagreed.

Reviving Implementation. The good news in Sarajevo was that the joint institutions actually existed; the bad news was that they barely functioned.

The joint presidency, composed of Izetbegovic, Krajisnik, and Zubak, was one of the most important litmus tests of Dayton. I was gratified to see that our decision to limit the presidency to three people—one from each ethnic group—had been correct, but the joint presidency was still a limited operation. It had been in a state of suspension for over a month as a Serb protest against the British operation on July 10 in Prijedor—the most important military action since Dayton—which had resulted in the capture of one indicted war criminal and the death of another. The dead Serb had been one of Karadzic's closest allies, the Prijedor police chief, a notorious killer during the 1992 "death camp" phase of the war, and his death had been a serious blow to the Bosnian Serbs. Only our trip to Sarajevo had forced Krajisnik to attend.

The meeting began in an unlikely manner. Looking directly at me, Krajisnik said that he wanted to make an opening comment. "At Dayton," he said, "I opposed the agreement. I was wrong. I opposed the deployment of IFOR. I was wrong. Dayton is a good thing for Bosnia. I want to make this clear, especially to Ambassador Holbrooke."

This statement was not as promising as it sounded. Krajisnik's "Dayton" was not what we had in mind; his was a way station on the path to partition, ours was an agreement for a single country. He may have signed the agreement, but he still refused to accept its central thesis.

Krajisnik was immovable on every issue. Fed up, we ended the meeting and asked to see him alone. Gelbard and I angrily told him that his behavior was unacceptable, and obviously incompatible with his opening statement of support for Dayton. I said we had not come all this way just to participate in a meaningless meeting. We scheduled a second meeting for that evening at the National Museum in Federation territory. When Krajisnik protested the venue, we told him that if he did not come to the museum we would assume he was withdrawing from the joint presidency. This startled Krajisnik, and he backed down.

Another All–nighter. We resumed at about ten o'clock that evening, August 7, at the National Museum, and turned immediately to three unresolved problems: creating a single telephone system, getting the Standing Committee on Military Matters functioning, and agreeing on the distribution of ambassadorships among the three ethnic communities.

The meetings ended at four in the morning, with agreements on all these issues. The last carried equally great symbolic value, especially when the Muslims agreed that the ambassador in Washington would be a Serb, while they retained the position at the United Nations.

When the final documents were ready for signature, the acting High Representative, Gerd Wagner, brought them in for Krajisnik's signature. Wagner, whom I had known well in Bonn and Washington, was one of Germany's rising diplomatic stars. Krajisnik clearly disliked Wagner, and instead of signing the agreements, he began to pick a fight with the affable German diplomat. Furious at Krajisnik's abuse of Wagner, I leaned forward across the table and said, "I want to tell you something I have never said to anyone else in this long negotiating process: if you do not sign this paper now, as you already promised in front of witnesses, I promise we will never speak to you or deal with you again." I handed Krajisnik a pen, and he signed the agreements. The next morning, Wagner joined Gelbard and me at a press conference at the American Embassy to announce the agreements of the previous evening. It was a real achievement for Wagner, the highest-ranking German diplomat in Bosnia—but it was one of his last. A few weeks later, he and eleven other people, including five Americans, died when a Ukrainian helicopter crashed into the side of a hill. Once again, as at Mount Igman and Dubrovnik, the enforcing nations had paid the ultimate price for their efforts to bring peace to Bosnia. And once again, the dead were civilians, diplomats, policemen, and aid workers—not soldiers.

A few days later, *The New York Times* would criticize us for having "spent the bulk of [our] time haggling over telephone area codes and designs for a currency and the appointment of Bosnian ambassadors [instead] of dealing with the principal threats to a unified Bosnia." But the front-page article missed one of the main points of our trip, and indeed of the entire implementation process: to create a unified Bosnia, these seemingly small issues had to be solved, one by one if necessary—and this could be done only under external pressure. The parties themselves could not voluntarily agree on anything yet. *The Washington Post* got it right, reporting that "Holbrooke's efforts [were] seen as part of the campaign to end a sense of drift that had settled over the Bosnia peacemaking effort." Our trip helped revive the implementation process, and set the stage for further progress. Bob Gelbard would continue to travel to the region tirelessly, hammering the parties into slow but steady progress.

Banja Luka and Plavsic. Immediately after the press conference announcing the new agreements on August 8, we flew to Banja Luka to see Biljana Plavsic, who was now receiving international attention for her defiance of both the Pale Serbs and Milosevic. A biologist during the Tito era, she had been a Fulbright scholar in New York and spoke serviceable English. She was on her best behavior, trying hard to charm us. The United States, in turn, had put its weight behind her in her struggle against Pale. Nonetheless, we could not ignore her unsavory origins and close ties to Karadzic.

"I want you to know that while I am still a nationalist, I am also a good democrat," she began. This was a shrewd start. "But what we must ask you," I responded, "is whether you are still a separatist."

"No," she answered firmly, "I do not support a separate Serb state, I support Dayton." Later, although we had agreed to keep our conversation private, her staff made this exchange public. It represented a complete change for her since the days when Bosnian Serbs named tanks after her.

She told us she feared for her life at the hands of Pale thugs. She said that her meeting with Madeleine Albright in May had been critical in her decision to stand up to her former mentors. The day after that meeting, she said, she had gone to Pale to meet with Krajisnik, Buha—and Karadzic. "I told them we should comply with Dayton," she said, "and they attacked me, told me I had betrayed the revolution, and threw me out of the party."

When it was time to leave, the most revealing moment of the day occurred. Over one hundred journalists were waiting downstairs. We had assumed she would keep her distance from us in their presence. Instead, she announced that she would sit with us and participate. In addition, she asked David Lipton to explain to the press the price the Bosnian Serbs were paying in lost international aid because of Pale's refusal to participate in the joint institutions.

Mrs. Plavsic had crossed the Rubicon. It would be difficult for her to scramble back. She had chosen to defy Pale, and was clearly, publicly, counting on American support.

Belgrade, August 8. Once again, Milosevic had moved the meeting place, this time to the "White Palace," a magnificent royal dwelling in Belgrade unused for over a decade. The gardens were splendid, the food significantly better, and the walls filled with Old Masters, including a Rembrandt. But these cosmetic changes only emphasized that nothing else had changed. In fact, the sense of isolation felt greater.

Alone in the palace except for his faithful aide Goran Milinovic and one Deputy Minister, Milosevic said that Dayton was succeeding and that we should be satisfied, except for the troubles that Mrs. Plavsic was causing. We disagreed strongly, saying that Karadzic was now openly violating the July 18, 1996, agreement, and that, by backing Pale over Plavsic, Milosevic was undermining stability in Bosnia. The meeting meandered on, and even a private talk in the gardens was unproductive.

During dinner, Milosevic and I spoke alone in the reception room. "Mr. President," I said, "we have been wasting our time tonight. We are willing to return tomorrow if you wish to bring Krajisnik here so that we can try to make some progress." We finished the meal without any progress.

. . .

Gelbard and I returned to the White Palace the next morning alone, wondering if Krajisnik would appear. He had told us flatly in Sarajevo that he would not come to another meeting in Belgrade. But there he was, sitting quietly in a chair next to Milosevic, his demeanor quite different from what we had seen two days earlier.

We turned first to Radovan Karadzic, still the overriding issue. I showed the two men an interview that Karadzic had given the previous day to a German newspaper. Both Milosevic and Krajisnik professed to be unaware of the interview, but they readily agreed that it constituted a flagrant violation of the July 18 agreement. We warned that such actions would increase the chances of a military action to bring Karadzic to justice.

"If you take such action," Milosevic said emphatically, "it will be a disaster for all of us. Your nation will regret it." Gelbard and I shrugged. "That is your problem," I said. "You cannot threaten our nation. What happens in Bosnia is important to us, but not decisive. For you these events are life and death."

Krajisnik offered a guarantee that Karadzic "would henceforth comply fully with the July 18 agreement." We rejected this as no longer sufficient. "If you wish to affirm that the July 18 agreement is still valid, you may do so, and we will report it publicly," I said. "But we cannot make a second agreement with you. You signed the first one, and it has been violated."

We concluded the meeting by discussing several other issues that concerned us.* Then, after a press conference, we left for the United States. For the first time since Dayton, I felt that the implementation effort was being pursued with sufficient vigor and determination, thanks in large part to Gelbard and Clark. At a meeting in the Cabinet Room on Friday, August 15, I told the President and other senior officials that we were still far behind schedule, but progress was visible in many parts of Bosnia. At the local level, people were trying to live and work together again. But it was necessary to repeat a warning that was now nearly two years old: as long as the leaders who had started the war remained in power in Pale, the country would not be out of danger, and it would be almost impossible to withdraw our troops.

Milorad Dodik and the second elections. In a bold gamble, the United States and its Contact Group associates backed a proposal by Mrs. Plavsic to hold new elections for the Republika Srpska Assembly. In our August 1997 meeting, Gelbard and I had told Milosevic that we would back these elections despite his strenuous objections. Faced with this unyielding position, Milose-

* The bulk of the meeting concerned matters that are still "operational," and must therefore be omitted from this account.

vic changed course and began to deal with Plavsic, whom he had long
ridiculed publicly.

The results of the election, held in September 1997 under OSCE supervision, were stunning, and suggested more than any previous event the potential
that lay in aggressive implementation of the Dayton Agreements. Eighteen
members of the new Bosnian Serb assembly were Muslims, elected by Muslim refugees voting in their home areas under complex electoral provisions
hammered out at Dayton, over Milosevic's objections. These new legislators
combined with Plavsic's supporters to elect as Prime Minister—by one vote—
a thirty-nine-year-old businessman named Milorad Dodik, who had not been
involved in the war and who had only limited ties to the Bosnian Serb wartime
leadership. For the first time since the war began, the Bosnian Serb government was not controlled by the party of Radovan Karadzic. While Izetbegovic
and his government in Sarajevo watched skeptically, Dodik announced that he
would honor Dayton. In response, the United States and the European Union
began to release aid funds previously denied to the Bosnian Serbs. The dis-
mantling of the Bosnian Serb wartime capital of Pale, which we had long
hoped for, began as government offices moved, one by one, to Banja Luka.

The President Decides. On December 22, 1997, President Clinton made
his second trip to Bosnia. He took with him not only his family and members
of Congress but, in a brilliant display of bipartisanship, former Senator and
Mrs. Dole. Dole had told me in early September that he would support an extension of the American troop presence in Bosnia, information I promptly re-
layed, with Dole's blessing, to the President, and the two men, once political
adversaries, had found common ground over the need to stay the course in
Bosnia.

Two days before his trip, President Clinton held a news conference in
which he announced that the United States would keep American troops in
Bosnia past the original June 1998 deadline. The President accepted full responsibility for agreeing to the two earlier deadlines, and said he would set no
further deadlines.

This was a benchmark decision for the United States. The President had finally made it explicit that we would not walk away from Bosnia. Three days
later, he took that message directly to the people of the Balkans.

I talked often to the President and his senior advisors in the weeks prior to
his announcement and his trip, and I knew how difficult the decision was at
the personal level, especially since his political opponents were determined to
take advantage of it. But he knew that the original timetable would have done
enormous damage to the national interests of the United States and NATO. We
spoke again right after the trip, and it was clear that seeing Sarajevo for the

first time had had a powerful impact on him and his family. I had the sense that the trip had reaffirmed in his mind the correctness of his strategic decisions, and clarified for him the difficulties that still lay ahead.

Once it was clear that the United States had abandoned a specific NATO troop withdrawal schedule, the pace of implementation picked up. The first few months of 1998 saw more movement than in the previous two years. The common currency coupon and new coins, a unified telephone system, a single license plate, and limited air, rail, and truck traffic all began to function—although in many cases local officials resisted such reforms, as they would cut into their personal gains under the highly corrupt system that had developed during the war within each ethnic community.

In September 1998, another important nationwide election was held in Bosnia. In several meetings during the summer of 1998 at the White House, I stressed that these elections would be critical in deciding the country's future. The highest priority was the defeat of Momcilo Krajisnik, who was running for reelection as the Serb co-President of Bosnia and still represented the extreme rejectionism of Karadzic. His departure was, in my view, absolutely necessary for progress in Bosnia. This was especially true since, under the rotation system agreed to at Dayton, the next senior president of Bosnia-Herzegovina would be Serb—and Krajisnik would never convene a meeting of the three-person presidency if elected.

Gelbard added that Plavsic's reelection was equally important, although, given her origins as a founding member of the SDS, she still carried a highly unsavory legacy and was firmly opposed to the return of Muslim refugees to the Serb portions of Bosnia. Gelbard predicted that both elections would produce the desired outcome.

The election results were mixed. Krajisnik lost to a moderate, Zivko Radisic—a man with whom both the Bosnian Muslims and the international community could work. Furthermore, the vote of the extreme nationalist parties in all three communities declined, the first electoral indication that the people might at last be turning away from the leaders whose inflammatory ultranationalism had destroyed Bosnia. In the Republika Srpska Assembly, for example, the number of seats controlled by the SDS had dropped from forty-five to nineteen in just over a year.

But something went wrong with the second part of the scenario. Running a sloppy and complacent campaign, ignoring the advice of her advisors and of Bob Gelbard, Mrs. Plavsic lost her bid for election as president of Republika Srpska to an ultranationalist, Nikola Poplasen, who represented a party even more extreme than the SDS. In addition—and this was not unexpected—another nationalist, Ante Jelavic, won the election for the Croat co-President of Bosnia, reinforcing concerns that, in the long run, the greatest danger to a single functioning Bosnian state would come not from the Serbs but from the Croats, who could more easily carve parts of the west (where the bulk of the Croats lived) out of Bosnia and annex them formally to neighboring Croatia, which already exercised de facto control over much of the area through its representative and local thugs.

Poplasen and Jelavic were setbacks, but Radisic's victory was a step forward. As a result, Gelbard and I suggested in several meetings at the White House in late 1998 that a significant adjustment in policy was in order: henceforth, the implementing powers needed to seek ways to strengthen the *central* government, which had been virtually nonexistent while Krajisnik had been its senior Serb representative. Approving this policy shift, Washington and the EU planned to place more power in the central institutions in 1999, and remove as much as possible from the entities. Such a policy—I called it "back to the future"—was precisely what I had originally hoped for at Dayton, since a stronger central government would increase the chances of making Bosnia a viable single country. I urged that we now address the single greatest flaw in the Dayton Agreement—the existence of two opposing armies in a single country—by creating a centralized defense establishment.

Despite the mixed election results—and despite the fact that refugee return to minority areas, the single most critical indicator of progress, was still moving extremely slowly—even the most hardened critics of Dayton had to be impressed by evidence that the country seemed to be gradually coming together, especially economically. At the end of 1997, Gelbard and the Contact Group decided, as an incentive for further progress, to offer Milosevic a "road map" for normalizing Yugoslavia's relations with the international community: a series of actions that the U.S. and the Contact Group would take to "reward" Belgrade for supporting strict implementation of Dayton. The steps were primarily economic: the phased removal or suspension of most of the remaining economic restrictions on Yugoslavia, keyed to progress in Bosnia. Beyond that lay Belgrade's ultimate goal: political acceptance, U.N. and OSCE membership, U.S. recognition.

In March 1999, the Western powers took two important steps, demonstrating their continued resolve. First, Roberts Owen finally made his long-awaited ruling on the town of Brcko, "awarding" it neither to the Federation nor to the Serbs. Rather, he established a special zone, the "Brcko District," that would be administered directly by the central government. On the same day, High Representative Carlos Westendorp fired Nikola Poplasen as President of Republika Srbska because of his continual efforts to destroy the Dayton Agreement.

But long before these events, indeed a year earlier, something that had long been feared occurred. Kosovo, the most difficult of all the problems of the region, the area where the crisis had begun, exploded again.

By the spring of 1998, Kosovo would create another crisis for—and between—America and its NATO allies and Russia, both proving again the necessity for American leadership and illustrating in the most brutal form the dilemmas created by the terrible and complex history of the Balkans. It would also bring me back to the region in the summer and fall of 1998 under the most difficult conditions in a desperate effort to prevent another Balkan war.

CHAPTER 21

America, Europe, and Bosnia

Providence has not created mankind entirely independent or entirely free. It is true that around every man a fatal circle is traced
beyond which he cannot pass; but within the wide verge of that circle he is powerful and free; as it is with man, so with communities.

—ALEXIS DE TOCQUEVILLE

FROM THE BEGINNING OF YUGOSLAVIA'S COLLAPSE, Americans divided into
two groups, broadly defined: those who thought we should intervene for either
moral or strategic reasons, and those who feared that if we did, we would become entangled in a Vietnam-like quagmire. As awareness of ethnic cleansing
spread, the proportion of those who wanted the United States to "do something" increased, but they probably never constituted a majority.

Nonetheless, in only eighteen weeks in 1995—when the situation seemed
most hopeless—the United States put its prestige on the line with a rapid and
dramatic series of high-risk actions: an all-out diplomatic effort in August,
heavy NATO bombing in September, a cease-fire in October, Dayton in November, and, in December, the deployment of twenty thousand American
troops to Bosnia. Suddenly, the war was over—and America's role in post–
Cold War Europe redefined.

Had the United States not intervened, the war would have continued for
years and ended disastrously. The Bosnian Muslims would have been either
destroyed, or reduced to a weak landlocked ministate surrounded by a Greater
Croatia and a Greater Serbia. Fighting would eventually have resumed in eastern Slavonia. Europe would have faced a continued influx of Balkan refugees.
And tens of thousands more would have been killed, maimed, or displaced
from their homes.

This was a substantial achievement. But legitimate questions remain: Was
American involvement in the national interest? How did it affect America's role
in the world? Did Dayton bring peace to Bosnia, or only the absence of war?
What might we have done better? Can Bosnia survive as a single multiethnic
country, as called for in Dayton, or will it eventually divide into two or three
ethnically based states? These issues, and others, deserve further attention.

American Leadership. By the spring of 1995 it had become commonplace to say that Washington's relations with our European allies were worse than at any time since the 1956 Suez crisis. But this comparison was misleading; because Suez came at the height of the Cold War, the strain then was containable. Bosnia, however, had defined the first phase of the post–Cold War relationship between Europe and the United States, and seriously damaged the Atlantic relationship. In particular, the strains endangered NATO itself just as Washington sought to enlarge it.

The Clinton Administration was severely criticized for reneging on our commitments to European security and for lowering the general priority accorded to foreign affairs—in short, for weak leadership in foreign policy. These charges deeply troubled the Administration's senior foreign-policy officials, especially when, ironically, they often came from those who opposed American involvement in Bosnia. In its own eyes, the Clinton Administration had laid down a strong track record in post–Cold War Europe: it had built a new relationship with Russia and the other former Soviet republics; started to enlarge NATO; tackled the Irish problem; strengthened American ties with the Baltic nations and Central Europe; and gained congressional approval for the NAFTA and GATT trade agreements. Nonetheless, the perception that Washington had turned away from Europe at the end of the Cold War was hard to shake as long as we did nothing about Bosnia.

Dayton changed this almost overnight. Criticism of President Clinton as a weak leader ended abruptly, especially in Europe and among Muslim nations. Washington was now praised for its firm leadership—or even chided by some Europeans for *too much* leadership. But even those who chafed at the reassertion of American power conceded, at least implicitly, its necessity. As I suggested at the time, this was not a serious problem; it was better to be criticized for too much leadership than for too little.

After Dayton, American foreign policy seemed more assertive, more muscular. This may have been as much perception as reality, but the perception mattered. The three main pillars of American foreign policy in Europe—U.S.-Russian relations, NATO enlargement into Central Europe, and Bosnia—had often worked against each other. Now they reinforced each other: NATO sent its forces out of area for the first time in its history, and Russian troops, under an American commander, were deployed alongside them. "Clinton managed to pull off the seemingly impossible," wrote Russia's former Prime Minister, Yegor Gaidar, "to implement NATO enlargement without causing irreparable damage either to democratic elements in Russia's political establishment or to U.S.-Russian relations."[1] De Charette had it right: "America *was* back."

Strategic considerations were vital to our involvement, but the motives that finally pushed the United States into action were also moral and humanitarian.

After Srebrenica and Mount Igman the United States could no longer escape the terrible truth of what was happening in Bosnia. A surge of sentiment arose from ordinary Americans who were outraged at what they saw on television and from senior government officials who could no longer look the other way. Within the Administration, the loss of three friends on Mount Igman carried a special weight; the war had, in effect, come home.

Despite American pride over Dayton, our own record in the former Yugoslavia was flawed. The tortured half-measures of the United Nations and the European Union had been inadequate, to be sure, but they had kept the Bosnian Muslims from complete destruction for several years. And the Europeans continued to pay the bulk of the bills, without getting sufficient credit from the American public or the Congress, which, immediately after Dayton, told the Europeans that they would have to carry the burden for civilian reconstruction. Thus, the richest nation in the world, in the midst of its strongest economic performance in thirty years, offered the former Yugoslavia a relatively insignificant amount of aid. Furthermore, despite valiant efforts by John Kornblum, implementation of the Dayton agreement was initially halfhearted. Only in mid-1997, with the arrival of Bob Gelbard and General Clark, did the implementation effort begin to show the energy required.

A final report card on Dayton is not yet possible. When President Clinton visited Sarajevo in December 1997, he said, as I had, that implementation was running about a year behind schedule. But there had been no fighting for two years; the three communities had begun rebuilding ties at the local level; Sarajevo was reunified and rebuilding; a large number of Bosnian Serb weapons had been destroyed; four airports had opened for civilian traffic; a few refugee "open areas" had been created; the odious Pale television transmitters had been silenced; and Banja Luka had begun to replace Pale. At the same time, Carlos Westendorp, the High Representative, did what should have been done two years earlier: he simply decreed the design for a new common currency. On January 22, 1998, American soldiers made their first arrest of a war-crimes suspect in Bosnia: Goran Jelisic, a Bosnian Serb who liked to refer to himself as "the Serbian Adolf." If such actions continued, the anti-Dayton forces would be progressively weakened, and the chances of creating a peaceful, viable state would dramatically improve.

Still, while the bloodlust of 1991–95 had begun to subside, it was far from gone; all sides carried deep scars and many still sought revenge instead of reconciliation. Most troubling, the same leaders who had started the war were still trying to silence those who called for multiethnic cooperation. The two most dangerous men in the region, Radovan Karadzic and Ratko Mladic, remained at large more than three years after Dayton. With Karadzic's overt involvement, the rearguard forces of Pale still sought to thwart cooperation between the two parts of Bosnia. They had discovered this strategy almost by accident when, "amid large-scale arson and police intimidation while IFOR troops stood by," they drove most local Serbs out of Sarajevo in March 1996, in what one experienced observer called "the greatest stain on the peace process."[2] As Michael Steiner explained at the end of his tour as Deputy High Representative in late 1997, "The Pale leadership has only one aim, and that is to separate from Bosnia-Herzegovina. Short of that, they are fighting for as autonomous a position as possible within the common state."[3] As long as Pale had residual powers, the threat would be alive.

Flaws. No one knew the weaknesses of Dayton better than those who had participated in the negotiations. But these were not necessarily the same as those mentioned by outside critics, many of whom confused the peace agreement with its implementation. When I looked back on the negotiations, I invariably returned to several key moments or issues:

- The most serious flaw in the Dayton Peace Agreement was that it left two opposing armies in one country, one for the Serbs and one for the Croat-Muslim Federation. We were fully aware of this during the negotiations, but since NATO would not disarm the parties as an obligated task, creating a single army or disarming Bosnia-Herzegovina was not possible.

- A second problem was our agreement to allow the Serb portion of Bosnia to retain the name "Republika Srpska."* The decision, it will be recalled, was forged in the dramatic late-night meeting with Izetbegovic in Ankara on Labor Day, with the Geneva Foreign Ministers meeting only three days away and the resumption of the bombing still in doubt. "Republic" does not necessarily connote an independent country in the Balkans and eastern Europe, but nonetheless, to permit Karadzic to keep the name he had invented was more of a concession than we then realized.

- The timing of the end of the bombing will always remain disputed. The negotiating team would have welcomed its prolongation for at least another week. But when the military told us in the second week of September that they had only about three days of targets left, we had to negotiate before the bombing ended on its own. Warren Christopher questioned the military's statement privately, but neither he nor the ne-

---

* See Chapter 8.

gotiating team was able to learn the full facts.* Informal discussion between us and General Michael Ryan, who commanded Deliberate Force, would have allowed more informed decisions at a critical moment. But such contact was apparently barred by Admiral Leighton Smith, even through General Clark.[4]

- The creation of a weak International Police Task Force had especially serious consequences. This was the result of several factors, including European objections to a strong international police force, and Washington's refusal, during a huge budget confrontation with the new Republican Congress, to ask for sufficient American funds for the police. We had identified the problem before Dayton but could not overcome our internal difficulties.

- In his memoirs, Carl Bildt wrote that, in regard to the mandate of the High Representative, "the Americans initially stressed purely military aspects and did not want any cohesive civilian or political authority."[5] Bildt's observation is valid, although the position he criticizes was not that of the negotiating team, which argued this point by phone with NATO throughout the first ten days at Dayton. Even the compromise position we reached with General Joulwan was a mistake. Bildt's mandate should have been stronger. On the other hand, when the Bosnian Serbs defied Dayton, the United States urged Bildt to interpret the authority granted him by Dayton more broadly, at which point, ironically, resistance came from the Europeans, who, having correctly criticized us initially for limiting Bildt's mandate, then reined him in.

- Finally, there were the two arbitrary time limits cited earlier: one year for IFOR; eighteen months for SFOR. They left the impression that the Serbs might be able to outwait the enforcing powers, thus encouraging delaying tactics. By laying out self-imposed time limits, the United States only weakened itself. Everyone closely associated with implementation knew this from the outset. As Madeleine Albright said in a speech in January 1998, "The mission should determine the timetable, not the other way around."[6] When the President dropped the time limits in December 1997, he sent the strongest possible signal that the United States would stay the course, with immediate results.

One Country or Two (or Three)? The most serious criticism of the peace agreement came from those who questioned its central premise, that Bosnia should, or could, be reconstructed as a single, multiethnic country. It was fash-

---

* See Chapter 10.

ionable for critics of Dayton to contend that this was not achievable and that the United States should accept, if not encourage, the partition of Bosnia along ethnic lines. While Dayton was a successful cease-fire agreement, this argument went, its political provisions—giving refugees the right of return and affirming a single country and a central government—could never be implemented. Skeptics—including many old Yugoslav hands—had warned us from the outset that it would be impossible for a multiethnic state to survive in Bosnia. But most of those who opposed a multiethnic Bosnia after Dayton had been proven wrong at least twice: first, in 1991, when they believed that Yugoslavia could be held together, then again when, for the most part, they opposed military action or American intervention.

Still, as implementation slipped seriously behind schedule in 1996–97, some criticized Dayton as a partition agreement, while others criticized it precisely because it was not one. The most distinguished and influential American proponent of the latter view was Henry Kissinger, who argued that Bosnia had never existed as an independent nation and that we should not try to create it now.[7] The negotiating team did not share this view. It was not that we underestimated the difficulties of getting the leaders of the three ethnic groups to cooperate; no one knew this better than those of us who had conducted the negotiations! But every other choice was worse. Dividing the country along ethnic lines would create massive new refugee flows. Serbs, Croats, and Muslims who still lived as minorities in many parts of the country would be forced to flee their homes, and fighting would be certain to break out as the scramble for land and houses erupted again. Thus, contrary to the arguments of the partitionists, the chances of fighting would be increased, not decreased, by partition and the relocation that would follow. In addition, there was a moral issue: the United States and its European allies could not be party to creating more refugees and legitimizing the Serb aggression. As *The Economist* wrote two years after Dayton,

> Partition would almost certainly provoke mass migration and further bloodshed. . . . And the fighting might not be confined to Bosnia. The spectacle of a partitioned Bosnia would hearten every separatist in the Balkans. In areas of ethnic instability like Macedonia and Kosovo, who would listen to the West as it urged the merits of sinking differences and living together in harmony? . . . Fans of partition tend to ignore the situation in central Bosnia, where many Croats live in enclaves surrounded by Muslims. Knowing they would be left in a Muslim-dominated state, most of these Croats dread partition.[8]

Of course, as I had written to President Clinton after Dayton, no vital national interest of the United States was directly affected by whether Bosnia was one, two, or three countries. We did not oppose a voluntary change in the international boundaries in Bosnia-Herzegovina or its eventual division into more than one country—if that was the desire of a majority of each of the three ethnic groups at some future date. Other countries had broken up peacefully in recent years, including Czechoslovakia and the Soviet Union. But this could be decided only by *elections free of intimidation,* something that was not possible in the aftermath of the war, while the ultranationalist parties, preaching separatist ethnic hatred, were in control of the media and the police. In all three ethnic groups, the men who started the war in 1991–92 were still in power. They have to disappear to make way for a new generation of leaders willing to reach out to one another. If more leaders like Dodik and Radisic emerged, and survived, Bosnia would survive as a single state.

AMERICA, STILL A EUROPEAN POWER

The end of the Cold War did not mean the end of America's strategic and national interests outside its own borders. This was not self-evident to most Americans, who assumed, or at least hoped, that the need for direct involvement in Europe—and for that matter, in most of the rest of the world—would decline sharply with the fall of the Soviet Union at the end of 1991.

But once the United States became, to use an oddly ambiguous boast that was often heard after the fall of the Soviet Union, "the world's only superpower," its involvement in major events in the rest of the world could no longer be limited to crusades against fascism or communism. The American economy, once heavily centered on its own domestic markets, was now more dependent on global markets than ever before. How could the United States, in a world growing steadily smaller and more interdependent, disengage from the political, strategic, and moral issues that increasingly impinged on its once-splendid isolation?

This was not to argue that the United States had to become the world's policeman. Not every issue was equally susceptible to American leadership or American-led solutions; even the world's only superpower had its limits, and knowing where they were would be a central test of a new generation of Washington policymakers. Each and every American involvement overseas required the support, or at least the passive acceptance, of Congress and the American people. This was one of the many lessons of Vietnam, and it still applied a quarter century after the fall of Saigon.

Nonetheless, as not only Bosnia but the Mideast and Northern Ireland showed, there was a real need for active American leadership in addressing complex problems that, left to their own devices, might fester indefinitely or explode into more serious crises. Sometimes, as in Cyprus, where I spent a great deal of time from 1997 to 1999 as President Clinton's special emissary, the efforts did not produce solutions to long-standing and seemingly intractable problems. But even Cyprus—widely regarded by experts and scholars as virtually insoluble—benefitted greatly from the engagement of the Clinton Administration, in close coordination with the United Nations and the European Union. Without such continuous pressure and involvement, the situation in Cyprus might have exploded into direct conflict at several points in the last decade of the century. The Russian missiles purchased by the Greek Cypriots, for example, would surely have been deployed in late 1998 with potentially disastrous results if not for a massive international effort led by the United States. Instead, the government of Cyprus wisely diverted the missiles to the island of Crete, part of Greece itself, thus averting a crisis. This was the latest in a series of American efforts, often in conjunction with the United Nations and the European Union, to defuse or resolve thorny issues in the region. The resolution of the bitter dispute between Greece and the former Yugoslav republic of Macedonia in September 1995 during the Bosnia shuttle, as described earlier in this book, and our equally successful effort to resolve border disputes between Greece and Albania earlier in 1995, and between Hungary and two of its neighbors in 1996, were other examples of the role that could be played by an activist, hands-on foreign policy that addressed potentially explosive issues early, before they turned into other Bosnias. In the post–Cold War world, where foreign policy was no longer a zero-sum game in which the Soviet Union profitted from any American failure, it was often better to have tried and failed—when the stakes were high enough or the chances of success reasonable—than never to have tried at all.

At the end of the century, deep, if intangible, factors bound America and Europe, ties of history and culture, as well as common interests, humanitarian, economic, and strategic. Most Americans, including many whose families had fled Europe,wanted nothing more to do with Europe's internal squabbles. But history, which had pulled the United States into a deep engagement on the European continent three times during the twentieth century—in two world wars and in the Cold War—would not permit us to turn our backs on Europe so easily. After each of the first two involvements, the United States withdrew, or began to withdraw, from the continent: first, in 1919–20, when it decided not to join the League of Nations even though the driving force behind its creation had been President Wilson; second, in 1945–46, when the United States began a rapid withdrawal of its forces from Europe, only to be confronted by the challenge of Soviet expansionism. When the initial postwar American policy, based on an effective United Nations, failed because it required the positive participation of the Soviet Union, the Truman Administration quickly revised its view of Moscow and entered into the century's third American engagement in Europe, putting into place the Cold War policies that would be known as containment. Perhaps no peacetime foreign policy in history was ever as successful. Despite domestic debate, quarrels with our allies, and the immense tragedy of Vietnam, containment led to the collapse of the Soviet Union at the end of 1991 and prevented a general European war for over forty years.

That Americans, after three major wars and fifty years of continuous and contentious engagement in the world, then wanted to focus on domestic priorities and disengage from international obligations was understandable. World War II, Korea, Vietnam, and the Cold War had cost the nation hundreds of thousands of lives, a staggering amount of money, and a series of often vicious domestic struggles over policy, from the debate over Who Lost China? to McCarthyism and Vietnam. But the hope that international conflicts would fade into the background after the collapse of the Soviet Union and no longer require American leadership was dangerous and unrealistic.

Well before the Bosnian negotiations, I argued that "an unstable Europe would still threaten essential security interests of the United States."[9] But in the absence of a clear and present danger, a Hitler or Stalin who could personify an evil system that we had to oppose, few in Washington felt the need to invest in European security or to play a part in its reshaping when, for the first time since 1917, Russia needed to be included in the general European security system, rather than excluded from it. But despite the desires of many to build this new European security structure with minimal American participation, the fact was that a stable post–Cold War structure could not be built while an integral part of it, the former Yugoslavia, was in flames. Thus, settling Bosnia was necessary, although not sufficient, for stability in Europe. But Europe found that it could not do this without American support and involvement, while the United States learned that our interests still included stability and peace in Europe.

The visionary policies of the 1940s had produced unparalleled peace and prosperity for half a century—but for only half a continent. With the war over in Bosnia, NATO, long the private preserve of the nations on one side of the Iron Curtain, could gradually open its doors to qualified Central European nations. It was essential that this be done in a manner that neither threatened Russia nor weakened the alliance. Meanwhile, a new role for Russia, Ukraine, and the other nations of the former Soviet Union was being defined through new agreements like the Founding Act, which created a formal relationship between Russia and NATO yet did not give Russia a veto over NATO activities. Other existing institutions, like the Organization for Security and Cooperation in Europe (OSCE) were strengthened and expanded; in October 1998 the OSCE would be given a role in Kosovo far larger than any ever attempted before.

Leadership Without Unilateralism. The great architect of European unity, Jean Monnet, once observed, "Nothing is possible without men, but nothing is lasting without institutions." It has become commonplace to observe that achieving Monnet's vision is far more difficult in the absence of the unifying effect of a common adversary. But we should not wax nostalgic for the Cold War. It is now institutional and structural problems that inhibit progress on both sides of the Atlantic.

The United States has survived divided government between the Executive Branch and the Congress for much of the last two decades. But a bloated bureaucratic system and a protracted struggle between the two branches have eroded much of Washington's capacity for decisive action in foreign affairs and reduced our presence just as our range of interests has increased. The United States continues to reduce the resources committed to international affairs even as vast parts of the globe—the former Soviet bloc, China—and new issues that once lay outside its area of direct involvement now take on new importance and require American attention. One cannot have a global economic policy without a political and strategic vision to accompany it, as the 1997–98 economic crisis in East Asia has shown.

If the search for a process that can produce coherent policies is difficult in Washington, it seems to be even harder in the new Europe. Carl Bildt has made a useful observation: the United States, he points out, has to harmonize "institutional views" while Europe has to coordinate "national views." Bildt, who saw the two systems from a unique vantage point, observed:

> In Washington everything has to be formulated and shaped in a continuous compromise between the State Department, the Defense Department, the Treasury, intelligence agencies, and purely domestic factors. The rivalry between these various interests sometimes runs very deep. A great deal of blood can be spilt in the course of inter-agency debates in Washington. *But when this apparatus finally decides on a policy, the United States then has the resources to implement its policy which is almost completely lacking in Europe* [emphasis added].[10]

A QUESTION OF EVIL

Advocates of realpolitik, like three of its most famous American practitioners, Richard Nixon, Henry Kissinger, and George Kennan, have long argued that American advocacy of human rights conflicted with America's true national security interests, amounted to interference in the internal affairs of other nations, and weakened the nation's strategic and commercial interests. In his book *Diplomacy,* Kissinger portrayed American foreign policy as a constant struggle between realism, symbolized by Theodore Roosevelt, and idealism, as epitomized by Woodrow Wilson. Kissinger, who strongly favored TR, wrote, "The American experience has encouraged the belief that America, alone among the nations of the world, is impervious and that it can prevail by the example of its virtues and good works. In the post–Cold War world, such an attitude would turn innocence into self-indulgence."[11]

Under Presidents Nixon, Ford, and Bush, such "realist" theories were in the ascendancy. (The Carter Administration and the Reagan Administration, after the forced departure of Secretary of State Al Haig, took much more assertive positions on human rights.) But based on personal experiences in the late 1970s with authoritarian leaders like Ferdinand Marcos of the Philippines and Park Chung Hee of South Korea—both of whose corrupt strongman regimes were peacefully replaced by democracies—I came to the conclusion that the choice between "realists" and "idealists" was a false one: in the long run, our strategic interests and human rights supported and reinforced each other, and could be advanced at the same time. In short, American foreign policy needed to embrace *both* Theodore Roosevelt and Woodrow Wilson. These thoughts were never far from my mind as we searched for a way to end the war.

Throughout the negotiations, I thought often of the refugees I had visited in 1992: how they knew many of the men who had killed and raped their families; how some of the killers had been their co-workers for twenty years; and how they had hardly been aware of ethnic hatred until 1990. Some people offered what had happened during World War II as proof that ethnic hatred was in the Yugoslav bloodstream. But the bloodbath and fighting of 1941–45 were a product of the larger struggle and genocide Hitler had unleashed. The rest of Europe found a path to peace and reconciliation, but Yugoslavia suffered a bad case of arrested development under communism. Then demagogic and criminal leaders seized power.

The killers were driven by ethnic prejudice rekindled by ultranationalists and demagogues. How could adults do such things to their neighbors and former classmates? After a while, the search for explanations failed. One simply had to recognize that there was true evil in the world.

The full ferocity of that evil so stunned most Europeans and Americans that they could not at first comprehend it. Then, as Carl Jung had warned, they did not know "what to pit against it." There was confusion over whom to blame, and disputes about what was happening; this increased as the war continued, since atrocities were committed by members of all three ethnic groups. But although Croats and Muslims were also guilty of atrocities, the Bosnian Serbs remained the primary perpetrators of the actions that made the phrase "ethnic cleansing" a part of the English language.

It was easy to conclude, as Eagleburger did, that nothing could be done by outsiders. Or that all Serbs were inherently evil. Such judgments allowed people to justify their own inaction. But drawing either inference would be to share the fundamental mistake of the people of the Balkans themselves, imputing to an entire ethnic group the attributes of its worst elements. For more than fifty years people had debated the degree to which the entire German people shared culpability for the Holocaust, and now a similar question arose: was the entire Serb "nation" responsible for the actions of its leaders and their murderous followers?

I often received letters, primarily from Serbs or Serbian Americans, charging that my remarks, or those of other American officials, lumped all Serbs together with a few indicted war criminals. This was a fair criticism of comments that could not always be precise. In fact, the majority of Serbs in the former Yugoslavia were ordinary people who did not kill anyone, although, like many "good Germans" during the Third Reich, a large number remained silent or passive in the face of something they admitted later they knew was wrong. But others were courageous opponents of the fires that raged across their land, and some even fought on the Muslim side. One of contemporary Europe's great visionaries, Czech President Vaclav Havel, addressed this issue in an eloquent essay:

> I consider it an offense against the Serbian people and betrayal of the civic notion of society when evil is identified with Serbian nationality. But I find it equally misguided when evil is not defined at all, for fear of hurting Serbian feelings. All peoples have their Karadžićs and Mladićs, either real or potential. If such men—as the result of a mix of historical, social, and cultural circumstances—gain greater influence than they have in other parts of the world, it does not mean that they come from a criminal people. . . . [This] is a conflict of principles, not of nationalities. . . . In other words, let us beware of attempts to lay the blame for evil on whole peoples. That would be tantamount to adopting the ideology of the ethnic fanatics.[12]

WAS BOSNIA UNIQUE?

After Dayton we came full circle, back to an uncertainty about how much to invest in Bosnia. Having put American prestige on the line in 1995 to end the war, the United States and its allies were uncertain in 1996 and early 1997 about how hard to try to make Dayton work. The result was halfhearted implementation that led critics and cynics to call for scaled-back objectives in Bosnia. Failure to squash the separatist Serb movement immediately after Dayton, when it lay in disarray, seemed to some to prove that partition was inevitable. Such preemptive defeatism could have led to the permanent partition of Bosnia, followed by more refugees and more fighting. The best course remained vigorous enforcement of the Dayton agreement. At the end of 1997,

President Clinton's decision to remove the time limit for U.S. troops dramatically enhanced the chance of success. In 1998 the main constraint was no longer the separatists of Pale, who were beaten, corrupt, and in disarray. Success was within sight, but it would take hard work and a firm commitment from the leaders of the international community—and time.

The circumstances that led to the collapse of Yugoslavia were so extraordinary that it is difficult to conceive of their recurrence. Yet if history teaches us one thing, it is that history is unpredictable. There will be other Bosnias in our lives, different in every detail but similar in one overriding manner: they will originate in distant and ill-understood places, explode with little warning, and present the rest of the world with difficult choices—choices between risky involvement and potentially costly neglect. But if during the Cold War Washington sometimes seemed too ready to intervene, today America and its allies often seem too willing to ignore problems outside their heartland.

There will be other Bosnias in our lives—areas where early outside involvement can be decisive, and American leadership will be required. The world's richest nation, one that presumes to great moral authority, cannot simply make worthy appeals to conscience and call on others to carry the burden. The world will look to Washington for more than rhetoric the next time we face a challenge to peace.

Acknowledgments

IN APRIL 1968, AVERELL HARRIMAN AND CYRUS VANCE asked me to join the negotiating team they were assembling for the first direct talks with the North Vietnamese. I arrived in Paris a few days later, a twenty-six-year-old Foreign Service officer caught up in the excitement of the world's most closely watched negotiation. In Paris I read with fascination *Peacemaking 1919,* Harold Nicolson's diary of his experiences on the British negotiating team at Versailles. But, lacking his discipline, I left Paris in the summer of 1969 without having kept any personal record of my experience.

Still, the memories remained—of Averell Harriman, at the age of seventy-seven, tirelessly trying to convince President Johnson to stop the bombing of North Vietnam; Cyrus Vance sleeping on the floor of his office to ease the pain of a slipped disc; secret talks in Paris suburbs with the North Vietnamese; private emissaries from Vice President Hubert Humphrey asking if he should break with LBJ over Vietnam and resign; and visits from a Harvard professor (and Administration advisor) named Henry Kissinger. During the dramatic final week of the campaign President Johnson halted the bombing of the north, and Richard Nixon won a paper-thin victory over Humphrey amidst a welter of accusations over Vietnam. An opportunity to end the war—and not just the bombing—suddenly slipped away, and the conflict continued for another four years. Contrary to most accounts of this seminal period in American history, it was neither foreordained nor inevitable that the war should continue, with another twenty-five thousand Americans and countless Vietnamese dead. A negotiated end to the war in 1968 was possible; the distance to peace was far smaller than most historians realize.

When, twenty-seven years later, President Clinton and Secretary of State Christopher asked me to take over the Bosnia negotiations, my friend and teacher Fritz Stern urged me to keep a detailed personal record. History was becoming harder to preserve and reconstruct, he pointed out; internal memoranda, telegrams, and other traditional forms of communication had been replaced by secure telephone calls and private faxes that were lost to history.

Of course, he was right. But the pace and intensity of the negotiations left me and most of my colleagues with neither the time nor the energy to keep a detailed record, not even at Dayton. My own cables to Washington were extremely rare, and although my Pentagon colleagues did send regular messages to their superiors, these were incomplete, often intentionally so. The best I could do was to dictate a few thoughts occasionally, and preserve a handful of random notes.

But I remembered the failure to record the 1968 story when its memories were still fresh. Encouraged by my friend and agent, Mort Janklow, and guided by the superb editorial team at Random House—Jason Epstein and Joy de Menil, and, until their departures, Harry Evans and Peter Osnos—I set out to tell the story of these negotiations before the details had receded in my mind.

For a better understanding of events, especially those that did not involve our negotiating team, I consulted as many former colleagues (and journalists) as possible. Some simply responded to a specific question; others spent hours going through their records or journals to help reconstruct events. Many participants offered specific suggestions for revision or rewording, almost all of which I accepted. Others—including some not involved directly in the negotiations—took time to read all or part of the manuscript, and made important suggestions.

Valuable work of historical preservation was done in 1996–97 at the direction of Warren Christopher and Tom Donilon. Recognizing that the publication of State Department documents in the annual Foreign Relations of the United States (FRUS) series was no longer adequate alone, they established an experimental unit within the State Department's Historical Division, to produce a history based both on written records and on supplemental oral histories. They chose Bosnia as the first subject for this experiment, and asked Derek Chollet, a young Columbia University historian, to write the study. When declassified, it will provide an invaluable resource for other historians. I am especially grateful to Derek for his subsequent assistance to me as a researcher, general advisor, and friend throughout the latter part of this project.

I am indebted to many others who offered information, editorial suggestions, or general assistance, including: Morton Abramowitz, Sheppie Abramowitz, Marshall Adair, Madeleine Albright, Walter Andrusyzyn, Kofi Annan, Don Bandler, Marsha Barnes, Reginald Bartholomew, Richard Beattie, Sandy Berger, Carl Bildt, Joachim Bitterlich, Alan Blinken, Donald Blinken, General Charles Boyd, Robert Bradtke, John Burns, Nick Burns, General George

Casey, Warren Christopher, General Wesley Clark, Hillary Rodham Clinton, President Clinton, James Collins, Admiral William Crowe, Tom Donilon, Sandy Drew, Linda Bird Francke, Katharina Frasure, Bennett Freeman, Dan Fried, Leon Fuerth, Peter Galbraith, Ejup Ganic, Judy Gelb, Philip Goldberg, Vice President Gore, Marc Grossman, Sir David Hannay, the late Pamela Harriman, Chris Hill, Chris Hoh, Robert Hunter, Douglas Hurd, Maxine Isaacs, Wolfgang Ischinger, Cati James, Ellen James, James A. Johnson, Vernon Jordan, General George Joulwan, Lena Kaplan, Sir John Kerr, Major General Donald Kerrick, Joe Klein, John Kornblum, Gail Kruzel, Tony Lake, David Lipton, Jan Lodal, Colonel Robert Lowe, Endre Marton, Ilona Marton, Mike McCurry, John Menzies, Judy Miller, Tom Miller, Tom Niles, Victoria Nuland, James O'Brien, Roberts Owen, James Pardew, Rosemarie Pauli, Rudy Perina, William Perry, David Phillips, Tom Pickering, Sir Robin Renwick, Jamie Rubin, Miriam Sapiro, Aric Schwan, Tom Schick, Arthur M. Schlesinger, Jr., Robert Schrum, General John Shalikashvili, John Shattuck, Brooke Shearer, Doug Shoen, Tom Siebert, Haris Silajdzic, Walter Slocombe, George Soros, James Steinberg, George Stephanopoulos, Fritz Stern, Elizabeth Stevens, George Stevens, Loucas Tsilas, Cyrus Vance, Jon Vanden Heuvel, Sandy Vershbow, Elie Wiesel, Frank Wisner, and Warren Zimmermann.

Jim O'Brien at the State Department and Don Kerrick at the NSC were especially helpful in obtaining the necessary clearances for the publication of this book, and also gave valuable advice along the way.

Among those who offered advice and assistance, I must single out Strobe Talbott, who despite his backbreaking schedule as Deputy Secretary of State gave generously of his time to offer detailed criticism and corrections. I am deeply grateful both to him and to his wife, Brooke Shearer, for their support and friendship. I also owe special thanks to Les Gelb, my friend and confidant of over thirty years, who offered wise advice and insight during the negotiations, encouraged this project from the outset, and made invaluable editorial suggestions.

I must also express my deep appreciation to my colleagues at Crédit Suisse First Boston—Rainer Gut, Jack Hennessy, Lucas Muhlmann, Allen Wheat, and Chuck Ward—for their understanding and support. Without their forbearance, especially when this project ran longer than anticipated, it could never have been completed. As always, I owe Beverly Snyder special thanks for carrying out so many administrative and secretarial tasks, big and small but always "urgent," with such skill and charm.

It is commonplace to end acknowledgments with a few words about one's family. In this case it is hard to find the proper words to describe what I owe to my wife, Kati, who lived every twist and turn of this story, often participating directly. Perhaps because she was born in nearby Hungary, she had an almost intuitive understanding of the people of the region. She also played an important role in Bosnia on her own, as chair of the Committee to Protect Journalists, promoting press freedom during several trips to the region. Some of her contributions are mentioned in the text, but not the most important—the intangible ones of love and support.

My two sons, who endured the Carter years as children, are now grown and successful in their own careers. They are a constant source of pride and joy, and their support for my efforts was enormously important. Anthony appeared in this story unexpectedly at a critical moment right after the fall of Srebrenica, and performed with the skill and courage that makes a father proud. His older brother, David, gave me love and encouragement when it was most needed. Kati's two wonderful children, Elizabeth and Christopher, also got into the spirit of the project, even helping with some of the final editing.

I am grateful to everyone for their help. Still, I expect that many readers, especially those who lived through parts of this story, will come forward with suggestions or corrections. I look forward to incorporating them in any future edition of this work.

Cast of Characters

Yasushi Akashi   Senior U.N. Envoy to the Former Yugoslavia (1993–95)

Madeleine Albright   U.S. Ambassador to the U.N. (1993–97); Secretary of State (1997–   )

Kofi Annan   U.N. Undersecretary-General for Peacekeeping (1993–97); Secretary-General (1997–   )

Arkan (Zeljko Raznatovic)   Leader of paramilitary Serbs

James Baker   U.S. Secretary of State (1989–92)

Samuel (Sandy) Berger   U.S. Deputy National Security Advisor (1993–96); National Security Advisor (1996–   )

Carl Bildt   European Union Peace Envoy, High Representative in Bosnia (1995–97)

Jacques Blot   French Representative to the Contact Group (1995–1998)

Boutros Boutros-Ghali   U.N. Secretary-General (1990–97)

Aleksi Buha   Bosnian Serb "Minister of Foreign Affairs"

Momir Bulatovic   President of Montenegro, Federal Republic of Yugoslavia (1992–97)

Nicholas Burns   Spokesman, U.S. State Department (1994–97)

Jimmy Carter   President of the United States (1977–81)

Hervé de Charette   Foreign Minister of France (1995–97)

Jacques Chirac   President of France (1995–   )

Warren Christopher   U.S. Secretary of State (1993–97)

Wesley Clark   Lieutenant General, U.S. Army; Director for Strate-
                                     gic Plans and Policy, JCS (1993–96); Supreme
                                     Commander, NATO (1997–   )

William Jefferson Clinton   President of the United States (1993–   )

William Crowe   U.S. Ambassador to Great Britain (1994–97)

John Deutch   Director, Central Intelligence Agency (1995–97)

Milorad Dodik   Prime Minister, Republika Srpska (1998–   )

Tom Donilon   U.S. Assistant Secretary of State for Public Affairs
                                     and Chief of Staff to the Secretary of State
                                     (1993–96)

S. Nelson Drew   Lieutenant Colonel, U.S. Air Force; Senior Staff
                                     member, National Security Council (1995)

Lawrence Eagleburger   Deputy Secretary of State; later Secretary of State
                                     (1989–93)

Robert C. Frasure   U.S. Deputy Assistant Secretary of State for Euro-
                                     pean and Canadian Affairs (1994–95)

Leon Fuerth   National Security Adviser to Vice President Gore
                                     (1993–   )

Peter Galbraith   U.S. Ambassador to Croatia (1993–97)

Ejup Ganic   Vice President, Bosnia-Herzegovina (1992–97);
                                     President, Federation (1998–   )

Robert Gelbard   U.S. Special Representative for the Implementation
                                     of the Dayton Accords (1997–1999)

Kiro Gligorov   President of former Yugoslav Republic of Macedo-
                                     nia (1991–   )

Albert Gore   Vice President of the United States (1993–   )

Pavel Grachev   Russian Defense Minister (1992–97)

Mate Granic   Foreign Minister of Croatia (1993–   )

Pamela Harriman   U.S. Ambassador to France (1993–97)

Chris Hill   Director, Office of South-Central European Affairs,
                                     U.S. Department of State (1994–96)

Robert Hunter   U.S. Ambassador to NATO (1993–97)

Wolfgang Ischinger   Political Director, German Foreign Ministry; Rep-
                                     resentative to the Contact Group (1994–   )

Igor Ivanov   Russian Deputy Foreign Minister; Representative to
                                     the Contact Group (1995–   )

Alija Izetbegovic	President of Bosnia-Herzegovina (1992–)
Bernard Janvier	Lieutenant General of France, Commander of all U.N. forces in the former Yugoslavia (1995–96)
George Joulwan	General, U.S. Army; Supreme Commander of Allied Forces Europe (NATO) (1993–97)
Radovan Karadzic	President of Bosnian Serb Republic (1992–96)
Donald Kerrick	Brigadier (later Major) General, U.S. Army; Senior staff member, NSC; later, Deputy to the National Security Advisor (1995–96; 1997–)
Nikola Koljevic	"Vice President" of Bosnian Serb Republic (1992–96)
John Kornblum	U.S. Deputy Assistant Secretary of State for European and Canadian Affairs; later Assistant Secretary of State (1994–97)
Andrei Kozyrev	Foreign Minister of Russia (1992–96)
Momcilo Krajisnik	Speaker of Bosnian Serb Assembly; later Co-president of Bosnia (1996–1998)
Joseph Kruzel	U.S. Deputy Assistant Secretary of Defense for International Security Affairs (1993–95)
Anthony Lake	U.S. National Security Advisor (1993–96)
Jean-David Levitte	Foreign policy advisor to President Chirac of France (1995–)
David Lipton	U.S. Deputy Assistant Secretary of Treasury for International Affairs (1993–96); Undersecretary of Treasury (1997–)
Jan Lodal	Principal Deputy Undersecretary of Defense for Policy (1993–)
John Major	Prime Minister of Great Britain (1990–97)
Mike McCurry	White House Spokesman (1994–1998)
John Menzies	U.S. Ambassador to Bosnia-Herzegovina (1995–97)
Slobodan Milosevic	President of the Republic of Serbia (1989–97); President of the Federal Republic of Yugoslavia (1997–)
Milan Milutinovic	Minister of Foreign Affairs, Federal Republic of Yugoslavia (1995–97); President of Serbia (1997–)
Ratko Mladic	General, Commander of Bosnian Serb Army (1992–96)

Pauline Neville-Jones   Contact Group Representative from the United
                                 Kingdom (1993–96)

Roberts Owen   Legal advisor on shuttle team

William Owens   Admiral, U.S. Navy; Vice Chairman of the JCS
                                 (1994–96)

Leon Panetta   White House Chief of Staff (1994–97)

Andreas Papandreou   Prime Minister of Greece (1981–89, 1993–96)

James Pardew   Director, Balkan Task Force, Department of De-
                                 fense (1995–97)

Rosemarie Pauli   Department of State; Executive Assistant to the au-
                                 thor (1993–96)

Rudy Perina   U.S. Chargé d'Affaires, Belgrade (1993–96)

William Perry   U.S. Secretary of Defense (1993–97)

Thomas Pickering   Undersecretary of State for Political Affairs (1997–   )

Biljana Plavsic   "Vice President" of Bosnian Serb Republic;
                                 Co-president of Republika Srpska (1996–1998)

Malcolm Rifkind   British Defense Secretary, later Foreign Secretary
                                 (1992–97)

Muhamed Sacirbey   Foreign Minister of Bosnia-Herzegovina, Ambas-
                                 sador to the U.N. (1992–97)

John Shalikashvili   General, U.S. Army; Chairman of the Joint Chiefs
                                 of Staff (1993–97)

John Shattuck   Assistant Secretary of State for Humanitarian Af-
                                 fairs (1993–1998)

Haris Silajdzic   Prime Minister of Bosnia-Herzegovina (1992–   )

Walter Slocombe   U.S. Undersecretary of Defense for Policy
                                 (1993–   )

Leighton Smith   Admiral, U.S. Navy; Commander of NATO forces,
                                 Southern Europe; Commander, IFOR (1995–96)

Rupert Smith   Lieutenant General, British Army; Commander of
                                 U.N. forces in Bosnia-Herzegovina (1994–96)

James Steinberg   Director of the Policy Planning Staff, U.S. Depart-
                                 ment of State (1994–96); Deputy National Security
                                 Advisor (1997–   )

Michael Steiner   Deputy German Representative to the Contact
                                 Group; Deputy High Representative (1996–97)

Thorvald Stoltenberg	U.N. Representative to the International Conference on the Former Yugoslavia (1993–95)
Gojko Susak	Defense Minister of Croatia (1992–1998)
Strobe Talbott	U.S. Deputy Secretary of State (1994–)
Peter Tarnoff	U.S. Undersecretary of State for Political Affairs (1993–97)
Franjo Tudjman	President of Croatia (1991–)
Alexander (Sandy) Vershbow	Senior Director for Europe, U.S. National Security Council (1994–97); U.S. Ambassador to NATO (1998–)
John White	Deputy Secretary of Defense (1996–97)
Boris Yeltsin	President of Russia (1991–)
Warren Zimmermann	American Ambassador to Yugoslavia (1989–92)
Kresimir Zubak	President of the Muslim-Croat Federation in Bosnia; later Co-president of Bosnia-Herzegovina (1996–1998)

Notes

Chapter 1: The Most Dangerous Road in Europe

1. Warren Zimmermann, *Origins of a Catastrophe: Yugoslavia and Its Destroyers* (New York: Times Books, 1996), p. 22.

Chapter 2: "The Greatest Collective Failure . . ."

1. "America, a European Power," *Foreign Affairs,* March–April 1995, p. 40.
2. Warren Zimmermann, *Origins of a Catastrophe: Yugoslavia and Its Destroyers* (New York: Times Books, 1996), pp. 151–53.
3. Noel Malcolm, *Bosnia: A Short History* (New York: New York University Press, 1994), p. 252.
4. Zimmermann, p. 174.
5. David C. Gompert, "The United States and Yugoslavia's Wars," in *The World and Yugoslavia's Wars,* Richard H. Ullman, ed. (New York: Council on Foreign Relations, 1996), pp. 122, 134. Gompert's essay is courageous in its candor.
6. James A. Baker III, with Thomas M. DeFrank, *The Politics of Diplomacy* (New York: G. P. Putnam's Sons, 1995), p. 483.
7. Zimmermann, p. 216.
8. Laura Silber and Allan Little, *Yugoslavia: Death of a Nation* (London: Penguin Books/BBC Books, 1996), p. 201.
9. Baker, p. 637.
10. Gompert, pp. 127–28.
11. Silber and Little, p. 166.
12. Ibid., pp. 171–72.
13. Baker, p. 637.
14. Zimmermann, p. 177.
15. Silber and Little, pp. 211–12.

Chapter 3: A Personal Prelude

1. Henry A. Kissinger, *Diplomacy* (New York: Simon & Schuster, 1994), p. 225.

Chapter 6: Pale's Challenge

1. *The Wall Street Journal,* September 20, 1993.
2. Robert Scheer, "Clinton's Globetrotter," *Los Angeles Times Magazine,* February 21, 1995.

Chapter 7: Bombing and Breakthrough

1. Bernard-Henri Lévy, *Le Lys et la Cendre: Journal d'un Écrivain au Temps de la Guerre de Bosnie* (Paris: Grasset, 1996), pp. 464–70. Translated for the author by Kathe Rothe.

Chapter 10: The Siege of Sarajevo Ends

1. Mira Markovic, *Night and Day: A Diary* (Belgrade, 1995), pp. 17–18.
2. Warren Zimmermann, *Origins of a Catastrophe: Yugoslavia and Its Destroyers* (New York: Times Books, 1996), p. 175.

Chapter 13: Cease-fire

1. Laura Silber and Allan Little, *Yugoslavia: The Death of a Nation* (London: Penguin Books/BBC Books, 1996), p. 224.

Chapter 15: Decisions with Consequences

1. Colin Powell, with Joseph E. Persico, *My American Journey* (New York: Random House, 1994), p. 149.

Chapter 17: "Peace in a Week"

1. Pauline Neville-Jones, "Dayton, IFOR, and Alliance Relations in Bosnia," *Survival,* Winter 1996–97, pp. 50–51.
2. Ibid., p. 51.

Chapter 21: America, Europe, and Bosnia

1. *Foreign Policy,* Winter 1997–98, p. 66.
2. Christopher Bennett, "No Flying Colors for Dayton—Yet," *Transitions,* December 1997, p. 37.
3. *Transitions,* August 1997, "Don't Fool Around with Principles."
4. This issue is addressed in a valuable study by the United States Air Force, *DELIBERATE FORCE: A Case Study in Effective Air Campaigning,* a study directed by Colonel Robert C. Owen. In the unclassified conclusion, Colonel Owen writes:
   Contacts between military leaders and some key diplomats did not seem to have kept up with the pace of events just before and after DELIBERATE FORCE. . . . Ambassador Holbrooke and General Ryan made plans and took actions in ignorance of one another's positions in key areas. [Published in *Airpower Journal,* Fall 1997, pp. 21–22.]

5. Carl Bildt, *Uppdrag Fred* [Assignment Peace] (Stockholm: Norstedts, 1997); translation provided by the author.
6. Speech to the Center for National Policy, January 13, 1998.
7. An extended example of the first view can be found in Radha Kumar's *Divide and Fall? Bosnia in the Annals of Partition.* The author's generic criticism of partition from Korea to Cyprus is insightful, but she misstates the goals of Dayton and confuses the Dayton agreement with the way it has been implemented.
8. *The Economist,* December 6, 1997, p. 16.
9. "America, a European Power," *Foreign Affairs,* March–April 1995, p. 138.
10. Bildt; translation provided by the author.
11. Henry A. Kissinger, *Diplomacy* (New York: Simon & Schuster, 1994), pp. 833–34.
12. Vaclav Havel, *The Art of the Impossible* (New York: Alfred A. Knopf, 1997), pp. 232–34.

Bibliography

Air Force Materiel Command. "Special Collectors' Edition." *Leading Edge,* February 1996. Wright-Patterson Air Force Base, Ohio: Air Force Materiel Command, 1996.

Ash, Timothy Garton. "The Way out of Kosovo," *The New York Review of Books,* January 14, 1999.

Baedeker's Touring Guide to Yugoslavia. New York: Macmillan Company, 1964.

Baker, James A. III, with Thomas M. DeFrank. *The Politics of Diplomacy.* New York: G. P. Putnam's Sons, 1995.

Bildt, Carl. *Peace Journey: The Struggle for Peace in Bosnia.* London: Weidenfeld and Nicholson, 1998.

Blanchard, Paul. *Yugoslavia Blue Guide.* New York: W. W. Norton, 1989.

Boutros-Ghali, Boutros. *Egypt's Road to Jerusalem: A Diplomat's Story of the Struggle for Peace in the Middle East.* New York: Random House, 1997.

Boyd, Charles G. "Making Bosnia Work," *Foreign Affairs*, January–February 1998.

Brodie, Bernard. *War and Politics.* New York: Macmilllan Company, 1973.

Cohen, Philip J. *Serbia's Secret War: Propaganda and the Deceit of History.* College Station, Texas: Texas A & M University Press, 1996.

Cohen, Roger. *Hearts Grown Brutal: Sagas of Sarajevo.* New York: Random House, 1998.

Committee on Armed Services, United States Senate. "Hearings on Bosnia," June 7, 8, 14; September 29; October 17; November 28; December 6, 1995. Washington, D.C.: U.S. Government Printing Office, 1996.

Department of the Army. *German Antiguerrilla Operations in the Balkans (1941–1944).* Washington, D.C.: Department of the Army Pamphlet No. 20-243, August 1954.

Drew, Elizabeth. *On the Edge: The Clinton Presidency.* New York: Simon & Schuster, 1994.

Gjelten, Tom. *Sarajevo Daily: A City and Its Newspaper Under Seige.* New York: HarperCollins, 1995.

Glenny, Misha. *The Fall of Yugoslavia: The Third Balkan War.* 3rd rev. ed. New York: Penguin Books, 1996

Gow, James. *Triumph of the Lack of Will.* New York: Columbia University Press, 1997.

Gutman, Roy. *A Witness to Genocide.* New York: Macmillan Publishing Company, 1993.

Hall, Brian. *The Impossible Country.* New York: Penguin Books, 1994.

———. "Rebecca West's War." *The New Yorker,* April 15, 1996.

Havel, Vaclav. *The Art of the Impossible.* New York: Alfred A. Knopf, 1997.

Honig, Jan Willem, and Norbert Both. *Srebrenica: Record of a War Crime.* New York: Penguin, 1997.

Hutchings, Robert L. *American Diplomacy and the End of the Cold War.* Washington, D.C.: Woodrow Wilson Center Press, 1997.

Ignatieff, Michael. *The Warrior's Honor: Ethnic War and the Modern Conscience.* New York: Metropolitan Books, 1997.

International Commission on the Balkans. *Unfinished Peace: A Report.* Foreword by Leo Tindemans. Washington, D.C.: Carnegie Endowment for International Peace, 1996.

Kadare, Ismail. *The File on H.* New York: Arcade, 1998.

Kaplan, Robert. *Balkan Ghosts: A Journey Through History.* New York: Vintage Books, 1993.

Kissinger, Henry A. *Diplomacy.* New York: Simon & Schuster, 1994.

———. *White House Years.* Boston: Little, Brown & Co., 1979.

Kumar, Radha. *Divide and Fall? Bosnia in the Annals of Partition.* New York: Verso, 1997.

Kurspahic, Kemal. *As Long As Sarajevo Exists.* Stony Creek, Connecticut: Pamphleteer's Press, 1997.

Lampe, John R. *Yugoslavia as History: Twice There Was a Country.* New York: Cambridge University Press, 1996.

Lengvai, Paul. *Eagles in Cobwebs: Nationalism and Communism in the Balkans.* Garden City, New York: Doubleday & Company, 1969.

Lévy, Bernard-Henri. *Le Lys et la Cendre: Journal d'un Écrivain au Temps de la Guerre de Bosnie.* Paris: Grasset, 1996.

Maass, Peter. *Love Thy Neighbor: A Story of War.* New York: Alfred A. Knopf, 1996.

Malcolm, Noel. *Bosnia: A Short History.* New York: New York University Press, 1994.

———. *Kosovo: A Short History.* New York: New York University Press, 1998.

Markovic, Mira [Mrs. Slobodan Milosevic]. *Night and Day: A Diary.* English translation by Margot and Bosko Milosavljevic. Belgrade: Privately printed, 1995.

Marton, Kati. *A Death in Jerusalem.* New York: Pantheon, 1994.

————. *Wallenberg: Missing Hero.* New York: Arcade, 1995.

May, Ernest R. *"Lessons" of the Past: The Use and Misuse of History in American Foreign Policy.* New York: Oxford Univeristy Press, 1973.

Murray, Rupert Wolfe. *IFOR on IFOR.* Foreword by Richard Holbrooke. Edinburgh, Scotland: Connect, 1996.

Neustadt, Richard E., and Ernest R. May. *Thinking in Time: The Uses of History for Decision-Makers.* New York: Free Press, 1986.

Neville-Jones, Pauline. "Dayton, IFOR, and Alliance Relations in Bosnia." *Survival* 38:4 (Winter 1996–97), pp. 45–65.

The New Republic, ed. *The Black Book of Bosnia: The Consequences of Appeasement.* Edited by Nader Mousavizadeh. Afterword by Leon Wieseltier. New York: A New Republic Book–Basic Books, 1996.

Nicolson, Harold. *Peacemaking 1919.* New York: Grosset & Dunlap, 1965.

O'Hanlon, Michael. "Turning the Bosnia Ceasefire into Peace." *The Brookings Review,* Winter 1998.

Owen, David. *Balkan Odyssey.* New York: Harcourt Brace & Company, 1996.

Powell, Colin, with Joseph E. Persico. *My American Journey.* New York: Random House, 1994.

Quandt, William B. *Camp David: Peacemaking and Politics.* Washington, D.C.: Brookings Institution, 1986.

Remak, Joachim. *Sarajevo: The Story of a Political Murder.* New York: Criterion Books, 1959.

Renwick, Sir Robin. *Fighting with Allies: America and Britain in Peace and at War.* New York: Times Books, 1996.

Ridley, Jasper. *Tito: A Biography.* London: Constable, 1994.

Rieff, David. *Slaughterhouse: Bosnia and the Failure of the West.* New York: Touchstone, 1996.

Rohde, David. *Endgame: The Betrayal and Fall of Srebrenica, Europe's Worst Massacre Since World War II.* New York: Farrar, Straus and Giroux, 1997.

Rose, Gideon. "The Exit Strategy Delusion," *Foreign Affairs,* January–February 1998.

Rosegrant, Susan. "Getting to Dayton: Negotiating an End to the War in Bosnia." A Case Study from the John F. Kennedy School of Government, Harvard University, 1996.

Silber, Laura, and Allan Little. *Yugoslavia: Death of a Nation.* Rev. ed. London: Penguin Books/BBC Books, 1996.

Sobel, Dava. *Longitude: The True Story of a Lone Genius Who Solved the Greatest Scientific Problem of His Time.* New York: Penguin Books, 1995.

Sudetic, Chuck. *Blood and Vengeance.* New York: W. W. Norton, 1998.

Talbott, Strobe. *Deadly Gambits.* New York: Alfred A. Knopf, 1984.

Tanner, Marcus. *Croatia: A Nation Forged in War.* New Haven: Yale University Press, 1997.

Thompson, Mark. *A Paper House: The Ending of Yugoslavia.* New York: Pantheon Books, 1992.

Ullman, Richard H., ed. *The World and Yugoslavia's Wars.* New York: Council on Foreign Relations, 1996.

United States Air Force. *DELIBERATE FORCE: A Case Study in Effective Air Campaigning.* Edited by Colonel Robert C. Owen. To be published by the Air University Press; excerpts in *Airpower Journal,* Fall 1997, pp. 21–22.

Vance, Cyrus. *Hard Choices.* New York: Simon & Schuster, 1983.

Vickers, Miranda. *Between Serb and Albanian: A History of Kosovo.* London: Hurst & Company, 1998.

Vickers, Miranda, and James Pettifer. *Albania: From Anarchy to a Balkan Identity.* London: Hurst & Company, 1997.

Volkan, Vamik. *Bloodlines: From Ethnic Pride to Ethnic Terrorism.* New York: Farrar, Straus and Giroux, 1997.

Wedgwood, C. V. *History and Hope: Essays on History and the English Civil War.* New York: E. P. Dutton, 1987.

West, Rebecca. *Black Lamb and Grey Falcon.* New York: Penguin Books, 1982.

Westendorp, Carlos. "Speech by the High Representative to the Peace Implementation Council," Bonn, December 9, 1997.

Woodward, Bob. *The Choice.* New York: Simon & Schuster, 1996.

Woodward, Susan L. "Avoiding Another Cyprus or Israel," *The Brookings Review,* Winter 1998.

———. *Balkan Tragedy.* Washington, D.C.: Brookings Institution, 1995.

Zimmermann, Warren. *Origins of a Catastrophe: Yugoslavia and Its Destroyers.* New York: Times Books, 1996.

Index

Page numbers in *italics* refer to maps.

ABOUT THE AUTHOR

RICHARD HOLBROOKE began his diplomatic career in Vietnam in 1962, serving in the Mekong Delta and the American embassy in Saigon. After a tour on President Johnson's White House Staff in 1966–67, he wrote one volume of the Pentagon Papers, served as special assistant to Undersecretaries of State Nicholas Katzenbach and Elliot Richardson, and was a member of the American delegation to the Paris peace talks on Vietnam.

Holbrooke was Peace Corps director in Morocco from 1970 to 1972 and managing editor of *Foreign Policy* from 1972 to 1976. He served as Assistant Secretary of State for East Asian and Pacific Affairs (1977–81) and U.S. Ambassador to Germany (1993–94). He was Assistant Secretary of State for European and Canadian Affairs from 1994 to 1996, when he became the chief architect of the Dayton Peace Accords. He is co-author of Clark Clifford's memoir, *Counsel to the President*, and is currently a vice chairman of Crédit Suisse First Boston, based in New York. He is married to author Kati Marton and has two sons, David and Anthony.